D1603599

The Rise of Popular Literacy in Victorian England

The Rise of Popular Literacy in Victorian England

The Influence of Private Choice and Public Policy

David F. Mitch

University of Pennsylvania Press
Philadelphia

Library of Congress Cataloging-in-Publication Data

Mitch, David Franklin, 1951–
    The rise of popular literacy in Victorian England : the influence of private choice and
public policy / David F. Mitch.
        p.   cm.
    Includes bibliographical references (p.   ) and index.
    ISBN 0-8122-3075-2
    1. Literacy—Social aspects—England—History—19th century.   2. Working class—
Education—England—History—19th century.   3. Education and state—England—
History—19th century.   I. Title.
LC156.G72E56   1991
302.2′244—dc20   91-32072
                                                                                CIP

English people will not be driven,
but they may be won. It is worth
that will win them. They have their
eyes open, and they know what is good,
whether in things or people, and,
given a sufficient time for
discrimination of what is good and
what is not, they will secure it.

REV. J. R. BYRNE,
General Report to the Committee of
Council on Education for the year
1882 on schools in the counties of
Surrey and Middlesex (commenting on
the effectiveness of compulsory
schooling laws)

Contents

Figures

Tables

xii   Tables

Preface

THE RISE OF MASS EDUCATION has been one of the most remarkable changes in European society in modern times. Before 1500, less than 10 percent of the population of any European nation was able to read or write, and an even lower percentage was likely to have ever received formal schooling.[1] By 1900, the adult population of a number of European countries had, almost universally, achieved at least minimal literacy; sizable segments had attained considerably higher levels of education.[2] Historians of Europe have attributed fundamental consequences to the rise of mass education, from the acceleration of economic growth to the delineation of modern social classes.[3] In turn, the extent of mass education has been used as a barometer of social and economic development.[4]

In accounting for the rise of mass education, historians have traditionally focused on the educational efforts of the state, the church, and a variety of other groups whose overt motive was to foster general social progress.[5] This focus is easily justified by the obvious presence of these efforts and especially by their massive scale during the nineteenth and twentieth centuries. By the early twentieth century, school buildings, whose construction was financed in large part by public funds, had sprung up within easy access of virtually every city block and rural hamlet throughout Western Europe and North America. The teachers in these schools had most, if not all, of their salaries paid from public funds. Many of them had been trained in publicly run normal schools. Both the curricula they followed and the inspectors who assessed the results of their instruction were provided by centralized authorities. And teachers were not the only emissaries of public education; truant officers also became a common sight in urban slums and wherever parents were reluctant to send their children to school.[6]

Because of the scale of public efforts to promote mass education, historians have often simply presumed that these efforts had a significant educational impact. They have focused their attention instead on the groups in European and North American society that were responsible for these efforts and whether they were motivated by a desire to promote the general public interest or a desire to promote their own special interests.[7] One reason for the interest in the groups that publicly supported mass education is that the public provision of education, by at least some definitions of public, was not confined to the state. Various religious organizations, both centralized and local, as well as various secular philanthropic groups and individual philanthropists also provided financial and organizational support for popular elementary education. In this study, all of these nongovernmental groups will be deemed public rather than private on the grounds that their overt motive was the general improvement of society rather than the personal gain of group members, their families, or some other narrowly restricted group.[8] Although the term *public school* is commonly used in England to refer to an exclusive group of secondary schools for the upper classes, the term was also used in Victorian educational inquiries in the sense used here to refer to all elementary schools receiving nonfee income, whether from parliamentary grants, an endowment by a local philanthropist, or a contribution by a local clergyman.[9]

Historians have actively debated the nature of the motives of those who promoted public support for education. Progressive accounts have maintained that their motives were benevolent and aimed at furthering the interests of society at large. Revisionist accounts have argued the opposite case, that promoters of public education primarily sought to further the interests of the middle and upper classes by using mass education to instill values and behaviors in the working classes that would make them more docile and subservient. Despite their differences, the various accounts share the perception that the rise of mass education involved the passive response of the working classes to educational policies determined by an elite few.[10]

But, increasingly, historians have become disenchanted with ascribing a passive role to the working classes in the rise of mass education. To begin with, there is evidence that the demand of the working classes for education was growing independently of public educational policy. In many areas of Europe and North America, a majority of the population had acquired literacy even before public provision of education had become widespread. And, even as centralized public primary schooling became widespread throughout North America and Europe during the nineteenth century, private elementary schools with a working class clientele seem to have persisted, suggesting the strength of popular demand.[11]

Furthermore, public policy and popular demand could interact with each other in a variety of ways in influencing the rise of mass education.

Some historians of public educational policy have noted that popular attitudes toward education could directly shape public policy when that policy was subject to democratic control.[12] Others have found that popular attitudes toward education could influence the effectiveness of public educational policy.[13] And some historians have even argued that the public provision of schooling had a negligible or negative impact on mass education because it displaced private efforts.[14] The spread of public education could also shape the nature of popular attitudes toward education.[15] Indeed, the official rationale for public education was to reshape popular values; the desired values—whether piety, obedience, or a sense of civic duty—would seem to imply attitudes conducive to education.[16]

Strong interactions between popular demand and public educational policy imply that the evolution of one factor significantly shaped that of the other. The overall course of educational development could then have varied considerably depending on particular historical circumstances and influences on popular demand and public policy.[17] In other words, the possibility of strong interactions between popular demand and public policy suggests the importance of examining the historical process involved in order to explain the rise of mass education.

Politicians and policy experts as well as historians of education have been concerned with the interactions between public policy and popular demand for education. These interactions have been at the core of recurring oppositions and tensions in the development of educational policy: Should local autonomy or centralized control prevail? Should instructional provision respond to individual circumstance or should basic educational standards be established? Should educational standards be improved by choice and competition or by direct assistance to the educationally disadvantaged? These issues have recently emerged as central concerns in the United Kingdom as the Baker Plan has led to efforts to implement both a national curriculum for primary and secondary schools and provisions for parental management of individual schools.[18] And the United States in recent years has, on the one hand, seen a surge of support for voucher plans promoting parental choice but has, on the other hand, had its courts mandate that states and cities eliminate disparities in educational provision.[19]

Although diverging approaches to educational policy are inevitably based on differences in ideological disposition, the viability of a given policy alternative also depends on direct evidence about key premises of that approach. Do choice and competition among schools really improve educational performance? To what extent does such an approach leave the educationally disadvantaged behind? Can centralized direction really improve educationally disadvantaged areas, and can it compensate for the lack of local initiative and support for education? The laboratory of history provides an important source of evidence on the viability of policy alternatives. England, in the late nineteenth century as in the late twentieth century, attempted to implement a national curriculum. The complaints of "overpressure" made in the 1880s about efforts to get children through inspectors' examinations sound strikingly similar to complaints about the implementation of the standardized tests proposed by the Baker Plan of 1988.[20] Another concern about the Baker Plan has been that many areas would be deprived of adequate schooling for the less affluent if public resources were used to support private schools. This would seem similar to the demands for "filling in the gaps" that led to the English Education Act of 1870 to ensure that all children had access to schools that met nationally established standards.[21]

This study will examine the rise of literacy in Victorian England. This case is an apt one for considering the relative importance of popular demand compared with public policy in the rise of mass education. Literacy rates, as measured by the minimal standard of ability to sign one's name at marriage, had been stagnant at around 50 percent from the middle of the eighteenth century through the first third of the nineteenth century and then rose to over 95 percent by 1900, thus almost doubling within a sixty-year period.[22] The literacy rate of 50 percent by 1750 had been achieved in the absence of centralized public support for mass education, which suggests the initial presence of some combination of widespread popular demand and local philanthropic support for mass education. The rise in literacy rates in the last two-thirds of the nineteenth century coincided with the development of publicly provided mass schooling and circumstances that would seem to have increased popular demand for education, including rapid urbanization, rising working-class living standards, and the development of publications aimed at the working-class market.[23]

Both contemporaries and subsequent historians have debated the importance of the provision of schooling and popular demand in the rise of Victorian literacy. Proponents of a centralized state apparatus for the provision of mass schooling gained increasing influence during the Victorian period, and many historians have embraced their point of view.[24] Some contemporaries, however, have emphasized the role of popular demand and the possibility that it could achieve results through private provision of schooling, a view shared by some later historians.[25] Yet other historians have argued that the motives for government activity were based on class conflict.[26] Recently, historians have pointed to the interaction between public policy and private motives: that popular demand could influence the effectiveness of public policy and that, in turn, rising educational attainment resulting from public policy would further spur popular demand.[27] The importance of these two factors has yet to be established, however. This will be the central task of the following pages.

The reasons why a study of Victorian popular education would focus on literacy are clear. There was a dramatic rise in the percentage of the population mastering basic literacy skills and in the percentage of children enrolled in elementary school. And the vast majority of the English population during this period had little hope of receiving more than an elementary education.[28] But it is important to note that defining the term *literacy* is problematic, in particular, when proposing a stark dichotomy between the literate and the illiterate.

The most immediate problem with a simple literate/illiterate dichotomy is that literacy is commonly defined as the ability to both read and write.[29] Including two basic skills in the definition of literacy raises the possibility that a person could master one of the skills but not the other. Partial literates were most likely to be able to read but not write; because reading is a more passive skill, it is generally easier to master than the more active skill of writing. Also reading has commonly been taught before commencing instruction in writing. In societies where reading or writing was commonly acquired through informal instruction and where school attendance was often restricted to just a few months, it would not be surprising if many people could read but not write. In fact, surveys conducted by statistical societies in early Victorian England indicated that for a significant proportion of adults this was the case. Based on an examination of these surveys, Webb has concluded that the number who could read in early Victorian England was between one and a half times and twice the number who could write.[30] This intermediate category became less important over time as a growing percentage of the Victorian population received enough instruction to be able to write. Moreover, the syllabus put in place for public elementary schools by the Revised Code in 1862 provided for training in writing as well as in reading from the very first stage of instruction, thus more closely linking the two skills. Examination results in the last third of the nineteenth century indicate that similar proportions of students passed in writing as in reading.[31] To properly capture the range of reading and writing skills that prevailed during the Victorian period, however, definition and measurement of literacy would have to allow for those who could read but not write.

Although literacy is commonly defined to include only the skills of reading and writing, the commonplace of the three Rs points to how closely arithmetic, and the related notion of numeracy, is linked in popular thinking with reading and writing.[32] In the nineteenth and twentieth centuries, arithmetic has been placed with reading and writing to form the staples of the elementary school curriculum.[33] Despite this frequent association, reading and writing have been distinguished from arithmetic because they inherently involve the use of language. Arithmetic, in contrast, is viewed as involving the use of more abstract reasoning. Thus, W. B. Hodgson, a Victorian educational reformer, argued in an influential essay that "arithmetic holds a quite different position from [reading and writing]. Besides its actual uses in the working world, it is a science, capable of becoming the instrument of important training. . . . the doctrine of numbers may truly be regarded as at once a root science and a great power in education."[34]

The ability to count and do basic arithmetic neither follows from nor is required for the ability to read and write. Nevertheless, there does in fact appear to be a basic link between the actual use of numerical skills and the ability to read and write. People read and write when using numbers to keep written accounts because they need to decode and record written numerals. Although tally sticks and other methods can be used by illiterates to keep accounts, these tasks are greatly facilitated by the ability to read and write. Indeed, Jack Goody and Roy Harris have argued that the origin of writing systems and the earliest uses of literacy were in keeping numerical accounts.[35] This suggests that the desire to use numeracy, especially in keeping written accounts, may have provided an important incentive for acquiring the linguistic skills of reading and writing. Thus, while this study will focus on literacy defined as the ability to read and write, at some points the links of these skills with numeracy will also be considered.

Reading and writing involve a number of component tasks which can be performed at various levels of competence. It is plausible to separate these tasks into lower-order ones of decoding and transcribing and higher-order ones of interpreting and communicating. These considerations further complicate a simple literate/illiterate dichotomy by raising the question of what specific tasks must be mastered, and at what level of competence, in order for someone to be deemed literate. Victorian educational regulations implicitly provided some criteria. They indicated that children had to complete at least the first three stages of the elementary curriculum to be exempt from child labor and compulsory schooling laws. They also specified what skills were to be acquired in those stages.[36] Under the Revised Code introduced in 1862, a child completing the first three stages of the curriculum should be able to read "a short paragraph from an elementary reading-book used in the school," to write "a sentence from the same paragraph slowly read and then dictated in single words," and to do "a sum in any rule as far as short division."[37] But while the Revised Code may have provided a useful reference point, many educators were critical of it as the sole criterion of educational achievement, and the set of skills it incorporated can hardly be used as a universally accepted standard for literacy throughout the Victorian period.[38]

Indeed, as educational attainments have risen over time, so have the expectations of society as to what skills should be mastered in basic education. In the twentieth century, this rising standard has been reflected in the development of the notion of functional literacy, according to which one should have enough reading and writing ability to function effectively in daily life, whether at work, in social situations, or in one's personal affairs.[39] Inevitably, the skills required will depend on the average mastery of skills in society at large, leading to a continual upgrading of the requirements for functional literacy as educational attainment in general rises. Because this standard is continually rising, a certain proportion of society will always remain below this standard; accordingly, the notion of functional literacy has been criticized for being needlessly alarmist about the extent of illiteracy. Some measures of functional literacy imply that between 5 and 14 percent of professionals and managers in the United States in the 1970s were functionally illiterate, a dubiously high proportion.[40] Nevertheless, the notion of functional literacy is useful because it points to the importance of considering the context in which literacy skills are to be used in order to determine their appropriate definition.

Beyond the question of what specific skills are covered under the rubric of literacy, a deeper ambiguity lies in the significance of the mastery of the skills. All that literacy would necessarily seem to entail is mastery of specific tools for communication. Indeed, educational reformers have criticized centering primary education on the mastery of literacy on the grounds that this focus is too narrow. In the notable analogy of W. B. Hodgson, claiming that reading and writing alone are sufficient basis for an education is like offering somebody a meal by providing knife, fork, and plate but no food.[41] Nevertheless, various commentators have assigned a wide variety of consequences to the mastery of literacy. In early modern times, training in reading was used as a tool for mastery of the catechism.[42] In the late eighteenth and nineteenth centuries, primary education came to be viewed as a way of instilling socially desirable behavior. Some commentators argued that apart from conveying general enlightenment, the discipline involved in decoding the printed page and wielding a pen was conducive to orderly social behavior.[43] In the twentieth century, a person's acquisition of literacy has been viewed as pivotal in acquiring more general behaviors associated with modern, as opposed to traditional, ways of life.[44] Much has also been made of contrasting literacy with orality and exploring the possibility that each mode of communication involves different cognitive processes.[45] However, a well-established revisionist perspective disputes such stark contrasts and points to the importance of examining the particular context in which literacy is being used in order to evaluate its significance and consequences.[46]

Despite their many drawbacks, some simple dichotomous measures of literacy will be used in this study because they provide the only feasible means of comparing literacy levels across time and space. One particular measure that will be used extensively because of its ready availability for the Victorian period is signature ability on marriage registers. This measure offers the advantages of covering large segments of the population and of requiring objective performance of literacy ability. Historians of literacy have given extensive consideration to the sources of ambiguity in this measure. Although conceivably one could master signature ability without mastering other literacy skills, or alternatively, one might make a mark to avoid embarrassing one's spouse, there is little evidence to suggest that either of these possibilities was common. Rather, according to Roger Schofield, ability to sign one's name at marriage probably indicates at least moderate reading ability.[47] The main purpose of using the signature measure despite its limitations is that it is likely to provide a valid comparative indicator of literacy levels both across groups and over time. This is clearly an important advantage despite possible variability in the actual literacy skills that signature ability measures and despite the likelihood that over time these literacy skills improved relative to signature ability.

This study will use a cost-benefit approach to examine the impact of both public policy and private choice on the rise of literacy. This method assumes that the educational attainment of a population rises as an increasing percentage finds that the benefits of additional education exceed the costs. The basic premise is that the ultimate actors in the acquisition of literacy were families and individuals assessing whether it was worthwhile to obtain instruction in order to become literate. A cost-benefit approach indicates their perspective in balancing the various incentives to acquire literacy with the various costs, including those benefits and costs influenced by public policy. It thus provides a way of assessing the relative importance of the diverse factors influencing literacy rates.

This approach is subject to limitations and criticism. It could be argued that it is unlikely that working-class families actually performed explicit calculations of costs and benefits in making educational decisions. It seems particularly unlikely that they would have used present discounted values to do these calculations, as would have been required to do them properly. Indeed, it may be that school attendance or the acquisition of literacy was not a strictly rational, forward-looking decision made at a particular point in one's life. Rather, it was the result of numerous daily decisions about whether to attend school, reflecting basic attitudes toward education. But while it may be problematic to use a cost-benefit framework to capture the actual decision-making process of working-class families, this approach can still point to important forces that shaped general literacy trends. Balances of benefit relative to cost can capture tendencies in the general net advantage perceived to literacy and the consequent response. Even if few families were guided by explicit cost-benefit calculations, many of them probably did have at least a general awareness of the direction of this balance and were influenced by it.

A cost-benefit approach is subject to the broader criticism that, in focusing on individual choice, it does not directly incorporate the influence of societal forces in shaping the individuals making the choice. For example, neither peer pressure nor class conflict, factors often emphasized by social historians and sociologists of education, seems to be conveniently incorporated into a cost-benefit calculation. Nor is the role of historical evolution.[48] For these reasons it could be argued that this approach has a hidden agenda favoring forces that reflected individual choice rather than public policy or social change. But while admittedly a cost-benefit perspective does focus on the individual rather than on society, this can be defended on grounds that education is ultimately determined by individuals and that the influence of societal forces on educational attainment is mediated through individual choice. An attempt to consider what societal forces may be present can at least allow one to incorporate such forces into the individual's cost-benefit comparisons. Indeed, a cost-benefit calculation allows the possibility of comparing the impact of such societal factors with those of more direct individual significance.[49] In other words, the framework used here can be defended on grounds that it provides an important perspective on the acquisition of literacy, even if it is not the only significant one.

The study will proceed by examining trends in the benefits and then in the costs of acquiring literacy. In order to understand private response to public educational policy, it is important to understand the broader role education has played in working-class lives. And, in order to understand the impact of public policy, it is important to examine the implementation of that policy as it proceeded from the chambers of Parliament to the chalk face of the schoolhouse.

Part 1 of the book examines the benefits of literacy and how they changed during the Victorian period. Chapter 2 establishes that literacy offered opportunities for occupational advancement for some but not all of those of working-class origins and that those opportunities increased, although at a modest pace, during the last half of the nineteenth century. Chapter 3 considers the role of literacy in the daily life of the working classes. In the early Victorian period, working-class men and women had little occasion to read or write in their leisure and domestic activities. But by the end of the nineteenth century, even unskilled laborers and their wives were passing the time on Sunday afternoons with the weekly paper or a novelette. Since schooling and education decisions were made as much by parents as by individuals who were directly educated, Chapter 4 turns to the influence of the family on literacy trends. Although rising living standards and declining family size appear to have had little impact on literacy trends, the rise in the proportion who were literate in a given generation significantly increased the probability that the children of that generation would be literate.

Part 2 of the book examines the costs of acquiring literacy and how they were affected by public educational policy. Chapter 5 considers the marked improvement in the access of the working classes to subsidized elementary schools. Chapter 6 establishes that the way in which literacy was acquired shifted from informal instruction to formal schooling; it also finds that declining fees and rising instructional quality had a marked impact on enrollments in elementary schools. Chapter 7 finds that both the declining demand of the workplace for child labor and the enforcement of child labor and compulsory schooling laws improved the regularity of school attendance. The concluding chapter weighs costs against benefits

of acquiring literacy in Victorian England, in order to establish the importance of policy and popular demand in the rise of literacy.

In my own struggle with the written word in preparing this study, I
have received assistance from many quarters. A Spencer Fellowship from
the National Academy of Education allowed me to devote the 1987–88
academic year to researching and writing preliminary versions of this
book. An F. Leroy Hill Summer Faculty Fellowship from the Institute for
Humane Studies of George Mason University permitted me to devote the
summer of 1989 to the manuscript. Funds to assist in publishing tables
were generously provided by the Department of Economics, the Dean of
Arts and Sciences, and the Graduate School of the University of Maryland
Baltimore County. I received beneficial comments on individual chapters
from Richard Altick, Farley Grubb, Timothy Guinnane, Thomas Jordan,
W. Marsden, Clark Nardinelli, W. B. Stephens, David Vincent, and Maris
Vinovskis. The referees for the University of Pennsylvania Press provided
most helpful comments on the manuscript as a whole. The editorial exper-
tise of Elisa Diehl improved the manuscript considerably. The manuscript
benefited further from the skillful copyediting of Catherine Gjerdingen
and the advice of Mindy Brown, both of the University of Pennsylvania
Press. Useful assistance was provided by Jeanne Jennings in preparing the
bibliography, by Marty Taylor in editing the tables, and by Iris Hobbs in
typing the bibliography and tables. I owe a special debt to Rowena for her
patience and encouragement.

1. Interpreting the Rise of Literacy in Victorian England

DESPITE ENGLAND'S EMINENCE in the world of letters since the time of Chaucer, it was not until the second half of the nineteenth century that most working-class English men and women could read and write. Before 1500 perhaps only 10 percent of all English adults were literate.[1] This percentage gradually rose until 1750, when about half of all English brides and grooms could sign their names.[2] England's Industrial Revolution in the second half of the eighteenth century does not appear to have been accompanied by rapid educational progress. And, although England was preeminent as an economic and military power during the first half of the nineteenth century, the educational standing of its populace was undistinguished. Between 1754 and 1840, the signature rates of grooms at marriage appear to exhibit no clear upward trend, while the signature rates of brides increased by a modest 10 percentage points.[3] In 1840, one third of all grooms and half of all brides could not sign their names at marriage.[4] Literacy and school attendance rates in England in the mid-nineteenth century were about the same as in France and somewhat behind most of Germany, Scandinavia, and the United States.[5] Then, between 1840 and 1900, the educational attainment of the English population improved markedly. By 1900, virtually all brides and grooms were able to sign the marriage register.[6]

This improvement came during a period of extensive efforts by the state as well as by various religious and lay associations to establish a national system of elementary schooling. During the first third of the nineteenth century, religious organizations began to provide both day and Sunday school facilities. In 1833, Parliament began to provide funding for elementary schools; it subsequently established the Committee of Council on Education to oversee their operation. These efforts were accompanied by legislation that restricted child labor. Parliament prodded parents in a more direct way to send their children to school when the Education Act of 1870 gave authority to local school boards to require all children under their jurisdiction to meet minimum standards of school attendance. In the 1880s, all localities of England and Wales were required to set such standards. By 1900, elementary schools charging no tuition and meeting state-certified standards of instruction were within reach of the entire English and Welsh populations, and it became increasingly difficult for parents and children to violate the laws against truancy. The marked growth in public expenditure on elementary education during the nineteenth century makes it clear how extensive all these efforts were. At the beginning of the nineteenth century, expenditure by church and state on elementary education was negligible; by the end of the century, annual expenditure on elementary education by the state alone came to over six million pounds per year.[7]

This surge of activity not only by the state but by other groups with overtly public motives, including national religious organizations, local clergy and religious groups, and individual philanthropists, provides an obvious explanation for the rise of literacy in Victorian England. Indeed, the growth of a national system of elementary schooling and, during some periods, the sluggishness of that growth have been used as indicators of growing government involvement in social and economic affairs.[8] Yet both Victorian policymakers and recent educational historians have acknowledged that the story of rising educational attainment in Victorian England involved much more than the institutional development of educational policy. These observers have been aware that the effectiveness of educational policy measures depended on how the working classes responded to them. It was ultimately the children of working-class parents who had to attend schools and master their lessons if basic educational attainments were to improve. Subsidized schools would do little good if they were not attended, and laws requiring school attendance would do little good if they were not obeyed. From Horace Mann in his report for the 1851 Census of Education and the authors of the 1861 Newcastle Commission report to educational historians writing after World War II, low school attendance has been attributed to a large extent to parental apathy toward education.[9] A series of articles on Victorian school attendance written in the 1960s and 1970s acknowledged the importance of popular demand.[10] John Hurt's book on elementary education before World War I contains a chapter entitled "The Parental Consumer."[11] W. B. Stephens's detailed analysis of regional variation in education contains, for each region he examines, a section on "Attitudes to Education"; the attitudes he considers include those of working-class parents as well as those of middle- and upper-class supporters of education.[12]

Some historians have even argued that the rise of literacy reflected a

growing working-class demand for this skill. In support of such an interpretation, E. G. West has pointed to the widespread presence in the early
nineteenth century of private day schools financed only by the payments
of their working-class patrons.[13] This has led West to conclude that during
this period there was an extensive working-class demand for elementary
schooling, and that any growth in this demand could have been met
through the private provision of schooling. Similarly, Thomas Laqueur
has pointed to the development in the first half of the nineteenth century
of Sunday schools supported primarily by working-class communities.[14]
And, Philip Gardner has pointed to the persistence of private schools supported by working-class patrons well after state-supported schools became
pervasive.[15] These historians argue that working-class parents throughout
the Victorian period were actively seeking education for their children and
not simply responding to church and state efforts to provide schooling.

Yet none of these historians has examined in any detail trends in
working-class demand for literacy. Those emphasizing the importance of
educational policy measures have acknowledged, but not analyzed, the
influence of the demand for literacy by the working classes on their education. Those emphasizing the contribution of popular demand to the
growth of education have primarily pointed to active private markets for
schooling as evidence of widespread popular demand for literacy but have
not examined the characteristics of that demand.

It is difficult to attribute the rise of popular literacy to an increase in
working-class demand because of the lack of evidence on how much that
demand grew. It remains to be shown that the growth of popular demand
for literacy would have been sufficient to lead to almost universal adult
literacy in the absence of a church- or state-supported school system and
without the prodding of compulsory schooling legislation. Although the
existence of a private schooling market is suggestive of private, popular
demand for schooling, it does not establish whether the demand was rising over time. Indeed, private schooling for the working classes actually
declined over the nineteenth century, although this can largely be attributed to displacement by public schooling. E. G. West has used aggregate
evidence taken in part from other countries to argue that rising income
alone would have led to increases in literacy and schooling.[16] However, as
West acknowledges, this aggregate evidence does not establish whether
working-class demand was responding to income increases or whether rising per capita income was coincident with increased state provision of
schooling.[17]

The nature of working-class demand for literacy has been considered in some detail by historians interested in the role of literacy in the labor market and in working-class culture. Michael Sanderson's study of the education of the labor force in Lancashire during the Industrial Revolution examines the value of education in the labor market; however, his analysis stops before the mid-nineteenth century, when literacy rates began to rise decisively.[18] Richard Altick, Robert Webb, and Raymond Williams have examined reading materials during the Victorian period.[19] The important study by David Vincent considers how the working classes used literacy both in the workplace and in other aspects of their lives throughout the period.[20] But while Sanderson and Webb consider the interaction between popular demand for education and the development of educational policy, they do not consider the later Victorian period. Vincent, Altick, and Williams do consider the later Victorian period but do not explore in any detail the interaction between the development of educational policy and trends in popular demand.

Although the most conspicuous gaps in the explanation of the rise of literacy are on the demand side, issues also remain on the supply side, the most important of which is whether or not private schools, in the absence of publicly provided schools, would have been able to accommodate large increases in working-class demand. Critics of private working-class elementary schools have also questioned their quality as well as whether or not the majority of them were truly aimed at a working-class clientele.[21] This study will compare the relative importance of the rise of popular demand for literacy with the development of educational policy measures by church and state in contributing to the rise of working-class literacy during the Victorian period. It will consider the initial demand of the working classes for literacy and how much that demand grew. It will also consider how literacy rates were influenced by the development of a national system of elementary school provision and by the establishment of compulsory schooling laws. Finally, it will compare the influence of popular demand and educational policy on trends during the Victorian period in the costs and benefits of acquiring literacy.

Part 1

Private Choice and the
Benefits of Literacy

The most specific benefit attributable to literacy is the access it provides to the written and printed word. The ability to read allows direct decipherment of written and printed statements. The ability to write allows one to send written statements to others and to keep records that can later be used to remind and inform oneself as well as others. The benefits associated with these abilities range widely from a capacity to write letters to family and enhanced opportunities to acquire information about consumer prices and job openings, to the entertainment and insight provided by novels and the general information provided by newspapers. The importance of possessing literacy skills in acquiring access to the printed and written word should not be overstated; an illiterate can rely on others for access by having them read and write for him. But it is obviously much more reliable and convenient to have access without requiring an intermediary.[1]

Literacy may be valued not only because of its direct advantages in dealing with recorded statements but also because of a perception that it confers broader attitudinal and cognitive characteristics. These characteristics may be relatively narrow: literacy could make people quicker and more intelligent. But the characteristics could also include more amorphous tendencies associated with enlightenment and rationality—including behavioral features such as orderliness and more control over impulse.

Because the advantages of literacy can be so wide-ranging, it is hard to say much about their extent or tendency to change over time without considering specific situations where they would have been at work. Yet before turning to specific situations, one can pose a general question related to the changing value of literacy over time. To what extent was the value of literacy in communication enhanced as the proportion of the population that became literate increased? For the reader, the number of occasions to read could have increased with rising literacy rates; for the writer, there would have been more people who could understand written messages or street and shop signs. Accounts of such signs indicate that, during early modern times in England, tradesman used pictures and figures rather than lettered signs and numerical street addresses to indicate the nature and location of their businesses because of low levels of reading ability. In mid-eighteenth-century London, such signs were replaced by printed statements identifying type of business and numerical street addresses. One factor in the timing of this change seems to have been the rising rates of literacy in London.[2] Some segments of English society with high rates of illiteracy in the later nineteenth century and early twentieth century seem to have been aware of the problems of illiteracy when they found themselves in high literacy environments. One account of English canal boatmen in the early twentieth century comments on their illiteracy:

> So long as they remain afloat this constitutes no great hardship. It merely means that they can neither read books nor write letters—which they probably have no great desire to do in any case. When they go ashore, however, they are only a little better off than wanderers in a foreign field. . . . Since they cannot read, public notices mean nothing to them, and they cannot tell where the buses go or even in what street they are walking. All the time they must be asking questions of somebody. For the same reason, they are equally at a loss to understand their ration books and are unaware of what is due to them. Thus they must appeal to the grocer and the butcher to help them in their problems—questions, questions, questions! . . . In the old days, when country folk everywhere—and plenty of townspeople, too, for that matter—were uneducated, they never gave the subject a thought. Now that this sharp dividing line has developed, however, they are anxious to save their children from being in the way that they themselves must inevitably continue to be.[3]

One issue that Part 1 will consider is just how common it was in Victorian England for the rise of literacy itself to generate new uses for literacy and to lower the social standing of those who were illiterate.

Parliamentary investigators in early Victorian England as well as the employers they questioned were especially prone to inquire about and comment on the broad behavioral effects of elementary education, such as its tendency to instill habits of obedience and order. Such effects should be considered in examining public motives for improving Victorian elementary education. The term *public*, as stated in the Preface, is used to refer to interest in the consequences of an action for society at large. However, one might expect working-class men and women deciding whether to acquire literacy for themselves or their children would be more responsive to the immediate advantages of reading and writing. These advantages will be termed *private* in this study, since the primary motives for obtaining them are their consequences for the person acquiring literacy and his or her immediate family and friends. Part 1 establishes that these advantages, though limited, did exist and increased over the course of the nineteenth century. Chapter 2 finds that literacy improved prospects in the labor market, but only for a limited proportion of the working classes. It also finds that these prospects increased to some degree in the last half of the nineteenth century. Chapter 3 determines that reading and writing became increasingly pervasive in working-class leisure and domestic pursuits. Families rather than individuals probably most commonly made the decision as to whether it was worthwhile to acquire literacy. Chapter 4 concludes that the influence of the family lay not so much in providing resources for acquiring literacy but in shaping the value individuals placed on literacy, in particular through the impact of the literacy of parents on the literacy of their children.

2. The Benefits of Literacy in the Workplace

ON JANUARY 4, 1850, the Swan Brewers of Waltham Green advertised in the *London Times* for "a strong active, respectable looking man who can write plainly and who understands the management of a horse and cart." Those interested were to apply by letter in "the applicant's own handwriting." Writing could also be considered important for those who served up the brewer's product, as is evident from the Scarborough commercial hotel that advertised in the *Leeds Mercury* on August 26, 1854, for "a barmaid who thoroughly understands bookkeeping." Literacy in Victorian England, then, could be a precondition for employment, not just for the middle-class clerk or solicitor but also for more modest situations. These situations were accessible to those of working-class origins, even if to a limited degree. A growing proportion of English men and women may have wanted to learn to read and write to qualify for such situations and would thus have demanded places in the schools that the church and state were building. Over the course of the nineteenth century, the proportion of jobs in the English economy making use of literacy grew modestly; consequently, so did the incentives that the workplace offered to acquire literacy.

How Widespread Were the Advantages of Literacy in the Labor Market?

England's economy in the mid-nineteenth century was perceived to be one of the most technologically advanced in the world, with highly developed commercial and industrial sectors. One might presume that in such an economy, jobs rewarding the ability to read and write would have abounded, thus motivating workers to become literate. The presumption is supported by numerous studies of England and other regions of Europe in early modern times indicating a systematic variation in literacy rates across occupations.[1] There are serious grounds for challenging this presumption, however. It has been argued that the factories spawned by England's industrial revolution did not require workers who could read and write and, indeed, that the spread of the factory system actually lowered the working-class propensity to acquire literacy by raising the demand for child labor and hence the cost of acquiring literacy.[2] More generally, it has been argued that relatively few jobs in mid-Victorian England demanded reading or writing skills. For example, tending a spinning mule, puddling iron, plowing and hedging a field, and working a coalface provided virtually no occasion for reading, writing, or doing accounts. Although solicitors, accountants, and more prosperous merchants must have been able to read and write, they would also have required considerably more education than simple literacy, not to mention the advantages of either a prosperous family background or unusual ambition and native ability. These arguments, however, have not been based on any systematic survey of the Victorian labor force. Such a survey will be presented here in order to assess how plausible it was that literacy could have improved most workers' employment prospects.

Different occupations used literacy for different reasons and with varying degrees of flexibility. One can distinguish three basic ways in which literacy functioned in the workplace.

First, some jobs made direct use of the abilities to read, write, and cipher. For example, the Scarborough commercial hotel, mentioned above, wanted a barmaid to keep the books; and a compositor had to be able to read in order to set type. Among Victorian newspaper advertisements that referred to literacy, some simply stated that applicants "must be able to read and write." Writing was the most commonly mentioned skill, however, appearing in such phrases as "can write a good clear hand," and "apply in applicant's own handwriting." Advertisements also commonly mentioned bookkeeping skills, as in the phrases "keep books and accounts" and "quick writer and sharp with figures." Reports on adult evening schools in the 1860s and 1870s state that students were much more interested in mastering writing and arithmetic than reading because they perceived that the former two skills were more valuable in the labor market.[3]

Second, literacy could have been expected as a prerequisite or complement to other skills. Solicitors, physicians, and the clergy obviously would have been literate both because they would have completed levels of education far beyond primary schooling and because they performed far more intellectually demanding tasks than merely reading and writing. (On the other hand, it should be noted that one need not be literate to argue before a judicial body, heal the sick, or preach the Lord's word; it is probable that in earlier centuries, illiterates commonly did all three tasks.)[4] Literacy would also have been helpful, if not essential, for manual workers using designs, plans, and artistic patterns and models, for example, carpenters—who in the nineteenth century were perceived to be highly literate—and glass workers—for whom training in design was perceived to be of value.[5]

Third, some employers associated literacy and the schooling involved in acquiring literacy with general modes of behavior that they thought workers should possess. For example, some employers would advertise in newspapers for workers who were "respectable and well educated." Employers could perceive educated workers to be more disciplined, more intelligent, more willing and able to follow orders, and less prone to rebel or strike. While the level of a worker's education may have been viewed primarily as an indicator of fundamental behavioral characteristics, it also appears that some employers believed that education in itself played a role in producing the desired characteristics. In parliamentary inquiries (especially following incidents of labor unrest), employers commonly stated that educated workers behaved in a more manageable fashion than uneducated workers. After severe strikes and uprisings, employers sometimes appear to have increased the funding they gave to elementary schools, which would suggest that they believed education had a causal impact on worker behavior.[6]

However, it is also important to distinguish between the teaching of moral precepts and the teaching of literacy skills. Middle- and upper-class commentators on Victorian popular education on occasion expressed concern that schools taught reading and writing at the expense of moral training.[7] Whether or not a correlation was perceived between literacy and orderly behavior, and whether or not employers were willing to pay for schooling with the prospect of improving workers' behavior, the question remains of whether employers thought that education influenced workers' behavior by enough that they actually favored hiring more educated workers. In occupations such as mining, where strikes and unruly behavior were common, there seems to be little evidence that educated workers were hired over uneducated ones.

In a survey of the usefulness of literacy in the workplace, it is important to classify occupations according to the *degree* to which literacy was useful rather than to simply divide occupations into those using and not using literacy. Not only can degree of use vary at any point in time, but the requirements of specific occupations can change over time or across regions as the overall literacy rate of the labor force varies. For example, in the early Middle Ages some kings were illiterate, while in the twentieth century unskilled factory workers are often expected to be able to read and write.[8] In specifying varying degrees to which literacy was used across occupations, it should be acknowledged that occasions could conceivably arise in even the most unskilled occupations in which literacy would be useful. A day laborer could have occasion to read instructions or send a message. Nevertheless, the probability that literacy would be useful was far higher in some occupations than in others. It should also be noted that some economists argue that the economic value of education lies not so much in its functional use in performing specific tasks but in improving broad cognitive abilities.[9] But again the value of these abilities was likely to have been far greater in some occupations than in others.

    In Table 2.1, the Victorian labor force is divided into groups according to the extent to which literacy was useful in their occupations.[10] It reports estimates of the distributions of the male and female labor forces across occupational categories according to usefulness of literacy between 1841 and 1891. Table 2.2 reports estimates of actual literacy rates for each occupational category in the 1840s and indicates that literacy rates did vary between categories according to the usefulness of literacy. Appendix A reports the specific occupational titles that were included in each category of usefulness of literacy.

    Between 1841 and 1851, according to the estimates in Table 2.1, 5 percent of the male labor force and 2 to 3 percent of the female labor force were in occupations that strictly *required* literacy. In addition to lawyers, doctors, clerics, scientists, and writers, army and navy officers were required to be literate, and just after mid-century, the army began requiring that noncommissioned officers be able to read and write.[11] Teachers would obviously have needed to be able to read and write (although surveys of early Victorian education reveal that some teachers were unable to sign their names). Government civil servants, whose jobs intrinsically involved paperwork, must have been able to read and write. By the 1830s, policemen were commonly required to be able to read and write because they used charge sheets to report arrests and because they were expected to be familiar with legal procedures.[12] Individuals in banking, insurance, and

Table 2.1

Use of Literacy in the Victorian Labor Force (Percentage of Workers in Occupations Categorized According to Usefulness of Literacy)

Category of Occupational Usefulness of Literacy	1841	1851	1871	1891
	Male Workers			
Literacy required	4.9	5.6	7.9	11.1
Literacy likely to be useful	22.5	22.8	25.3	26.1
Literacy possibly useful	25.7	24.2	24.5	25.9
Literacy unlikely to be useful	46.9	47.0	42.3	37.0
	Female Workers			
Literacy required	2.2	3.0	3.7	5.6
Literacy likely to be useful	5.2	5.6	7.0	9.8
Literacy possibly useful	67.9	57.9	61.8	59.0
Literacy unlikely to be useful	24.7	33.4	27.6	25.5

Source: These figures are based on aggregates of the numbers reported by occupational category for census occupational reports as compiled in W. A. Armstrong, "Information About Occupation," Appendix D in Nineteenth Century Society, ed. E. A. Wrigley (Cambridge: Cambridge University Press, 1972), 253-83. The specific occupations included in each category of the usefulness of literacy are listed in Appendix A.

Table 2.2

Literacy Rates of Workers by Occupational Usage of Literacy, 1839-43

Category of Occupational Usefulness of Literacy	% Literate	N
	Male Workers	
Literacy required	99.1	215
Literacy likely to be useful	91.1	956
Literacy possibly useful	75.5	918
Literacy unlikely to be useful	43.0	1,554
	Female Workers	
Literacy required	100.0	7
Literacy likely to be useful	83.0	12
Literacy possibly useful	46.5	441
Literacy unlikely to be useful	9.4	74

Note: Literacy figures are based on the signature rates of brides and grooms reporting occupations for a given category in the marriage register sample described in Appendix B. The occupations included in each category of usage of literacy are listed in Appendix A. N indicates number of observations.

clerical occupations would also have needed to be literate because they kept written accounts. Railroad employees were required to be able to read and write relatively soon after the introduction of the railroad, both because they used printed timetables and instructions and because literacy was thought to be an indication of character and discipline.[13]

In some occupations, literacy might not have been strictly required but was *likely* to have been quite useful. For example, many businesses, especially those engaged in wholesale and retail sales, may have found it helpful to keep accounts, even if they were not always kept or strictly required. When a Mr. Bobbett advertised in *The Daily Bristol Times and Mir-ror* on September 21, 1881 for "a trustworthy young woman . . . to assist in baker's shop," he specified that she "must be a good writer and quick at figures" and that she should "apply by letter only." Street sellers and others engaged in small-scale sales activity were unlikely to have kept accounts.[14] But those engaged in dealing on a larger scale would have wanted to keep accounts to establish the operation's profits and to record outstanding credit and debt. Although the extent to which accounts were actually kept or kept competently is difficult to establish and will not be explored here, there is little question that they could be of value in operating a business.

It is important to note that the ability to read and write was neither a necessary nor a sufficient set of skills for keeping accounts. Illiterates improvised a variety of accounting systems from making marks on a stick to keeping counters in drawers.[15] And in the sixteenth and seventeenth centuries, there were lawyers and statesmen well trained in their letters who were unable to properly follow accounts because they had not mastered arithmetic.[16] Nevertheless, the ability to read and write would have greatly facilitated the keeping of accounts, especially in a business of any size and complexity. Some illiterate tradesmen in the eighteenth and nineteenth centuries lost considerable sums because they kept faulty records or because they affixed their mark to contracts whose meaning they did not understand.[17]

Self-employed proprietors such as builders, self-employed artisans such as many blacksmiths or bakers, and farmers also would have valued the ability to keep written accounts of business transactions. This is probably why in the January 4, 1850, *London Times* a lad seeking an apprenticeship to a plumber and glazier or painter indicates that he is "acquainted with bookkeeping and accounts and can measure well."

For farmers, the importance of accounts would have varied with the scale of the farm and the extent of its market orientation. Descriptions of nineteenth-century farm practice suggest that what accounts were kept were frequently not very detailed or systematic but were valuable nonetheless.[18] Farm bailiffs seem to have been required to read and write, which can be explained by the importance of keeping accounts.[19] Literacy should also have aided farmers in keeping abreast of new developments in agricultural technology. However, accounts of the spread of technology in nineteenth-century England have tended to emphasize the role of personal networks and contacts rather than the printed word.[20]

Factory overseers were also commonly expected to be literate.[21] One man advertising in the September 9, 1854, *Leeds Mercury* for a position as manager or overlooker in a woolen manufactory indicated that he could "write a good hand and understand bookkeeping." Contemporary statements indicate that literacy was of value to mine supervisors in reading and maintaining plans of underground works. On occasion, illiteracy could be a barrier for promotion to mine supervisor, although supervisors were frequently illiterate.[22]

In many occupations, workers received no formal training but learned by trial and error. Even in some of these occupations, however, written instructions were useful. Contemporary statements indicate that textile dyers were more productive if they could refer to written lists of ingredients and labels on pots. For this reason, they were sometimes required to be able to read.[23] However, dyers do not appear to have had very high literacy rates; they frequently used trial and error rather than written lists.[24]

A literate worker would have been able to use plans, designs, and models more effectively than an illiterate worker even if literacy was not strictly required for their use. Mayhew reported in the 1850s that carpenters wanted to educate their children because, in the course of their own work, they had come to appreciate the value of being able to mark with a pencil and to follow a design. Makers of glass, artifical flowers, and lace were more valued by their employers if they had mastered principles of design and possessed artistic ability. Even if training in art and design did not strictly require literacy, assessments of this training commonly stressed that it was ineffective when the students did not have a grounding in basic literacy.[25]

Between 1841 and 1851, according to the estimates reported in Table 2.1, 22 to 23 percent of the male labor force and 5 to 6 percent of the female labor force were in occupations where literacy was likely to have been useful but was not a strict requirement for employment.

In a wide range of additional occupations, literacy *might* have been useful, although the extent to which employers actually expected workers in these occupations to be literate is unclear. With available information, the value of literacy to workers in these occupations is *ambiguous*.

The value of literacy seems uncertain in those occupations in which workers were paid on a piece-rate basis, in other words, occupations in which workers were paid according to how much they produced. Piecework compensation was widespread in the Victorian labor market, being common in the manufacture of clothing, furniture, small metal products, and hardware.[26] These activities accounted for 14 percent of the male and 23 percent of the female labor force in 1851.[27] Miners were commonly paid by piece rate, and sometimes farm laborers were paid this way also.[28]

In piecework occupations, a written record of a worker's output was frequently used to determine the appropriate payment. Although such records were perhaps most commonly kept by the worker's employer, supervisor, or middleman, on occasion employers required or at least preferred literate workers because they could assist in keeping records of their output.[29]

A literate worker may also have found it advantageous to be able to check that his compensation was correct. Cases exist of apparently literate employees who kept independent records of their production and challenged employers on their compensation. In some of these cases the employer was willing to make a correction in the worker's favor. In others the employer refused. Employers may not have been cooperative in making records available or in correcting errors, and many workers may have been too timid to challenge their employers. Still, workers who had good reason to think that they were being treated unfairly by one employer were probably more likely to search for another who did pay fairly.[30] One witness before the 1871 parliamentary inquiry on the truck system mentioned large farmers who used account books to record payments to farm workers. He noted that the worker who could read would be able to verify that payment was fair.[31]

One important case involving the verification of accounts in piecework activity occurred during the third quarter of the nineteenth century. Miners and mine owners clashed on whether workers could have their own checkweighmen to verify the coal weights recorded by representatives of the owner. The intensity of the struggle suggests that much was at stake, with some estimates indicating that 10 to 40 percent of a worker's total earnings were involved.[32] In the case of nail making, employers were reputed to have exploited illiterate workers by shortweighing them.[33]

Parliamentary investigations into trades with piecework compensation made little mention of illiteracy as a source of worker exploitation, however. The notoriously low literacy rates of miners and the low value they apparently placed on the education of their children also raise doubts about whether literacy was of any significant value to piece-rate workers in assuring fair compensation. Thus, the actual value of literacy to piece-rate workers in Victorian England remains uncertain.

Domestic service was another major sector of the labor force in which literacy was of possible but uncertain use. Literacy was frequently expected of those in higher-level service positions that involved household administration, keeping accounts, issuing written instructions and orders, and making household purchases.[34] Employers may also have preferred literate servants becaused they believed that literacy was an indication of good character. One early nineteenth-century guide to household management even stated that no servant should be hired who could not read and write, although the relatively low literacy rates of domestic servants indicate that this principle was not commonly followed.[35] In the sample of marriage register entries from 1839 to 1843, described in Appendix B, only 42 percent of brides reporting the occupation "servant" signed their names. Furthermore, advertisements in Victorian newspapers for service positions did not mention literacy except occasionally for higher-level positions such as cook or housekeeper. In rural areas, however, parents seem to have believed that elementary schooling would improve their daughters' prospects of getting service positions.[36] The rural school may have provided a link to urban service positions through the reference of either the schoolmaster or the country parson.[37] This incentive for girls to attend schools has been offered as one explanation of why, in the second half of the nineteenth century, the signature rates of brides in many rural areas exceeded those of grooms.[38] Literate servants may also have found it easier to get information about job openings. The literate servant with access to newspapers would have been able to peruse ads for alternative employers without having to make her interest public by having someone else read the ads to her.

Literacy could have been of possible use in various other occupations. Masons and workers in other construction occupations may have made some use of plans, designs, and measurement, although they made less use of them than carpenters and relied more on practical experience. Smaller farmers and skilled agricultural laborers may have had some occasion for keeping accounts. Some carriers and other workers in road transportation may have had some occasion to read instructions, directions, and addresses, but it is uncertain how common this was.[39]

In the mid-nineteenth century, according to the estimates reported in Table 2.1, a quarter of the male labor force and between half and two-thirds of the female labor force were in occupations where literacy was of possible use. Thus, just over half of all male workers and two-thirds of all female workers were in occupations where literacy was definitely or possibly an asset.

Finally, workers in a number of occupations were *unlikely* to have made use of literacy. Although, as noted above, one cannot rule out any possible use, contemporary descriptions of some occupations indicate that they were unlikely to call for literacy with any frequency. Thus, the report to the Newcastle Commission on manufacturing districts in the Black Country of Warwick and Stafford stated: "All the operations are such as to require in the mass of the laborers employed great bodily strength and endurance, but little skill of any kind, and no kind of intellectual or moral cultivation."[40]

Agricultural and general laborers as well as fishermen fall under this category. In textile manufacture, only workers involved with dyes or patterns had any occasion to read or write. Other textile operatives, even skilled cotton spinners, had no reason to read or write in their jobs.[41] In iron and steel production as well as other manufacturing work, physical effort was the main requirement of workers.[42] What knowledge and skill were required in manufacturing occupations were typically acquired by experience. Road workers, coal heavers, general seamen, and inland watermen were not expected to be literate, and neither were the rank and file in the army and navy.[43] Despite the possible value of literacy in connection with piecework compensation, the low literacy rates of miners (58 percent of miners signed their names in the 1839–43 marriage register sample described in Appendix A) indicate that they also should be classified as unlikely to have used literacy in their jobs. An examination of data on earnings of shoploom weavers in Gloucester in the 1830s and agricultural laborers in Dorset in the 1860s indicates no wage premium within these occupations to literacy.[44] This suggests the absence of even general cognitive advantages in these occupations from acquiring literacy.

Between 1841 and 1851, according to the estimates reported in Table 2.1, nearly half of the male labor force and between a fourth and a third of the female labor force were in occupations where literacy would have been of no value. A minority of the Victorian labor force were clearly making use of literacy on the job. This would suggest that for the third of all grooms who made a mark in the 1840s, the workplace was making few demands on them to learn to sign their names. For the half of all brides who made a mark during this period, the opportunities to use literacy in the labor market can only be regarded as *possibly* more abundant.

However, although relatively few jobs demanded that workers be literate, one cannot infer that the labor market provided little incentive to acquire literacy. Even those from humble backgrounds would on occasion have discovered opportunities for promotion and advancement in which literacy would have been advantageous. One contemporary assessment of mid-Victorian education claimed that many workmen failed to be promoted for want of education.[45] Miners and factory workers seeking promotion to overseer, along with farm laborers seeking a promotion to bailiff, seem to have had considerably better chances if they could read and write.[46] As previously noted, women seeking higher-level positions as cooks and housekeepers and women in households of higher standing were also frequently expected to be literate. To see how much incentive to acquire literacy the Victorian labor market actually provided, one should directly compare the careers of literate and illiterate workers.

The Effect of Literacy on Economic Opportunity

The employment ads in Victorian newspapers mentioned above suggest that working-class men and women who could read and write would have had job opportunities that illiterates did not have. A sample of some eight thousand marriage register entries collected for this study from twenty-nine English counties for the years 1839 to 1843 and 1869 to 1873 provides more general evidence on the extent to which literacy improved employment prospects. This sample is described in more detail in Appendix B. The marriage register entries show the occupations of the bride and groom, and of their fathers, as well as whether the bride and groom signed the register or made a mark. With roughly 90 percent of the English population in the nineteenth century marrying at some point in their lives, the register entries allow comparison of the occupations of literates and illiterates for a broad segment of the English population.[47]

Aggregating and ranking the occupations reported by grooms and their fathers into five broad categories of occupational status indicates that for grooms with fathers of a given occupational status, those who signed their names tended to be in higher-ranking occupations than those who made a mark (see Table 2.3). Thus, in the 1839–43 sample for grooms with unskilled fathers (occupational status V), half of those who could sign their names reported occupations with a status higher than unskilled compared with only 20 percent of those who made a mark. These differences in status categories can be translated into differences in wages. By using one set of estimates of wage rates by occupation for 1867, the mean difference in wages between literate and illiterate sons of laborers for the

1869–73 sample can be estimated at 1.9 shillings per week. Such a difference would have been 13 percent of the weekly wage of an unskilled laborer for that time period.[48]

The occupational advantage of literacy reported in Table 2.3 was higher for grooms with fathers of relatively high or low status than for those with fathers in the middle of the social hierarchy. Thus, for sons of fathers of occupational status II (farmers, clerks, professionals, and merchants) from the period 1839 to 1843, 47 percent of literate sons reported occupations of occupational status I (aristocracy, high public office, and military officers) or II compared with 22 percent of illiterate sons. For sons of fathers of occupational status III (petty shopkeepers and skilled manual trades) in the same sample, however, 87 percent of literates reported occupations of occupational status III or higher, compared with 74 percent of illiterates. And, as noted above, for sons of unskilled fathers, 49 percent of literates reported an occupation with occupational status higher than unskilled, compared with 20 percent of illiterates.

One explanation for this pattern is that for those with fathers in relatively high-status occupations, literacy tended to be a prerequisite for entering such occupations while for those with fathers in low-status occupations, literacy helped to compensate for their humble background. In the comparisons of the occupations of literates and illiterates reported in Table 2.3, illiterates with relatively high social origins were much less likely than literates with the same origins to retain their father's status or even to enter more desirable manual work. Literate grooms from skilled and semiskilled manual backgrounds had much less of an advantage over illiterate grooms from the same backgrounds in retaining their fathers' status. Occupations in these categories probably tended to make less use of literacy than those of occupational status II, and the father's status as such may have served as a better guarantee than literacy that the son would match his father's status. For sons of those with the lowest occupational status (occupational status V), the comparisons reported in Table 2.3 indicate that literacy helped considerably in compensating for a humble background. Some illiterates were able to advance above the low occupational status of their fathers, but only half as frequently as literates were able to do so.

But if the comparisons reported in Table 2.3 indicate that literates had an advantage over illiterates in obtaining occupations of a higher status, they also indicate that literacy was neither strictly necessary for obtaining a high-status occupation nor a guarantee of avoiding a low-status

Table 2.3

Literacy and Occupational Status of Grooms by Father's Occupational Status
(Percentage in Each Occupational Category)

Occupational Status of Father and Groom's Literacy	Occupational Status of Groom					
	I	II	III	IV	V	N
Fathers with Occupational Status I						
1839-43						
Literate Grooms	34.7	35.5	28.1	0.8	0.8	121
Illiterate Grooms	50.0	0.0	50.0	0.0	0.0	2
1869-73						
Literate Grooms	35.4	37.8	23.2	3.7	0.0	82
Illiterate Grooms	0.0	100.0	0.0	0.0	0.0	1
Fathers with Occupational Status II						
1839-43						
Literate Grooms	2.8	44.3	32.0	10.6	10.2	537
Illiterate Grooms	0.0	22.0	26.8	15.9	35.4	82
1869-73						
Literate Grooms	1.9	41.8	38.9	11.3	6.1	524
Illiterate Grooms	0.0	24.1	31.0	10.3	34.5	29
Fathers with Occupational Status III						
1839-43						
Literate Grooms	0.6	5.2	80.8	8.8	4.6	1,263
Illiterate Grooms	0.0	0.6	73.8	12.8	12.8	321
1869-73						
Literate Grooms	0.8	7.0	75.3	9.7	7.4	1,334
Illiterate Grooms	0.0	0.0	67.7	11.6	20.6	189
Fathers with Occupational Status IV						
1839-43						
Literate Grooms	0.9	3.3	37.6	50.0	8.2	450
Illiterate Grooms	0.0	0.5	27.0	51.5	21.0	200
1869-73						
Literate Grooms	0.8	5.1	40.4	44.8	9.0	525
Illiterate Grooms	0.0	0.0	39.6	36.3	24.2	91
Fathers with Occupational Status V						
1839-43						
Literate Grooms	0.0	1.9	25.4	22.0	50.6	413
Illiterate Grooms	0.0	0.3	10.3	9.5	80.0	624
1869-73						
Literate Grooms	0.0	2.0	28.8	17.1	52.1	643
Illiterate Grooms	0.0	0.0	16.1	5.8	78.2	348

(continued)

Table 2.3 (continued)

Note: Figures are derived from the sample of marriages described in Appendix B. Types of occupations included in each of the five occupational status categories (also described in Appendix B) are as follows: (I) titled, high public office, military officers; (II) professions, commerce, clerical, farmers; (III) petty shopkeepers, skilled manual trades, mining, most transport occupations; (IV) semi-skilled manual labor; (V) unskilled labor. N indicates number of observations.

one. Thus, in the 1839–43 sample, 22 percent of the illiterate sons of fathers of occupational status II also reported occupations of occupational status II while 20 percent of the illiterate sons of fathers of occupational status V reported higher-status occupations than their fathers. In the same time period, 51 percent of literate sons of unskilled fathers (occupational status V) also reported working in unskilled occupations.

One explanation of why an individual literate worker would not have been guaranteed a higher-status occupation than an illiterate worker is that literacy had to be combined with other skills, attitudes, and aptitudes in order for literacy to provide an advantage. This is suggested by the extent to which various occupations made use of literacy. Only a small percentage of occupations strictly required literacy. Most occupations making use of literacy also involved other worker characteristics, such as manual skills for carpenters and blacksmiths or access to funds and business aptitude for shopkeepers and merchants. The comparisons reported in Table 2.3 suggest that for those seeking advancement, literacy alone was not sufficient to compensate for humble origins. The literacy rate for sons of unskilled fathers reporting occupations of higher status was lower than that of sons in higher-status occupations who had the advantage of fathers in such occupations. Thus, the literacy rate of grooms reporting occupations of occupational status III in the 1839–43 sample was 81 percent for those with fathers of occupational status III but only 62 percent for those with fathers of occupational status V.[49] Sons of unskilled fathers who were able to advance to occupational status III would seem to have had other characteristics in addition to literacy to offset the influence of lowly origins. But if occupations using literacy also made use of other worker characteristics, did literacy per se provide a real advantage in entering such occupations or does the advantage of literates over illiterates apparent in the comparisons in Table 2.3 merely reflect an association between literacy and other characteristcs more fundamental for success?

The survey of the uses of literacy in various occupations indicates that

at least some advantage in obtaining advancement can be directly attributed to literacy. Situations did arise in the Victorian workplace where otherwise able people would not have been promoted if they had not been
able to read and write. For example, parliamentary inquiries into agriculture mentioned cases of able but illiterate farm workers who were not
promoted to the position of bailiff until they learned to read and write.[50]
A report on technical training in the 1850s asserted that compared with
America, where education was more widespread, able workmen in England were frequently not promoted for want of education.[51] Literacy was
required for obtaining a position on the railways.[52] The role of the combined influence of education and family connections is evident in the following statement by a Welsh boy in 1870: "I am going to my 12, sir. I
can't read nor write. I've only been at school for a month, and this here
school master is good for nothing to teach anything. My father's going to
send me to Haverford-West to school and if I can get to be a scholar my
brother says he can get me a place in London, on the Great Western
Railway."[53]

An important indication that much of the apparent advantage of literates over illiterates can be attributed to literacy per se is that the types of
occupations where literates had the most advantage in entering were those
occupations where literacy was most likely to be used. The comparisons
reported in Table 2.4 are based on classifications of the types of occupations reported by literate and illiterate grooms whose fathers were in unskilled occupations (occupational status V) according to the likelihood
that literacy would be used. Of the higher probability of literate sons in
reporting an occupation other than unskilled (49.7 percent for literate
grooms versus 20.2 percent for illiterate grooms, implying a 29.5 percentage point difference), over 80 percent is attributable to an advantage in
movement into occupations where literacy was at least possibly useful
(37.6 percent for literate grooms versus 13.5 percent for illiterate grooms,
implying a 24.1 percentage point difference). The comparisons reported
in Table 2.4 indicate that although literates did have an advantage over
illiterates in entering textile manufacture, they had no advantage in entering mining, another important industry in which ordinary operatives had
no occasion to use literacy in their work.

Some mid-nineteenth-century observers asserted that education improved labor market prospects for only the more able and ambitious.[54]
Such assertions would seem to be confirmed by the high percentage (over
50 percent) of literate sons of unskilled workers who were also in unskilled

occupations in the comparisons reported in Tables 2.3 and 2.4. This group, despite their literacy, apparently lacked other qualities necessary to get on in the world. But, since it would seem likely that the least able and ambitious probably would have had relatively low literacy rates, this group would have been central in the move toward universal literacy during the second half of the century. And labor market incentives to acquire literacy would then seem to have had a limited, possibly negligible, impact on this movement.

However, the large proportion of literates apparently gaining no advantage in the labor market from their literacy could have been due to chance rather than to a lack of ambition and ability. Or parents may have been unable to assess whether their children would lack ambition and ability as adults when deciding to send them to school during childhood. An indirect indication of the influence of ability and ambition on the value of literacy can be seen by taking grooms marrying literate brides and those marrying illiterate brides and, for each of the two groups, comparing the occupational distributions of literate and illiterate grooms. The basic premise of this comparison is that grooms marrying literate brides were more able and ambitious or more likely to have possessed other character traits contributing to career success than grooms marrying illiterate brides. Within a given region, the advantage to literacy for grooms marrying literate brides had no tendency to be greater than for grooms marrying illiterate brides. For example, when the sample of marriages collected for this study was restricted to laborers' sons marrying in London during 1839–43, literate grooms were 20 percent less likely than illiterate grooms to be laborers, regardless of whether they married literate or illiterate brides. This suggests that chance was as important as differences in ability and character in influencing the extent to which literacy provided an advantage in the labor market.

The economic advantage literacy provided may also have varied across England because of regional differences in the labor market demand for literacy. The Newcastle Commission inquiry conducted in 1858 suggests marked differences between the specimen districts examined in the extent to which primary education enhanced workers' employment prospects. On the one hand, reports on London and port districts indicated that primary education was commonly perceived as markedly improving employment prospects. On the other hand, reports on districts in which textile manufacture, metal manufacture, mining, and agriculture predominated indicated that primary education did not improve employment

Table 2.4

Occupations of Grooms Whose Fathers Were in Unskilled Occupations, 1839-43 (Percentage in Each Category)

Category of Occupational Literacy Usage	Literate Grooms	Illiterate Grooms
Literacy clearly advantageous		
Clerical	0.7	0.0
Dealing	0.0	0.4
Farming	1.2	0.0
Police, teaching, other public service	1.0	0.0
Total	2.9	0.4
Literacy likely to be or possibly useful		
Artisanal proprietary	3.6	0.3
Construction	4.1	2.6
Domestic service	9.2	4.3
Skilled farm labor	1.5	0.5
Blacksmithing, other skilled metalwork	7.3	1.1
Other skilled manufacture (except textiles)	2.4	0.7
Small farming	3.9	1.3
Transport	2.7	2.3
Total	34.7	13.1
Literacy unlikely to be useful		
Enlisted military	0.2	0.3
Hawking, other petty sales	0.2	0.2
Mining	1.5	2.1
Semiskilled manufacture		
Metals	0.5	0.3
Textiles	6.8	2.6
Other	0.0	0.2
Skilled textiles	2.9	1.0
Total--occupations		
other than unskilled labor	12.1	6.7
Unskilled labor	50.4	80.1
Total	62.5	86.8
Total--all sons of unskilled fathers	100.1	100.3

(continued)

Table 2.4 (continued)

	Literate Grooms	Illiterate Grooms
Total N	413	624

Note: Figures are derived from the marriage register sample described in Appendix B. The particular sample used for Table 2.4 consists of all grooms whose fathers reported occupations assigned to occupational status category V, based on the occupational status categories described in Appendix B. Use is also made of the classification of occupations with respect to the usage of literacy described in Appendix B. Totals for all sons of unskilled fathers exceed 100 percent because of rounding. N indicates the number of observations.

prospects for the ordinary working-class person.[55] Comparisons between the occupational status of literate and illiterate grooms whose fathers were in unskilled occupations are reported in Table 2.5 for six types of districts. For four of the districts, literate grooms were noticeably less likely than illiterate grooms to be in unskilled occupations. The differences in status between literate and illiterate grooms were markedly lower in mining areas and the metalworking district of Halesowen, however.

Because of regional differences in the types of labor demanded, a sorting process may have emerged through which literate workers tended to be attracted to regions with relatively high demands for literate labor. The literate worker could have had a further advantage in such a sorting process because of the value of literacy to the migrant. Contemporary observers of agriculture in the 1860s and 1870s asserted that uneducated farm workers were less likely to migrate to high-wage regions because of "ignorance . . . as to the places where better paid employment was to be obtained, and as to the means of transfering themselves to such places."[56]

But, regional differences cannot fully explain why so many literate workers were in unskilled occupations. Even in Lancashire, the area with the lowest percentage of literates who were laborers, 38 percent of literate sons of unskilled fathers were themselves in unskilled occupations, according to the comparisons in Table 2.5. More generally, correlations across five of the six districts between literacy rates and various measures of the labor market advantage to literacy varied in sign.[57] The correlation between the literacy rate of grooms whose fathers were unskilled (occupational status V) and the difference in the percentage between literate and

Table 2.5

Literacy and Occupational Status for Grooms Whose Fathers Were in Unskilled
Occupations by Economic Activity of District, 1839-43
(Percentage in Each Category)

Literacy of Groom by Regional Economic Activity	Occupational Status of Groom					
	I	II	III	IV	V	N
Farming districts						
Literate grooms	0.0	1.7	18.6	20.3	59.3	59
Illiterate grooms	0.0	0.7	7.3	5.3	86.8	151
Major commercial and manufacturing metropolis						
Literate Grooms	0.0	0.0	29.2	18.1	52.8	72
Illiterate Grooms	0.0	0.0	11.7	14.9	73.4	94
Metalworking and iron-manufacturing district						
Literate Grooms	0.0	9.1	9.1	18.2	63.6	11
Illiterate Grooms	0.0	5.6	19.4	16.7	58.3	36
Mining districts						
Literate Grooms	0.0	0.0	100.0	0.0	0.0	3
Illiterate Grooms	0.0	0.0	100.0	0.0	0.0	11
Mixed market gardening, manufacture of lace and straw products, market towns						
Literate Grooms	0.0	1.2	22.8	12.9	63.2	171
Illiterate Grooms	0.0	0.2	3.6	4.4	91.8	478
Textile-manufacturing districts						
Literate Grooms	0.0	2.7	35.1	24.3	37.8	37
Illiterate Grooms	0.0	0.0	22.6	13.2	64.2	53

(continued)

illiterate unskilled sons of unskilled fathers was $+.19$. This positive correlation suggests that a relatively high premium on literacy encouraged
laborers' sons to acquire literacy. But the correlation between the literacy
rate of grooms whose fathers were unskilled and the percentage of literate,
unskilled sons of unskilled fathers was $-.38$. This correlation suggests
that a person's uncertainty as to whether or not he would benefit from
literacy sizably affected his incentive to acquire literacy.

Table 2.5 (continued)

Note: These figures are derived from the sample of marriage registers described in Appendix B. The samples used for Table 2.5 consist of grooms whose fathers reported occupations assigned to occupational status category V, based on the occupational status categories described in Appendix B. The specific occupations included under each status category are given in Appendix B and Table 2.3. The specific parishes sampled are described in Appendix B. The locations of the parishes for each type of district are as follows: Farming districts are from the counties of Buckinghamshire, Cumberland, Hertfordshire, and Wiltshire. Major commercial and manufacturing metropolis are from London, Kent, Middlesex, and Surrey parishes in the twenty-nine-county sample of marriages described in Appendix B. Metalworking and iron-manufacturing district is Halesowen in the county of Worcestershire. Mining districts are from the counties of Cornwall and Durham. Mixed market gardening, manufacture of lace and straw products, market towns are from the county of Bedfordshire. Textile manufacturing districts are from Lancashire parishes in the twenty-nine-county sample of marriages described in Appendix B. N indicates the number of observations.

Literacy did not guarantee improved labor market prospects. Nevertheless, literate and illiterate sons of laborers differed so noticeably in the occupations they reported as to suggest that literacy was of value not just to the most able and ambitious but also to those of more modest aspirations.

The comparisons of the occupations of literate and illiterate grooms reported in Tables 2.3 to 2.5 do not fully resolve the extent to which literacy improved labor market prospects. Because these tables are based on data from marriage registers, they reveal nothing about those who never married. Only 10 percent of any generation remained unmarried in the nineteenth century, however, and there is no reason to expect that the advantages of literacy would have been markedly different for those who never married.[58]

The marriage register comparison also provides no evidence on career experience before or after marriage. Opportunities for promotion in which literacy would have improved prospects were available to older, more experienced workers. Examples include the positions of farm bailiff, mine or factory overseer, shopkeeper, and artisanal proprietor. However, in the marriage register sample there was no obvious tendency for the advantage of literacy to rise with age of marriage (see Table 2.6). Admittedly, those marrying at older ages may have had different career paths than those marrying at younger ages. The more ambitious may have postponed marriage to pursue advancement, while the least able may have married later because of difficulty in attracting a spouse. Nevertheless, if the effect of labor market experience on the advantage to literacy had been

Table 2.6

Literacy and Occupational Status by Age at Marriage for Grooms Whose Fathers
Were in Unskilled Occupations, 1869-73 (Percentage in Each Category)

| | Occupational Status of Groom | | | | | |
Age at Marriage	I	II	III	IV	V	N
Ages 24 and under						
Literate Grooms	0.0	1.3	32.1	10.7	56.0	159
Illiterate Grooms	0.0	0.0	20.9	3.5	75.6	86
Ages 25 to 30						
Literate Grooms	0.0	1.0	32.6	23.2	43.2	95
Illiterate Grooms	0.0	0.0	18.4	10.5	71.0	38
Ages 31 and over						
Literate Grooms	0.0	4.4	34.8	19.6	41.3	46
Illiterate Grooms	0.0	0.0	24.1	13.8	62.1	29

Note: Figures are derived from the sample of marriage registers described in Appendix B.
The particular sample used for Table 2.6 consists of grooms whose fathers reported
occupations assigned to occupational status category V, based on the occupational status
categories described in Appendix B. The specific occupations included under each status
category are described in Appendix B and Table 2.3. N indicates the number of
observations.

marked, then the advantage to literacy reflected in marriage register comparisons would also have risen markedly with the age of marriage.

Literacy could have been advantageous to the worker not only in entering more desirable occupations but also in improving income and employment security within occupations. There is, however, evidence for a
number of occupations of little or no wage premium on literacy. This
evidence includes data on earnings of shoploom weavers in Gloucester in
the 1830s, agricultural laborers in Dorset in the 1860s, as noted above,
and also merchant seamen in the 1860s and 1880s.[59] It would be desirable
to have evidence for a broader range of occupations, especially those where
the use of literacy was likely or ambiguous but not required, such as for

those engaged in piecework or for self-employed artisans, proprietors, and farmers. Contemporary reports indicate that within a given trade, less educated workers, especially those who could not read or write, were most likely to be laid off in times of depression. These reports were made about both occupations in which piecework compensation was common and other occupations in which literacy may have been useful.[60] Thus, if the possibility of greater employment security associated with literacy is not taken into account, comparisons of the occupations of literate and illiterate grooms could understate the economic advantage of literacy.

Literacy also influenced the prospects of women in the labor market. Comparisons of the occupations reported by literate and illiterate brides are presented in Table 2.7. Literate brides were more likely to report occupations in service and clothing manufacture while illiterate brides were more likely to report occupations related to textile manufacture. Literate brides, not surprisingly, were far more likely than illiterate brides to enter occupations such as shopkeeping (classified as artisanal proprietor in Table 2.7) and school teaching (classified as low professional in Table 2.7), although only a small percentage of the female labor force held such occupations. In clothing and other workshop manufacture, some contemporary reports indicated that employers preferred female employees who were literate both because literate workers would be better able to handle designs and patterns and because they could assist in keeping records where piecework compensation was used.[61] In domestic service, as previously noted, literacy was not required but was useful in obtaining supervisory positions and was perceived in rural areas as providing an advantage in securing a position.

Although literate women tended to enter different occupations than illiterate women, it is uncertain whether the occupations entered by literates paid more than those entered by illiterates. For example, occupations in dress manufacture and domestic service—jobs that literate brides tended to report—paid more, according to some assessments, than did occupations in textile manufacture—jobs that illiterate brides tended to report. But other assessments are ambiguous on this point.[62] In textile districts, women of urban origin seem to have preferred factory work to domestic service because of the greater freedom in off hours that factory work allowed, while in rural areas placing daughters into service appears to have been desirable, perhaps because it facilitated migration to the city.[63] Shopkeeping and school teaching, occupations in which literacy was important, as indicated by the higher proportion of literate than illiterate

Table 2.7

Literacy and Occupation for Brides Whose Fathers Were Manual Workers (Percentage in Each Category)

	1839-43				1869-73			
	Father's Occupational Status							
	III		*V*		*III*		*V*	
	Bride's Literacy							
Bride's Occupation	S	X	S	X	S	X	S	X
Farm Laborer	1.1	1.1	0.0	1.5	0.0	0.0	0.0	0.0
Dealer	0.0	1.1	0.0	0.0	0.0	0.0	0.0	0.0
Dressmaker	25.3	15.6	12.5	8.2	17.7	2.4	14.7	7.1
Farmer	1.1	1.1	0.0	0.0	0.0	0.0	0.0	0.0
Hawker	0.0	0.0	0.0	0.5	0.0	0.0	1.5	2.4
Low professional	2.2	0.0	1.3	0.0	1.3	0.0	0.0	0.0
Miner	0.0	1.1	0.0	0.0	1.3	0.0	0.0	0.0
Industrial laborer	0.0	1.1	0.0	0.0	0.0	0.0	0.0	0.0
Metalworker	1.1	2.2	0.0	1.5	1.3	2.4	0.0	0.0
Artisanal proprietor	9.9	1.1	1.3	0.0	3.8	0.0	1.5	0.0
Servant	58.2	56.7	80.0	66.8	51.9	23.8	69.1	38.1
Textile Worker	1.1	16.7	2.5	5.6	22.8	71.4	10.3	45.2
Titled Lady	0.0	0.0	0.0	0.0	0.0	0.0	0.0	0.0
Transport Worker	0.0	0.0	0.0	0.5	0.0	0.0	0.0	0.0
Unskilled Laborer	0.0	2.2	2.5	15.3	0.0	0.0	2.9	7.1
N	91	90	80	196	79	42	68	42

Note: Figures are derived from the sample of marriage registers described in Appendix B. The specific occupational groups included in occupational status categories III and V are described in Appendix A and Table 2.3. Brides with fathers in occupational status IV, figures for whom are excluded in Table 2.7, constituted only 13 percent of all brides with fathers in manual occupations in 1839-43 and 18 percent in 1869-73. S indicates brides who signed their names on the marriage register. X indicates brides who made a mark on the marriage register. N indicates number of observations.

brides in Table 2.7 reporting occupations classified as artisanal proprietor and low professional, paid far more than female manual occupations. But the comparisons in Table 2.7 indicate that only a small percentage of brides from working-class origins reported occupations classified as artisanal proprietor or low professional.[64]

The incentives the labor market would have offered women to acquire literacy were dampened by women's low participation in the labor force. Census reports indicate that in the second half of the nineteenth century only 30 to 40 percent of women over twenty reported an occupation, compared with over 90 percent of men. Participation rates were markedly higher for women aged fifteen to twenty five; however, in the 1861 census, two-thirds of women aged fifteen to twenty reported an occupation, as did 59 percent of those aged twenty to twenty-five.[65] Relatively high rates of participation in the labor force by younger women would increase labor market incentives to acquire literacy because the period of labor force participation was close to the period when literacy was likely to be acquired. Brides from lower-class origins were more likely to report an occupation at marriage, suggesting that labor market incentives may have been more important to this group (see Table 2.8). It should be noted, however, that the proportion of brides who reported an occupation on the marriage register was markedly lower than the proportion of women who reported an occupation on the census. Thus, marriage register entries are at best an uncertain source of information on the labor force participation of Victorian women.

The incentives offered by the labor market for females to acquire literacy would have been dampened not only by the more limited time women spent in the labor force but also by the more limited variation in the usefulness of literacy across the occupations that Victorian women pursued compared with those of Victorian men (see Table 2.1). But these factors were largely offset because those occupations that women did pursue were more likely to make use of literacy than those pursued by men. Thus, the marriage register evidence reported in Tables 2.4 and 2.7 indicates that of those literates who married in 1839–43 and whose fathers were unskilled, approximately half of the grooms compared with less than 3 percent of the brides were employed as unskilled laborers. Since men had the advantage of superior strength and manual skill, women were more likely to enter occupations in which basic education was of value. For example, one historian of women's work notes that in London

Table 2.8

Brides Reporting an Occupation by Father's Occupational Status (Percentage of Brides with Fathers of a Given Occupational Status Who Reported an Occupation on the Marriage Register)

	Brides Reporting An Occupation	
Father's Occupational Status	1839-43	1869-73
I	4.6	0.0
II	11.2	5.7
III	11.5	7.5
IV	17.0	13.9
V	25.4	11.1

Note: Figures are derived from the sample of marriage registers described in Appendix B. The specific occupations included under each occupational status category are described in Appendix B and Table 2.3.

"shopkeeping had always been women's work. The wives of small crafts-men or tradesmen traditionally handled the retail and financial side of the workshop."[66]

The Victorian labor market offered incentives to both men and women to acquire literacy. If the majority of jobs did not require workers to read and write, those workers who did learn to do so, regardless of how humble their family origins, improved their prospects for advancement. On average, literate workers from all social origins were more likely to move into higher-status occupations than their illiterate counterparts. On the other hand, many literate workers found that the ability to read and write did not guarantee them well-paid and respectable jobs. Whether, during that period of their lives when literacy was most likely to be ac-quired, working-class children had already been segregated, either by themselves or by their parents, according to the perceived value of literacy in their subsequent careers is a critical issue, but one that is difficult to resolve. (The comparisons in Table 2.5 suggest that, to a limited degree, it depended on where in England the children were being raised.) In short, literacy offered both men and women enhanced but uncertain work prospects.

The Rising Literacy of the Victorian
Labor Force: Demand or Supply?

Although the English labor market of the 1840s offered some incentives to those of working-class background to acquire literacy, this alone cannot explain why, over the next sixty years, the proportion of brides and grooms able to sign their names grew, when that proportion had been stagnant during the previous six decades. The demand of the Victorian labor market for literate workers must have been growing for it to have contributed to rising Victorian literacy rates. It has been argued, however, that England's industrialization may actually have lowered demands for even modestly educated labor by substituting the routine and mechanization of the factory for the craft and skill of the artisan's workshop.[67] This argument, although it focuses on certain segments of the manufacturing sector, such as cotton textiles, and on the late eighteenth and early nineteenth centuries rather than on the Victorian period, raises the issue of the extent to which the Victorian economy changed course from the early Industrial Revolution so as to increase the demands for educated labor. Although a worker did not have to be literate to run a spinning mule in a cotton factory during the early nineteenth century, he did in order to run a railroad locomotive or deliver letters in the last half of the nineteenth century.

On net, the composition of the English labor force in the last half of the nineteenth century was shifting toward activities likely to have made use of literacy. The estimates in Table 2.1 present the distribution of the English labor force across occupations between 1841 and 1891 according to the usefulness of literacy. The percentage of men in occupations either requiring or likely to use literacy skills rose by 9 percentage points between 1851 and 1891 while the percentage in occupations unlikely to use literacy fell by 10 percentage points. The percentage of women in occupations either requiring or likely to use literacy rose by 7 percentage points between 1851 and 1891 while the percentage in occupations unlikely to use literacy fell by 8 percentage points.

Some of these changes in composition may have been induced by the increased availability of literate workers, but exogenous forces were also involved. Thus, the decline of agriculture in the Victorian economy was due, by many accounts, to the decline in international transport costs and the repeal of the corn laws, combined with the greater abundance of land in North America than in England. Urbanization, growing regional specialization, and the expanding scale of the English economy along with technological advance in transportation spurred the growth of the transport and dealing sectors. And rising living standards and changes in the nature of politics probably spurred the growth of the professional and public service sectors. Moreover, the Victorian labor force did not shift uniformly toward occupations likely to use literacy. The mining sector, an activity that made little use of literacy, grew markedly in the second half of the nineteenth century.[68]

Shifting 8 to 10 percent of the labor force from occupations making no use of literacy to those likely to use literacy accounts for only a modest part of the 33-percentage-point rise in literacy rates for grooms and the 50-percentage-point rise for brides in the last half of the nineteenth century. Even if changes in the composition of narrower subsectors are taken into account, this conclusion is not substantially altered. The rest of the rise in male literacy was due to rising signature rates for given occupations.[69]

If the demand for literate workers increased less than the supply during the Victorian period, any wage premium paid for literacy is likely to have fallen. In fact, the difference in wages for males between occupations likely to have used literacy and those unlikely to have used literacy as a proportion of average wages in occupations in which literacy would not have been useful fell from 1.115 in 1851 to 0.966 in 1871 and to 0.575 in 1891.[70] This marked fall in the wage premium suggests that the supply of literate male workers was increasing faster than the demand for them in the Victorian labor market. Less information on women is available, but there is evidence that in domestic service and teaching—two occupations making at least some use of literacy—women's wages rose faster than in other occupations between 1870 and 1890. Between 1850 and 1870, wages for teachers were also rising relative to the average for women, but those for servants relative to other occupations were close to level.[71] These trends suggest that the demand for literacy in female occupations may have been increasing more than in male occupations.

Because the labor force shifted only modestly toward occupations using literacy and because the wage premium for literacy apparently fell for males during the Victorian period, it is difficult to explain the rise in popular literacy solely by an increasing demand for literate workers. Nevertheless, changes in occupational composition do account for a significant amount of the rise in literacy rates.

Labor market opportunities may have contributed in less obvious ways to rising literacy rates. As literacy became widespread, reading and writing may have become incorporated into more and more occupations. Thus, farm laborers were increasingly expected to be able to read in order to understand the instructions for operating the steam machinery that was introduced in the 1870s.[72] By the end of the nineteenth century, according to one account, ordinary workers in iron and steel production were expected to be able to read dials and instructions on machinery, whereas in mid-century they had not been expected to be literate.[73] Even in mining, the value of being able to read safety rules and instructions was becoming evident.[74] Gradually, between the mid-nineteenth century and the first third of the twentieth century, literacy became required of enlisted men in the army and navy, spreading from the higher ranks down.[75] Not until well into the twentieth century, however, was reading and writing ability expected of workers in most manufacturing occupations.[76]

As children of the unskilled increasingly gained access to literacy, they were better able to compete with people of higher-status origins for higher-status jobs. Such competition seems to have characterized the market for clerks. Throughout the last half of the nineteenth century, contemporary observers noted that men of lower middle-class origins seeking clerical positions found increasing competition for openings because of improved working-class education.[77]

If one considers how the Victorian labor market absorbed the increasing percentage of sons of the unskilled who were literate, one can better evaluate the importance of the increasing use within occupations of literacy and the competition for higher-status occupations by children of the unskilled. In the sample of marriages collected for this study, the signature rate for grooms with fathers in category V (unskilled occupations) rose from 40 percent for those married between 1839 and 1843 to 65 percent for those married between 1869 and 1873.[78] Between these two periods, grooms whose fathers were unskilled but who themselves were both literate and reporting occupations of higher status than unskilled rose from 19.7 percent to 31.1 percent of all grooms whose fathers were unskilled.[79] Thus, while literacy rates for sons of the unskilled rose by 25 percentage points (65 − 40) between 1839–43 and 1869–73, the proportion of sons of the unskilled who were able to acquire literacy and move to an occupation of higher status than unskilled rose by 11.4 percentage points (31.1 − 19.7). How was the Victorian labor market able to accommodate this upward mobility despite the marked rise in the proportion of sons of the unskilled who were literate and hence competing with each other for higher-status jobs involving literacy?

Part of the increase in upwardly mobile literates can be attributed to a decrease in upwardly mobile illiterates. Between 1839–43 and 1869–73, the proportion of sons of the unskilled who were illiterate and upwardly mobile fell by 4.35 percentage points, from 12.05 percent to 7.7 percent of all sons of unskilled fathers.[80] But this decline can be attributed to the decline in the percentage of sons of the unskilled who were illiterate (from 60 percent to 35 percent). The upward mobility rate for illiterate sons of the unskilled actually rose slightly, from 20.1 percent to 21.9 percent (see Table 2.3). In other words, the rising literacy rate among sons of the unskilled was associated with a rising literacy rate for that percentage of sons of the unskilled who were upwardly mobile. Between 1839–43 and 1869–73, the literacy rate for upwardly mobile sons of the unskilled rose from 62 percent to 80 percent.[81] Part of this rise may reflect an increased use of literacy for occupations of higher status than unskilled. But it should be noted that the change in the literacy rate of sons of the unskilled who were also in unskilled occupations was even greater: it rose from 29.5 percent in 1839–43 to 55.2 percent in 1869–73.[82] Nevertheless, the rise in literacy for the upwardly mobile suggests that literacy was increasingly being incorporated into job specifications.

The other part of the increase in upwardly mobile literate sons of the unskilled can be attributed to an increased proportion of positions of higher status that opened up for sons of the unskilled. This proportion can be estimated by the difference between the total increase in the proportion of sons of the unskilled who were upwardly mobile and literate (11.4 percent) and the decrease in the proportion of sons of the unskilled who were upwardly mobile and illiterate (4.35 percent)—a difference of 7.05 percent. This increase in access to positions of higher status can in part be attributed to a fall in the proportion of unskilled workers in the Victorian economy. In the sample of marriage registers described in Appendix B, the proportion of all grooms who were of occupational status V fell by 6.20 percent between 1839–43 and 1869–73.[83] However, the proportion of grooms with unskilled fathers who were themselves unskilled fell by an even larger proportion, 10.28 percent.[84] The difference in these two proportions can be interpreted as reflecting an increase in the proportion of sons of unskilled fathers who were successfully competing with sons of higher-status origins for higher-status jobs. This increased proportion was 2.80 percent.[85]

In sum, of all grooms with unskilled fathers, the percentage of grooms who were literate and upwardly mobile increased by 11.4 percentage points between 1839–43 and 1869–73. This increase can be attributed to three factors, apportioned as follows: (1) the decrease in the percentage of unskilled jobs in the Victorian economy, $(6.20/10.27) \times (7.05/11.40) = 37.3$ percent; (2) the increased success of sons of the unskilled in competing for higher-status jobs, $2.80/11.40 = 24.6$ percent; and (3) the decrease in upwardly mobile illiterates, $4.35/11.40 = 38.2$ percent. Each of these three factors made a significant contribution, with no one factor accounting for a majority of the increase. This would suggest that labor market incentives to acquire literacy for those with origins of relatively low status would have increased during the second half of the nineteenth century not only because of the shift of the Victorian economy toward occupations that were more likely to make use of literacy but also because existing occupations were increasingly changing to make use of literacy and because people of humble origins were becoming better able to compete for higher-status positions.

Conclusion

A teenager who looked for employment in the *London Daily Chronicle* of September 22, 1881, under the heading "Apprentices and Boys" would have found that of 117 listings, 14 mentioned the ability to read or write. This is consistent with the finding in the first part of this chapter that a minority of the Victorian labor force were in occupations clearly making use of literacy. In the early Victorian period, almost half of the male labor force and at least a quarter of the female labor force were in occupations where literacy was unlikely to have been used at all. Literacy did not guarantee respectable employment. A sizable proportion of literate workers were in unskilled occupations. But for the teenager and for Victorian workers generally, literacy did expand employment opportunities. The second part of this chapter found that literate workers irrespective of social origins were more likely to enter higher-status occupations than illiterate workers.

Furthermore, the demand of the labor market for literate workers was increasing. Throughout the Victorian period, employment on railways, in the post office, in shops, and in other activities where employers valued literate workers was increasing relative to employment for farm workers, cotton spinners, and in other occupations where literacy did not improve employment prospects. As literacy increasingly became accessible to the sons of laborers, they became better able to compete with the sons of skilled artisans and shopkeepers for positions as clerks or even schoolteachers. Victorian commentators indicated that more parents were putting their children in schools and more adults were attending evening classes so that they could compete for jobs that required literacy. And as literacy became increasingly widespread, occupations were increasingly redefined to incorporate literacy skills. The newspaper began to be used as a clearinghouse for working-class employment during the Victorian period, reflecting the spread of working-class literacy. Thus, the spread of literacy itself could in some ways increase its value to individual working-class men and women.

The marked rise in literacy over the Victorian period is not completely explained by the pull of a rising demand for literate workers, however. The difference in wages in 1891 between occupations that used and those that did not use literacy fell in the last half of the nineteenth century. According to the estimates presented earlier in this chapter, the wage premium associated with literacy in 1891 was only half of the premium in 1851. Furthermore, even the signature rates for grooms who were unskilled laborers rose, from 34 percent in 1839–43 to 57 percent in 1869–73.[86] Because literacy rose so markedly for this group, other incentives than the advantages literacy provided in the labor market would seem to have contributed to the rise over the Victorian period in working-class educational attainments. The next chapter turns to the benefits outside of the workplace that literacy may have offered.

3. Literacy as an Equipment for Living

By 1840 the majority of brides and grooms in England and Wales were able to sign their names, as were 35 percent of the sons and daughters of laborers in a national sample of marriages from the early 1840s.[1] Since school attendance at this time was not compulsory, these figures suggest that English men and women commonly placed a positive value on the ability to read and write. Although the previous chapter concluded that a high proportion of those from working-class backgrounds would have found that the ability to read and write had little effect on their earnings, there were many conceivable occasions outside of the workplace where they would have found literacy to be useful, ranging from reading shop signs to writing love letters. Although such occasions were infrequent in the early Victorian period, they became increasingly common over the course of the nineteenth century.

What Contact Did the Working Classes in Early Victorian England Have with the Written and Printed Word?

Reading a book or newspaper or writing a letter were probably not common activities for literate working-class men and women in early Victorian England. A rural clergyman testifying before a parliamentary investigation on newspaper taxes in 1851 stated that in small towns and agricultural villages in Devon and Suffolk, "you will not find one person in 50 that sees a newspaper."[2] And historians of the English press have found that it was not until the second half of the nineteenth century that reading newspapers became a widespread habit among the working classes. An 1839 survey of 151 peasant families in Kent indicated that only 15 of the parents questioned reported opening a book "after the labours of the day were closed."[3] According to post office statistics, only four letters per capita were delivered in 1839. And the average number of letters per working-class person must have been considerably smaller when allowance is made for commercial and middle- and upper-class correspondence. Gravenor Henson, a spokesman for Nottingham hosiery and lace makers, reported to the Committee on Postal Reform in 1838 "that they [the working classes] never write unless it is almost upon life or death, unless they can send their letter free of charge."[4]

It should be noted that surveys taken in the 1840s do indicate that in London and other large cities, book *ownership* (as opposed to actually reading books with any frequency) and at least occasional newspaper reading were common among the working classes. An 1843 survey of the St. George's Hanover Square district in London found that 43 percent of the 1,439 families surveyed read newspapers. An 1848 survey of St. George's-in-the-East found that only 29 of 1,260 families reporting did not read a newspaper.[5] Of 1,954 families reporting on book ownership in the St. George's-in-the-East survey, 71 percent owned at least one book. For those families that owned books, the average holding was ten books per family. Even 71 percent of the 363 common laborers surveyed in this district possessed at least one book. In the households of laborers who owned books, the average holding was eight per family.[6] An 1840 survey of a Westminister district in London found that 63 percent of the 5,113 families surveyed owned at least one book.[7] A survey by the Manchester Statistical Society in the 1830s reported sales in Manchester of periodicals aimed at working-class readers of some three thousand per week.[8]

But newspaper reading and book ownership appear to have been much less common outside of the major cities. One nineteen-year-old boy from the South Stafford coal field did report to the Commission on Children's Employment in Mines in the 1840s that he "read[s] the Bible, books about Turpin and Jack Shephard: I read Bell's Life in London; it is much read in this part; but some houses do not take it in."[9] But other mining boys reported that their reading was largely confined to religious literature, in part because little else was available. Another nineteen-year-old from South Stafford stated that, while he had looked at a few sixpenny books, he primarily looked at Wesleyan tracts because the Wesleyans would replace the tracts from Sunday to Sunday.[10] A thirteen-year-old boy from Shropshire reported reading only his Psalter.[11]

Although surveys of rural areas indicate that the Bible, the Psalter, and similar religious materials were commonly found in homes of farm workers, few nonreligious printed materials were to be found. The 1839 survey of 151 peasant families in Kent, cited above, found that 86 families owned the Bible or similar religious material.[12] In Norfolk, 60 out of 66 farm laborer families surveyed owned basic religious books, as did 144 out of 174 families surveyed in Essex and 467 out of 596 surveyed in Hereford.[13] But the survey of Kent reported that only 8 of 151 families owned nonreligious books, and the three other surveys make no mention of nonreligious material.[14] Observers for the four surveys cited commented that in many homes they suspected that the Bible was rarely, if ever, opened.

Although the working classes in early Victorian England were often illiterate, they still could have had access to printed and written materials. In her survey of 200 working-class households in Middleborough in the early twentieth century, Florence Bell reported seven cases of illiterates who had others in their family read to them.[15] Throughout the nineteenth century, illiterates were able to get others to read or write letters for them; for example, street stationers in London performed this service. Flora Thompson described how she performed the same service in the later nineteenth century as postmistress in a rural Oxford village.[16] Gravenor Henson reported to the Select Committee on Postage in 1838 that during the Napoleonic Wars many people made a good living by writing letters for soldiers' wives; he indicated that there were still almost a dozen people in Nottingham who supported themselves in that way.[17]

There were occasions other than making use of books, newspapers, or the postal system when it was helpful to be able to read and write, yet in which getting the assistance of others may have been inconvenient, if not impossible. Shirley Heath's ethnographic study of mill families and middle-class townspeople in the American South in the 1970s revealed that the most frequent uses of literacy involved immediate, instrumental tasks of daily life. These tasks included deciphering street signs, street numbers, price tags at stores, clock dials, telephone dials, calendars, notices, directions, announcements, and labels on products, and jotting down telephone numbers, recipes, notes on calendars, and grocery lists and other lists.[18]

Some occasions for using literacy in daily life may also have been encountered by the working classes in early Victorian England. Street numbering became common in London in the mid-eighteenth century.[19] F. Parnell, a Methodist religious leader from Lancashire born in the late eighteenth century, taught himself to read from gravestones.[20] The use of time clocks at work and the placement of clocks on public buildings have been traced to the 1840s.[21] Printed poster advertisements had become pervasive in London and other major cities by the 1840s; according to one estimate, some 150 billstickers were at work in 1851 in London alone.[22]

Under the so-called truck system used in many mining towns, workers were paid by credits to their accounts at an employer-run store; credits could not be converted into cash. The parliamentary inquiry into the truck system in 1871 mentions an instance in which a literate (and presumably numerate) miner detected discrepancies in his account and was able to obtain rectification from his employer.[23]

There is little evidence that these tasks played an important role in working-class life in early Victorian England, however. People probably made their way around the streets by habit rather than by following signs or a numbering system. Census evidence on the distribution of billstickers suggests that posters were largely concentrated in major cities.[24] Despite the low rate of literacy that prevailed among miners, illiteracy is not mentioned in parliamentary inquiries as an important cause of unfair treatment under the truck system. In the small transactions that many working-class households would have encountered, keeping accounts may have called more for numeracy than literacy. A curate in Devonport suggested in 1858 that one could not maintain literacy skills solely by keeping accounts: "A large proportion of those who are between the ages of about 18 to 40 have lost the power to write and to make any calculations except such as arise out of the management of their small weekly incomes, or the every day transactions of their manual work."[25]

Educational and social inquiries in early Victorian England frequently mentioned cases where people had learned to read and write as children and had then lost the skill by early adulthood because of lack of use. One may infer from this that people had little occasion to read and write. In the parliamentary investigation on newspaper taxes it was reported that in agricultural areas "many learn to read as children and then having nothing to read forget how to read as adults." Similar instances were reported in mining areas.[26] Gravenor Henson expressed to the Committee on Postal Reform in the 1830s his concern about "many persons, who when I first knew them, wrote an excellent hand, on account of their scarcely ever practising, now write very badly."[27] Samuel Smiles testified to the Select Committee on Public Libraries in 1849 that "one great obstacle to reading books is the want of a sufficient supply of books, and that that is the cause of many who have learned to read when they were young, forgetting even the art of reading in their adult years."[28] Thus, in the mid-nineteenth century it seems that large segments of the English population *at some point had been taught to read and write* but had had little occasion to read or write in their daily lives.

The Falling Price and Rising Use of
Books, Newspapers, and the Mails

An obvious reason for the infrequent use of books, newspapers, and the mails among the working classes in early Victorian England was their high price relative to working-class earnings. Farm laborers at this time could expect to earn money wages of fifteen to twenty-five pence a day; urban laborers, perhaps thirty-five to forty-five pence.[29] By 1815 the stamp tax on newspapers had reached four pence a copy, and there were further taxes on advertising.[30] In 1830 a copy of the *London Times* cost seven pence. Popular periodicals in the 1840s such as *Lloyd's Weekly Newspaper* sold for three to four pence a copy.[31] In the first third of the nineteenth century, the monopoly of the Royal Post Office was used to generate revenue over and above cost. Rowland Hill estimated that in the late 1830s the average fee for sending a letter was more than six pence.[32] Although printed ballads, broadsheets, and eight-page chapbooks were available on the streets of major cities for a penny or so, more substantial reading matter, in both length and content, was considerably more expensive in the early Victorian period.[33] Charles Knight estimated that in 1828 the average price of a complete book, such as a major new novel, was sixteen shillings. Henry Mayhew stated that used copies and remainders of serious books were selling in London in the mid-nineteenth century for one to two shillings each. Such material was middle- and upper-class fare. But even the "poor man's gothic novel," a leaflet of some thirty to forty pages, would typically go on the streets for sixpence.[34]

The high prices of books, newspapers, and postage prevented the working classes from using what literacy skills they had acquired. Thus, George Dawson, a lecturer in a mechanics institute, told a committee of Parliament in 1849 that "we give the people in this country an appetite to read, and supply them with nothing. For the last many years in England everybody has been educating the people, but they have forgotten to find them any books."[35] The high cost of postage and the procedure whereby the recipient paid the postal fee made people reluctant to use the mails. Gravenor Henson stated before the Committee on Postal Reform in 1838 that "the general feeling of the working classes is this: that the high rate of postage is beyond their means of communicating with one another."[36] And Richard Cobden testified before the same committee that the working classes in Lancashire "are at present excluded from the benefits of the Post-Office by the high rates of postage."[37] Advocates of postal reform underscored the burden of making the recipient pay the postal charge by circulating stories of "mothers pawning their clothes to pay the postage of a child's letter."[38]

As the nineteenth century progressed, the prices of books, newspapers, and postage fell markedly. Newspaper prices fell because of the removal of the stamp and paper taxes as well as because of improvements in printing technology and paper manufacture. In 1836 the stamp tax was lowered from four pence to one pence, and in 1855 it was abolished. Correspondingly, newspaper prices fell. Whereas in 1830 a copy of the *London Times* had cost seven pence, in 1870 it cost only three pence. Popular periodicals such as *Lloyd's Weekly Newspaper* sold for three to four pence a copy in the 1840s; following the removal of the stamp tax in 1855, it cost only a penny a copy.[39]

The fall in postal rates was even more marked than that for newspapers. In the 1830s the cost of sending a letter within England could exceed ten pence, the cost varying with the distance sent and the number of sheets in the letter.[40] After reform of the postal system was initiated by Rowland Hill in 1839, the cost of sending a letter within England fell to the uniform price of a penny for the first half ounce.[41]

The introduction of the steam press, the replacement of machine-made for handmade paper, the lifting of paper duties, and the decision of publishers to aim for the mass market were all lowering book prices throughout the nineteenth century. Charles Knight estimated that the average price of a complete book fell from sixteen shillings in 1828 to eight shillings in 1853. The introduction of reprints and novels in serial form during this period lowered the effective price even further. Eight shillings was still more than the working classes were willing to pay for a book, but the same forces lowering the prices of books for society's wealthier elements also seem to have improved the quality of the one- to sixpenny literature aimed at the working classes. In 1820 a penny bought a broadside consisting of a few doggerel verses describing the trial of Dick Turpin. By 1850 a penny could buy a Gothic romance of fifty to one hundred pages written in reasonably fluent prose.[42]

As the prices of books, newspapers, and the mails fell, their use increased markedly. With the reduction of the stamp tax from four pence to one pence in 1836, the number of newspaper stamps issued increased from 32 million in 1836 to 44 million in 1847.[43] Purchase of stamped newspapers was disproportionately concentrated among the middle and upper classes. However, the circulation of *Lloyd's Weekly Newspaper*, a leading paper aimed at the lower middle class and the skilled manual class, also rose markedly as the stamp tax was removed. In 1843 when *Lloyd's* was first published for three pence, its weekly circulation was 21,000 copies. Its circulation increased to 90,000 copies in 1853. Following the lifting of the stamp tax in 1855, *Lloyd's* lowered its price from three pence to two pence; consequently its circulation grew to 170,000 in 1861. In that same year, anticipating the removal of the paper duty, *Lloyd's* reduced its price to a penny. Over the next two years its circulation more than doubled, reaching 350,000 in 1863. It took more than twenty years for *Lloyd's* circulation to double again and reach its 1886 level of 750,000.[44]

The impact on popular purchases of lowering the stamp tax is suggested by the emergence in the 1840s of other newspapers that successfully catered to the popular market, such as the *Illustrated London Newspaper*.[45] In his report on "Western Agricultural Districts," James Fraser stated to the Newcastle Commission on Popular Education in 1861 that "the enormous circulation of cheap newspapers is an evidence that education is intellectually leavening classes who, twenty years ago, were entire strangers to its influence. You will hardly find a village now in which two or three newspapers do not circulate."[46]

The increase in book usage, especially books aimed at the working-class reader, is harder to document. Both Fraser reporting on "Western Agricultural Districts" and Thomas Hedley reporting on "Eastern Agricultural Districts" to the Newcastle Commission noted that it was difficult to obtain fiction and other light reading matter in rural areas.[47] Henry Mayhew reported, however, that in the 1860s increasing numbers of book hawkers were making their way through country districts.[48] Flora Thompson's description of an Oxfordshire hamlet in the 1880s suggests ready access to cheap fiction:

> Most of the younger women and some of the older ones were fond of what they called "a bit of a read" and their mental fare consisted almost exclusively of the novelette. Several of the hamlet women took in one of these weekly, as published, for the price was but one penny, and these were handed round until the pages were thin and frayed with use. Copies of others found their way there from neighbouring villages, or from daughters in service, and there was always quite a library of them in circulation.[49]

In 1840, the first year of the penny post, the number of letters delivered was more than double the number delivered in 1839. By 1845, deliveries had risen to almost four times the 1839 level. Nevertheless, this increase did not meet the expectations of the advocates of postal reform. Gravenor Henson had reported expectations that working-class use of the mails would increase ten times with the introduction of the penny post.[50] Rowland Hill, the architect of postal reform, had assured Parliament that deliveries would rise by the five and a half times necessary to maintain revenues in the face of an equal percentage cut in price. With actual volume only slightly more than doubling in the first year after reform, revenues actually fell. Not until the 1850s did volume increase by five and a half times to match Hill's expectations. Not until the 1860s were revenues restored to their 1839 level. And not until the 1870s were profits restored to their prereform level.[51]

The number of letters per capita delivered by the Royal Post Office in England eventually increased from four in 1839 to four hundred in 1881.[52] Much of this increase may have been due to increased commercial, along with middle- and upper-class, usage.[53] Still, in 1861, James Fraser reported of rural districts that "if in these penny post times they [servants] do write rather more letters than their predecessors did twenty years ago, even if they be love-letters . . . I think that education may bear the blame, without suffering much in consequence in the estimation of dispassionate judges.[54] A curate from Devonport reported to the Newcastle Commission that "the cheapness of postage now causes all to desire to learn to write and keep up the art."[55] In the last half of the century, special occasion cards enjoyed a surge of popularity. Cards for Valentine's Day were the first to experience this surge, then Christmas cards, and finally, spurred by the introduction of the halfpenny postcard in 1870, picture postcards sent by the vacationer.[56]

Historians of the English press disagree about just how widespread newspaper reading was among the working classes by 1900, and this disagreement will be considered further below. Nevertheless, a number of accounts state that by the early twentieth century, newspaper reading had become habitual for many of the working classes in both urban and rural areas. According to H. W. Massingame's account of the press in 1892, "The penny and especially the halfpenny newspaper, is to be met with in the common lodging house, and the furnished room of the worst slums, just as it is in the rural labourer's cottage."[57] Bell found in her survey of turn-of-the-century Middleborough that three-quarters of all workmen read newspapers and more than a quarter of them read books as well.[58] A number of descriptions of working-class life at the end of the century suggest that reading the Sunday paper had become a regular part of working-class routine.[59] B. Seebohm Rowntree, in compiling his minimum poverty budget, indicated that doing without a halfpenny Sunday newspaper was one indication of deprivation.[60] One account of rural districts of the lake counties of northwest England asserted that "by the 1880's . . . at least half of the adult population were regular and assiduous newsreaders."[61] A Cambridge farmer testified before the Royal Labour Commission in the 1890s that almost all farm laborers were getting weekly newspapers.[62] Nor was it uncommon for working-class women to read newspapers. P. J. Lucas's study of mid-Victorian Furness in Lancashire concluded that newspapers were read by working-class women.[63] A survey of slum districts in turn-of-the-century Manchester found that because women were interested in horse racing, "the shops were besieged by women at midday for the early edition of the sporting papers."[64]

The working classes in the late nineteenth and early twentieth centuries, according to a number of accounts, also frequently read inexpensive novelettes. Bell's survey of Middleborough in the early twentieth century found that of two hundred households surveyed, fifty read novels only, compared with fifty-eight where only newspapers were read.[65] Novelettes were especially popular among women. This is indicated by Flora Thompson's description, cited above, of the club that women formed in her hamlet to share novelettes.[66] And in a survey of an industrial district of Lancashire in the very early twentieth century, John Leigh found that women preferred novelettes to newspapers.[67] The weekly novelette, Leigh suggests, had an advantage over the Sunday newspaper in that it was sold throughout the week.[68]

Although reading newspapers and novelettes was widespread among the literate working classes at the end of the nineteenth century, it was almost surely not universal. The above-mentioned survey of Middleborough indicated that 25 percent of the workmen in the sample read neither books nor newspapers.[69] Even fewer of the wives of the workmen were found to read.[70] Robert Roberts made this assessment of Salford at the turn of the century: "In the houses of innumerable members of the lower working class one would not find a book of any sort. Indeed I have heard men say that after leaving school they never opened a book again."[71] But then, even in the mid-twentieth century, there seem to have been at least some members of the working classes who seldom had occasion to read or write, and Richard Hoggart has noted that working-class families in the mid-twentieth century infrequently wrote letters.[72]

Yet, Roberts, despite his pessimistic assessment, also states that even those who did not have occasion to read or write on the job and who had forgotten how to write still "kept up some reading skill in leisure." He noted that many adult prisoners who were taught to read indicated that "the heaviest penalty of their ignorance had been their previous inability to read the *News of the World*." [73]

With a newspaper in 1900 selling for one-eighth of its cost in 1830, it is hardly surprising to find reports from the late nineteenth century that most farm laborers were reading the Sunday paper. Nor, with the postage for a letter in 1900 costing one sixth of what it had in 1830, is it surprising to find it reported of the working classes that "if a member of the family is away, a weekly letter is painfully put together." [74]

Religion, Politics, Urban Life, and Sports

The fall in price was not the only reason why the use of books, newspapers, and the mails may have increased during the Victorian period. Living standards were also rising, which helped to put these commodities within reach of working-class budgets. The spread of Methodism, with its emphasis on individual piety and religious study, may have fueled the desire of weavers and tin miners—occupational groups particularly active in the Methodist movement—to study the Bible and prayer books. [75] The upsurge of Chartism and other activist working-class movements may have put copies of radical publications such as William Cobbett's *Political Register* or Thomas Wooler's *Black Dwarf* in the hands of farm laborers and stockingers who had previously not seen the printed word. [76] The rising flow of population from rural areas to cities and abroad may have increased the proportion of the English population using the mails to contact distant relatives and friends. [77] Patterns of leisure and recreation may have changed in such a way as to make reading and writing more important, as can be seen in the growing popularity of the novelette and the sporting press. But how much did these activities actually influence the frequency with which reading and writing occurred in daily life? [78]

Working-class incomes by some estimates almost doubled in the last half of the nineteenth century. [79] However, if the prices of books, newspapers, and postage had remained at their early Victorian levels, even a doubling of incomes might have had at best a modest impact on working-class expenditures for these items. And rising income was not necessarily sufficient to stimulate the working classes to read newspapers or send letters. In coal-mining and metalworking areas, there were reports of low literacy rates and little apparent interest in books or newspapers despite high wages.[80] In 1849, William Dawson reported to the Select Committee on Public Libraries that in Staffordshire "high wages and heavy feeding rather than anything intellectual have been the characteristics of the mining population."[81]

The 1848 survey on St. George's-in-the-East in London reports for families grouped by occupation: average income, the proportion of families that owned books, and the number of books they owned. The simple Pearson correlation was only $+.15$ between average book ownership and average income, and was actually $-.006$ between the proportion of each group owning books and average income. However, the Spearman rank order correlation was $+.4$ between average book ownership and average income. One interpretation of these results is that book ownership did respond to income levels, hence the not insubstantial Spearman coefficient; however, the response was quite weak, hence the low Pearson coefficient. Rising income alone does not seem to explain an increase in the propensity to buy books.

In the first half of the nineteenth century, many of the books and pamphlets aimed at a working-class audience were about religious or political topics. The surveys of working-class book holdings in the 1830s and 1840s cited above indicated that religious tracts, pamphlets, and the Bible were among the printed materials most commonly found in the houses of the humbler classes. And Chartism and other radical political activism led to some of the most conspicuous journalistic activity aimed at the working classes in the second third of the nineteenth century.

Religious and political movements probably did not influence the rise of literacy during the second half of the nineteenth century, however. After 1840, the Church of England regained strength relative to Methodism and other dissenting sects, while Chartism gave way to trade unionism and a willingness among working-class activists to work within the existing political order.[82] Large segments of the working classes in the second half of the nineteenth century, according to many studies, had at best weak ties with organized religion.[83] James Obelkevich has asserted of the relation between religious practice and literacy in South Lindsey:

> In the period of greatest religious excitement, before 1850, large minorities of both men and women were illiterate; after 1850, literacy increased and

religious excitement decreased. Other evidence suggests that literacy and religious practice in rural England were inversely related. But it remains an
open question whether the religious revival contributed towards the final
conquest of illiteracy or was undermined.[84]

Virtually all surveys and reports on working-class reading matter in
the nineteenth century indicate that it was of a light and entertaining nature. Sensational crime reports and light fiction seem to have been especially popular. More concern was expressed in upper- and middle-class
circles over the indecency of working-class literature than over its heretical
or insurrectionary character.[85] The exception that may have proved the
rule was mid-nineteenth century Wales, where many religious periodicals
were published in response to an unusually strong lower-class interest in
religion and theology. Even there the demand was not sufficient to keep
these publications in business. The small and dispersed population of Wales
probably contributed to the lack of success of these publications. But if
religious publications could not make a go of it amid the atmosphere of
pious fervor that existed in Wales, it is doubtful that they would have fared
well elsewhere. Meanwhile, in the rest of England, sensational periodicals
such as the *Terrific Register* and *Reynolds' Miscellany* were thriving.[86]

Although working-class political and religious movements probably
peaked during the first half of the nineteenth century, urbanization and
migration were increasing during the second half, in approximate correspondence with increases in literacy. At first glance, regional differences
also suggest that urbanization had a strong positive influence on literacy.
Throughout the nineteenth century, London was consistently one of the
counties with the highest proportion of brides and grooms who were able
to sign their names at marriage. The Newcastle Commission report in
1861 indicated far more favorable attitudes toward education not only
in London but also in the commercial and port cities of Bristol and Hull,
compared with the rural and strictly industrial districts surveyed. However, the correlations reported in Table 3.1 between measures of urbanization and measures of literacy and schooling indicate that urbanization
was not a dominant influence on literacy.[87]

When the extreme cases of London on the one hand and Wales on
the other were excluded (that is, when only thirty-six English counties
were considered), the correlations between urbanization and *illiteracy* in
the 1850s were not statistically different from zero at less than the 10
percent level (see Table 3.1). Although urbanization was negatively correlated with illiteracy in the 1850s, it was also negatively correlated with

Table 3.1

Correlations Between Urbanization and Education
(Pearson Correlation Coefficients)

	Correlation between	
	Urbanization in 1851 and Illiteracy in 1857	*Urbanization in 1871 and Illiteracy in 1871*
For 36 English counties[a]		
Male and female illiteracy	-.044 (.798)	.341 (.042)
Male illiteracy	-.251 (.139)	-.065 (.707)
Female illiteracy	-.142 (.409)	.550 (.001)
For 40 English counties[b]		
Male and female illiteracy	-.379 (.016)	—
Male illiteracy	-.503 (.001)	—
Female illiteracy	-.212 (.188)	—
For 36 English counties and 12 Welsh Counties[c]		
Male and female illiteracy	—	-.034 (.820)
Male illiteracy	—	-.075 (.612)
Female illiteracy	—	.002 (.990)

(continued)

1851 school enrollments, counter to what would be expected if urbanization favored the use of literacy. Furthermore, the 1871 urbanization
measure was actually positively correlated with 1871 overall illiteracy and
female illiteracy, with a probability of under 5 percent of being equal to
zero. Although urbanization was negatively correlated with male illiteracy

Table 3.1 (continued)

	Correlation between Urbanization and School Enrollment in 1851
For 36 English counties[a]	-.307 (.070)
For 40 English counties[b]	-.243 (.130)

Notes and Sources: Urbanization is measured by the percentage of population in a county residing in a settlement of over 2,500 in a given year. Urbanization in 1851 is taken from "Census of Gt. Britain, 1851, Population Tables I, Appendix to Report," PP 1852-3, vol. 85, [1631], cvi (Table 17). Urbanization in 1871 is taken from "Census of England and Wales, 1871, General Report, Vol. IV, App. A," PP 1873, vol. 71, pt. II, [C.-872-I], 33 (Table 34). Illiteracy rates for males and females are measured by the proportion of grooms and brides who made marks rather than signed their names at marriage. These proportions are taken from 20th ARRG (Abstract for 1857), PP 1859, vol. 12, sess. 2, [2559], viii; and 34th ARRG (Abstract for 1871), PP 1873, vol. 20, [C.-806], lxvi. School enrollment in 1851 was measured by the proportion of the total population in a county reported by the 1851 census as enrolled in school. These proportions are taken from "Census of Gt. Britain, 1851, Education," PP 1852-3, vol. 90, [1692], 4-7.
[a]Excludes Wales as well as Yorkshire, London, and the nonmetropolitan areas of Kent, Middlesex, and Surrey.
[b]Excludes Wales, combines the three ridings of Yorkshire into one county, and allocates London among Kent, Surrey, and Middlesex.
[c]Includes 12 Welsh counties and excludes Yorkshire, London, and the nonmetropolitan areas of Kent, Middlesex, and Surrey.
Numbers in parentheses indicate the probability that a correlation coefficient is equal to zero.

in 1871, the coefficient had a probability of greater than 70 percent of being equal to zero.

With London added to the sample, the correlation was negative between urbanization and all three illiteracy measures and had a probability of under 5 percent of being equal to zero for both overall illiteracy and male illiteracy (see the results for forty English counties reported in Table 3.1). But, the correlation was still negative between 1851 school enrollment and illiteracy. With the twelve Welsh counties added and London excluded from the sample, the probability that each of the coefficients was equal to zero was greater than 60 percent (see the results for thirty-six English counties and twelve Welsh counties reported in Table 3.1).

These results raise the question of what incentives to acquire literacy the city may have actually offered. The urban environment had more situations where print would have been encountered, such as, on street signs and in street advertising. But, the relatively high literacy rates in London and port towns may also have primarily reflected the mix of occupations that the labor markets in these areas were demanding. Industrial and mining towns were notorious for low literacy rates. The Newcastle Commission report on Staffordshire noted more apathy toward education in the pottery and iron districts than in surrounding agricultural districts.[88] In contrast, northern farm counties such as Cumberland and Northumberland had some of the highest signature rates for both brides and grooms. Moreover, the most marked improvement in female literacy (arguably more subject than that of males to environmental influences apart from occupation) after 1840 throughout England occurred in rural counties.[89] The more consistent relation (see Table 3.1) between urbanization and literacy for males than for females is further evidence that the high literacy rates in London and port towns was primarily due to the occupational composition of these cities and not to environmental influences.

Ambiguity about the relative importance of environmental versus occupational factors on literacy is suggested by comparing the signature rates for sons and daughters of unskilled workers marrying in London with those marrying in farm areas (see Table 3.2). As previously noted, brides and grooms marrying in London were more likely to be able to sign their names than were those marrying in farm areas. And in the early period (1839–43) covered in the sample, the difference was much greater for brides than for grooms. One can conjecture that male literacy was significantly influenced by occupational demands whereas female literacy may have been more influenced by environmental conditions associated with urbanization. The greater gap in literacy between London and farm areas for females than males would then point to the importance of environmental influences on literacy. But in the later period (1869–73) the difference in literacy rates between London and farm areas was greater for grooms. And signature rates rose far more rapidly for brides marrying in farm areas than for those marrying in London. The rise of female rural literacy could have been induced by the expectation of migration to urban areas, but the rapidity of this rise indicates that an urban environment was not a prerequisite for rising literacy. The weak correlations between literacy and urbanization reported in Tables 3.1 and 3.2 do not completely

Table 3.2

Literacy of Brides and Grooms in London and Farm Districts Whose Fathers Were in Unskilled Occupations (Percentage Signing Their Names at Marriage)

Region	Grooms		Brides	
	1839-43			
London[a]	42.6		51.9	
		(188)		(189)
Farm districts[b]	28.0		16.4	
		(211)		(213)
	1869-73			
London[a]	75.1		76.0	
		(213)		(204)
Farm districts[b]	55.4		61.7	
		(186)		(211)

Note: Figures in parentheses are the base number of observations for the adjacent percentages. Literacy rates are measured by the percentage of brides and grooms who signed their names on the marriage register sample described in Appendix B. The particular sample used for Table 3.2 consists of brides and grooms whose fathers reported occupations assigned to occupational status category V, based on the occupational status categories described in Appendix B.
[a]Parishes sampled from London are listed in the description of the 29-county sample in Appendix B.
[b]Farm districts include parishes from the counties of Buckinghamshire, Hertfordshire, Cumberland, and Wiltshire.
The parishes sampled are listed in Appendix B.

contradict the possibility that an urban environment per se had a positive influence on literacy, but they do suggest that its influence was not dominant enough to offset the influence of other factors associated with literacy and, further, that it was not a prerequisite for rising literacy.

After 1840 internal migration in England was on the rise and overseas migration soared. The proportion of English men and women residing outside their county of birth rose from 16 percent in 1841 to 25 percent in 1881.[90] The number of passengers going abroad per thousand English population increased by more than half between 1851–70 and 1871–90.[91] The perception that emigration influenced the demand for literacy skills was evident in the minutes of the Select Committee on Public Libraries in 1849, which reported of inhabitants of some Scottish villages that "the inclination amongst them for reading works which will give them information regarding the countries to which they intend to go has been very great."[92] The committee also argued that one reason for forming village libraries throughout England was to provide "the most exact and ample information" on subjects related to emigration.[93]

A more immediate, and perhaps more plausible, effect of migration on the demand for literacy skills is evident in contemporary statements that illiterates would get others to write letters to distant relatives. Joseph Arch, the famous agricultural union organizer, noted in his autobiography, "A great many of the poor people who had children and relatives away from home, but who could not write to them, used to come to my mother and ask her to write letters for them."[94] Flora Thompson, in the description cited above of her duties at a turn-of-the-century post office, mentions how migrant laborers from Ireland would ask her to write letters to send home.[95] Yet these cases also suggest that although migrants wanted to communicate with distant friends and relatives, they were not motivated enough to actually *acquire* literacy. If a farm laborer could get a postal clerk to handle correspondence with his children in London, and if the letters he sent or received were few and far between, the incentive for him to learn to read and write was not likely to have been strong. It is, in fact, difficult to determine how strong and pervasive such incentives may have been.

Other general secular forces, though, may have increased the number of occasions calling for reading and writing. The keeping of accounts by poor people may have become more common between the mid-nineteenth century and World War I. This would have called for numeracy as well as literacy, but as noted previously, the ability to read and write would have considerably facilitated the maintenance of reliable accounts. Roberts mentions that in the store his mother kept in Salford just before the First World War, credit customers were given a small notebook in which to keep a record of their accounts. His mother had to make entries for illiterate customers.[96] Illiterates would on occasion devise schemes for reckoning without using numbers or the alphabet, such as making marks in a doorway or putting tokens in a drawer.[97] They were obviously awkward in comparison with written accounts.[98] Bell noted of some of the Middleborough households she surveyed in the early twentieth century, "I have been given the details of expenditures in various households, which make one marvel at the skill with which small funds are administered." Yet she also notes, "We must not assume that such skill reigns in all the households we are considering. It is obvious that it is only the skillful and thrifty managers who administer accounts with such a nicety that they can put them down on paper."[99]

The growing intrusion of bureaucracy on working-class life in the early twentieth century may have increased the number of occasions where the working classes would have had to fill out forms and hence make use of literacy. Roberts, describing the impact of World War I on literacy, states that "communications from husbands and sons, official forms, and, later, ration books all made hitherto unknown demands upon the unlettered or near illiterate."[100] And a Birmingham girl found on the eve of World War I that she had to assist her illiterate parents in filling out forms to apply for her to receive free school clothing.[101] Although migration, the keeping of accounts, and the encroachment of bureaucracy may have had an important impact on the incentives for the working classes to acquire literacy, their influence is difficult to observe.

More noticeable influences on literacy can be traced to changes in working-class leisure habits. Several historians have argued that fundamental changes occurred over the nineteenth century in how the working classes occupied their leisure hours, most notably in rural areas.[102] According to recent accounts of life in the Victorian countryside, there was a shift away from rowdy, spontaneous activity based on drinking and on cruel games such as bullbaiting toward more organized and orderly activities, including attending concerts, participating in choruses and brass bands, and socializing in pubs.[103] Rising living standards in the later Victorian period led to more hours of leisure and, even if to a limited degree, made novelettes and newspapers more affordable for the working classes.[104] Lamps and paraffin in the 1880s began to replace candles and rushlights in farm workers' cottages, thus facilitating evening reading.[105]

Of the various changes in Victorian leisure pursuits, the rise of organized sport had particularly important consequences for popular literacy. The spread of the telegraph and the railroad made possible a national network for a variety of sports. With improved transportation, competitors from all across the nation could more easily face off. With the development of the telegraph, a contest's outcome could be published throughout

England on the same day it took place. A national horse racing network emerged by the early nineteenth century and continued to develop through 1900. Cricket had achieved some degree of popularity by the 1860s, and football emerged and developed as a national sport from the 1870s onward.[106] In the last half of the nineteenth century, sporting news became a central feature of halfpenny papers aimed at popular audiences.[107]

One factor that spurred working-class interest in sporting news was the eagerness to place bets, especially on horse races. Indeed, popular interest in gambling has frequently been described as more important to the development of sporting coverage in newspapers than popular interest in sports as such. Betting on the horses was pervasive among the lower classes by the end of the century, causing enough concern to become the subject of a parliamentary inquiry.[108] And, as previously noted, betting attracted the interest of women as well as men.[109] Betting on sports does not appear to have become widespread until the late nineteenth century, well after popular literacy was beginning to rise.[110] But the surge of betting activity in the 1880s and 1890s may have played an important reinforcing role for those on the margin of acquiring literacy. Although the following passage from Roberts probably exaggerates this role, it does suggest how powerful this incentive may have been to some.

> There was a flood of cheap print devoted entirely to racing form and tipsters' views and forecasts . . . the sport of kings drew many along the road to literacy. When the ability to read offered a chance of sudden wealth through the mere deciphering of "Captain Cole's Special Selection," with some the need for basic education grew urgent. Many a man made the breakthrough to literacy by studying the pages of the *One o'Clock*.[111]

Thus the development of sports, rising incomes, migration, and other secular trends were stimulating the working classes to purchase books, newspapers, and postage. Not only did these trends directly increase people's incentives to acquire literacy, but they also implied that the working classes would benefit from the falling prices of books, newspapers, and postage.

How Much Was the Ability to Read and Write During Leisure Hours Worth?

Even by 1900, when reading newspapers and writing letters had become commonplace among the working classes, they may still have regarded these activities as largely frivolous. How much value did the working classes in the second half of the nineteenth century place on reading books and newspapers and writing letters? And how great was this value relative to the costs of acquiring literacy? One can measure the value to the consumer of using books, newspapers, and the mails by examining the impact on consumption of the marked fall in their prices between 1830 and 1900. This in turn measures the value that literacy (or at least access to those who were literate) provided to the consumer by making possible the use of books, newspapers, and the mails. This measure is calculated by assessing the gain to someone who would not have purchased books, newspapers, or postage at the high prices prevailing in the early nineteenth century, but who would have purchased them after their prices fell to their 1900 levels.

This measure can be defined, in economic terminology, as the consumer's surplus derived from purchasing books, newspapers, and the mails at their 1900 prices. The consumer's surplus can be estimated directly on the assumption that consumers had linear demand curves. In Figure 3.1, the triangle below the demand schedule, but above the rectangle of expenditure for the product, provides an estimate of the value net of cost the consumer received from using the product. Thus, if at a price of 7 pence a letter, the consumer made virtually no use of the mails, but at a price of 1 pence, he would have written six letters a year, then .5 × 6 × 6 = 18 pence was the consumer's surplus, or value net of cost, derived from being able to send the letters.

Table 3.3 presents estimates of the consumer's surpluses derived from using newspapers, books, and the mails. Estimates of the consumer's surplus for each of these items can be made from assumptions about (1) the change in price, (2) the quantity purchased after the fall in price, (3) life expectancy, and (4) the discount rate between present and future consumption. Appendix C further explains the calculations and the evidence supporting the range of prices, quantities, life expectancies, and discount rates considered in the consumer's surplus estimates reported in Table 3.3.

These estimates do not allow for many other conceivably important uses of literacy, ranging from reading street signs to keeping accounts. Thus the estimates of total consumer's surplus from books, newspapers, and the mails reported in Table 3.3 understate the total value of literacy. Since there was no charge to the individual associated with these other uses of literacy, however, it is difficult to put an exact value on them. But although Heath has emphasized the importance of these alternative uses

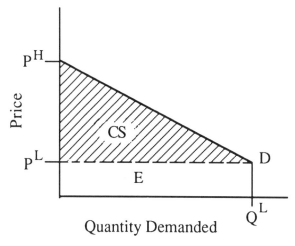

Figure 3.1. Consumer's surplus from fall in price of
newspapers, books, and postage. At high price, the
consumer does not purchase the item; at low price, the
consumer buys a positive amount. P^H = high price.
P^L = low price. Q^L = quantity purchased at low price.
CS = consumer's surplus. E = consumer's expenditure
on the item purchased. D = consumer's demand curve
for newspapers, books, or postage.

in twentieth-century South Carolina, these uses, as suggested above, were
probably far less important in nineteenth-century England. Indeed, the
evidence considered previously suggests that for the late Victorian working classes, reading the Sunday newspaper was the most common occasion
for using literacy. While books and letters were used less frequently, evidence is available on the price and usage of books and letters as well as
newspapers and, hence, on their value.

To assess the incentives to acquire literacy offered by the consumer's
surplus gains estimated in Table 3.3, these gains can be compared with the
cost of acquiring literacy and with the gain in earnings that literacy may
have provided in the labor market. The cost of acquiring literacy was probably no more than a few pounds; the magnitude of this cost will be considered in subsequent chapters. In the previous chapter, it was suggested
that the son of a laborer might expect to increase his wages by two shillings a week by acquiring literacy. Appendix C gives intermediate values
for the discount rate and career length as 25 percent and twenty-five years,

Table 3.3

Present Value of the Consumer's Surplus from Newspapers, Books, and Letters (In English Pounds)

Newspapers

	$r = .05; n = 50$			$r = .25; n = 25$			$r = .5; n = 25$			$r = \infty; n = 1$		
	Q^L											
$P^H - P^L$	20	52	365	20	52	365	20	52	365	20	52	365
0.31	0.24	0.62	4.33	0.05	0.13	0.94	0.03	0.07	0.47	0.01	0.03	0.24
0.62	0.47	1.23	10.18	0.10	0.27	1.88	0.05	0.13	0.94	0.03	0.07	0.47
3.31	2.53	6.58	46.21	0.55	1.43	10.05	0.28	0.72	5.03	0.14	0.36	2.52

Books

	$r = .05; n = 50$			$r = .25; n = 25$			$r = .5; n = 25$			$r = \infty; n = 1$		
	Q^L											
$P^H - P^L$	0	20	52	0	20	52	0	20	52	0	20	52
2.31	0.00	1.77	4.59	0.00	0.38	1.00	0.00	0.19	0.50	0.00	0.10	0.25
5.31	0.00	4.06	10.56	0.00	0.88	2.30	0.00	0.44	1.15	0.00	0.22	0.58
11.31	0.00	8.65	22.50	0.00	1.88	4.89	0.00	0.94	2.45	0.00	0.47	1.23
22.62	0.00	17.33	44.99	0.00	3.76	9.78	0.00	1.88	4.90	0.00	0.94	2.45
51.72	0.00	39.56	102.87	0.00	8.60	22.37	0.00	4.31	11.20	0.00	2.16	5.60

(continued)

respectively. These values, together with a fifty-week work year, imply that the present value for the wage gain from literacy was twenty pounds.

Newspapers were perhaps the most common reading material of the three types under consideration here and were therefore most likely to have influenced the incentives to acquire literacy. If purchased daily, reading a halfpenny paper at the moderate discount rate of 25 percent would

Table 3.3 (continued)

	Letters											
	$r = .05; n = 50$			$r = .25; n = 25$			$r = .5; n = 25$			$r = \infty; n = 1$		
	Q^L											
$P^H - P^L$	5	25	100	5	25	100	5	25	100	5	25	100
0.31	0.06	0.30	1.19	0.01	0.06	0.26	0.01	0.03	0.13	0.01	0.01	0.06
0.62	0.12	0.59	2.37	0.03	0.13	0.52	0.01	0.06	0.26	0.01	0.03	0.13
1.62	0.31	1.55	6.20	0.07	0.34	1.35	0.03	0.17	0.68	0.02	0.08	0.34
5.56	1.06	5.32	21.27	0.23	1.16	4.62	0.12	0.58	2.32	0.06	0.29	1.16

Note: P^H = maximum price (in pence) a consumer would pay for a product. P^L = price (in pence) after price fall. Q^L = annual quantity of product a consumer would consume after price fall. r = discount rate. n = life expectancy or, alternatively, number of years a consumer would use a given type of product. Evidence on the values of P^H, P^L, Q^L, r, and n that were common for working-class consumers during the Victorian period is reviewed in Appendix C.

have had a lifetime present value of one pound. This seems significant relative to the cost of a few pounds for acquiring literacy. But purchase of a weekly paper, with a maximum price of one or two pence and at a 25 percent discount rate, would have had a present value of only a tenth to a quarter of a pound. Thus, weekly purchases of a penny paper, encouraged by the repeal of the stamp tax in 1855, would seem to have had, at best, a marginal impact on one's decision to acquire literacy. The Sunday paper would have provided a substantial consumer's surplus gain only for those willing to pay more than one or two pence per paper or with a discount rate of 5 percent or less. These people were probably the most likely to have acquired literacy even without the fall in price considered here. Thus, the spread of daily papers among the working classes at the end of the nineteenth century probably had a substantially greater influence on the decision to acquire literacy than the earlier spread of weekly papers.

Although people more commonly purchased newspapers than books, those who did purchase books with any frequency probably had substantially greater incentive to acquire literacy than those who read newspapers only. The estimates of consumer's surplus in Table 3.3 indicate that this is because book buyers were probably willing to pay more for a book than newspaper buyers were willing to pay for a newspaper. For example, at a 25 percent discount rate, according to the estimates in Table 3.3, those who would have been willing to buy a novelette every third week (twenty times a year) for three pence would have derived a lifetime consumer's surplus of more than a third of a pound. Those who purchased a novelette every week would have derived a consumer's surplus of one pound. Book purchases probably were not common for the majority of readers, although increasing numbers of female readers may have purchased them, thus contributing to the rise in female relative to male literacy. At a discount rate of 5 percent, the value of books would have been far greater (see Table 3.3). At a 5 percent discount rate, even those buying a book every third week would have derived a consumer's surplus of at least 1.77 pounds. But readers with such a low discounting of future relative to present uses of literacy were probably also the most likely to have acquired literacy even before the prices of books fell.

The use of the mails would seem to have been of only marginal value. For people with a discount rate of 25 percent, the lifetime consumer's surplus would probably have been less than one third of a pound (see Table 3.3). The cases that were exceptions were those people who were sending or receiving more than one letter every other week or those people who were willing to pay postal fees as high as those that prevailed before the postal reform. These people were probably more likely than most to have acquired literacy under any circumstances. Even at a discount rate of 5 percent, the consumer's surplus from using the mails exceeded a pound only for those using the mails more than every other week or placing a value of more than two pence on a letter. In general, the estimates reported in Table 3.3 suggest that under any given set of assumptions, the mails provided the lowest consumer's surplus of the three kinds of material considered. This low consumer's surplus can be attributed to the low frequency with which letters were usually sent or received and to the relatively low value attached to a letter.

Those on the margin as to whether to acquire literacy may have had the higher discount rates and lower usage rates considered in Table 3.3. For these people, the fall in the prices of books, newspapers, and postage during the Victorian period had at best a marginal impact on their decision to acquire literacy. The lifetime present value of consumer's surpluses reported in Table 3.3 appear small relative to even the annual value of five pounds that literacy, according to the estimates in Chapter 2, may have offered in the labor market (the value of five pounds assumes a two shilling per week premium on literacy and fifty weeks of work per year). However, the shift from readership of Sunday to daily papers probably became increasingly common among the working classes by 1900. The estimates reported in Table 3.3 do indicate that this shift offered a significant consumer surplus gain relative to the cost of acquiring literacy. The weekly purchase of novelettes offered another significant gain.

Moreover, the consumer surplus estimates reported in Table 3.3 were clear *changes* in the value of literacy. They reflected incentives to acquire literacy that did not exist before the second half of the nineteenth century. The estimates reported in Table 3.3 suggest that a lifetime consumer's surplus of a pound or so may well have been quite frequent. A consumer's surplus of this magnitude may account for the growing proportion of those who would probably have perceived no labor market gain from literacy, such as females, but who still decided to learn to read and write.

Were the Incentives to Acquire Literacy Self-Generating?

Did Illiterates Feel Increasingly Isolated?
Rising literacy itself could have generated further incentives to acquire literacy. As working-class literacy rates were rising, illiterates may have increasingly felt ostracized and inferior relative not only to their superiors but also to their peers.

Some features of the marriage behavior of illiterates suggest that if any stigma was attached to illiteracy, it did not increase as literacy rates rose. David Vincent has found that as literacy rates rose in nineteenth-century England, the probability within a given social class that a literate would marry an illiterate spouse remained high until illiteracy rates fell below 10 percent. Furthermore, for the period 1899–1914, when signature rates at marriage were well over 95 percent, Vincent found that in almost all marriages in which one spouse was illiterate, the other spouse was literate.[112] Of course, since during this period the literacy rates among marriage partners exceeded 95 percent, the forces segregating literates and illiterates would have to have been strong for illiterates to primarily marry among themselves. But Vincent's results indicate that such strong tendencies toward segregation were not present. Furthermore, the marriage samples examined in the present study indicate that for illiterates of a given social background, prospects for upward mobility by marriage did not decline as literacy rates rose. Such a decline would be expected if in fact a social stigma on illiteracy were increasing in Victorian society.

Comparison of the occupational status of the husbands of literate and illiterate brides in the sample of marriages described in Appendix B indicates no decline between 1839 and 1873 in the prospects for upward mobility of illiterate brides. For brides whose fathers reported occupations of a given status, literate brides tended to marry spouses in higher occupational categories than did illiterate brides (see Table 3.4).[113] But the percentage of illiterate brides, with fathers of a given occupational status, marrying higher-status rather than lower-status husbands did not decline between 1839 and 1873 even though the literacy rates of brides from each social background rose markedly (see Table 3.4).

The absence of a decline in the social status of the spouses of illiterates, despite rising literacy rates in Victorian society, can be attributed in part to a general redistribution of the Victorian labor force away from lower-status categories. But, as the figures reported in the rows for all brides in Table 3.4 indicate, this redistribution was not marked and would not have been sufficient to offset any marked decline in the social status of illiterates.

However, comparison of the age of marriage of literate brides and grooms with those who were illiterate does suggest that in some circumstances a stigma may have been attached to illiteracy as literacy rates in Victorian society rose. The mean age at which illiterate brides married rose by a little more than a year between the 1839–43 sample and the 1869–73 sample (24.8 to 26.0), while the age of marriage for literate brides fell by more than two years (from 26.4 to 24.2). For illiterate grooms, the age of marriage rose by half a year. T-tests indicate that this increase was statistically significant at the 94-percent level for brides but only at the 48-percent level for grooms. When the sample was stratified by the social status of the fathers of the brides and grooms, the age of marriage for illiterate daughters of fathers in social class II rose substantially between the two time periods (from 25.0 to 29.7) as it did for illiterate sons of fathers in social class IV (from 23.4 to 27.6). T-tests indicate this change was statistically significant at the 95-percent level. The rise in the age of marriage for daughters of fathers in class II is especially significant because their literacy rate between the two periods rose from 76.7 percent

Table 3.4

Literacy and Occupational Status of Husband for Daughters of Manual Workers
(Percentage of Brides Marrying Grooms of Each Occupational Status)

Bride's Literacy		*Occupational Status of Groom*					
		I	II	III	IV	V	N
Brides with Fathers of Occupational Status III							
1839-43							
Literate		1.7	13.7	64.4	11.7	8.5	922
Illiterate		0.0	3.3	64.4	13.7	18.6	671
All brides		1.0	9.3	64.4	12.6	12.7	
Literacy rate	57.9						
1869-73							
Literate		0.6	12.1	64.4	11.4	11.6	1,269
Illiterate		0.0	4.1	66.4	11.6	18.0	345
All brides		0.4	10.4	64.8	11.4	13.0	
Literacy rate	78.6						
Brides with Fathers of Occupational Status V							
1839-43							
Literate		0.0	4.8	41.5	9.2	44.5	337
Illiterate		0.0	2.0	24.1	11.9	62.1	751
All brides		0.0	2.9	29.5	11.0	56.6	
Literacy rate	31.0						
1869-73							
Literate		0.2	2.0	37.4	11.6	48.9	656
Illiterate		0.0	1.2	31.5	10.3	57.0	330
All brides		0.1	1.7	35.4	11.2	51.6	
Literacy rate	66.5						

(continued)

Table 3.4 (continued)

Notes: Figures are derived from the sample of marriage registers described in Appendix A. The occupations included under Categories III and V are described in Appendix B. Brides with fathers in occupational status IV, figures for whom are excluded in Table 3.4, constituted only 13 percent of all brides with fathers in manual occupations in 1839-43 and 18 percent in 1869-73. N indicates the number of observations.

to 89.6 percent. This increase in the age of marriage could be interpreted as indicating that, as literacy became close to universal within a given social group, an increasing stigma became attached to illiteracy. For illiterate sons and daughters of fathers in all other social groups, however, no statistically significant rise in the age of marriage occurred.

The interpretation of these results is made problematic by the fact that the proportion of marriages reporting age rose markedly from 12 percent in the 1839–43 sample to 43 percent in the 1869–73 sample. And the percentage of marriages reporting age rose by more for both brides and grooms whose fathers were in lower-status occupations and who were illiterate rather than literate.[114] Thus, changes in the age of marriage between time periods could reflect changes in the representativeness of the sample.

At any rate, the existence of any stigma attached to illiteracy seems to be more directly measurable by the influence of illiteracy on the social status of marriage partners than by its influence on the age of marriage. Factors other than a social stigma associated with illiteracy could also have affected the age of marriage. If nothing else, the trend in the social status of the marriage partners of illiterates reported in Table 3.4 suggests that if the working classes attached a stigma to illiteracy during the Victorian period, they did not go so far as to ostracize illiterates.

*Did the Rise of Popular Literacy Lead to the Rise of
Cheap Popular Publications?*
As the number of working-class readers rose, publishers should have found that it was increasingly lucrative to develop novelettes and periodicals to attract these readers. Thus, rising literacy itself could have contributed both to the falling prices of books and newspapers and to the greater variety of material written for working-class readers.

Indeed, the argument that the rise of mass education stimulated the development of mass literature and newspapers was made within a few decades of the Education Act of 1870. Publishers in the 1880s and 1890s such as Newnes and Northcliffe, according to this view, perceived that the spread of elementary schooling had created a new class of consumers who had very limited reading ability and who found existing newspapers difficult to comprehend. To appeal to these readers, these publishers developed newspapers and periodicals such as the weekly *Tit-Bits*, which featured short articles on subjects of popular interest written in easily comprehensible prose.[115]

Beginning with an article by Harold Perkin in 1958, however, much recent scholarship on the history of the popular press has dismissed the impact of rising literacy rates on the development of popular newspapers and periodicals.[116] Perkin and subsequently Raymond Williams have argued that throughout the nineteenth century the number of active readers was far less than the number of literate adults in the British population.[117] This disparity would seem to preclude illiteracy as a constraint on the development of popular publications. Perkin and Williams have also challenged the notion that publications specifically aimed at the working classes emerged in response to rising working-class literacy rates. Their position is that by the mid-nineteenth century, a press already existed that reached down to working-class readers.[118] Furthermore, Perkin, Williams, and Lucy Brown have argued that the real problem in developing working-class publications in Victorian England was not the small number of those in the working classes who could read, but the small number of those who could read who actually bought newspapers and other publications.[119]

Alan Lee, however, has estimated that the gap between newspaper circulations and the number of literates was much narrower and may not have existed at all. Lee arrives at this conclusion by making a much lower estimate of the number of literate adults and a much higher estimate of newspaper circulations than Perkin or Williams. This discrepancy suggests the general uncertainty behind these estimates. The greatest uncertainty probably surrounds total newspaper circulations in Victorian England.[120]

Nevertheless, the estimates of Perkin, Williams, and Lee all imply that the minimum circulation required for a profitable publication was well under the total number of active readers or even (to allow for multiple readers per copy) of active buyers in Victorian England. Williams's estimates imply that by the mid-nineteenth century, daily newspapers had combined circulations of several hundred thousand, and weeklies had combined circulations of over a million.[121] Lee estimates that by 1870 newspaper readership may have been as high as six million.[122] At the same time, Louis James and Lee have estimated that circulations of only one to two thousand were necessary for a newspaper to be viable in the 1830s. Even for the 1880s, when advances in technology had increased capital costs of publication, Lee estimates that a provincial newspaper required a circulation of twenty thousand to forty thousand to be profitable.[123] There is direct evidence that the low number of readers in Victorian England did not preclude the development of publications with large circulations. Popular newspapers, such as *Lloyds', News of the World*, and the *Daily Telegraph*, were able to achieve circulations of a hundred thousand or more soon after mid-century.[124]

As a symptom of the existence of many potential readers who did not usually buy papers, Lucy Brown has noted how newspaper sales would soar above normal levels on occasions of exceptional public interest.[125] Many of the cheap publications supposedly aimed at a "mass audience" were in fact, according to the revisionists, aimed at a lower middle-class audience of clerks and shopkeepers and perhaps also more skilled artisans.[126] Examples of such publications include the penny Sunday papers that gained prominence in the 1850s and 1860s, such as *Lloyds' Weekly* and the *Telegraph*, and the halfpenny daily papers of the 1890s such as the *Daily Mail*. Lucy Brown has also argued that newspapers in the last half of the nineteenth century "made no attempt . . . to adjust their presentation of the news to people of limited education."[127]

What is left, Perkin and subsequent revisionists have argued, of the claim that rising mass literacy was important to the development of a mass newspaper market is nothing but, to use Perkin's phrase, the "egregious truism" that people have to be able to read if they are to read newspapers regularly.

There may be more to the claim than this, however. As some revisionists themselves recognize, the volume of sales required for a popular publication to be viable rose markedly over the nineteenth century. Inexpensive popular newspapers began to require large circulations, both to justify their low prices and to cover the large capital costs that became associated with rapid publication in large volume.[128] New developments in publishing technology, such as the rotary press, the composing machine, and stereotyping, greatly increased the speed and lowered the cost per paper of publishing large numbers of papers. While these technical developments facilitated the growth of large-circulation daily and weekly newspapers, they also greatly increased the capital expenditures required for publication.[129] Costs independent of circulation were further increased by the growing importance of telegraph communications and of maintaining contact with a geographically dispersed network of news correspondents.[130]

These developments substantially increased the capital required to start up a newspaper. Lee estimates that in 1850 only one or two thousand pounds was required to start up a provincial daily. In the 1880s, according to Lee, a provincial weekly could still be started with working capital of a few hundred pounds, but provincial dailies required a start-up capital of twenty to thirty thousand pounds. And for a London daily, Lee estimates that the start-up capital went from twenty-five thousand pounds before 1850 to at least a hundred thousand pounds by 1870.[131]

The increase in capital expenditures accounts for the increase in break-even circulations for mass newspapers noted above.[132] By the early twentieth century, successful halfpenny dailies had circulations in the hundreds of thousands.[133] And the rise in capital costs with the consequent importance of increasing circulations seems to have held for weekly papers aimed at the working classes as well as for dailies aimed at the middle classes.[134]

Revisionists such as Perkin have probably understated the extent to which newly literate groups were important for ensuring the large circulations required for the profitability of popular publications. According to Perkin, it is improbable that "the early half-penny London dailies were chiefly supported by the third or less of the population which became literate between 1870 and 1900."[135] He argues that this group was too poor to have supported the new papers. And, he also queries, if this segment was being tapped at this point in the late nineteenth century, what group contributed to the further expansion in daily newspaper readership in the early twentieth century? [136] But this newly literate group could have added substantially to sales in the later nineteenth century; although relatively poor, its members may still have been able to afford newspapers. Indeed, B. Seebohm Rowntree includes means to buy a paper as a requisite of even a poverty budget.[137] Rising living standards, as Perkin himself mentions, surely allowed even humble groups to purchase newspapers.[138] Furthermore, as long as a sizable number of those newly literate—not necessarily the majority—purchased newspapers, these purchases could have greatly increased the odds for many publications of reaching break-even circulations.

Virginia Berridge, in a detailed study of the mass circulation Sunday papers that emerged in the 1850s, finds that at least some of these papers, especially *Reynolds' Newspaper*, drew primarily from a working-class audience. Moreover, she finds that at least some of this audience were farm and urban laborers. She argues that revisionists have overstated the extent of the lower-middle-class audience for these papers relative to working-class support.[139] In fact, she argues, the publishers of these papers were motivated by the pursuit of large profits and sought to reach mass audiences.[140] The extent to which publishers sought to attract mass audiences is suggested by the statement attributed to the manager of *Lloyd's* in the 1840s: "We sometimes distrust our own judgement and place the manuscript in the hands of an illiterate person—a servant or machine boy, for instance. If they pronounce favourably upon it, we think it will do."[141]

Some simple calculations illustrate why the argument of Perkin and other revisionists may understate the contribution of rising literacy to circulation levels. Total circulation can be viewed as the product of three factors: adult population size (either total population or one segment of the population, such as the working classes), the literacy rate of the population (either the total or the particular segment under consideration), and the proportion of literates that bought newspapers (to capture demand tendencies). Estimates of these three factors for different dates in the nineteenth century are reported in Table 3.5.[142] Table 3.6 reports how much an increase in one component would have increased circulation levels if the other two components had remained at their initial levels.[143]

The estimates in Tables 3.5 and 3.6 provide some support for the revisionist argument. With the proportion of literates buying newspapers so low in the 1840s and the rise in the proportion over the next century so large, it is hard to argue that literacy rates as such constrained the size of the working-class publishing market. It is true that prevailing purchase rates and literacy rates in the 1840s would not have supported the development of many publications with circulations of a hundred thousand and over. But major increases in circulation awaited publishers who could tap into the existing number of readers in the 1840s. Indeed, publishers such as Edward Lloyd amply demonstrated the gains in circulation and consequent profits that were possible.[144] Moreover, as the calculations reported in the Table 3.6 indicate, the increase in circulation resulting from the rising proportion of those already literate who purchased papers was several times larger than the increase resulting from rising literacy.[145]

However, the estimates in Table 3.6 also show that increases in the literacy rate alone sizably increased the circulation of working-class newspapers. Even after price reductions had substantially increased purchase rates in the 1870s, the total working-class circulation was still only several

Table 3.5

Factors Influencing Newspaper Circulations among the Lower Working Classes during the Nineteenth Century

Year	Adult Population (millions)	Literacy Rate (%)	Proportion of Literates Purchasing Newspapers	Newspaper Circulations (thousands)
1840	6.1	41	.02-.04	50-100
1870	8.7	70	.06-.20	365-1,200
1900	13.2	85	.10-.20	1,000-2,500

Notes and Sources: To estimate the working-class population in a given year, figures on the midyear population aged fifteen and over, taken from Mitchell and Deane, *British Historical Historical Statistics*, are multiplied by .6. This procedure is based on the estimate in R. Dudley Baxter, *National Income: The United Kingdom* (London: Macmillan, 1868), 50-51, 52, 79, that 60 percent of English adult males in 1867 were in the lower skilled, agricultural laborer, and unskilled groups. Literacy rates of the lower working class for 1840 and 1870 were calculated from signature rates of brides and grooms whose fathers were of occupational statuses IV and V. The signature rates were calculated from the marriage register sample described in Appendix B. The occupations included under categories IV and V are also described in Appendix B. The ratio of purchases relative to literates were calculated from the estimates in Raymond Williams, *The Long Revolution*, rev. ed. (New York: Harper and Row, Harper Torchbooks, 1966), 167, 176, 191, 193, 199, 204, 209. Estimates of newspaper circulations were taken from A. P. Wadsworth, "Newspaper Circulations, 1800-1954," *Transactions of the Manchester Statistical Society*, session 1954-55 (March 1955): 3-23; and Williams, *Long Revolution*, 164, 177, 199, 204. Adult population, literacy rate, and proportion of literates are for lower working classes only; newspaper circulations are for the entire population.

hundred thousand to a million. This level of total working-class newspaper circulation was small enough to have constrained the rise of publications with threshold circulations of a hundred thousand or more; it was smaller still if each copy was passed to several different readers. Admittedly the contribution of rising literacy alone, at initially prevailing purchase rates, was modest in easing this constraint. The low initial purchase rates clearly limited the impact of rising literacy per se on increasing circulations. But the *interaction* between rising literacy and the increased purchase rate of

Table 3.6

Estimates of the Contribution of Various Factors to the Rise in Victorian
Newspaper Circulations (Changes are in thousands of newspapers per year)

Time Period	Estimates for Change in Newspaper Circulations (1)	Change Due to Increase in:			
		Literacy Rate (2)	% of Literates Purchasing Newspapers (3)	Adult Population (4)	Interactions (5)
1840-1870	+265-+1150	35-70	+50-+400	21-43	159-637
1870-1900	-200-+2135	78-261	-609-+853	189-630	142-391
1840-1900	+900-+2450	54-107	+150-+450	58-116	638-1785

Notes: The estimated ranges for circulation changes were calculated from the circulation estimates reported in Table 3.5. For the period 1870-1900, the lower estimate for circulation change is negative because the circulation estimates in Table 3.5 indicate the possibility of a drop in newspaper circulations. The estimates of the contribution to circulation changes of increases in literacy, proportion of literates purchasing newspapers, and the adult population were calculated as follows. The level of newspaper circulation at any one date is viewed as the product of the adult population size, the literacy rate of the adult population, and the proportion of literate adults purchasing newspapers. The increase in circulation attributed to each of these three components is estimated by calculating the change in a given component from the figures in Table 3.5 and multiplying that change by the values at the intial date for the other two components. The range of estimates for the contribution of each component is calculated by taking the lowest and highest possible contribution implied by the ranges for figures in Table 3.5. In the case of the impact of the change in the proportion of literates purchasing newspapers between 1870 and 1900, the lower estimate is negative because the figures for the proportion of literates purchasing newspapers in Table 3.5 indicate that this proportion could have fallen between 1870 and 1900. Interaction effects in column 5 were calculated by taking the change in circulation in column (1) for each time period and subtracting the entries in columns 2 through 4.

literates, along with interactions between these two factors and rising population size, was *more* important than the contribution of a rising purchase rate alone.

Perkin and Williams have made an important point in emphasizing that the small number of literates did not directly constrain the development of working-class publications in early Victorian England. Increasing the proportion of literates buying newspapers may have been more important to the development of the popular press than increasing the number of literates. But mass publications did have high fixed costs, which in turn implied high break-even circulations. Rising literacy would have contributed to the number of publications meeting break-even levels.[146] Indeed, Williams himself has on occasion acknowledged this point, as has Lee.[147]

But although rising literacy did facilitate the emergence of publications aimed at the working-class market, it does not seem to have ultimately facilitated the diversity of these publications. One might have expected that increasing the number of publications would have increased the variety of journalistic styles available to the working-class reader. And as various segments of the working-class readership saw the emergence of publications catering to their particular interests, this could have induced individual readers to increase their total purchases of publications of any sort. But historians of the popular press have argued that in response to the increasing size of the popular market, publishers sought to appeal to the lowest common denominator in order to obtain the largest market share. The result, according to this view, was "the new journalism," with more uniformity in style. Alan Lee has described the change: "No longer was the paper 'to inform,' but merely 'to Interest'; no longer was it 'to instruct,' but 'to Elevate'; no longer was it 'to amuse' but 'to Amuse.'"[148] Furthermore, in the early twentieth century, despite an increase in overall circulation, the number of mass-circulation newspapers in England declined.[149] Private publishers motivated by profit were not the only ones in Victorian society concerned about the size of the working-class readership. Among the arguments used by advocates of both postal reform and the abolition of newspaper taxes was that these measures would encourage working-class education. Gravenor Henson, in the testimony cited above before the Select Committee on Postage in 1838, argued that high postal rates were a major impediment to the progress of education. One consequence of high postal rates, he asserted, was that many who at one point had learned to write subsequently forgot how to do so because of lack of practice.[150] Taxes on newspapers were referred to as "taxes on knowledge" by advocates of their repeal. Both reform movements have been commonly viewed by historians as motivated primarily by the broader program of radical social reform.[151] Their arguments about the value of their reforms in promoting education may to a large extent have been rhetorical. Nevertheless, these arguments point to an awareness that the effect of public policy on the popular demand for education could have had as much consequence as public policy for the provision of education. The *Times* printed the following argument in an 1854 editorial: "We make a great stir about teaching everybody to read, and the state—that is the nation—pays a quarter of a million a year in teaching children to do little more than read. Then we proceed to tax the very first thing that everybody reads."[152]

The calculations reported in Tables 3.5 and 3.6 indicate that the arguments of reformers were more than rhetorical flourish. The late Victorian factory worker spending his Sunday poring over news of the latest football match or sensational murder in his penny paper could thank not just his local school board for teaching him how to read but also those who had fought more than a quarter of a century earlier to eliminate the taxes on knowledge so that he could afford the paper.

Conclusion

Although most working-class households in the early Victorian period owned a Bible, they spent very little of their leisure time with that or any other form of the printed or written word. But, during the next sixty years, as postal fees fell to one-sixth of their initial level and newspaper taxes were eliminated, the working classes sent letters and read newspapers on a regular basis. Religion, politics, urbanization, and peer pressure appear to have offered few incentives to most working-class men and women to acquire literacy. But following the latest football match or horse race, relaxing with a novelette, or spending Sunday afternoon with the paper did become a regular part of working-class routine by the end of the nineteenth century.

Eagerness to read the Sunday paper may have offered little incentive to attend school. The value placed by the working classes on reading newspapers probably did not surpass the cost of acquiring literacy until most of them began in the early twentieth century to read newspapers daily. By this time literacy, at least as measured by signature ability at marriage, was close to universal. Still, the battle over cheap newspapers in the mid-nineteenth century helped to ensure that the working classes could make regular use of skills they had learned as schoolchildren. The worker reading about a sensational murder in his Sunday paper in the 1890s may have filled his mind with thoughts just as gruesome as those of a farm laborer half a century earlier spending his Sunday afternoon baiting dogs. But at least the worker saw more readily the value of sending his children to school.

4. The Influence of the Family on Literacy Trends

JOHN STUART MILL VIEWED EDUCATION as one of the few areas where government interference with private choice was appropriate; he recognized the extent to which parents determined their children's education and argued that government intervention was frequently required to prevent parents from neglecting it.[1] There was in fact a strong association between the occupational status of one's parents in Victorian England and the likelihood of being literate. And a number of changes in Victorian society could have affected the choices parents made. Working-class incomes by most accounts rose markedly between 1840 and 1900; some suggest they may have doubled. Falling birthrates over the same period led to smaller families. The combination of rising incomes and smaller families meant that families had more resources to support their children's education. Mortality rates also fell over the nineteenth century. This raised the probability that parents would see a return on investing in their children's education, whether in the form of support in old age from a child with a successful career or in the form of satisfaction that their child survived childhood and used his education to improve his life. Finally, the spread of literacy implied that more and more parents would be literate and thus more likely to pass literacy on to their children.

Nevertheless, only the last of these changes had a strong enough impact to markedly influence literacy trends. Despite an apparent association between social origins and literacy, the income of one's parents during childhood, after controlling for other influences, had only a weak impact on the likelihood of being able to sign one's name during adulthood. The downturns in mortality and fertility occurred either too early or too late to have much influence on Victorian literacy trends, and the direct impact of these factors on family educational decisions was weak. Still, because the impact of parental education on the likelihood of literacy was strong and the role of the family in the decision to acquire literacy was central, the influence of the family on literacy trends warrants extended consideration.

Parental Status and Children's Literacy

One immediate indication that parents influenced the literacy of their children is the ranking of signature ability of brides and grooms according to measures of the social status of their parents. For the national sample of marriage registers from the mid-Victorian period described in Appendix B, the signature ability of brides and grooms rose as the occupational status of their fathers rose (see Table 4.1).

Although this ranking of children's literacy according to parental occupational status clearly suggests parental influence on education, it raises the questions of whether the ranking reflected the association of parental status with other more direct influences on literacy—perhaps the native intelligence of the child—and of what forces led to the connection between parental status and literacy. Indeed, historians of literacy have focused more on how literacy rates varied for those who actually held various occupations than on how literacy rates of children varied according

Table 4.1

Literacy of Brides and Grooms by Father's Occupational Status
(Percentage Signing Their Names at Marriage)

Occupational Status of Father	Brides' Literacy		Grooms' Literacy	
	1839-43	1869-73	1839-43	1869-73
I	99.1	98.8	98.4	98.8
	(109)	(81)	(124)	(83)
II	76.7	92.0	87.2	94.7
	(716)	(662)	(698)	(629)
III	57.9	78.7	79.3	87.9
	(1,605)	(1,620)	(1,696)	(1,650)
IV	44.4	71.9	65.0	81.7
	(419)	(402)	(471)	(420)
V	31.0	66.5	39.9	64.9
	(1,094)	(990)	(1,041)	(996)

Note: Figures are derived from the sample of marriage registers described in Appendix B. The occupations included under each occupational status category are described in Appendix B and in the notes to Table 2.3. Figures in parentheses are the base number of observations for the adjacent percentages.

to the occupations of their fathers. This suggests that the influence of the father's occupation apparent in the comparisons in Table 4.1 may have been indirect, reflecting the influence of the father's occupation on his child's occupation and in turn the influence of the child's occupation on the degree to which literacy was mastered. Controlling for the groom's occupational status in the marriage register sample substantially weakened the association between fathers' status and sons' literacy (see Table 4.2).

For grooms with occupations of status I and II in both time periods examined and for grooms with occupations of status IV in the later time period, literacy rates did not uniformly rise with the occupational ranking of the father. Moreover, in the comparisons reported in Table 4.2 there is at least as much variation in literacy rates for grooms with fathers of a given status as there is in literacy rates for grooms of a given status; in other words, the range of literacy rates is as great across rows as down columns.[2] These results suggest that occupational destination may have had at least as powerful an influence on literacy as parental status. Thus, grooms who achieved occupational status II and whose fathers were in category V had a higher rate of literacy than grooms whose fathers were in category II but who themselves had occupations in category V. Selection forces were probably at work in producing this result. Only the more able of those from humble origins would have been able to move their way into high-status occupations. The only offspring of high-status fathers who would have been likely to move into low-status occupations would have been those who were lacking in ability, ambition, or good fortune. The presence of these intervening factors provide one explanation for why, in the comparisons reported in Table 4.2, the literacy rates for sons of fathers with a given occupational status varied as much as literacy rates for sons with a given occupational status. But if parental influence on literacy was not as strong as may appear at first glance, what factors determined its strength?

The Contribution of Rising Living Standards

The amount of money a family had would seem one obvious influence on the education of its children. Indeed, a number of historians of nineteenth-century education, including Roger Schofield and E. G. West, have pointed to the rise in working-class living standards as a likely contributor

Table 4.2

Literacy of Grooms According to Their Own and Their Fathers' Occupational
Status (Percentage Signing Their Names at Marriage)

Father's Occupational Status	Groom's Occupational Status				
	I	II	III	IV	V
			1839-43		
I	97.7	100.0	95.5	100.0	100.0
	(43)	(56)	(22)	(1)	(1)
II	100.0	92.9	88.0	81.4	65.6
	(18)	(309)	(234)	(43)	(90)
III	100.0	95.0	80.5	73.9	57.5
	(9)	(100)	(1,325)	(142)	(113)
IV	—	100.0	72.5	62.8	44.1
	(0)	(10)	(178)	(223)	(59)
V	—	72.7	63.2	59.2	29.5
	(0)	(11)	(193)	(125)	(708)
			1869-73		
I	100.0	97.2	100.0	100.0	—
	(29)	(36)	(17)	(1)	(0)
II	100.0	97.5	96.2	93.0	72.0
	(13)	(285)	(237)	(43)	(50)
III	100.0	98.4	89.1	84.9	72.6
	(8)	(123)	(1,216)	(146)	(153)
IV	100.0	100.0	82.5	82.5	66.7
	(3)	(16)	(188)	(166)	(45)
V	—	100.0	78.3	83.0	55.2
	(0)	(14)	(276)	(94)	(607)

Note: Figures are derived from the sample of marriage registers described in Appendix B.
The occupations included under each occupational status category are described in
Appendix B and in the notes to Table 2.3. Figures in parentheses are the base number of
observations for the adjacent percentages.

to the rise in working-class literacy. Eric Hobsbawm has even suggested using literacy trends as a barometer of standard-of-living trends.[3] A considerable amount of evidence indicates that working-class living standards rose in the second half of the nineteenth century, and historians generally accept George Wood's estimate of an 80-percent rise between 1850 and 1900 even if they disagree about the extent to which particular working-class groups experienced gains above or below this benchmark.[4] But the extent to which working-class education responded to changes in living standards has been much less carefully considered and indeed some evidence indicates that the response may have been weak.

*Quantitative Evidence on the Impact of Income
on Literacy and Schooling*
Quantitative estimates of the response of education measures to income are available for six different micro data sets for a wide range of occupations in nineteenth-century England.[5] The data sets include surveys of factory weavers in Gloucester and handloom weavers in the west of England, both conducted in the 1830s for the parliamentary commission on handloom weavers; a survey of a London district conducted in 1848 by the London Statistical Society; surveys of parents in Macclesfield and in Hanley published in the factory inspectors' report for 1866; and a national sample of marriage registers. The two weaver data sets and the London data set provide information on children's school attendance; the two factory inspector data sets and the marriage register data set provide information on literacy. Estimates of income elasticities were obtained by regressing these education variables on measures of parental income and converting the estimated coefficients on income into elasticity form. Where possible, variables were entered for parental education and life-cycle stage of the family, to control for proportion of children outside the ages when school was most commonly attended, and a dummy variable was entered for region to control for such regional factors as availability of subsidized schooling.

One set of estimates for the income elasticity of education come from regressions of the proportion of children in school on family income and other variables for a sample of 315 handloom weavers in the west of England in the 1830s.[6] A regression of the proportion of children in school on family income and a life-cycle variable implied an income elasticity slightly greater than 1. But when dummies were entered for region, the estimated income elasticity fell to 0.7 and the regression coefficient on income was statistically different from zero only at the 80-percent level. One limitation of the data was that children's earnings could not be distinguished from adult earnings in the family income measure. As school enrollment was probably negatively correlated with children's earnings (unless older children financed the schooling of younger children), this limitation may lead to an understatement of the influence of income. Even so, the influence appears sizable.

Another set of estimates for the income elasticity of education uses data for 158 Gloucester factory weavers in the 1830s.[7] A simple regression of school enrollment on father's income for this data set implied an income elasticity of 1.3. When controls were entered for father's education and life-cycle stage (father's experience as a weaver), the implied income elasticity fell to 1, and the coefficient on income was statistically significant only at the 90-percent level. Including the wife's earnings in the regression, either separately or in the form of a total adult earnings variable, increased the income elasticity to 1.3, and the coefficient on income was statistically significant at the 1-percent level. Although these results suggest a sizable effect of income on school attendance, controlling for region substantially lowered this effect. In regressions with dummy variables for region, the implied income elasticities were generally below 0.1, and the coefficients on income were not statistically significant even at the 90-percent level. The one exception was when the wife's earnings were entered in the regression. When the wife's earnings variable was entered separately, the coefficient on husband's income was still statistically insignificant and implied an income elasticity below 0.5, but the coefficient on the wife's earnings variable was statistically significant. When a combined adult earnings variable was entered, the coefficient was statistically significant at the 98-percent level, and the implied elasticity was close to 1. These results suggest that for families in which the wife worked, schools served primarily to mind the children.

The 1848 survey of St. George's-in-the-East, a London parish, provides another source of evidence on the relationship between school enrollment and family income.[8] This sample included families of substantially higher income levels than the previous two samples considered (average family income of 26.5 shillings per week, compared with 12.8 shillings for the handloom weavers and 13.4 shillings for the shoploom weavers) and most likely of higher educational levels as well. The data for the published survey were not reported by family but as averages for all family heads of a given occupation; the families were classified across a total of twenty-eight occupations. Variables for book ownership were entered in the regressions estimated with this sample as a proxy for parental education or, alternatively, as a measure of "taste" for education. The estimated income elasticities were far lower than for the samples of weavers. The estimated income elasticities were no higher than 0.25 and fell as low as 0.11. Furthermore, in no case was the estimated regression coefficient on income significantly different from zero with a probability of 90 percent or greater. As with the the shoploom weavers, the coefficient on total adult income was higher than on father's income, and the coefficient on father's income increased when a variable for wife's income was entered. Total adult income may be a better measure of resources available for schooling than father's income alone; alternatively, the earnings potential of a wife may have increased a family's incentive to use school as a child-minding service.

The lower response of schooling to income in the London sample than in the weaver samples could reflect, in part, the higher level of income in the former sample. Most of the difference was eliminated when controls for parental education and region were entered in the weaver data. With one exception, the estimated elasticities fell below 0.1. The one income elasticity that remained near 1 in the shoploom weaver data after controls were included was for total adult earnings. When the earnings of husband and wife were entered separately in the regression, the coefficient on husband's earnings became statistically insignificant, suggesting that family income influenced schooling primarily because of the wife's demand for child-minding services.

Evidence is also available on the relationship between literacy and parental income. One source of data comes from reports of literacy and parental income contained in surveys in 1866 of parents of children applying for work in Macclesfield and Hanley.[9] As with the London sample, the data were reported as averages for all parents of a given occupation. The data did not provide information on possible controls to enter in the regressions. The implied income elasticity from the estimated coefficients was 0.121 for Macclesfield and 0.341 for Hanley.

The national sample of marriage registers described in Appendix B provides another source of data for estimating the response of literacy to father's income. As the sample provides information only on father's occupation, R. Dudley Baxter's estimates of mean wage rates by occupation were used to estimate father's income.[10] These estimates for 1867 were used for both the 1839–43 and the 1869–73 samples because they covered a fuller range of occupations than did data available for the 1830s and 1840s, and because the relative ordering of wages by occupation was probably unchanged over this period. The literacy rate at marriage was likely to have reflected decisions by parents some ten to twenty years earlier. Thus these estimates assume that Baxter's 1867 wage estimates capture the wage structure between 1820 and 1840. The basic observations used in these regressions are occupational group averages, not the underlying observations on individual marriages. The marriage register sample provided direct estimates of the mean literacy rates for brides and grooms with fathers of a given occupation. The average literacy rate for grooms of a given occupation was used to estimate the literacy rate of fathers of brides and grooms reporting a given occupation. The sample sizes used in estimating these occupational literacy rates varied across occupations, thus leading to variation in standard errors and heteroskedasticity. Therefore, regressions were run when more than fifteen observations were available to estimate the occupational literacy rates so that those observations with the largest standard errors could be eliminated. Simple regressions of literacy of bride or groom on income of their fathers yielded estimated income elasticities as high as 0.72, but when controls were entered for father's literacy, the estimated income elasticities fell markedly and, in six of eight cases, were below 0.2. Furthermore, no case that controlled for father's literacy had a coefficient on income statistically different from zero at even the 90-percent level.[11]

The estimates of the income elasticity of school enrollment or literacy in the six samples just reviewed vary considerably, ranging from under 0.1 for some estimates from the marriage register sample to over 1 in the two samples of weavers. The differences can be explained partly by differences in mean incomes across the samples: the estimated income elasticities tended to fall as mean income rose. Income elasticities from the weaver samples, which were by far the lowest income groups with family income averaging about 13.5 shillings per week, were generally above 1. For the marriage register samples, with father's mean income averaging about 25 shillings per week, the estimated income elasticities ranged from 0.01 to 0.72. For the London sample, with father's mean income averaging 23 shillings per week, the estimated income elasticities averaged about 0.2. When controls were entered for parental education, life-cycle stage, and regional effects, however, these differences were to a large extent eliminated, and estimated income elasticities generally fell to a modest 0.2 or lower.

Statements by Contemporary Observers

Contemporary testimony about the influence of income on education supports the conclusions from the quantitative evidence just surveyed: on the one hand, income elasticities were highest for those at high income levels; on the other hand, for the most part the impact of income was weak.[12]

Some observers perceived that school attendance suffered when parents were experiencing hard times. Some reports indicated that school attendance fluctuated with the state of trade. For example, a statistical society report in Birmingham in 1840 noted that school attendance was particularly low due to the depression of trade.[13] A survey of Brentford in rural Middlesex in 1843 stated that "the desire to educate their children is one of the first symptoms of improved circumstances among the poor."[14] Witnesses before parliamentary inquiries into children's employment conditions in textile manufactures (lace, hosiery, and cotton in particular) also observed that school attendance varied directly with the prosperity of trade.[15] More generally, observers—for example, witnesses before the commissions on women and children in agriculture—noted that poverty hindered school attendance.[16] Parents themselves, in statistical society surveys, frequently cited poverty as the reason for not sending their children to school. Of 513 parents surveyed in Pendleton in 1838, 265 cited poverty; of 133 parents examined in Hull in 1839, 116 cited reasons related to poverty.[17]

Other observers denied that poverty was a serious barrier to school attendance, however. The summary reports for both the 1851 Census of Education and the 1861 Newcastle Commission argued that poverty was more an excuse than a cause for low school attendance and both reports referred to parents in highly paid occupations who neglected their children's education while parents of far more modest means made sacrifices so that their children could be educated.[18]

In an 1863 hearing on children's employment, a lace finisher near Nottingham stated that, to her knowledge, "there are many very poor parents who send their children to school and others who earn much better wages, who send them to work very young and drink all their earnings."[19] Miners, despite their relatively high pay, were frequently observed to neglect the education of their children. One colliery agent stated, "families of pitmen are very generally well fed and clothed and in all respects in as good a circumstance as those of other labouring people, education excepted."[20] Although evidence contained in the parliamentary commission on handloom weavers indicates that the deterioration of weavers' earnings had lowered their children's school attendance, a number of witnesses noted that, despite earning lower wages than other occupations, weavers were *more* inclined to provide schooling for their children. According to one report from Dorset, "The weavers in this district are a well conducted and orderly set of men: they have neither the leisure to cultivate, nor the pecuniary means of obtaining any intellectual pursuits, but are not unwilling to sacrifice a small portion of their very limited means of subsistence in order to bestow an education on their children, being generally sensible of the advantage they may hereafter derive from it."[21]

The 1867–69 Commission on the Employment of Women and Children in Agriculture had many witnesses—including farmers, clergymen, and other upper-class residents of rural areas—who denied that poverty was a serious obstacle to school attendance. Of some 208 witnesses examined on the role of poverty, only 51 stated that poverty was a major barrier to school attendance, while 98 stated that poverty was not at all a barrier, 36 that it was not a major barrier, and 11 that parental indifference was a more serious problem than poverty.[22]

The Impact of Rising Living Standards
Despite the large apparent gains in working-class living standards in the second half of the nineteenth century, the weak response of literacy and school enrollment implies that the contribution of these gains to literacy was modest. Of the estimates of income elasticities surveyed above, twelve of the fifteen estimates that controlled for parental education were between 0.05 and 0.3. Even with working-class living standards rising by an average of 80 percent, the income elasticity estimates would imply school enrollment or literacy increases of only 4 to 24 percent. Such a contribution appears modest relative to the doubling in school enrollment rates and the two-thirds increase in literacy rates that occurred between 1840 and 1900.

One indication that the gains in living standards made no more than a modest contribution to increased literacy was the failure by observers of rural areas to acknowledge that the contribution of rising living standards was important. Reports for the 1867–69 Commission on the Employment of Women and Children in Agriculture repeatedly made reference to improvements in both living standards and educational conditions, yet observers perceived no link between the two.[23] The summary report on Wales for the 1870 Commission on the Employment of Women and Children in Agriculture noted that the income of the agricultural laborer had improved substantially over the previous twenty-five years and yet had produced virtually no improvement in schooling.[24]

A low income elasticity of education, then, appears to have prevented gains in living standards from making more than a modest contribution to the rise of literacy.

Births, Deaths, and Education

Although income's direct influence on education was weak, it could have had an indirect influence by affecting life expectancy and fertility rates.

Both birth rates and death rates fell over the nineteenth century. Reports of the Registrar General indicate that birth rates for women of child-bearing age fell from 134 per 1,000 in 1840 to 116 per 1,000 in 1900. Death rates for the English population fell from 22.9 per 1,000 in 1840 to 18.2 per 1,000 in 1900.[25] Both trends could have influenced literacy rates. The more children in a family at a given income level, the fewer the resources available per child for schooling. The longer the life expectancy of a child about to enter school, the more years he would have had to enjoy the benefits of his schooling. The longer the life expectancy of his parents, the more years they would have benefited from an educated child's increased earnings if the child supported them in their old age.

Nevertheless, the timing of demographic changes suggests, at best, an uncertain impact on literacy trends. E. A. Wrigley and Roger Schofield have found that a substantial increase in life expectancy at birth occurred in England between 1781 and 1826; during the following fifty years, however, trends in life expectancy were almost level.[26] Marriage typically occurred around the age of twenty-five, implying that the rise in life expectancy would be reflected in marriage register signature rates between 1806 and 1851.[27] But signature rates for England as a whole during this period were almost level.[28]

Mortality rates for those between the ages of five and thirty-four declined by half between 1840 and 1890, however. Mortality rates in this age range were the most important for the schooling decision because this period in the life cycle would be less heavily discounted at the point at which the schooling decision was made compared with later periods in the life cycle.[29] But the initial mortality rate in 1840 for those between the ages of five and thirty-four appears to have been too low for subsequent declines to have had much impact on the literacy decision: the rate fell from ten per thousand in 1840 to five per thousand in 1900. The impact of this change on the present value of the benefits of literacy can be gauged by assuming a constant annual rental rate attributable to literacy, a constant annual discount rate, and acquisition of literacy instantaneously at the age of ten.[30] The change in the expected present value of literacy benefits brought about by the mortality decline can be estimated under alternative assumptions about the discount rate. At a 5-percent discount rate, the present value would have been raised by only 5 percent, at a 20-percent discount rate, by only 3 percent.[31]

There is stronger evidence that changes in literacy were related to changes in fertility. Wrigley and Schofield's estimates indicate that English fertility rates fell between 1815 and 1846.[32] Assuming an average age of marriage of twenty-five, this period of declining fertility may have influenced literacy rates for those marrying between 1841 and 1871. This was the period when national literacy rates began to rise. Furthermore, Michael Teitelbaum, a demographer, has found consistently strong, statistically significant positive correlations between literacy levels and the date of onset of fertility declines across counties in England and Wales during the nineteenth century.[33] Other demographic studies of many European countries have found that illiteracy is the one variable that shows a consistently significant relationship with the onset of a substantial decline in marital fertility.[34]

It should be noted that demographers who have reported the negative relationship between literacy and fertility have emphasized the influence of literacy on fertility.[35] Economists, such as Gary Becker and H. G. Lewis, however, have argued that decisions by households on the number of children to have and on their education are interdependent.[36] They point out that, on the one hand, increasing the level of education per child raises the cost to the family per child and thus tends to lower fertility. And, on the other hand, lowering the number of children in the family lowers the total cost to the family of raising the average educational level of each child. Thus, they refer to a quantity-quality trade-off between numbers of children and the level of education given each child.

This quantity-quality trade-off could explain the high observed negative correlation between literacy and fertility. Not only do literacy rates across counties correlate highly with the onset of the fertility decline in Victorian England, but also fertility rates across counties correlate highly with literacy rates at marriage for the same cohort some twenty years later. Indeed, the level of fertility in 1841 explains over half of the variance in female literacy across counties in 1861.[37] If this quantity-quality trade-off was strong, then fertility declines could have contributed to rising literacy.

But the correlations just described do not necessarily reflect the presence of a trade-off; they could reflect mutual correlations with other factors. This possiblity always arises when using observations at an aggregate level, such as the county, to make inferences about individual families' decisions concerning education or numbers of children. For example, the correlation between literacy and fertility could be accounted for by the intercorrelation between fertility, literacy, and child labor. Counties with abundant opportunities for child labor would have offered parents incentives to have large families. But abundant child labor opportunities would also have discouraged school attendance and hence literacy. Literacy and child labor force participation rates were negatively correlated across counties, while fertility and child labor measures were positively correlated.[38] Indeed, George Boyer and Jeffrey Williamson, using pooled cross-section time series data across counties from 1851 to 1911 and entering controls for other determinants of fertility, report only a weak association between literacy and fertility.[39]

Moreover, an economic model of fertility and education does not necessarily imply a negative correlation between these two variables. If a family's decisions about numbers of children and education per child are based solely on income, and if other things are equal, raising income raises the demand for both numbers of children and education per child. Then, if the effect of income on both goods is strong enough, numbers of children and education per child in families can rise together. It is only if the effect of income on one good is much weaker than on the other that a quantity-quality trade-off is generated. Furthermore, if allowance is made for the earnings contribution of children, then increasing numbers of children can increase the capacity for older children in a family to support the education of younger children.

This theoretical ambiguity about the relationship between fertility and education is supported by a range of empirical studies. The ambiguity is apparent, for example, in twentieth-century studies. Developed countries in the twentieth century have been found to have a negative relationship between education and number of children per family.[40] Developing countries, however, have been found to have a much weaker relationship between income and numbers of children and, in some cases, even a positive relationship.[41] Some studies of countries that are now developed suggest that a negative education-fertility relationship emerged and became stronger after these countries reached a threshold level of development.[42] A number of surveys have concluded that across developed countries, there was not a strong correlation between initial literacy levels and the date of onset of declining fertility rates.[43] At lower levels of development, therefore, a greater value may have been placed on numbers of children and a lower value on education, thus weakening the quantity-quality interaction.

This may have been the situation of Victorian England. David Levine has argued that the fertility decline in late Victorian England was due to changing working-class economic strategies and consequent changes in values. He has asserted that these changes did not incorporate more positive working-class attitudes toward education.[44] In an alternative interpretation of the post-1870 fertility decline in England, J. W. Innes concluded that the largest downturns in fertility were initially in upper-class families.[45] If Innes is correct, this would reinforce the tendency for the fertility downturn to have a weak effect on literacy.

Three separate nineteenth-century English data sets on individual families suggest a much weaker interaction between education and fertility than that suggested by aggregate correlations across counties. One data set is from a survey of a London district in 1848, the other two from surveys of factory and handloom weavers in the 1830s.[46] For all three data sets, regressions of the number of children per family on family income reveal a positive coefficient on income. Furthermore, correlations between number of children per family and school enrollment variables in six of eight instances yielded positive values, although in only 1 instance was the positive coefficient significantly different from zero at the 10-percent level.[47] The magnitude of the quantity-quality trade-off for the nineteenth century, then, does not appear to have been large enough to offset the direct positive effect of income on the number of children per family. The disparity between the results from family-level versus aggregate data sets is consistent with findings from data on twentieth-century developing countries, in which aggregate data sets also indicate stronger quantity-quality trade-offs than do data on individual families.[48]

In sum, the evidence on the impact of fertility trends on literacy is conflicting. Wrigley and Schofield's estimates do indicate that there was a fertility decline in the first half of the nineteenth century, in contrast with previous studies, which had found less evidence for such a decline.[49] Both Teitelbaum's study and the other cross-county evidence described above do indicate high correlations between literacy and fertility.[50] These correlations could reflect the presence of intervening variables rather than a trade-off between fertility and literacy, however. The former possibility is suggested by the weak associations between fertility and literacy when more controls are entered and with family-level data.

Changes in Family Ties and Family Strategies

The changes in income, fertility, and mortality considered thus far still may not capture basic changes that occurred in the nature of the family over the course of the nineteenth century, changes that may have had an important influence on the education individuals acquired. In fact, there has been considerable disagreement among historians over how the Western family has changed during the past few centuries. It would be well beyond the scope of this study to undertake to resolve this controversy or to attempt to establish the broader changes that occurred in the nature of the family during the Victorian period. Nevertheless, this literature has developed to a point that it is useful to ascertain to what extent literacy trends could have been influenced by some of the major changes that are thought to have occurred.

In an influential survey, Michael Anderson distinguished three different types of approaches to the history of the family: (1) demographic approaches, (2) approaches that emphasize changes in what Anderson calls "sentiments," and (3) approaches that emphasize family economic strategies, especially over the life cycle and across generations.[51] Some historians have added another type of approach to these three, one labeled by Louise Tilly and Miriam Cohen as the hegemonic/institutional approach.[52] Each type of approach suggests ways in which changes in the family could have influenced educational trends.

Demographic approaches focus on basic descriptive characteristics of the household, especially on household size and on the relations between its members. Of particular interest has been whether household size and the extent of the nuclear family have been stable over time. Two related issues that have implications for educational trends are what trends have occurred in the proportion of children of school age who were residing with at least one parent and thus had someone to support them in school, and what trends have occurred in the age at which children left home and thus also left the direct control of their parents.

Turning to the first trend, mortality declines over the eighteenth and nineteenth centuries could have increased the proportion of children with at least one parent alive. Anderson has reported, based on a sample from the 1851 census, that in 1851 approximately 10 percent of children aged five to twelve were not residing with at least one parent, whereas in 1979 the proportion had fallen to under 5 percent.[53] Of course this still leaves open the question of how much of the decline occurred during the Victorian period. But Anderson's results, which imply a rise in the proportion of children with at least one adult present to attend to their education, at least suggest that a change may have occurred.

Richard Wall examined evidence on the second trend—changes in the age that children left home—and concluded that between 1841 and 1861 the age may have risen, although he finds little evidence of any trend in the century and a half before that.[54] This suggests that parental influence and control over children could have been rising and may have included increased influence over their education. But even during the early Victorian period, the percentage of children of school age (roughly ages five through twelve) living with at least one parent was already so high that it is unlikely that it could have increased still further by enough to have been a significant influence on trends in education. In a large sampling from the 1851 census, Anderson found that only 7.6 percent of children aged five to nine (the age range with the highest rates of school attendance) had no parent present at the time the census was taken.[55] Thus, currently available evidence on simple demographic trends suggests that they had no major impact on the role of the family in education.

Historians using what Anderson calls "the sentiments approach"— Lawrence Stone, Edward Shorter, and Philippe Aries among others— have argued that in modern times parents have developed an increased emotional attachment to their children. Stone attributes this in part to falling child mortality, implying that parents risk less emotional loss from developing an attachment to their children. Aries emphasizes the emergence of childhood as a distinct stage of life, an emergence he attributes in part to the rise of schooling. Shorter argues that rising living standards freed mothers from working and thus allowed more time for mothering, which in turn led to the development of maternal love. The arguments of Stone and Shorter, in particular, suggest that with increased parental affection and love for their children, parents were more likely to expend scarce resources for their well-being, including education. Indeed, J. H.

Plumb has argued that a "gentle and more sensitive approach to children" by the middle and upper classes in the eighteenth century led to a marked increase in their expenditure on their children's education.[56]

The sentiments approach has been extensively criticized because it is so difficult to verify that changes have occurred in families' emotional ties and because historians using the approach have taken the broadest of social trends as evidence that changes occurred.[57] Moreover, the evidence seems especially weak for changes in sentiments among the working classes. One major concern of critics has been that this approach unfairly presumes that the poverty of the lower classes dehumanized them and minimized emotional ties among family members.[58] Because of these difficulties, the case would hardly seem strong for using the approach to account for rising working-class literacy.

Yet the approach is useful, as even its critics have acknowledged, for revealing how changes in emotional attachments may accompany and reinforce other forces leading to social change. Thus, the ways in which shifts in sentiments may have influenced family behaviors with regard to education merit further attention. The possibility even exists that some changes in emotional ties during the Victorian period could actually have weakened family commitments to education. Anderson notes arguments that industrialization may have weakened the family, although for the most part he challenges such arguments. For example, the increasing separation of workplace and household with industrialization could conceivably have led wage earners to increase expenditure on drink at the expense of the family.[59]

Connecting sentiments to specific social and economic changes leads to the third type of approach suggested by Anderson. The household economics approach focuses on how a family defines its relationships in order to achieve its economic objectives. Advocates of this approach have developed the concept of "family strategies" to refer to the various decisions families make to achieve those objectives.[60] These strategies can involve education because the contribution of children—both immediately and in the future—to household finances is involved. Parents would be weighing their children's immediate earnings contribution to the family's resources against the children's future ability to support the family and to lead successful lives of their own.[61] A critical issue in this regard would be to what extent parents could rely on a share of any increased earnings their children received due to literacy.

W. B. Stephens's extensive survey of regional variation in schooling and literacy and in particular his discussions of parental attitudes toward schooling and literacy indicate regional variation in parental strategies toward children and schooling. In many regions of England, child labor opportunities influenced parents' decisions about schooling. The role of parental strategies is especially evident, however, in the South Midlands, such as in Bedford, where Stephens indicates that the poverty of parents made child labor especially important as a source of family earnings, and in Buckingham and Northampton, where farmers put pressure on agricultural laborers to send their children to work.[62] Parental expectations concerning future earnings might have been important in rural areas where emigration was sizable because parents might have expected that education would improve the ability of their children to find jobs in the city. One reason that has been given for why female literacy rates overtook male literacy rates in rural areas is that girls were motivated to attend school by the desire to obtain domestic service positions in urban areas. Indeed, even in textile areas such as Rochdale, domestic servants seem to have been heavily recruited from rural areas.[63]

Although such differences in strategies may well have occurred, they are inherently difficult to verify, as Louise Tilly has noted, because one cannot directly observe the expectations or plans associated with them.[64] It is also difficult to generalize at the national level about such strategies, for as Anderson indicates, they are likely to vary considerably with local conditions.[65] One indication of how specific family economic strategies contributed to rising literacy is the variation in literacy increases according to the occupational status of the fathers of the brides and grooms in the national sample of marriage registers.

If changes in the family strategies of specific groups contributed significantly to literacy increases, then the increases should be clustered among individuals with fathers of particular occupational categories. It would seem appropriate to consider the reduction in *illiteracy* to control for those groups that had already reached high literacy levels. The percentage reduction between 1839 and 1873 in brides and grooms making marks according to the occupational category of their fathers is reported in Table 4.3. On the one hand, considerable variation is evident across family backgrounds, but on the other hand, a substantial reduction of some sort did occur for all social groups. The former finding suggests some differences in strategies with respect to literacy across occupational groups, but the latter finding suggests increasing homogeneity of attitudes toward children and their strategic role.

Table 4.3

Reduction between 1839-43 and 1869-73 in Illiteracy of Brides and Grooms by Father's Occupational Category (Change in the Proportion Making a Mark between 1839-43 and 1869-73 as a Percentage of the Proportion Making a Mark at Marriage in 1839-43)

Father's Occupational Category	Reduction in Illiteracy among:	
	Brides	Grooms
Professional	58.5	66.7
Sales	56.4	61.7
Farmer	67.3	62.3
Small Farmer	62.3	76.5
Supervisory	44.9	-32.5
Skilled	51.7	50.8
Semiskilled	48.3	43.4
Service	62.4	75.5
Transportation	51.9	57.8
Miner	38.7	27.8
Unskilled	51.5	37.0

Note: Figures are derived from the sample of marriage registers described in Appendix B.

It has also been argued that industrialization led to a shift in family strategies that strengthened family ties. If this shift occurred, it could have increased the family's control over education. It could also have increased the extent to which parents could anticipate receiving a share of their children's enhanced earnings due to literacy. Anderson, for example, has argued that industrialization may have strengthened family ties by creating more of what he calls "critical" situations in which family support was important to getting an individual through difficult times or important periods of transition.[66] And, Stephen Ruggles has argued that the importance of the extended family may have increased with industrialization. Ruggles differs from Anderson in attributing the growing strength of family ties to rising affluence and cultural change rather than to increased reliance on the family in time of personal crisis.[67] Whatever the reason for stronger family ties, this strengthening could have increased the influence that parents had on the education of their children. And children could have found that their families were increasingly willing to support their education. Both evidence and arguments are conflicting on whether parental control over children increased over time and on whether changes in the family strengthened or weakened the interest that parents took in their children's education, however. Although Anderson has suggested that parental control over children may have increased, some contemporaries argued that increased child labor opportunities in textile areas actually put children in a position to challenge parental authority.[68] And although it could be argued that increased migration weakened the ties between parents and children and lowered the probability that children would support their parents in their old age, it is also possible that greater opportunities for migration increased the return to education and that improvements in transportation and communications sustained the possibility of contact and support for parents who had invested in their children's education.[69]

Rising income levels to the marked degree that occurred in Victorian England may have been part of a broader set of forces that changed the strategic role of children in the family and, with it, attitudes toward their education. This possibility is suggested by John Caldwell's theory of fertility decline, where he suggests that large-scale cultural and economic forces, such as rising income levels, may change the strategic role of children in families from providing a positive flow of resources to their parents to being on net positive recipients of resources; the latter direction could be associated with rising education levels of children.[70] Instead of expecting children to be net contributors to the family's resources, for example through child labor, parents may have become increasingly willing to invest in their children's education—even for primarily altruistic motives—thus making the direction of the net contribution flow from parents to children.

The fourth type of approach, the hegemonic/institutional approach, considers the conflict between the family and societal institutions, a conflict that may have arisen because the family felt its influence threatened by the schools that were promoted by institutions outside the family.[71] Neil Smelser has described how, in textile areas, the rise of the factory system separated working children from the control of their parents and how, subsequently, child labor laws prescribed children's education.[72] Philip Gardner has argued that control of schools by the state led to opposition from parents.[73] Although it seems unlikely that resentment by parents was sufficient to completely offset the impact of state subsidies to education, consideration should be given to the possibility that working-class hostility toward public control of education limited the extent to which public institutions could promote education. David Levine, in his work cited previously on quantity/quality trade-offs, has combined the household economics and institutional/hegemonic approaches. He has argued that changes in household strategies with consequent changes in values can account for declining fertility. But he also argues that the working classes resisted adopting a favorable attitude toward public education, in part because of hostility toward middle-class culture.[74] The issue of public involvement in education will be considered in Chapters 5 and 6.

It could be argued that the degree of direct parental control over decisions regarding education had only minimal consequences for literacy trends on the grounds that parents were simply responding to underlying forces for change. But the responses of parents, and of the family more generally, to these forces could have influenced how much impact these forces had.

The Influence of Parental Literacy on the Literacy of Their Children

The family did have at least one important influence on long-term literacy trends: the education of parents had a sizable impact on how much education their children received. A number of studies of twentieth-century

societies and of earlier times have found a clear influence of parental education on children's education.[75] There are several explanations for this
influence. Better educated parents were likely to have better information
on how education could benefit their children, and they might have provided some instruction directly to their children. Moreover, better educated parents may have been able to provide a home environment more
conducive to learning, even if they provided no direct instruction. Finally,
better educated parents may have had a greater "preference" for educated
children compared with less educated parents.

If the influence of parents' education on their children's education
was strong, it would have contributed to an acceleration in the spread of
literacy. An exogenous change that raised the literacy rates of one generation would have led to higher literacy rates for the children of that generation *over and above* the impact of the initial change. Even children who were
not induced to acquire literacy because of the direct effect of the exogenous change could have been induced to do so because their parents were
literate. The influence of parental literacy, then, tended to make the rise of
literacy self-generating. There is in fact evidence that in nineteenth-century
England, children with literate parents were significantly more likely to
acquire literacy than were the children of illiterate parents.

In a study of the village of Shepshed in Leicester between 1754 and
1851, David Levine linked marriage registers over time and was able to
compare signature rates of parents and children who both were married
in Shepshed.[76] His results imply that for those who had at least one parent
who could sign, 70 percent of grooms and 45 percent of brides could
also sign, whereas for those brides and grooms for whom neither parent could sign, only 48 percent of the grooms and 22 percent of the brides
could sign (see Table 4.4). Thus, the differential signature rate between
those with at least one parent who could sign and those with neither parent who could sign was 22 percent for grooms and 23 percent for brides.

The national marriage register sample can also be used to examine the
relation between the literacy of the father and the literacy of the bride and
groom. This can be done in two ways. First, the marriage register gives
the names of the fathers of the bride and groom as well as the names and
signatures (or marks) of two witnesses. In 12 percent of the marriages in
the 1839–43 sample and in 16 percent of the marriages in the 1869–73
sample, the name of one of the fathers and of one of the witnesses were
the same. If one assumes that a father and a witness of the same name
were the same person, the signature rate of witnesses can provide a

Table 4.4

Literacy of Brides and Grooms by Literacy of Their Parents in
Shepshed, 1754-1844 (Percentage Signing Their Names at Marriage)

	S/S	S/X	X/S	ONE S	X/X
Grooms	75.3	65.4	73.2	70.0	48.3
	(81)	(107)	(26)	(214)	(120)
Brides	59.0	37.2	32.1	45.2	21.9
	(105)	(137)	(28)	(270)	(123)

Source: Calculated from David Levine, "Education and Family Life in Early Industrial England," *Journal of Family History* 4 (1979): 376 (Table 3). The figures from Levine's article are used here with the permission of JAI Press, Greenwich, Connecticut.
Note: Definitions of Variables: S/S = both parents could sign. S/X = only father could sign. X/S = only mother could sign. ONE S = at least one parent could sign. X/X = neither parent could sign. Numbers in parentheses are the base number of observations for the adjacent percentages.

measure of literacy of the fathers. Second, the occupational literacy rates of grooms can be used to estimate the occupational literacy rates of fathers.

Comparisons of the literacy rates of brides and grooms according to whether witnesses with the same name as the father signed their names or made marks are reported in Table 4.5. The implied differential in literacy rates between children of literate and illiterate parents is generally greater than in Levine's sample, although the discrepancy is much smaller in the 1869–73 sample than in the 1839–43 sample. Levine's results show that the literacy differential between sons of literate and illiterate fathers was 17 percentage points, whereas the results reported in Table 4.5 indicate a 55 percentage point differential in the 1839–43 sample and a 26 percentage point differential in the 1869–73 sample. For daughters, Levine's results show a 23 percentage point differential between those of literate and illiterate fathers, whereas the results reported in Table 4.5 indicate a 43 percentage point differential in the 1839–43 sample and a 33 percentage point differential in the 1869–73 sample. Controlling for father's occupational status narrows the differential considerably except for those with fathers of occupational status V in 1839–43 (see Table 4.6).

These results must be treated with caution for two reasons. First, in only a minority of marriages did witnesses have the same name as the

Table 4.5

Literacy of Brides and Grooms by Literacy of Witness to Marriage
(Percentage Signing Their Names at Marriage)

	Literate Witness	*Illiterate Witness*
	1839-43	
Grooms	94.3 (122)	39.1 (46)
Brides	81.9 (292)	38.8 (49)
	1869-73	
Grooms	88.7 (142)	63.0 (27)
Brides	92.9 (451)	59.6 (47)

Note: Figures are derived from the sample of marriage registers described in Appendix B. Numbers in parentheses are the base number of observations for the adjacent percentages.

father of the bride and groom; such marriages may have been atypical in other respects and thus subject to sample selection bias.[77] Second, the assumption that a witness with the same name as the father of a bride or groom was in fact the father is tenuous.[78]

Thus, although using the occupational literacy rates of grooms as estimates of the occupational literacy rates of their fathers employs a less direct source of information than the first approach, it is not subject to the potential biases of the first approach. The key assumption of the second approach, that the ordering of literacy rates by occupation was the same for grooms as for fathers of brides and grooms, seems plausible. The

Table 4.6

Literacy of Brides and Grooms by Literacy of Witness to Marriage and by Occupational Status of Father

	Occupational Status of Father				
	I	II	III	IV	V
	1839-43				
Grooms					
Literate	100.0	100.0	94.8	91.7	85.7
witness	(11)	(30)	(58)	(12)	(7)
Illiterate	—	75.0	75.0	0.0	23.1
witness	(0)	(4)	(12)	(3)	(26)
Brides					
Literate	100.0	92.7	78.7	87.0	60.0
witness	(14)	(82)	(127)	(23)	(35)
Illiterate	—	50.0	56.3	40.0	24.0
witness	(0)	(2)	(16)	(5)	(25)
	1869-73				
Grooms					
Literate	100.0	95.6	89.7	94.7	68.2
witness	(7)	(23)	(68)	(19)	(22)
Illiterate	—	—	75.0	50.0	56.3
witness	(0)	(0)	(8)	(2)	(16)
Brides					
Literate	100.0	98.1	92.3	85.4	88.6
witness	(19)	(107)	(221)	(48)	(44)
Illiterate	—	0.0	55.0	33.3	68.2
witness	(0)	(1)	(20)	(3)	(22)

Note: Figures are derived from the sample of marriages described in Appendix B. Occupations included under each occupational status category are described in Appendix B and in Table 2.3. Numbers in parentheses are the base number of observations for the adjacent percentages.

second approach can be used to estimate regressions explaining variation in brides' and grooms' literacy with fathers' literacy rates by occupation being used as independent variables in the regressions. The probability that the child of a literate father would be literate was again somewhat greater in these regressions than in Levine's sample, with the differential probability ranging from 0.21 to 0.38, compared with 0.22 to 0.23 in Levine's sample.[79]

The shoploom weaver regressions described above indicate far more uncertainty over the influence of a father's literacy on the proportion of his children in school.[80] The coefficients on the dummy variables for whether the father could read only or both read and write were negative, implying that the control group of fathers who could neither read nor write had higher proportions, on average, of children in school than those who could read or write. Furthermore, in most instances the coefficients on the fathers' education dummies were not significantly different from zero at even the 90-percent level. The coefficient on the dummy variable for fathers who could both read and write had a smaller negative value than the dummy variable for fathers who could read only, however. The result could reflect either a low value placed on education even by those fathers who could read or write or, possibly, the use of informal home instruction.

One limitation of both the marriage register and the shoploom samples is that they provide information only on the father's education, even though the mother's education might be expected to have a greater influence on the child's education because of the greater amount of time she probably spent in child rearing.[81] But twentieth-century studies of developing countries have found conflicting results on whether the mother's or the father's education had a stronger effect on the child's education.[82] And Levine's results for England are also mixed on this issue. Grooms with literate mothers but illiterate fathers in Levine's sample had an average literacy rate 24 percentage points higher than grooms whose parents were both illiterate. For grooms with literate fathers but illiterate mothers, the advantage over grooms with neither parent literate fell to 17 percentage points. For brides, however, father's literacy appeared more important than mother's literacy. Brides with literate fathers but illiterate mothers had, on average, a 5 percentage point higher literacy rate than brides with literate mothers but illiterate fathers.

In London, which might be regarded as a high literacy environment, there is indirect evidence that literary propensities of the family influenced the children's school attendance. The survey of London from 1848 described above reports book ownership per family as well as school attendance of children and family income. When various measures of book ownership are used as explanatory variables in regression estimates, they all have a positive impact on the proportion of children enrolled in school, and the estimated coefficients are all significantly different from zero at the 90-percent level or greater.[83] The variables for average book holdings account for about 40 percent of the variation in school enrollment per family.

The quantitative evidence reviewed here that the parents' education influenced the education of their children is reinforced by contemporary statements that better-educated parents were more likely than uneducated parents to attend to the education of their children. The Vicar of Walsell stated in 1864, "From 20 years' experience, I should say that education has advanced very considerably through the operation of the privy council grants. Many of the parents themselves are now educated, and value education for their children, and make great sacrifices to obtain it for them."[84]

The evidence just reviewed suggests that it is reasonable to suppose that a literate parent had at least a 20-percent higher probability than an illiterate parent of having a literate child. If this differential probability of 20 percent in fact existed, then it can be shown mathematically that the impact of any exogenous factor that increased literacy in one generation would have been further amplified by 25 percent in subsequent generations.[85]

Constraints Versus Preferences

Many of the findings of this chapter have minimized the impact of the family on literacy trends. The influence of parental status on literacy was not as strong as would appear from an initial consideration of the evidence. Forces that constrained a family's resources for education do not seem to have been important determinants of educational attainment in Victorian England. The estimates of both the response of education to income levels and the impact of the quantity-quality interaction between education and numbers of children indicated that both effects were modest.

Nevertheless, the attitudes of parents toward education did have an important influence on the literacy of their children. The literacy and school enrollment regressions considered in this chapter indicate that a substantially larger proportion of the variance in literacy and school enrollment was accounted for by parents' education than by their income.[86] And parental influences on education implied that the impact of changes in the literacy of one generation would persist onto the subsequent generation. These findings confirm Mill's concern that parental apathy and ignorance in nineteenth-century England were the major barriers to the advance of popular education. And they also suggest that apathy and ignorance were eroded by the rise of literacy itself.

Part 2

Public Policy and the Costs of Acquiring Literacy

L iteracy could be acquired by a variety of methods ranging from self-instruction spread over several decades of adulthood to a rigid curriculum in a formal school for several years during childhood. The costs of acquiring literacy could vary markedly depending on which method or mix of methods was used. As Chapter 6 argues, however, beginning in the mid-Victorian period, literacy was primarily acquired through formal schooling during childhood. This implied that there were three primary determinants of the cost of acquiring literacy: first, the fees and physical proximity of local schools; second, the quality of instruction offered in those schools; and third, the opportunity costs of the time used in attending school.

Secular economic trends could influence all three of these factors. Trends in the demand for adult labor could influence not only the salaries that teachers could command and hence the costs of offering instruction but also the abilities of prospective teachers. Trends in the demand for child labor would obviously have influenced the opportunity costs of attending school. The influence of these secular forces will be considered in Part 2. But as the chapters that follow argue, the cost of acquiring literacy during the Victorian period was predominantly influenced by the development of public educational policy; hence, Part 2 will focus on its impact.

By the early nineteenth century, a long-standing tradition of philanthropic assistance to primary education existed in England. As early as the late seventeenth century, the Society for the Preservation of Christian Knowledge attempted to organize a national effort to provide education for the poor. But for the most part, assistance consisted of scattered local endowments and efforts of better-off community members to provide subscriptions to build schools, pay teachers, and subsidize the tuition of needy or worthy students.[1]

With the spread of Sunday schools in the late eighteenth and early nineteenth centuries, and with the establishment of the National Society for Promoting the Education of the Poor in the Principles of the Established Church by Anglican groups and of the British and Foreign School

Society by non-Anglican groups in the early nineteenth century, national efforts to establish public elementary schools for the working classes developed significant momentum. Early in the nineteenth century, the British and Foreign School Society and the National Society also introduced the monitorial method of instruction in which older pupils were used to teach younger ones. In the second third of the century, Parliament began providing funds to assist in the building and, subsequently, the operation of elementary schools that had been established primarily through local effort and, to a large extent, in affiliation with the National or British and Foreign School societies. During this period the Committee of Council on Education was also established. In addition to administering government grants to support elementary schools, the committee developed a standard curriculum, a system of teacher certification, normal schools to train teachers, and a system to monitor instruction.[2]

For England and Wales as a whole, publicly provided primary schooling increased markedly over the nineteenth century (the term *public* refers not only to schools receiving funds from the government but also to those receiving funds from religious groups or individual philanthropists). As already noted in the Preface, this follows mid-Victorian usage and indicates that some of the funds for public schools were coming from those with overt motives of acting in the interests of society at large rather than for any specific person or narrow group of people. Since public schools were receiving at least some of their income from sources other than fees, or in other words from subsidies, the terms *public schools* and *subsidized schools* will be used interchangeably in what follows. Between 1820 and 1880 the proportion of the population enrolled in elementary day schools that received some form of subsidy increased fivefold, while between 1830 and 1880, the annual subsidy per child in subsidized schools at least doubled.[3] Subsidized schools had additional educational objectives besides teaching reading, writing, and other cognitive skills. Advocates of public education, especially in the first half of the nineteenth century, argued for the importance of religious indoctrination and the inculcation of orderly social behavior.[4]

In 1870, the state became even more involved in elementary education by enabling and, in many instances, requiring local districts to establish school boards for operating elementary schools financed by local taxes.[5] As early as 1802, legislation was enacted to restrict the employment of children, and it was extended and developed throughout the rest of the century.[6] In the last third of the century, compulsory schooling laws were set in place along with the means to enforce them.

Because of the sheer scope of this activity, it has been presumed that public efforts were central to the rise of popular literacy during the second half of the nineteenth century. As early as the 1860s, W. L. Sargent was willing to attribute rising signature rates at marriage to the activities of the National Society and the Committee of Council on Education.[7] Subsequent histories of nineteenth-century English education have also tended to focus on the role of government policy.[8]

Nevertheless, the scope of public efforts did not guarantee that they would be effective. Although annual government expenditure for elementary schooling rose from £20,000 in 1833 to £813,000 in 1861, the Newcastle Commission still concluded in 1861 that there were areas of England and Wales inadequately provided with subsidized schools.[9] Publicly funded schools were sometimes half empty.[10] Those who attended school as children were not necessarily able to read or write as adults. Indeed, a survey of Pendleton in 1838 indicated that the majority of adults surveyed who could not read had attended day school at some point in their lives.[11] Schools may have taught ineffectively and literacy may have been acquired outside the classroom. Providing subsidized school places may have had little impact on enrollments or on literacy in areas where parents and children lacked motivation to acquire literacy. The Newcastle Commission report on the Black Country districts of Staffordshire suggests that working-class apathy was more responsible for low educational attainment than inadequate school supply.[12] Equally important for discouraging school attendance was the value of children's time outside the classroom, whether they were earning money or doing domestic tasks. Nor did compulsory schooling laws guarantee full classrooms; they could be ignored by magistrates as well as by parents.[13]

Thus, the impact of public efforts to promote popular literacy may have depended not only on national policies but also on the efforts of local school boards, clergymen, and philanthropists to fund and operate schools and enforce schooling laws. The responses of parents and children to these efforts may have been even more fundamental to the success of public education. Part 2 examines these local efforts and the responses of parents and children to them. Chapter 5 presents evidence that the local provision of public schooling became more equally distributed across England and Wales over the nineteenth century. Chapter 6 establishes that increased access to public schools had a sizable impact on school enrollment rates and that increased school enrollment rates in turn had a sizable impact on literacy rates. Chapter 7 finds that both a secular decline in the demand for child labor and the enforcement of compulsory schooling laws also increased school enrollment rates.

5. The Geographical Distribution of Public Schooling

THE EFFORTS that went into assuring that all segments of the English population had access to subsidized schools by the end of the nineteenth century reflected the belief that popular education would develop only if more schools were built. Thus the chairman of the Ragged School Union was asked by the Cross Commission in 1887 which provision of the Education Act of 1870 was more important: establishing the obligation of rate payers (i.e., local taxpayers) to provide schools, or compulsory school attendance. He replied, "the obligation to provide schools. Compulsion would be useless without the schools that must follow."[1]

Throughout the nineteenth century, the funding and management of elementary schools depended heavily on local support, in spite of increasing centralized national control over the financing and operation of elementary schools.

Before 1870, the initiative to establish a school or apply for national sources of funding had to come primarily from local agencies. At the beginning of the nineteenth century, local endowments and groups of local subscribers were virtually the only sources of support for primary schooling. During the first third of the nineteenth century, both the British and Foreign School Society and the National Society for Promoting the Education of the Poor in the Principles of the Established Church began to fund and organize elementary schools at the national level. The National Society in particular was well placed to organize local efforts, since its Anglican connections allowed it to call upon the Church of England diocesan and parish organization to develop educational activity.[2] These organizations could do much to reinforce local efforts. But they also required that any school receiving their funds for building receive at least an equal amount of money from local sources. And before 1833 virtually all of the funding for the ongoing operation of a school had to come from local sources.[3]

In 1833, Parliament began providing funds to build schools. Initially, school sponsors were required to apply through the British and Foreign School Society or the National Society for these funds, and to qualify, a school had to have at least half of the cost of construction financed by local private contributions.[4]

In 1846 Parliament provided grants to teachers who passed certification examinations; it also funded a program for students aged thirteen to eighteen to train as pupil-teachers.[5] These students served an apprenticeship under the supervision of approved, qualified adult teachers. Both students and teachers received parliamentary grants. Teachers who were capable of meeting certification standards and standards for supervising pupil-teachers generally commanded higher salaries than other teachers. To qualify for parliamentary grants to teachers and pupil-teachers, schools had to come up with funds from local sources to cover the remainder of the relatively high salaries of their teachers.

The tension between local initiative and central direction in the provision of public schools that recurred through the nineteenth century is a fundamental one that persists to the present day. On the one hand, local initiative facilitates the responsiveness of schools to individual circumstances and their accountability to the parental consumers of education. On the other hand, complete reliance on local initiative would seem treacherous in areas that are either impoverished or apathetic to education. Despite shifts in the balance between local and central control in the provision of public education, the English government throughout the nineteenth and twentieth centuries has made allowance for these competing considerations in determining that balance. During the Victorian period, the provision of public education came increasingly under centralized control. Yet even in the last quarter of the nineteenth century, the immediate management of schools was accomplished either by local school boards or by local managers for individual Church of England and other nonboard public schools. In the late 1980s and early 1990s, the English government has attempted to revive the role of local initiative in public education by allowing individual schools receiving government funds the possibility of "opting out" from control by regional educational authorities while still retaining a role for those authorities.

In considering the issue of how government funds for education should be distributed, the examination of the Victorian experience that follows in this chapter confirms the wisdom of balancing the advantages of local initiative and central direction. The policy of rewarding local initiative that prevailed in the early Victorian period did result in a tendency for school subsidies to go to regions with relatively high initial educational attainments. Yet despite this, the more educationally destitute regions of England also made marked progress during this period in the provision of subsidized schooling. But the Education Act of 1870 also appears to have amplified this progress by causing government funds to be more likely to go toward those regions where illiteracy was more prevalent.

The Regional Distribution of Support for Public Education before 1870

Because schools needed local support to qualify for matching national grants, it is hardly surprising that mid-nineteenth century-commentators frequently noted that school subsidies were most likely to go to areas where educational conditions were already good. According to the National Society report for 1842, "cases of greatest urgency and destitution are in general the latest to present themselves."[6] And a Devon clergyman, speaking in the 1860s of the parliamentary grant system, noted that "under the present system of granting aid rich localities who are able to pay certificated masters get all, the poorer who are not get none."[7] The 1857 National Society report stated that parliamentary grants were "not calculated to afford sufficient assistance to a country subjected to so many disadvantages as Wales; their tendency being to aid wealthy districts in undue measure, or to state the case more accurately, to afford insufficient help to districts in which the population is necessitous or dispersed over a wide area."[8]

National and regional agencies did make efforts to channel funds toward areas in which local initiative appeared to be lacking. As early as the 1820s, the National Society, with the collaboration of Anglican diocesan officials, was active in funding and organizing schools in Lancashire. In the early 1840s, the National Society set up the Special Fund for the Establishment and Support of Schools in the Manufacturing and Mining Districts, and on net, National Society funds do seem to have moved toward these districts.[9] In 1846 the National Society established the Welsh Education Fund.[10]

Although funds from these sources did help channel resources toward targeted areas and, in Lancashire, regional organizations further

supported and coordinated local schooling activity, such efforts were ultimately limited by the extent of local activity. Despite the focus of the
National Society on industrial counties such as Lancashire and Staffordshire and the net transfer of funds toward those counties, their public
school enrollment rates in 1851 were below the average for England and
Wales. Enrollment per population was 7.4 percent in Lancashire, 7.3 percent in Staffordshire, and 7.84 percent in England and Wales as a whole.[11]
According to a Church of England school report, the nonfee income per
head of population in 1857 was 2.81 pence in Lancashire and 4.8 pence
in Staffordshire, compared with 5.76 pence in England as a whole.[12] In
Lancashire, National Society activity probably had some effect because the
percentage of the population residing in areas where, owing to deficiencies
in provision, the Department of Education after 1870 ordered that school
boards be established was only 6 percent, compared with a national average of 16 percent.[13] However, in Staffordshire, also the site of extensive
National Society activity, the percentage was 26.6 percent; local apathy
there dampened the impact of national and regional efforts.

The Committee of Council on Education also attempted to give special consideration in awarding grants to rural areas with low population
densities. In 1853 it provided that rural schools could receive a grant for
each student attending more than a given number of times per year under
the condition that a minimum proportion of students were able to pass
inspectors' examinations. Then in 1855 these grants were made available
to schools in all regions.[14] To increase the supply of teachers in rural areas,
the National Society issued in 1858 its "Regulations for Teachers of an
Humble Order," which provided for funds to train teachers who were
unlikely to pass the certification examination.[15] Nevertheless, the 1861 report of the Newcastle Commission indicated that rural areas with low
population densities continued to experience difficulties in supporting
public schools. Even in the 1880s the Cross Commission gave attention
to the issue of supporting schools in districts with low populations.[16]

If local apathy toward education in some communities was thwarting
the efforts of national and regional agencies, the agencies could have responded by intensifying their efforts to direct funds to areas that lacked
schools. But it was commonly argued that educational subsidies would be
most productive if sent to areas where a serious local effort was already
advancing education. The Newcastle Commisssion report stated the
following:

Another proposal still more objectionable is that the assistance of the government be proportioned to the want. . . . This is to ask the whole system of the Committee of Council be not merely changed but reversed; that the grant be proportioned not to the amount but to the deficiency of local effort; that the carelessness or illiberality of the proprietors be encouraged. . . . We may dismiss these proposals with no further comment.[17]

The policy of rewarding local effort was evident in the Revised Code that went into effect in 1862. It incorporated a policy of "payment by results," according to which the government grant a school received was based on how its students performed in examinations given by the Department of Education. Although the policy was criticized for emphasizing rote learning and putting too much pressure on students, it persisted into the 1890s. Rather than having "the assistance of the government be proportioned to the want," stated Robert Lowe, architect of the Revised Code, "if the new system will not be cheap it will be efficient, and if it will not be efficient it will be cheap."[18]

The reliance on local initiative for establishing and operating public schools during the first two-thirds of the nineteenth century seems to have made areas with relatively high school enrollments and literacy levels initially the most likely to obtain further support for public schools (see Table 5.1). The Spearman rank order correlation coefficient reported in Table 5.1 between the level of nonfee income per capita in Church of England schools in 1857 and school enrollment rates in 1833 and 1851 across counties was positive (+ .4996 with 1833 enrollment and + .619 with 1851 enrollment) and statistically different from zero at the 1-percent level. (The Spearman coefficient compares the ranking of counties for the variables considered as opposed to the numerical values of the variables themselves.) This positive correlation between initial education levels and further subsidies to schools occurred in the presence of marked differences across counties in the level of subsidy per capita. Parliamentary grants per capita for the period 1833–59 ranged from 10.8 pence per capita in Radnor to 69.6 pence per capita in Surrey.[19] For Church of England schools, nonfee income per capita reported for 1857 ranged from 2.25 pence in Lancashire to 11.23 pence in Oxford.[20]

The tendency for a positive association with existing educational conditions appears to have been much stronger for subsidies paid by local sources than for subsidies from parliamentary grants. The Spearman correlation coefficient across counties between 1857 illiteracy and income

Table 5.1

Correlations between Subsidy Sources per Capita and Educational Conditions
(Spearman Rank Order Correlation Coefficients)

	1833 School Enrollment	1851 School Enrollment	1841 Illiteracy	1857 Illiteracy
Nonfee income, 1857	.500 (.001)	.619 (.001)	-.433 (.001)	-.566 (.001)
Subscription income, 1857	.384 (.001)	.507 (.001)	-.310 (.025)	-.426 (.002)
Endowment income, 1857	.372 (.007)	.465 (.001)	-.410 (.003)	-.508 (.001)
Government income, 1857	.258 (.065)	.318 (.022)	-.018 (.902)	-.086 (.547)
Cumulative parliamentary grants, 1833-59	-.022 (.878)	.011 (.937)	.046 (.747)	.033 (.815)
Percent assisted by government, 1866	-.356 (.010)	-.333 (.016)	.231 (.099)	.268 (.055)

Sources: "Abstract of Returns on the State of Education in England and Wales, vol. III,"
PP 1835, vol. 43, [62], 1326-29; "Census of Gt. Britain, 1851, Education," PP 1852-3,
vol. 90, [1692], 4-7; National Society, "Summaries of Returns to the Inquiry into the State
and Progress of Schools during the Years 1856-7"; National Society, "Statistics of Church
of England Schools for the Poor in England and Wales for the Years 1866 and 1867";
"Report of Commissioners on Popular Education," PP 1861, vol. 21, pt. I, [2794-I], 585;
7th ARRG (Abstract for 1843), PP 1846, vol. 19, [727], 40-41; 20th ARRG (Abstract
for 1857), PP 1859, vol. 12, sess. 2, [2559], viii.
Note: Observations are by county and include 40 English and 12 Welsh counties. In the
English counties, London is divided between Middlesex, Kent, and Surrey, and the three
ridings of Yorkshire are combined into Yorkshire as a whole. Numbers in parentheses
indicate the probability that the true coefficient equals zero.

sources per capita in Church of England schools in 1857 was $-.426$ for subscription income and $-.508$ for endowment income but only $-.086$ for government grants. (Subscription and endowment income came from local donors.) These results are based on forty English counties and twelve Welsh counties. If just the English counties are considered, the differences between national and local funding sources in correlation coefficients with educational conditions appear to be weaker and in some cases disappear.[21] Based on this evidence, it appears that in Wales, where illiteracy rates were far higher than in England, it was particularly difficult to raise local funds to subsidize schools in areas where educational activity was initially low.

The difference between national and local sources of funds in their correlation with measures of educational conditions can be accounted for by differences in the determinants of the two types of funding sources. According to the Newcastle Commission report, as well as other nineteenth-century sources, the extent of local subsidies for schooling was largely determined by the activity of the local parson and by landowners' wealth and whether or not they resided in the area.[22] The parliamentary grants that initially funded school building in the 1830s gave a preference to "such applications as come from large Cities and Towns, in which the necessity of assisting in the erection of schools is most pressing."[23] Although the Committee of Council on Education in 1853 provided an allowance for smaller rural communities, in 1855 it provided a similar allowance for all communities.[24]

These differences between local and national sources of funding are evident in regression analysis across counties of the determinants of levels of support per capita for various sources of funding. The regressions reported in Table 5.2 explain variation in levels of funding, on the one hand, by variables that reflect the propensity to supply funding: measures of the influence of the Church of England and the percentage of land held by the larger gentry; and, on the other hand, by variables likely to reflect demands for popular education as a way of dealing with social tension: crime rates, the extent of mining and industrial activity, and urbanization.

For local sources of income, from subscriptions and endowments, the variable with the most explanatory power was that for Church of England strength. Government sources of income were more influenced by variables reflecting social tension: urbanization, industrialization, and crime rates. Thus, while there were similarities between government and local sources of support, there were also notable differences. Furthermore, the availability of government funds may have reduced the perceived

Table 5.2

Regressions Accounting for Variation in Subsidies for Elementary Education across Counties

Independ. Variables	Dependent Variables				
	Parl. Grant33-59	Govt. Grant57	Govt. Aid66	Subscrp. per cap.	Endow. per cap.
Intercept	0.147 (2.76)	0.001 (.679)	0.259 (1.76)	-0.239×10^{-3} (0.02)	0.004 (0.36)
Urb51	0.001 (1.96) [.380]	0.25×10^{-5} (.331) [.068]	— — —	-0.13×10^{-3} (1.53) [-.214]	-0.001 (1.45) [-.267]
Urb71	— —	— —	0.003 (2.41)* [.413]	— —	— —
Crime4	7.619 (2.42)* [.508]	— —	— —	— —	— —
Crime5	— —	0.065 (1.08) [.239]	15.150 (1.48) [.231]	0.858 (1.29) [.194]	-0.0754 (1.04) [-.206]
Com4	-0.001 (1.009) [-.229]	— —	— —	— —	— —
Ind6	— —	0.74×10^{-5} (.545) [-.136]	0.004 (1.50) [.272]	-0.14×10^{-3} (0.94) [-.159]	0.73×10^{-4} (0.45) [.100]
Gent	-0.001 (.623) [-.119]	0.66×10^{-5} (.329) [.068]	-0.49×10^{-3} (.147) [-.021]	0.23×10^{-3} (1.02) [.143]	-0.31×10^{-3} (1.28) [-.238]
Angseat	-0.090 (1.157) [-.246]	0.30×10^{-3} (0.26) [.061]	-0.071 (.370) [-.059]	0.038 (3.00)* [.473]	0.030 (2.14)* [0.444]
R^2	.286	.111	.587	.590	.287
F	2.319	0.724	8.245*	8.347*	2.339
d.f.	(5,29)	(5,29)	(5,29)	(5,29)	(5,29)

(continued)

Table 5.2 (continued)

Sources and Definitions of Variables: Parl. Grant33-59 = the cumulative grant by Parliament for school building between 1833 and 1859 per capita. From "Report of Commissioners on Popular Education," PP 1861, vol. 21, pt. I, [2794-I], 585. Subscrp. per cap. = subscription income in Church of England schools in 1857 per capita. From National Society, "Summaries of Returns to the Inquiry into the State and Progress of Schools during the Years 1856-7." London: National Society, 1858. Endow. per cap. = endowment income in Church of England schools in 1857 per capita. From ibid. Govt. Grant57 = income from government grants in Church of England schools in 1857 per capita. From ibid. Govt. Aid66 = percentage of Church of England schools in 1866 receiving assistance from the Department of Education. From National Society, "Statistics of Church of England Schools for the Poor in England and Wales for the Years 1866 and 1867." Urb51 = percentage of population living in towns of over 2,500 people in 1851. From "Census of Gt. Britain, 1851, Population Tables I. Appendix to the Report," PP 1852-3, vol. 85, [1631], cvi. Urb71 = percentage of population living in towns of over 2,500 in 1871. From "Appendix A to Report. General Report, Vol. IV. Census of Gt. Britain, 1871," PP 1873, vol. 71, pt. 2, [C.-872-I], 33. Crime4 = number of persons committed for trial or bail as a percent of the population between 1842 and 1846. From "Judicial Statistics, Tables Showing the Number of Criminal Offenders in the Year 1846," PP 1847, vol. 47, [807], 65. Crime5 = percent of population committed or bailed for trial between 1854 and 1858. From "Judicial Statistics 1858, pt. I," PP 1859, vol. 26, [2508], 105. Com4 = percentage of employed persons engaged in commerce, trade and manufacture. From "Population: Occupation Abstract, Census of Gt. Britain, 1841," PP 1844, vol. 27, [587], 22. Ind6 = percentage of all employed persons 20 years and older engaged in industrial occupations. From "Census of England and Wales (1861), General Report, Appendix," PP 1863, vol. 53, pt. 1, [3221], 123, 131-32. Gent = percentage of land area occupied by estates of 3,000 to 10,000 acres in 1873. From F. M. L. Thompson, *English Landed Society in the Nineteenth Century* (London: Routledge and Kegan Paul, 1963), 114. Angseat = percentage of sittings in all churches that were in Church of England churches. From Census of Gt. Britain,1851, Religious Worship, PP 1852-3, vol. 89, [1690], Table G, Summary Tables, cclxxiv-cclxxv.

Note: The observations are for 35 English counties. London, Kent, Surrey, Middlesex, Yorkshire, and Monmouth were excluded because of missing information. Figures in parentheses are T-statistics. Figures in brackets are beta (or standardized) coefficients. The beta coefficients are obtained by multiplying the coefficient estimate for each independent variable by the standard deviation of that variable and then dividing by the standard deviation of the dependent variable. F = F-statistic. d.f. = degrees of freedom.

* Statistically different from zero at the 5-percent level.

importance of local charity.[25] The rank order correlation across thirty-five English counties between government grants per capita in 1857 and subscription income per capita was + .523, indicating some correspondence between the two funding sources. But the correlation between government income and endowment income was only + .097.[26]

Surprisingly, the system of "payment by results" introduced in 1862, which tied government payments to school examination performance, does not appear to have diverted government funds away from areas of high illiteracy. A measure of government support for 1866 (proportion of Church of England schools receiving government aid) was more highly correlated with illiteracy and low school attendance than measures of government support for earlier years (see Table 5.1). One explanation is that larger urban schools that happened also to be in areas of relatively high illiteracy were in a better position to qualify for government support. An alternative explanation, offered to explain why in Devon only 26 percent of subsidized schools were on the government grant list, is that "the limited grant then available seems in most cases to have been thought not worth the loss of independence and the expense of complying with the Department's requirements on buildings and staff."[27]

Centralized sources of funding, whether from government grants or National Society special funds, may have been more likely than local philanthropy to reach areas where educational attainment was low. But in the first two-thirds of the nineteenth century, local philanthropy was still the dominant source of subsidies for primary schools.[28] The reliance on local sources thus seems to have restricted the tendency for funds to go where school provision was the most deficient.

The Rising Availability of Public Schooling before 1870

Despite the regional disparity in access to funds and the limited tendency to channel funds to the most educationally backward areas, there is evidence of widespread improvement in access to subsidized schooling even before it was mandated by the Education Act of 1870.

Surveys of schools taken for Parliament in 1818 and 1833 suggest that public schooling was already widely available in England and Wales during the first third of the nineteenth century. Although these surveys have been regarded as unreliable, this is largely because of a tendency to undercount schools: public schooling may have been even more widely available than these surveys suggest.

These two surveys describe the schools of each parish of England and Wales. To avoid having to analyze all eighteen thousand parishes in the surveys, a sample of eight English counties will be used here: Durham, Gloucester, Hereford, Lancashire, Lincolnshire, Middlesex, Nottingham, and Stafford. These eight counties contained one-third of the English population in 1811, and their leading economic activities ranged from textile manufacture in Lancashire to mining and metal manufacture in Durham and Stafford to agriculture in Hereford and Lincolnshire. The signature rates at marriage in the eight counties were similar to those for England as a whole. In 1839, 30 percent of the grooms and 46 percent of the brides made marks on the marriage register, compared with 33 percent for grooms and 50 percent for brides for England as a whole.[29]

At least 30 percent of the population in the sample counties in 1818 lived in parishes with subsidized schooling.[30] This is a lower-bound measure because it includes only parishes identified by the survey as having at least one subsidized school (in many cases descriptions of schools were unclear on this point) and for which margin comments for the parish stated that "the poor were sufficiently provided with education." In the 1833 survey, only 14 percent of the population in the eight counties resided in parishes in which the survey made no mention of the presence of subsidized schools.[31]

In certain regions such as Wales, subsidized schools may have been less widely available in the first third of the nineteenth century than they were in the eight counties just considered. Still, the 1833 survey indicates that in the six Welsh counties of Brecon, Cardigan, Carmarthen, Glamorgan, Merioneth, and Radnor, 63.7 percent of the population resided in parishes that had at least one subsidized school.[32] However, in Cardigan, only 35 percent of the population resided in parishes having subsidized schools, and in Brecon, only 39 percent.

Between the 1833 parochial survey of education and the 1851 census of education, enrollment rates in subsidized schools more than doubled, from 3.8 percent of the population of England and Wales in 1833 to 8 percent in 1851. Some of this rise may reflect undercounting of public schools in the 1833 survey. But, the degree of undercounting suggested by critics of the 1833 survey has ranged from 10 to 50 percent, explaining only a small part of the observed increase between the two dates.[33] Although some of the increase in enrollment could reflect a rise in popular demand for schooling, simply to maintain subsidy levels per student in the face of rising enrollments in subsidized schools would have required an increase in the availability of subsidies. And subsidy levels per student appear to have been rising.[34] Moreover, an increase in demand would have increased enrollments in private schools also. But the percentage of all scholars enrolled in public schools rose from 42 percent in 1833 to 67 percent in 1851.

The percentage of the population enrolled in subsidized schools affiliated with the Church of England also rose markedly between 1837 and 1867. In England the proportion of the population enrolled in day or evening schools associated with the Church of England rose from 3.1 percent in 1837 to 5.7 percent in 1847, and to 7.7 percent in 1867. In England and Wales as a whole, the proportion of the population enrolled in Church of England day schools rose from 5.55 percent in 1847 to 7.03 percent in 1867.[35]

Even in the regions of England and Wales that had the fewest public school places per capita in the first third of the nineteenth century, public school enrollments rose markedly between 1833 and 1851. In the ten English counties with the lowest enrollment rates in public schools in 1833 (Bedford, Buckingham, Chester, Cornwall, Lancashire, Monmouth, Northumberland, Nottingham, Somerset, and the West Riding), public school enrollment per head of population rose from 2.9 percent in 1833 to 7.43 percent in 1851. And in these same counties the proportion of all scholars enrolled in public schools rose from 35 percent in 1833 to 65.5 percent in 1851. In Wales, which lagged behind England throughout the nineteenth century in both school enrollments and literacy rates, public school enrollments rose from 2.9 percent of the population in 1833 to 6.5 percent in 1851. The proportion of all scholars enrolled in public schools rose from 42 percent in 1833 in Wales to 74 percent in 1851. In Cornwall and Nottingham, which, of the bottom ten English counties in public school enrollments in 1833, experienced the slowest public enrollment growth between 1833 and 1851, public school enrollments rose by over 80 percent. In Cornwall public school enrollments grew from 2.8 percent to 5.3 percent, and in Nottingham, from 3.2 percent to 6.5 percent.

Within individual counties, the rise in enrollment rates was not confined to just a few registration districts but appears to have been general. In 1851 only 5.1 percent of the English population lived in registration districts in which public enrollment rates were below the 1833 rate for England as a whole (4 percent). None of the registration districts in North Wales in 1851 had public school enrollment rates below the 1833 English average. In 1851 only 18.5 percent of the population of South Wales resided in registration districts in which public school enrollment rates were below the 1833 average for England.[36]

The Perceived Gaps in Public
School Provision in 1870

In its 1861 report, the Newcastle Commission acknowledged that marked progress had been made in educational provision since 1800. Nevertheless, the majority of the Commission concluded that the existing system of local philanthropy supplemented by government grants was inadequate and left many areas insufficiently provided with public schooling. A minority of the Commission, however, continued to support a system emphasizing the role of voluntary charity, thus maintaining a controversy that continued to the end of the century.[37]

Although the majority of the Newcastle Commission agreed that the existing provision of schools was inadequate, the Commission's report indicated that there were few areas totally without school buildings or where the population had no access to subsidized schools. In a survey of specimen districts, waiting lists for schools were common in only one London district; a few schools in Ipswich were also reported to have had waiting lists. In all the other districts, accommodations in public schools far exceeded enrollments.[38]

But the Commission's report pointed out that the apparent availability of school places in many areas frequently disguised the poor distribution of schools. In Bradford, it was reported that "some schools are but half filled, while others are inconveniently crowded."[39] In Somerset, the parish of Hinton had a school with room for two hundred but only sixty children enrolled, while the parish of Lopen, less than three miles away, had no public day school despite "loud and earnest demands."[40] The report for Wales stated :

> Schools in that district [North Wales] are established and school rooms built on a principle altogether erroneous; the school promoters aim at making the schools centre points of education to extensive districts, whereas the physical character of the country and the distribution of the population over its area point to a greater number of schools, of perhaps humbler pretensions, as the desideratum for supplying what is the great deficiency in the condition of education in North Wales, the more equal distribution over the country.[41]

Furthermore, many of the clergy replying to Newcastle Commission inquiries stated that only because new schools had been built recently had problems of overcrowding or inconvenient location of schools been solved.[42]

In 1870 Robert Forster made a sufficient case against the existing system of leaving the supply of public schools to voluntary charity to enable him to maneuver through Parliament the landmark Education Act of 1870. The act provided for the establishment of local school boards in areas where existing provision was deemed inadequate. "Filling in the gaps" was the phrase used to justify such a policy, although in part the phrase reflected a desire to avoid ruffling the feathers of those who wished to maintain the existing system of schools funded through voluntary charity.[43]

The 1870 Education Act itself provides a reference point as to what gaps were perceived to exist. It ordered a survey of schools in England and Wales and, as just mentioned, required school boards to be established in inadequately provided areas. School boards could use funds from local taxes to build and operate the schools that they managed, which were to exist alongside schools financed by philanthropy. In civil parishes in the counties of Cornwall and Northumberland, both of which had relatively low enrollment rates in subsidized schools in the first half of the nineteenth century, the 1870 survey indicated that only 4.3 percent of the population lived in settlements that had no subsidized schools and where no mention was made of children attending schools in neighboring areas.[44] In the Welsh counties of Cardigan, Merioneth, Brecon, and Radnor the survey indicated that 4.5 percent of the population in civil parishes resided in communities with no subsidized schools and where children did not attend schools in neighboring communities. According to the survey, more schools or expansion of existing facilities was required in communities incorporating 28 percent of the population of civil parishes in the English counties of Cornwall, Northumberland, and Nottingham (another county with relatively low enrollment rates in public schools in the first half of the nineteenth century), and 25 percent of the population in civil parishes in the four Welsh counties just mentioned.

Subsidized schools in civil parishes in the three English counties and four Welsh counties, according to the survey, had sufficient seating to accommodate 10 percent of the population in the areas surveyed. This compares quite favorably with the 3.8 percent of the population reported enrolled in public schools in the 1833 parochial survey and the 7.9 percent reported enrolled in the 1851 Census of Education. However, it is also below the 12.5 percent enrollment goal suggested in 1838 by the Select Committee on Education and the 16.6 percent goal advocated by educational policymakers throughout the second half of the nineteenth century.[45]

The 1870 survey may have been too harsh in its assessment of the existing provision of schools. The Education Department could find that the existing provision was insufficient not only because of a shortage of school places but also because some of the schools providing these places were not "efficient" or not "suitable." In his speech to Parliament proposing the Education Act of 1870, Forster defined "efficient" schools as those with "good buildings and good teaching" and "suitable" schools as those "suitable to the religious views of the parents of the children."[46] Partisans of existing voluntary schools supported by religious groups and local philanthropy thought that these criteria of efficiency and suitability were so vague as to allow the Education Department to arbitrarily mandate school boards. Their fear was that the boards would then build schools that would compete with and displace existing voluntary schools.[47] In other respects, however, the 1870 survey may have overstated how much was accomplished before school boards were established. The 1870 Education Act initiated a flurry of voluntary school building both to avoid competition from board schools and to keep down local taxes. School boards were also established voluntarily in areas which probably would not have complied with Education Department standards in the absence of the boards.[48]

Nevertheless, the proportion of the population residing in areas where the Department of Education required that school boards be formed reflects how much of a problem remained with school provision in the view of at least one group of policymakers. In 1891, 16.8 percent of the English population and 36 percent of the Welsh population resided in areas where the Education Department in the 1870s had ordered that school boards be formed.[49]

How Many Gaps Did School Boards Fill?

Communities that were compelled by the Education Department to establish school boards do seem to have had populations with relatively low levels of educational attainment in 1870. The rank order correlation across forty English counties (excluding London) and twelve Welsh counties between the proportion of a county's population in areas that the Education

Department ordered to form school boards—because of either existing deficiencies or likely deficiencies—and illiteracy in 1871 was positive and statistically different from zero at the 5-percent level (see Table 5.3). If the English counties are considered alone, the correlation is still positive, but lower, and no longer statistically different from zero at even the 10-percent level. The proportion of the population under any type of school board, including both those formed voluntarily and those that had been compelled, had an even higher rank order correlation across counties with illiteracy in 1871 than did the proportion of the population in areas forced to form school boards (see Table 5.3). This result held for both England and Wales as a whole and for the English counties alone. It seems, then, that the school boards authorized by the Education Act of 1870 were relatively more active in areas where education was inadequate than were previous efforts by the Department of Education to supplement and supervise local activity with grants. And school boards of all types were active in this manner, not just those compelled by centralized authorities.

Indeed, simply ordering the establishment of a school board did not guarantee that the board would do much of consequence or more than the bare minimum, if that. It is true that school inspectors could report school boards that were inactive or not complying with Department of Education standards. And of some 2,470 boards established between 1870 and 1895, relatively few were completely inactive or in default. By 1887 only 33 boards were declared in default, and in only a further 10 cases were new boards required to be elected.[50] But boards could vary considerably in how they pursued their task. In some rural areas, boards were made up of major rate payers and could be "at least as much concerned to keep down the rates [local taxes] as to keep up the school."[51] Still, according to one assessment of rural Devon, "the glaring deficiencies of a few school boards, which stand out in the records from the uneventful respectability of the majority, should be regarded as a caution against, rather than a basis for, generalization."[52]

Such an assessment is supported by the fact that the rank order correlation across the counties of England and Wales between school board nonfee income per capita of population and illiteracy in 1884 was higher ($+.327$) than the correlation between government grants per capita to Church of England schools and illiteracy in 1857 ($-.0855$) or between parliamentary grants between 1833 and 1859 per capita and illiteracy rates in 1841 ($+.046$) (compare Tables 5.1 and 5.3). The impact of school

Table 5.3

Correlations across Counties between Population under School Board Control and Illiteracy (Spearman Rank Order Correlation Coefficients)

	English and Welsh Counties		English Counties Only	
	1871 Illiteracy	1884 Illiteracy	1871 Illiteracy	1884 Illiteracy
Percentage of population in areas forced to form school boards, 1871 to 1895	.281 (.043)	.324 (.019)	.160 (.326)	.208 (.199)
Percentage of population in 1895 under school boards	.472 (.0004)	.468 (.0005)	.336 (.034)	.310 (.051)
Nonfee school board income per capita, 1885	.322 (.020)	.327 (.018)	.279 (.082)	.271 (.091)

Sources and Definition of Variables: 1871 Illiteracy and 1884 Illiteracy = percentage of brides and grooms in a county making marks in 1871 and 1884. From 34th ARRG (Abstract for 1871), PP 1873, vol. 20, [C.-806], lxvi; 47th ARRG (Abstract for 1884), PP 1886, vol. 17, sess. I, [C.-4722], xli. Percentage of population in a county in areas forced to form school boards from 1871 to 1895. Calculated from percentage of 1891 population in a county in districts where a school board was compelled to be formed because of a deficiency in provision or under section 12 (anticipating a deficiency because of a school closing). From "List of School Boards and Attendance Committees in England and Wales," PP 1895, vol. 76, [C.-7687], 8-111. Percentage of population in a county in 1895 under jursidiction of a school board. Based on 1891 population. From ibid., 4-7. Nonfee school board income per capita, 1885. Calculated by subtracting fee income in school boards from total income of school boards and dividing by 1881 population. From AR 1885-86, PP 1886, vol. 24, [C.-4849-I], 2-91.

Note: Observations exclude London. The three ridings of Yorkshire are combined into Yorkshire as a whole. The numbers in parentheses report the probability that the correlation coefficient equals zero.

boards seems to have been further sustained by the fact that the correlation between school board income and illiteracy was only slightly below the correlation between the percentage of the population in a county under jurisdiction of a school board and illiteracy, although it was greater than the correlation with the percentage of the population in areas where the Education Department had ordered establishment of a school board (see Table 5.3). Not only were school boards more likely to form where illiteracy rates were higher, they were also better able to raise money in such areas without requiring the prodding of central authorities to do so.

The Roles of Local Initiative and Central Direction in the Provision of Public Schools

It is testimony to how much was accomplished in the first two-thirds of the nineteenth century that over 80 percent of the English population and almost 67 percent of the Welsh in 1870 lived in areas that met the standards for school provision specified by the Education Act of 1870. The effort involved is evident in the some 287 schools built in Devon between 1821 and 1870, compared with the founding of 30 new voluntary schools, the construction of 70 new buildings for schools already in existence, and the establishment of 47 new board schools between 1870 and 1900. Many of the schools founded between 1821 and 1870 replaced already existing schools, but even so, the pre-1870 effort was considerable compared with what followed.[53]

Nevertheless, at least 15 percent of the English and 33 percent of the Welsh population in 1870 were in areas deemed deficient in school provision, suggesting that by that date substantial gaps remained. The establishment of school boards in conjunction with the 1870 Education Act allowed the national educational system to allocate funds more directly to the areas with the greatest need for more schooling than the previous system based on local philanthropy had been able to. Even so, Gillian Sutherland's history of the Education Department between 1870 and 1900 also underscores what a major administrative undertaking the centralized direction of school provision was. It was subject to continual conflict between the Department of Education and the Treasury over how much was to be spent and over how money was to be distributed to individual schools.[54] The amount of administrative effort involved and the bureaucratic conflict that arose suggest that the task of setting in place a system of local school boards in the last third of the nineteenth century would have been far more difficult without the establishment during the first two-thirds of the century of a network of schools financed in large part by voluntary charity.

The Improvement in Access to Public Schools During the Nineteenth Century

The widespread increase throughout England and Wales during the nineteenth century in the availability of funds for public schools made it increasingly easier for working-class people to attend them. At the very least, the 12 percent of the population that, in 1818, lived in parishes in the eight counties described above that had no public schools would have acquired access to public schools over the course of the nineteenth century. But this estimate surely understates by a considerable degree the improvement in access to schooling because much of the remaining 88 percent of the population in 1818 probably lived in localities where public schools were either too small or too inconveniently placed to accommodate all children who wished to attend. At the other extreme, one can note that enrollment rates in public schools in 1818 were only 15 percent of what they were in 1899, suggesting that 85 percent of the population may have gained access to public schooling.[55] But this figure almost surely overstates the increase in *access* by not taking into account the role of rising popular demand for education. Relatively low public school enrollments in 1818 may have reflected lack of demand as well as lack of access.

The rise over time in the percentage of students enrolled in public schools, from 42 percent in 1818 and 1833 to 67 percent in 1851, to 85 percent in 1870, indicates a marked increase in access to public schooling. If just *working-class* students are considered, the proportion enrolled in public schools may have been as high as 60 percent in 1818 and as high as 87.5 percent in 1851, still suggesting a marked improvement in access.[56] Some students who attended private rather than public schools may have done so because of preference rather than lack of access.[57] An estimated 8 percent of all working-class students were enrolled in private schools in 1871; one recent study suggests that this estimate understates the extent of private schooling.[58] Some allowance, however, should be made for children who had no access to schools; one indication of the size of this group is that 10 percent of the English population resided in communities of under six hundred in 1881.[59] Communities this small would have had difficulty supporting a full-time school.

By the mid-1880s, places in public schools were abundant throughout virtually all of England and Wales. Admittedly, witnesses before the Cross Commission reported deficiencies in some urban areas, especially those with rapidly growing populations and perhaps most noticeably in London. And problems of support in rural areas were still evident in the Cross Commission investigations of the mid-1880s. But there was a general sense of adequacy, which is supported by the high level of accommodation and enrollment in public schools in every county of England and Wales. By 1882 even the ten counties that had the lowest public enrollment rates in England in 1833 reported accommodation equal to 18 percent of the population. Of that group, even the two counties with the lowest public enrollments in 1882 had public schools that could accommodate more than 17 percent of their population and that actually enrolled at least 15 percent of their population. And in Wales in 1882, accommodation in public schools was equal to 18.3 percent of the population, and enrollment, to 17.3 percent. This compares with the 3.8 percent of the population of Wales reported enrolled in public schools in the 1833 parochial survey and the 7.9 percent reported in the 1851 Census of Education.[60]

These trends suggest that over the course of the nineteenth century about 40 percent of the English population gained access to subsidized schools. This estimate is based on a comparison of the 50 to 60 percent of working-class students who were probably enrolled in public schools in the 1830s with the almost 100 percent who were enrolled in 1900. A more generous estimate can be based on the 1818 parochial survey, which indicated that 70 percent of the population in the eight counties considered above resided in areas with inadequate access to schools. This suggests, compared with the estimates from the 1830s, that even more progress must have been made to allow all English children in 1900 access to public schools. Either estimate implies that over the course of the nineteenth century, the combination of voluntary charity and government decree substantially increased the proportion of English children that could attend public elementary schools.

6. The Impact of Increased Public School Provision on Literacy Trends

PROVIDING MORE SCHOOLS in the regions of England where illiteracy was most prevalent did not guarantee the eradication of illiteracy. If the majority of the population in these regions were uninterested in learning to read and write, most children may never have attended the newly provided public schools. And those children who did enroll may have attended so infrequently as to be unable to read and write as adults. Even when farm laborers or miners or cotton spinners began to want their children to be literate, they may have chosen other means of instruction than public schools. They may have preferred private venture schools financed solely by student fees in order to avoid the moral and religious indoctrination that public schools often emphasized. For those with the motivation to learn to read and write but who could not afford the fees of a private school, a nearby relative or an acquaintance from work may have been able to give occasional instruction in the evening. Over the course of the nineteenth century, literacy was increasingly acquired through schools rather than through informal instruction. For the most part, the private schooling market catering to the working-classes could have offered the additional instruction required by rising popular demand for literacy. Public schools may have offered superior instruction in literacy, compared with private schools, though it is uncertain how pervasive or sizable this superiority was. But the markedly lower fees that public schools charged, along with the increased access to public schools that occurred in the second half of the nineteenth century, led to a sizable increase in elementary school enrollment rates.

The Relation between Schooling and Literacy

During the seventeenth and eighteenth centuries, literacy appears to have been commonly acquired through informal instruction, possibly reinforced with occasional formal schooling. This point has been made by Margaret Spufford, among others, and the case she cites of Thomas Tryon illustrates how sporadic instruction could be in early modern times. Tryon was born in 1634 in Oxfordshire, the son of a village tiler and plasterer. He was sent to school at age five but was quickly withdrawn and put to work. Tryon provided the following account of how he learned to read and write:

> All this while, tho' now about Thirteen Years Old, I could not Read; then thinking of the vast usefulness of Reading, I bought me a primer, and got now one, then another, to teach me to Spell, and so learn'd to Read imperfectly, my Teachers themselves not being ready Readers: But in a little time having learn't to Read competently well, I was desirous to learn to Write, but was at a great loss for Master, none of my Fellow-Shepherds being able to teach me. At last, I bethought myself of a lame young Man who taught some poor people's Children to Read and Write and having by this time got two Sheep of my own, I applied myself to him, and agreed with him to give him one of my Sheep to teach me to make the Letters, and Joyn them together.[1]

Working-class biographies from the late eighteenth and early nineteenth centuries also suggest the importance of informal instruction. In a collection of biographies from Lancashire compiled by Michael Sanderson, only 7 of 18 (39 percent) of those born before 1800 had ever attended day school, although all mentioned some form of instruction. Of those born between 1810 and 1830 in Sanderson's collection, 18 out of 29 (62 percent) had attended day school.[2] But even in this latter group, other forms of instruction were common. Of the 18 who received day school instruction after 1810, only 8 reported this as the only form of instruction. Five of the remaining 10 combined Sunday and day school instruction; 2 combined formal day school with self instruction; and 3 combined evening with day school instruction.

In a comprehensive collection of working-class autobiographies from all regions of England and Wales by John Burnett, David Vincent, and David Mayall, 12 of the 57 born before 1800 indicate instruction largely through informal means—help from a co-worker or self-instruction—with no attendance whatever at a day school.[3] And 13 of the 45 autobiographies of those born before 1800 that do indicate day school attendance also mention other forms of instruction, such as Sunday school or the help of a relative. Of the 107 people born between 1800 and 1830 in the collection, the autobiographies indicate that 16 did not attend a day school and relied primarily on informal instruction. And of the 82 people born in the same period who did mention attending a day school, 33 also mentioned receiving other forms of instruction.

The significance of methods of literacy instruction other than day schooling in the first half of the nineteenth century is also suggested by the role of Sunday schools in working-class education. Sunday schools began to appear in England in the 1780s. In 1818, the parochial survey of education indicated that enrollment in Sunday schools was 70 percent of enrollment in day schools. The 1833 parochial survey of education indicated that Sunday school enrollment had reached 1.2 times day school enrollment. The 1851 Census of Education reported that Sunday school enrollment was 1.12 times day school enrollment.[4]

In the first half of the nineteenth century, Sunday schools taught reading and, to a lesser extent, writing as well as religious doctrine. Manchester Statistical Society surveys between 1834 and 1843 indicate that 98 percent of the Sunday schools surveyed taught reading, although only about 20 percent taught writing and a mere 5 percent taught arithmetic.[5] In some cases it appears that even when church officials wanted to offer instruction only in religious doctrine and reading, those who attended exerted pressure to have instruction in writing. An 1835 report to the National Society from Macclesfield states,

> the number of children in our Sunday schools have much diminished in consequence of the instruction which is given in writing upon the Lord's day in some other Sunday schools. The practice was given up in all the Sunday schools; but the dissenters have reverted to the plan, and it serves to increase their schools very much to the injury of ours, at least for the present.[6]

After 1850 there are indications that Sunday schools were used primarily for teaching religion; both the 1861 Newcastle Commission report and the 1867 National Society survey of Church of England schools describe Sunday schools in this way.[7]

Autobiographies and surveys of the working classes suggest the importance of Sunday schools in their education in the first half of the nineteenth century. In Sanderson's collection of Lancashire biographies, 11 out of 58 of the subjects born before 1830 were described as having been educated exclusively in Sunday schools, while a further 23 indicated that they received at least some Sunday school instruction. In the Burnett, Vincent, and Mayall collection, Sunday schools were less important, suggesting that they were more important in Lancashire than in England generally. Still, of 107 people mentioned in this collection born between

1800 and 1830, 9 indicated that they were educated exclusively or predominantly in Sunday schools, and 13 others indicated that they attended Sunday schools as well as day schools. In an 1842 survey of 60 mining boys, 27 had no instruction other than in Sunday school.[8]

That Sunday schools were a substitute for day schools in the first half of the nineteenth century is suggested by the negative correlation across counties that prevailed between Sunday school and day school enrollments. In 1818, the correlation was +.638, which could indicate that when Sunday schools were first established, they required the accompanying support of a day school. In 1833 the correlation was −.474, and in 1851, −.337. For the enrollment rates reported by the 1858 Newcastle Commission survey, however, the correlation across counties between public schools and Sunday schools was +.21. This suggests that by early in the second half of the nineteenth century, Sunday schools were no longer serving primarily as substitutes for day schools.[9]

By the mid-nineteenth century, formal day schooling during childhood appears to have acquired a central although not exclusive place in working-class education. In the autobiographies collected by Burnett, Vincent, and Mayall, of 161 people born between 1830 and 1870, only 17 did not attend a day school. But 69 people attended Sunday school or received evening or informal instruction in addition to attending day school. Of 199 people born between 1870 and 1895, only 3 did not attend a day school. But 73 people indicated that, in addition to attending day school, they also received instruction in Sunday school or by some other means.[10] Many of the people who received instruction outside of day school were probably receiving either religious instruction in Sunday schools or education more advanced than basic literacy instruction, however.

Surveys by statistical societies and parliamentary commissions confirm the importance of day schools in working-class education in the mid-nineteenth century. An 1839 survey of 20,000 adults in Hull reported that 69 percent had attended a day school at some point in their lives; of 417 who had had no formal instruction, none could read or write.[11] An 1838 survey of 5,000 adults in Pendleton reported that 88 percent had attended day school; of the adults in the survey who could read, write, or cipher, over 99 percent had attended day school.[12] The 1842 survey of 60 mining boys suggests that day school played a lesser role in their education, although it was still important for those who could read or write. Only 22 of the boys had ever attended day school, and for 27 of them, Sunday school was their only educational experience. Of 18 boys who could read but not write, 13 had attended day school. Of the 3 boys who could both read and write, all had attended day school. In an 1867 survey of 45 agricultural laborers, 18 of 24 men, 9 of 13 boys, and 6 of 8 women reported that they had attended day schools.[13] Of the 36 laborers who could read and write, 32 had attended day school.

A different survey of miners, also done in 1842, indicates unambiguously the importance of day schools in teaching writing.[14] The survey asked 150 miners who could sign their names how they acquired this ability. Seventy-one percent said through day schooling, 11 percent said through evening school, and 18 percent said through self-instruction. Forty-six percent said they had learned to sign before they were ten; 20 percent learned between the ages of ten and fifteen; 9 percent, between the ages of fifteen and twenty; and 9 percent, over the age of twenty.

Profiles of literacy rates by age in the mid-nineteenth century provide evidence that instruction occurred primarily at younger ages. Studies of eighteenth-century literacy patterns have found a tendency for literacy rates to rise with age into adulthood, suggesting the importance of informal instruction after childhood.[15] A survey of children conducted in the 1840s, however, indicates that the proportion who could read rose from 18 percent for those aged seven to nine, to 46 percent for those aged ten and eleven; it then remained level for those aged twelve to fifteen.[16] The proportion who could read rose to 55 percent for those aged sixteen to seventeen. For writing ability, 4 percent of children aged seven to nine could write, and 20 percent of those aged twelve and thirteen could write, after which the proportion remained constant. These comparisons do not control for the general rise of literacy during this time period, and the small gap between younger and older ages may in part reflect this rise.[17] Nevertheless, the survey shows a marked rise in literacy rates for children from the age of seven to the age of eleven, the period of childhood when school attendance would have been most likely.

For a sample of orphan boys apprenticed to the Marine Society between 1710 and 1873, literacy profiles by age exhibit a tendency for literacy rates to rise for boys between the ages of thirteen and sixteen who were apprenticed between 1770 and 1824.[18] For boys apprenticed between the years 1809 and 1812, 39 percent of thirteen-year-olds compared with 54 percent of sixteen-year-olds could read and write. For boys apprenticed after 1824, however, the percentage that could read or write did not rise appreciably between the ages of thirteen and sixteen. For boys apprenticed between 1824 and 1844, 71 percent of thirteen-year-olds and 68 percent of sixteen-year-olds could read and write. Thus, instruction after childhood may have played a greater role in the late eighteenth and early nineteenth centuries than it did later.

The connection between day schooling and literacy is suggested by the extent to which variations in day school enrollment rates across counties can account for variations in signature rates of brides and grooms in 1841, 1851, and 1866 (see Table 6.1a-b). The standardized coefficients in Table 6.1a-b indicates that from 30 to 70 percent of the variance in literacy rates across counties and 30 to 40 percent of the variation across registration districts can be accounted for by variations in school enrollments.

There are several explanations for why the working classes around the middle of the nineteenth century may have shifted toward learning to read and write primarily by means of day school instruction received during childhood. Elite sponsors of day schools may have begun to put less emphasis in the curriculum on religious and moral indoctrination and more emphasis on basic literacy instruction.[19] This tendency may have been reinforced as the state took the responsibility for administering public schools away from religious groups. Finally, the shift may reflect the basic superiority of full-time formal day schooling compared with more casual methods of instruction. As places in day schools became more accessible because of increased public subsidies for education, parents and their children would then have been induced to shift to the superior mode of instruction. But an increased popular demand for literacy could also have led to a shift to day school instruction to take advantage of its superiority. As parents became increasingly eager to have their children learn to read and write, they would have been increasingly willing to come up with the necessary fees to put them in school.

Did Schools Have to Be Publicly Provided?

If schools offered a service that parents wanted and if parents were willing to pay part of the cost of subsidized schools, why could the service not have been provided by private schools (where private schools are defined as those financed solely by fees charged to students)? In fact, the 1833 parochial survey of education indicates that 58 percent of all students were

Table 6.1a-b

Regressions of Literacy on School Enrollment Rates

Table 6.1a Regressions of Literacy on School Enrollment Rates for Every 10th Registration District in England and Wales

Independent Variable	Dependent Variable ODMLIT66	Independent Variable	Dependent Variable ODFLIT66
Constant	-2.57	Constant	-1.77
	(-1.23)		(-1.10)
ERM	9.21	ERF	9.02
	(3.44)		(3.79)
	[.365]		[.346]
ARM	4.80	ARF	3.23
	(2.16)		(1.87)
	[.248]		[.176]
SSRM	-2.41	SSRF	-6.81
	(-2.45)		(-6.60)
	[-.259]		[-.597]
EVERM	-67.85	EVERF	-32.30
	(-2.95)		(-0.89)
	[-.318]		[-.078]
PUBM	-1.18	PUBF	0.19
	(-1.63)		(0.35)
	[-.188]		[.034]
R^2	.407		.562
F-Statistic	7.94		14.90
Degrees of Freedom	(5,58)		(5,58)
N	64		64

(continued)

enrolled in schools financed solely by student fees.[20] Although a sizable proportion of the students in these private schools may have come from middle-class families, surveys conducted by the Manchester and London statistical societies in the 1830s and 1840s also indicate that private, for-profit schools aimed at a working-class clientele were widespread.[21]

Table 6.1 (continued)

Table 6.1b Regressions of Literacy on School Enrollment Rates: Value-Added Approach

	Dependent Variables	
Independent Variables	ODLIT66ᵃ	ODLIT66ᵇ
Constant	0.610	0.720
	(8.28)	(8.02)
ODLIT51	0.826	0.763
	(13.32)	(10.99)
	[.863]	[.871]
CHD35	4.110	-2.115
	(1.80)	(-0.74)
	[.112]	[-.071]
CHS35	-2.630	-.640
	(-3.09)	(-.039)
	[-.190]	[-.029]
CHP35	0.024	0.458
	(0.13)	(1.85)
	[.008]	[.168]
R²	.825	.799
F-statistic	57.80	36.66
Degrees of Freedom	(4,49)	(4,49)
N	54	54

(continued)

Indeed, one National school in Manchester in the 1830s appears to have had enrollments well under its seating capacity while several private venture schools operated within a few hundred yards of it.[22]

This comparison of the importance of the two types of schools assumes that they offered similar types of instruction—a dubious assumption according to many contemporary observers and subsequent historians. These doubters have argued that many private schools were primarily intended for child minding rather than instruction.[23] Whether their children were being taught to read and write may have been far from the minds of harried mothers eager to get their offspring out of the way before rushing to a long day in a workshop or factory. Critics have argued

Table 6.1 (continued)

Sources for Tables 6.1a-b: "Abstract of Returns on the State of Education in England and Wales, vol. III," PP 1835, vol. 43 [62], 1326-29; "Census of Gt. Britain, 1851, Education," PP 1852-3, vol. 90, [1692], 4-49; 14th ARRG (Abstract for 1851), PP 1852-3, vol. 40, [1665], vii; 29th ARRG (Abstract for 1866), PP 1867-8, vol. 19, [4006], vii, 6-25.

Note: The dependent variable is put in the form of the logarithm of the odds ratio in order to obtain a variable that is not bounded in its range.

Definition of Variables: ODMLIT66 = log[MLIT66/(1-MLIT66)] where MLIT66 is the proportion of grooms signing the marriage register in 1866. ODFLIT66 = log[FLIT66/(1-FLIT66)] where FLIT66 is the proportion of brides signing the marriage register in 1866. ODLIT66 = log[ALIT66/ALIT66)] where ALIT is the average of the proportion of brides and grooms signing the marriage register in 1866. ODLIT51 = as with ODLIT66 but for 1851. ERM = percentage of the male population enrolled in day school in 1851. ARM = percentage of male day school students enrolled who were attending school on day of the 1851 census. SSRM = percentage of male population enrolled in Sunday School in 1851. EVERM = percentage of male population enrolled in evening school in 1851. PUBM = of all males enrolled in day school in 1851, the percentage who were enrolled in public school. ERF = percentage of the female population enrolled in day school in 1851. ARF = percentage of female day school students enrolled who were attending school on day of the 1851 census. SSRF = percentage of female population enrolled in Sunday School in 1851. EVERF = percentage of female population enrolled in evening school in 1851. PUBF = of all females enrolled in day school in 1851, the percentage who were enrolled in public school.

CHD35 = change in percentage of population enrolled in day school between 1833 and 1851. CHS35 = change in percentage of population enrolled in Sunday School between 1833 and 1851. CHP35 = of all students enrolled in day school, the change between 1833 and 1851 in the percentage enrolled in public school. Numbers in parentheses are T-Statistics. Numbers in brackets are beta coefficients. The beta coefficient is calculated by multiplying each coefficient estimate for an independent variable by the standard deviation of that variable and then dividing by the standard deviation of the independent variable. The beta coefficient indicates how much of the variation in the dependent variable can be explained by variation in a given independent variable.

*The unit of observation is the registration county. The sample consists of 42 English and 12 Welsh counties. Among the English counties, London is allocated among Middlesex, Kent, and Surrey, while the three ridings of Yorkshire were each treated as separate counties.

b The sample is composed of 42 English counties only. Among the English counties, London is allocated among Middlesex, Kent, and Surrey, while the three ridings of Yorkshire were each treated as separate counties.

---

further that even if parents wanted their children to be taught to read and write, private venture schools were poorly equipped to undertake such a task. Private school teachers, it appears, only rarely had any formal training in pedagogy; in some cases they may have been unable to read or write.[24] Thomas MacCaulay labeled the elementary school teachers of his day "the refuse of all other callings."[25] This label is consistent with the portrayals in the surveys by statistical societies of failed tradesmen who took up teaching as a last resort or crippled soldiers and elderly widows who were given situations as teachers as a type of pension.[26]

A common name for private schools for the working classes, especially those intended for younger children, was "dame school." The elderly dames who ran these schools typically held classes in their homes and were reputed to have crowded their hot kitchens or dank cellars with pupils so that they could pursue assorted household tasks while conducting classes. Not surprisingly these descriptions made little mention of formal textbooks, instead suggesting that scraps were used from whatever book or pamphlet came to hand. Dame schools have been depicted as highly ephemeral; one dame would start a school, only to be replaced after a few months by another down the street.[27]

In contrast to the depictions of squalor, laxity, and incompetence that were often used to characterize private venture schools, both denominational school societies and the Committee of Council on Education emphasized certain standards that had to be maintained in the schools they sponsored.[28] Beginning in the early nineteenth century, the National Society published, in its annual reports, the architectural plans that it recommended for school buildings. The Committee of Council on Education gave attention to how much space should be allotted per student and scrutinized ventilation and privy facilities. To ensure the competence and respectability of teachers, the British and the National Societies established normal schools in the first half of the nineteenth century. A program of teacher certification was set in place by the Committee of Council on Education that reviewed the qualifications even of teachers who had not attended a normal school. To encourage certification, the Committee of Council set in place a salary scale for certified teachers that raised their earnings well above those of private teachers. Curriculum guidelines, textbooks, and other instructional materials were developed for public schools. To qualify for funds from Parliament or the denominational school societies, schools had to agree to periodic inspection to verify that instructional standards were being met. These efforts by public educational organizations to establish standards for instruction and facilities were reflected in the average expenditure per pupil in public schools. From evidence in a survey conducted by the Newcastle Commission, it can be estimated that in 1858 public schools were spending 35.4 shillings per pupil compared with 24 shillings per pupil in private schools.[29]

The disrespect with which private schools for the working classes have been viewed may reflect not so much actual deficiencies in the instruction provided in private schools as a bourgeois disdain for working-class habits, however. This disdain may have been based on a bourgeois penchant for neatness and formality not shared by the children and parents who patronized private schools.[30] The use of a kitchen for a classroom or the absence of a lesson plan may have been shocking to an observer for the Manchester Statistical Society but of no consequence to a mother whose children were learning to read while attending the school. As one school inspector stated in the early 1870s, "It certainly will be very difficult at first to convince a Yorkshire father that the school is not 'efficient' when his child is 'getting on' very well in it. It will be very difficult to convince him of the slow but sure mischief caused by crowded, ill-ventilated rooms, by want of light, want of drainage, by filthy offices and by unhealthy 'surroundings.'"[31] Even some middle-class observers conceded that students in private schools could read well; they expressed concern primarily about the lack of instruction in religious and moral doctrine.[32]

Private schools were also criticized because their teachers were elderly and because the schools themselves were transitory. Phil Gardner's recent book has argued that these concerns have been overstated. By examining manuscript census material for Bristol, Gardner found that the average age of the city's private school teachers was 40.3 in 1851, 43.5 in 1861, and 37.1 in 1871.[33] Gardner has argued that the transitory character of the schools has been overstated because of a failure to allow for schools that changed their locations or for teachers who changed their names because of marriage. In a collection of statistical society surveys fom the 1840s, Gardner found that 54.8 percent of the private schools surveyed had been in existence for at least five years.[34]

Even if it were granted that most private schools did a poor job of teaching reading and writing, this failure can be explained by a lack of working-class demand for literacy rather than an inherent deficiency in what the private market was able to supply. The emphasis on child minding reported in many private schools could have reflected the preferences of their clientele or the fact that private schools catered to teaching younger children and public schools to somewhat older ones.[35] Since private schools were financed solely by fees, if parents were actively concerned about their children's mastery of reading and writing, private schools had ample incentives to respond to these concerns. In fact, Gardner's study cites cases where parents transferred their children from public to private schools because the latter were more successful in teaching literacy skills.

One mid-nineteenth-century observer was told by a private teacher "that she had several scholars from the National schools, because their parents said they learnt nothing there by clapping hands and singing."[36]

Some working-class parents seem to have had reservations about public schools because of their greater emphasis on religious and moral indoctrination than on basic literacy skills. This emphasis may have been unattractive to working-class parents not only because they considered it a waste of time and money, but also because they resented the attempt to impose middle-class values and doctrines on their children.[37] Moreover, working-class parents probably had more rapport with a teacher from a background similar to theirs. According to observers for the Newcastle Commission, "frequently the preference [in choosing a school] is determined by friendship for the master or mistress. . . . Some [parents] would rather help and trust a neighbour of their own grade, than place their children under the care of a stranger and superior."[38]

The informality of private schools that so disturbed many middle-class observers may have been more attractive to working-class parents than the middle-class routine and discipline that characterized public schools, as the following comments by contemporary observers suggest:

> My own impression is that the vitality of these schools is owing in great measure to the fact, as I believe, that the children can come and go when their parents chose.[39]

> To a poor and ignorant woman living in an irregular hand-to-mouth way, and accustomed to employ her children on trifling errands, or to yield weakly to their wishes, the discipline of a good public school and the persistent enquiries after absentees are very irritating; she escapes all this by sending the children now and then whenever she can spare the money to a so-called private school where no questions will be asked.[40]

> A dame, when asked by one of your Committee what was the reason she did not supply herself with some of the "Society's Cards," in preference to the torn leaves of a Dictionary, from which the children were learning to spell, replied that such a measure would immediately be followed by the removal of all the children from the school.[41]

Private schools, in addition to offering teachers both who were eager to please parents and who shared a common culture with their clientele, also offered a lower pupil-teacher ratio than public schools. According to an 1861 Newcastle Commission survey, there were, on average, twenty-five students per teacher in private schools surveyed compared with sixty-two students per teacher in public schools.[42] Small class sizes permitted private teachers to pursue the "individual method" whereby each child was given his or her own assignment and progress was monitored during the school day by the teacher. Although public school officials disdained this method, many working-class parents seemed to prefer it.[43]

The most relevant criterion for comparing the educational effectiveness of private and public schools was not whether teachers had received formal training or whether they had a rapport with working-class families or whether they offered a set curriculum. It was, rather, their ability to teach their students to read and write. Schools did teach other subjects besides reading and writing; moreover, some historians argue that instilling behavior acceptable to the middle classes was the real objective of public schooling for the working classes. Nevertheless, by the mid-nineteenth century, reading and writing had become the core of the public school curriculum, while private schools were faulted for their inability to teach these skills at a basic level, let alone higher subjects. If public schools did a superior job of teaching reading and writing, then higher proportions of their former students should have been able to sign their names at marriage than former students from private schools. This superiority, however, is only partially in evidence in comparisons across regions of school enrollment rates with subsequent ability of brides and grooms in such regions to sign their names.

Regression estimates of the relationship across counties and registration districts between signature rates at marriage and school enrollment and attendance rates fifteen years earlier are reported in Table 6.1a–b. Across registration districts, the estimated coefficients on day school enrollment and attendance rates were positive for both males and females, and these variables explained a sizable amount of the variation in both male and female literacy (as indicated by the beta coefficient estimates). The estimated impact of both Sunday and evening school enrollment was negative. One interpretation of this result is that students enrolled in Sunday and evening schools to compensate for infrequent day school attendance. In areas where this was common it was because factors such as the demand for child labor discouraged day school attendance, which in turn discouraged the acquisition of literacy. The estimated impact on literacy of raising the proportion of students enrolled in public schools was negative for males. For females, the impact was positive, but the probability that the coefficient was actually zero was over 70 percent, and the beta coefficient accounted for under 5 percent of the variation in literacy rates across registration districts.

The apparently weak and even negative impact of the proportion of students enrolled in public schools on subsequent variations in signature rates across registration districts could reflect the offsetting influence of other factors for which the comparisons do not control, however. One such factor may be a correlation between the relative importance of private schooling and the relative share of middle-class enrollments in total enrollments. This is suggested when a "value-added" approach is used to estimate the impact of factors that affected literacy rates across counties.[44] The value-added model explains variation in literacy in 1866 across counties by *changes over time* in various schooling variables after controlling for the level of literacy in 1851. The estimated equations reported in Table 6.1b consider the impact on literacy in 1866 of changes between 1833 and 1851 in: (*a*) day school enrollment rates, (*b*) Sunday school enrollment rates, and (*c*) the proportion of day scholars enrolled in public schools.

When English and Welsh counties together are considered, differences between counties in the change in day school and Sunday school enrollments accounted for a sizable part (as measured by the beta coefficients) of variation across counties in literacy rates in 1866 after controlling for their literacy rates in 1851 (see Table 6.1a–b). But the estimated impact of differences in the change in the proportion of scholars enrolled in public schools accounted for less than 1 percent of the variation in literacy, and the probability that the coefficient on this factor was equal to zero was over 70 percent. When the English counties alone are considered, however, the impact of changes in the public school proportion becomes much more significant, explaining 17 percent of the variation in literacy rates in 1866 and with a probability of less than 10 percent that the coefficient on this factor was equal to zero. Moreover, in this case the impact of changes in day school enrollment rates actually becomes negative, while the probability that the coefficient on this factor is equal to zero was over 30 percent.

These results suggest that, in English counties, public schools may have been more effective than private schools in teaching reading and writing. The claims of the superiority of instruction in public schools may have been based on more than bourgeois arrogance. No superiority of instruction is evident when the Welsh counties are also included in the analysis, however, and the impact of any superiority is apparently swamped by initial background conditions when registration districts are considered; thus, it would be rash to dismiss the ability of mid-Victorian private schools to transmit literacy.[45]

One clear advantage of public schools was that their fees were generally lower than those of private schools. In the mid-nineteenth century, public schools received three-fourths of their income in the form of subsidies. This enabled public schools not only to spend more per pupil than private schools but also to charge lower fees. The Newcastle Commission conducted a survey of specimen districts in 1858, which indicated that fees in private schools offering literacy instruction to the working classes averaged six shillings per week compared with two shillings per week in public schools.[46] At the very beginning of the century, many public schools charged no fees whatever.[47] In the second half of the nineteenth century, fees in government-inspected schools doubled in real terms.[48] This does not imply that the impact of subsidies on fees declined, however. An increase in the supply price of teachers because of rising living standards along with the increasing size of the schooling sector would imply that, in the absence of competition from subsidized schools, fees would also have risen in private schools.

In areas of low population density or of general apathy toward education, the cost of instruction per pupil could have made private working-class schools unviable. Given the low enrollments that a school in such areas was able to attract, the fees necessary to provide the sole source of funds for a school would have been so high as to discourage anyone from enrolling. Not surprisingly, then, contemporaries frequently mentioned the difficulty of financing schools in low-population density or apathetic areas.[49]

For settlements of less than 500 to 600 people, it was probable that not enough children would have attended to sustain a full-time school solely by fees. If a fee of four pence per child had been charged, then for a teacher to earn the ten shillings per week commonly earned by a farm laborer in the mid-nineteenth century, 30 children per week would have had to attend a school. If all children between the ages of five and fifteen in a village attended the school, this would imply a total population in the village of 135 people, using the ratio of total population to those aged five to fifteen reported by the 1851 census. But the length of school life was at best six years and more commonly two to three years. Thus three to five times the village population of 135 would be required to insure a reasonable expectation of 30 children attending per week. Although at best approximate, these calculations suggest why, when a settlement size fell below 600, it became difficult to support a full-time private school.[50]

In 1881, 6 to 9 percent of the English and 7 to 10 percent of the Welsh population lived in parishes with a population of under 500.[51] It is difficult, using published census tables, to estimate what this percentage was earlier in the century. Census tables do indicate, however, that in the counties with relatively low population densities—Derby, Dorset, Hereford, Hertford, Huntingdon, Leicester, Rutland, and Westmoreland—the proportion of the population living in communities of less than 600 inhabitants was 44.7 percent in 1801 and 27.55 percent in 1851.[52] In the Welsh counties of Anglesey, Brecon, Pembroke, and Radnor, the proportion living in such communities was 62.4 percent in 1801 and 42 percent in 1851.

In the long term, the problem of areas with low population density would have been alleviated by urbanization without parents having to resort to sending their children to public schools. But even where population density continued to be low to the end of the century, private schools, with their greater flexibility, may have met local needs better than public schools, which had to conform to more rigidly defined standards. For example, part-time and itinerant teachers, who were not solely dependent on teaching for income, could teach in private schools.[53] It is notable that in areas with low population densities such as Lincolnshire and the East Riding, and in areas where the population was apathetic to education such as the Black Country of Staffordshire, schools, many of them private, were widespread even before 1870.[54] The Cross Commission noted in the 1880s that low-population-density areas had difficulty in funding voluntarily subsidized schools and, even more so, board schools. Indeed, the Cross Commission indicates that, despite the efforts of school boards to "fill in the gaps" between 1870 and 1885, areas with low population densities were still served predominantly by voluntary schools rather than by board schools.[55]

It is by no means certain that nineteenth-century attempts to improve the quality of public instruction through teacher training and certification or school inspection increased the probability that English schoolchildren would be able to sign their names at marriage fifteen or twenty years later. There is no question, however, that as public schooling spread, fees were sizably reduced. Still, the impact of fee reductions on literacy trends would have depended on the extent to which enrollments responded to the level of fees.

The Response of Enrollments to the
Introduction of Public Schools

For small changes in fees the response of enrollments may have been correspondingly small simply because fees may have been low relative to the opportunity cost of a child's time. Horace Mann stated aptly in the 1851 Census of Education, "it is not for the sake of saving a penny per week, but for the sake of gaining a shilling or eighteen pence per week that a child is transferred from the school to the factory or the fields."[56] Furthermore, insofar as parents were divided into those who were firmly persuaded of the importance of their children's education and those who were not, one might expect that moderate variations in fee levels would not have influenced either group's decision to send their children to school or to withdraw them. Raising fees to 10 percent or more of parental income, offering children meals for attending school, or putting their families on relief rolls surely influenced school attendance.[57] But less extreme changes would have been unlikely to draw much response for such clearly defined groups.

Much of the working-class population may have fallen into an intermediate category, however. Some assessments suggest that most Victorian children attended school at some point in their lives.[58] Whether or not they would be literate as adults may well have depended on how frequently or how long they attended school. Acquiring literacy would then not have been a simple one-time either/or decision. There are cases of people who claimed they learned to read and write as children and subsequently forgot for lack of use.[59] The presence of heterogeneity in the population without extreme polarization in attitudes toward education is suggested by the low correlation between school enrollment rates across counties and school attendance rates. Across a sample of every tenth registration district (sixty-four observations), the rank order correlation coefficient between school enrollment rates in 1851 and the percentage of enrolled students attending on the day of the census was $-.137$ and not statistically different from zero at the 10-percent level. With strong homogeneity, one would expect areas with high school enrollment rates and hence a generally high interest in education to also have had high attendance rates. With extreme polarization, high school enrollment rates might have led to low school attendance rates as an area attracted more apathetic groups into schools. The low correlation suggests an intermediate situation.

The level of school fees could have influenced the frequency and duration of attendance at school and hence literacy. Some observers thought that large changes in fees would influence school enrollments. One school inspector noted in 1864 that "it is obvious that there are many parishes where to double the weekly charge for admission to a school is simply to shut the children of the poor out of it."[60] According to one assessment in the 1857 National Society report, "as far as my own experiences goes, I observe that a school has the best chance of succeeding where a due proportion exists between the means of the parents and the rates of payments made for their children."[61] But for moderate changes in fees, observers suggested little influence on enrollments. A clergyman from a cathedral city stated in the 1839 National Society report that "our scholars are confined to the lowest ranks; the schools are gratuitous, 1 pence a week having been taken off last year; but no increase of scholars resulted from this measure."[62]

Quantitative evidence on how enrollment responded to fees is provided by three data sources that indicate how enrollment rates and fees varied across regions at given points in time. The 1847 "Inquiry Into Education in Wales" provides observations for the twelve counties of Wales.[63] A survey of fees in Church of England schools in 1857 and an estimate of total school enrollment rates for 1858 provide evidence for forty-four registration counties in England and Wales.[64] The Cross Commission report provides observations on ninety-two school districts for 1884–85.[65] Simple regression estimates of the impact of fees on enrollment rates are reported in Table 6.2a-b. To make allowance for simultaneous equations bias, estimates were also made of some simple demand and supply models of fees and school enrollments using two-stage least squares.

The estimates reported in Table 6.2a-b suggest a modest responsiveness of enrollment rates to fee changes since all the estimated elasticities of response, with the exception of the 1884–85 two-stage least squares estimate, are less than one.

Enrollment trends following the establishment of free schooling in 1891 also indicate how enrollments responded to changes in fees. In 1891 Parliament provided that compensation for fees in state-aided schools should be available to all who requested it. Consequently, average fees reported in state-inspected schools fell by 90 percent between 1891 and 1900.[66] Between 1891 and 1899 enrollments for children aged five to fourteen rose by 7 percent, whereas between 1861 and 1891 enrollments for the same age group rose by 11.6 percent.[67] This implies that the annual

Table 6.2a-b

Regressions of School Enrollments on Fees

Table 6.2a Simple Regressions of Enrollments on Fees (Dependent variable is the logarithm of the proportion of the population enrolled in day school)

Independent Variables	Data Set		
	(1)	(2)	(3)
Constant	-1.970	-2.340	1.630
	(-5.40)	(-19.76)	(-19.88)
Log (Fee)	-0.577	-0.188	0.169
	(-2.20)	(-1.81)	(2.09)
R^2	.326	.080	.047

Table 6.2b Two-Stage Least Squares Estimates (Dependent variable is the proportion of the population enrolled in day school)

Independent Variables	Data Set		
	(1)	(2)	(3)
Constant	0.372	0.193	0.371
	(2.76)	(3.50)	(3.04)
Fee	-0.463	-0.262	-0.505
	(-1.17)	(-0.78)	(-1.64)
Dense	5.85×10^{-4}	-4.35×10^{-5}	—
	(1.92)	(-1.53)	
R^2	.551	.071	.028
F-statistic	5.516	1.259	2.690
Degrees of Freedom	(2,9)	(2,33)	(2,92)
Implied Fee Elasticity	-0.3806	-0.3443	-1.1690

(continued)

Table 6.2 (continued)

Sources for Tables 6.2a-b: "Reports on the State of Education in Wales," PP 1847, vol. 27, pt. I, [870], 54-60; PP 1847, vol. 27, pt. II, [871], 75-77; PP 1847, vol. 27, pt. III, [872], 1-6; National Society, "Summaries of the Returns to the General Inquiries Made by the National Society into the State and Progress of Schools During the Years 1856-57 Throughout England and Wales" (London: National Society, 1858), 54-59; "Report of Commissioners on Popular Education," PP 1861, Vol. 21, pt. I, [2794-I], 596-616; "Statistical Report of the Commission on the Elementary Education Acts," PP 1888, vol. 36, [C.-5485-II], 175-487.

Note: Definition of variables: Fee = annual fee income in pounds divided by annual enrollment. Dense = population density per square mile. Numbers reported in parentheses are T-statistics.

growth rate in enrollments during the 1890s was more than double that of the previous thirty years.[68] While other factors may have contributed to the rise of enrollments in the 1890s, the sudden surge in enrollments following the establishment of free schooling in the 1890s would suggest its importance.

The implied elasticities of enrollment with respect to the change in fees between 1890 and 1900 were 0.05 for five- to fourteen-year-olds, 0.07 for five- to nine-year-olds and 0.28 for two- to four-year-olds. The elasticity estimate above for those five to fourteen years old is markedly lower than the estimates for earlier periods in the nineteenth century. A likely reason for this decline is the establishment of compulsory schooling legislation between 1870 and 1880; as a result of this legislation, the school enrollment decision by families was no longer an unrestrained weighing of costs and benefits but subject to coercion by the state. Children under five, who were not covered by compulsory schooling legislation, experienced much larger enrollment increases in the 1890s than did older children.

In sum, the response of school enrollments to changes in fees does not appear to have been large. Estimates of the elasticity of response for the first two-thirds of the nineteenth century indicate that it was around $-.4$ and at the end of the century, it may have been as low as $-.05$.

What Did the Rise of Public Schooling Accomplish?

During the first two-thirds of the century, additional public funding tended to be directed to areas that were already well provided with public schools—that is, schools receiving at least some funds from sources other than fees—or that had high literacy levels to begin with. Despite this tendency, funding rose by enough even in those areas that initially had the poorest supply of public schools to produce a marked increase throughout England and Wales in public school accommodation. For England and Wales as a whole, the proportion of the population that gained access to public schools over the course of the nineteenth century was between 40 and 70 percent.

Although many contemporaries argued that instruction in public schools was superior to that in private schools—that is, schools receiving income only from fees—this superiority was evident only to a limited extent in comparisons of the relation between school enrollment and literacy. This suggests that the main advantage of public schools may have rested in the lower fees they charged. In the mid-nineteenth century, public schools typically charged one-third of the amount charged by private schools that aimed at a working-class clientele. The response of enrollment to such lower fees is unclear; the estimates of the elasticity of response presented in Table 6.2a–b ranged from − .05 to − 1.2. The intermediate estimates ranged from − .25 to − .4.

The estimates of the increase in access to public schools, the reduction in fees associated with these schools, and the response of enrollments to lower fees can be combined to estimate the net impact of the rise of public schooling on total enrollments in nineteenth-century England. A midrange estimate of the proportion by which enrollments rose as a result of the development of public schooling would be $.4 \times .67 \times .4 = .107$. An upper estimate of the proportion would be $.7 \times .67 \times 1.2 = .563$. Both estimates are sizable relative to the approximate doubling in enrollment rates that occurred over the nineteenth century, even if they do not account for the total increase in enrollments.[69]

The influence of public schools on enrollment rates can be seen from the way enrollments did or did not keep pace with the increasing number of places in schools. Although some reports written between 1820 and 1840 indicate that public schools were full and even that waiting lists existed, reports from other areas written from the 1830s onward indicate that many public schools had large numbers of empty seats.[70] And the Newcastle Commission report suggested that "the surplus accommodation is not always provided in the places where the population requires it."[71] Still, according to the 1842 Report of the National Society, "It might have been supposed that many schools towards which the society had contributed would have failed entirely for want of scholars; but the fact is, that the returns made in 1838, the year of the general inspection prove satisfactorily that, except in four instances, of which no account whatever was received, all the schools built by the aid of the society were in operation."[72]

In the last half of the nineteenth century, the ratio of enrollments to accommodation in government-assisted schools stayed roughly level, even though the accommodation provided per capita more than doubled. In 1859, according to the Newcastle Commission, the ratio of enrollment to accommodation in government-aided schools according to the Newcastle Commission was 0.81.[73] The ratio reported by the Department of Education rose to 0.9 in 1870 and fell only slightly to 0.87 in 1890.[74] At the same time, accommodation per capita in government-assisted schools rose from 0.0835 in 1870 to 0.192 in 1890.[75] A good part of the rise in enrollments in these schools came at the expense of private schools and schools that received subsidies only from private charity rather than from Parliament. Demand for school attendance (even if prodded by compulsory schooling laws) must also have been rising or else utilization rates would have fallen. Still, additional places in public schools do not seem to have gone to areas where they were completely unwanted.

The estimates reported in Table 6.1a–b indicate that the frequency with which those students who were enrolled actually attended and the length of time they stayed in school (probably proxied in part by Sunday school enrollment rates) combined to explain more of the variation in literacy than did variation in enrollment rates. Increases in school enrollments did not necessarily translate into equivalent increases in literacy rates; this was particularly evident in the estimates for the value-added model reported in Table 6.1b. The importance of influences other than enrollment rates on literacy suggests that the motivations of children to attend school and the motivations of schools to teach influenced literacy levels as much as the number of children that passed through school doors.

But, as the estimates reported in Table 6.1a–b also indicate, variation in enrollment rates still accounted for about one-third of the variation across registration districts in literacy rates; getting the names of more children on the schools' books did influence literacy. During the nineteenth century between 40 and 70 percent of the English population gained access to schools whose fees were only a third of those commonly charged in private schools. It is hardly surprising that such a marked improvement in access made a marked contribution to the rise of literacy, even if it was not the only factor of significance.

7. The Changing Opportunity Costs of Acquiring Literacy: The Roles of Private Demand and Public Legislation

> It is not for the sake of saving a penny per week, but for the sake of gaining a shilling or eighteenpence a week that a child is transferred from the school to the factory.[1]
> Horace Mann, Report for the 1851 Census of Education

> "Times are bad, and we cannot afford it." The clergyman lowers his fee, but still they "cannot afford it." He offers to pay for their schooling; to oblige him they send the children to school for a week or two, but very soon they drop off again. "Times are bad, and they cannot afford it." Cannot afford what?—cannot afford to give up the value of their child's time. This was what they meant from the first. . . . Their time is worth 2s. or 3s. a week and this is what the parents grudge. . . . [T]he school fee is a mere trifle.[2]
> J. P. Norris, Report to the Committee of Council on Education, 1851–52

HORACE MANN AND J. P. NORRIS were not alone in their awareness of the value of children's time outside the schoolroom. Parliamentary commissions from the early nineteenth century onward and a constantly growing inspectorate from the 1830s onward were charged with examining child labor conditions. These efforts to monitor and restrict child labor and then, after 1870, to restrict all alternative uses of children's time through compulsory schooling legislation have been commonly viewed as central to the rise of popular schooling and, with it, popular literacy in Victorian England.

Yet these efforts may have been unnecessary if new technology was making the use of children in the workplace obsolete. And it is possible that child labor and compulsory schooling laws were not successfully enforced until after they had become redundant. If the demand for child

labor was buoyant and children's wages were high, then success in enforcement may well have been impossible.

The demand for child labor did in fact decline markedly in the second
half of the nineteenth century. Despite initial difficulties in enforcement,
child labor restrictions and compulsory schooling laws did contribute to
the rise in school enrollment rates. Although ultimately making a contribution, the impact of compulsion on the regularity of school attendance
met more initial resistance than did its impact on enrollments. Furthermore, teachers who instilled positive attitudes toward education among
the working classes may have contributed as much as truant officers to
both immediate compliance with the law and the long-term rise in school
attendance rates.

The Extent of Child Labor

Census evidence suggests that government efforts to restrict child labor
may have been far out of proportion to the actual magnitude of the problem. In the 1851 census, only 2 percent of boys and 1.5 percent of girls
five to nine were classified as "occupied," while 37 percent of boys and 42
percent of girls in this age group were classified as "at home."[3] A much
higher proportion of children ten to fourteen were classified as employed
(37 percent of boys and 20 percent of girls), but a large proportion of ten-
to fourteen-year-olds were also classified as "at home" (24 percent of boys
and 39 percent of girls). The large proportion of school-age children who
were neither at school nor at work suggests that failure to attend school
may have reflected the expense of school fees or apathy toward education
rather than children's earnings opportunities.

There is little reason to think that the census systematically under-
reported the number of children holding full-time jobs. Underreporting
could have occurred if parents feared harassment by civil authorities for
violation of child labor laws. One likely result of this fear would have
been a clustering of the reported ages of children at the minimum legal
age for employment. The published census reports exhibit no such clustering.[4] One study of nineteenth-century census-taking procedures found
a tendency for overreporting rather than underreporting the number of
children employed.[5] Overreporting was attributed to census takers' indis-
criminately assigning children the occupation of their fathers. This study
was based on records for only one district in Sheffield, and the results may

not generalize to the national level. But school registers from other areas of England also suggest that the census did not vastly underreport the numbers of children employed full time in the labor market. Some extant school registers from the nineteenth century report children's reasons for leaving school. Studies of these registers indicate that a substantial proportion of children left school to stay at home, a finding which is consistent with census reports.[6]

The low proportion of children reporting occupations can be accounted for by their limited usefulness to employers because of immaturity in physical and mental capacities. Reports on the use of Godfrey's cordial and other sedatives for young children provide gruesome testimony that the very young could subtract from, rather than add to, the productive time of the family. The frequent reports that working-class parents valued schools more for their child minding than for their educational functions suggest that even children over five did not always have productive uses for their time.[7] The role of immaturity in restricting employment opportunities is suggested by the marked rise in labor force participation rates of children with each year of age. A sample of 253,425 children reported in the 1851 Census of Education indicated that the labor force participation rates of boys rose from 1 percent at age seven to 6 percent at age nine, to 13 percent at age ten, and to 20 percent at age eleven. For girls, the labor force participation rates rose from 1 percent for seven-year-olds to 11 percent for eleven-year-olds. A recent sample from the 1851 census constructed by Carolyn Tuttle shows that labor force participation rates were only 1 or 2 percent for children of each year of age up to age ten, after which they rose markedly for each year of age.[8]

There are a number of indications, however, that children's time in Victorian England often did have significant opportunity costs and that these costs were frequently a serious impediment to schooling.

First, although the aggregate rate of child labor force participation was low, especially for children under age ten, it was subject to considerable regional variation.[9] In the county of Bedford in 1851, the census reported that 12 percent of boys aged five through nine and 21 percent of girls the same age were working. And Bedford had relatively high illiteracy rates throughout the nineteenth century. For example, in 1869, 70 percent of the grooms marrying in Bedford could sign their names, compared with a national average of 78 percent, while 64 percent of brides in Bedford could sign their names, compared with a national average of 75 percent. Altogether, four English counties reported that more than 5 percent of

boys five to nine were working (Bedfordshire, 11.8 percent; Buckinghamshire, 5.5 percent; Hertfordshire, 5.7 percent; West Riding of Yorkshire, 5.1 percent), and three counties reported more than 5 percent of
girls working in 1851 (Bedfordshire, 21.4 percent; Buckinghamshire,
11.1 percent; Hertfordshire, 7.4 percent). And W. B. Stephens has noted
that even more variation in child labor force participation probably existed
within individual counties.[10]

Parliamentary reports reveal how work opportunities rose with age
for children and how such opportunities were distributed across regions.[11]
The only activities reported by parliamentary investigators as commonly
employing children under the age of eight were lace making, straw plaiting, and hosiery, although there were also occasional reports of a three-
year-old scaring crows or a six-year-old trapper in coal mining.[12] These
activities were limited to a few regions: hosiery to Nottingham and Leicester, lace making and straw plaiting primarily to Bedford and Hertford.
Opportunities for eight- to ten-year-old children extended to a far wider
range of activities, including cotton and wool manufacture, coal mining,
pottery and earthenware manufacture, nail making, and, most important
of all, agriculture. Immaturity appears to have limited employment opportunities for this age group as well, however. This limitation was most evident in agriculture; the 1843 Commission on the Employment of Women
and Children in Agriculture noted many districts offering little or no employment for children before age ten and some offering no employment
until age twelve. Even at these older ages, many districts had no employment for girls. Although many nonagricultural activities were more likely
to employ children under the age of ten, parliamentary reports suggest
that even for these activities, children were not employed in large numbers
until after that age. The 1851 census reported that the numbers of children
employed in the most common occupations increased by some ten to
twenty times between the five to nine age group and the ten to fourteen
age group, and the number of female domestic servants increased by more
than forty times (see Table 7.1). Thus, if employment opportunities were
very limited for younger children, they were quite abundant for children
over the age of nine.

Where work opportunities were available, children's wages were substantial relative to adult wages. For example, in southwestern agricultural
districts in the 1840s, boys seven to ten were reported to earn 1.5 shillings
per week, rising to 2.5 shillings per week at age twelve.[13] Adult male agricultural laborers in the same region were reported to earn between 8 and

Table 7.1

Leading Occupations Employing Children, 1851

	Number of Boys Employed		Number of Girls Employed	
Occupation	Ages 5-9	Ages 10-14	Ages 5-9	Ages 10-14
Agricultural laborer	5,463	73,054	—	—
Domestic service	—	—	1,258	58,137
Farm service, indoor	—	25,667	—	10,085
Messenger, porter	2,158	38,130	—	—
Manufacture of				
Cotton	2,072	25,613	1,477	29,038
Lace	—	—	2,590	—
Silk	—	—	—	10,533
Straw plait	1,422	—	2,746	—
Wool cloth	1,161	—	—	—
Worsted	1,654	—	1,271	10,586
Coal miner	1,209	23,038	—	—
Laborer	—	13,478	—	—

Source: "Census of Gt. Britain, 1851, Education," PP 1852-3, vol. 90, [1692], cx-cxiv.
Note: The table gives the occupations most frequently reported by the census for each category of children listed. A dash indicates that the occupation was not a common one for children in that category, even though it may have been reported for a few of these children.

10 shillings per week. In West Riding coal mines in the 1840s, eight- and nine-year-old children were reported to earn 2.5 to 3 shillings per week, rising to 4 to 4.5 shillings per week for twelve-year-olds.[14] Adult coal miners in the same region were reported to earn 20 shillings per week. The Newcastle Commission report indicates that for England as a whole, children's weekly wages in the 1850s ranged from 2 to 4 shillings. According to other parliamentary reports, wages could range from as low as sixpence per week for young girls in lace-making districts to as high as 5 shillings per week for twelve-year-old boys in some coal-mining districts.[15] One study of a cotton enterprise found that in 1836, average earnings for ten- to twelve-year-old boys were 16 pence a week, compared with

139 pence per week for adult males, while for girls of the same age, average wages were 15 pence per week, compared with 55 pence for adult females.[16] (The marked rise in children's wages with age in these examples further supports the assertion that physical immaturity restricted the productive opportunities for younger children; the rise in wages probably reflected a rise in productivity on the job.)

Adult male wages in the 1860s ranged from as low as 9 to 15 shillings per week for agricultural laborers to as high as 20 to 30 shillings per week for cotton spinners, miners, and other skilled laborers. The demand for child labor was extensive enough to bid up the wages of a single child in the middle of the nineteenth century to between 10 and 30 percent of an adult male's wage. The wages of children were relatively high despite very limited labor force participation for a number of reasons. The supply of child labor was restricted because many working-class parents in some areas were reluctant to send their children out to work even if they did not send them to school. In urban areas, children were sometimes removed from jobs their parents perceived to be unhealthy.[17] In rural areas, a number of investigators noted that even if girls were not put in school, they were kept out of field work so that they would not become too coarse for future employment as domestic servants.[18] Nevertheless, other parents seem to have had few qualms about sending their children to work, and some, according to parliamentary reports, were eager to have their children employed as soon as employers would take them.[19] Investigators also noted that attitudes toward child labor varied among similar occupational groups. Thus, southwestern tin miners refused to send their children to work, while coal miners in other regions of England and Wales had few qualms about doing so.[20] Agricultural inquiries depicted a similar contrast between laborers in northern pasture districts and southern arable districts.[21] The limited supply of children would have driven up wages and, for those parents with no qualms about having their children work, provided further incentives for keeping their children out of the classroom.

A second, more pervasive reason why reported rates of child labor were low had to do with the value of children in domestic tasks and in casual and temporary work. This factor would imply that, despite low reported rates of regular child labor, the opportunity costs of children's time could have been a major barrier to school attendance. It would also account for the relatively high wages of children, despite their low rates of labor force participation. The census classification "at home" or, alternatively, "undescribed" leaves considerable ambiguity about how children so classified spent their time. While some may have played in the streets or idled at home, others surely looked after younger siblings while their parents worked, ran errands, or performed other odd jobs on a part-time basis. Furthermore, alternating between play, odd jobs, and domestic chores may have been the most common pattern for this category of children, perhaps even combined with stretches of school attendance or full-time work.

Parliamentary investigations suggest that idle play, domestic chores, and casual odd jobs were all common activities for children who neither attended school nor worked full time. A Sheffield police superintendent in the 1840s complained about the large numbers of vagrant children in the streets.[22] Edward Baines testified in the 1850s that one reason for low school attendance in textile-manufacturing areas was that girls kept house while their mothers worked in the mills.[23] An 1871 report on an Essex village indicates that children in poor families were often removed from school to look after the newly born.[24] The Newcastle Commission report on educational conditions in London in the 1850s refers to the abundant opportunities for casual employment available to children as street hawkers and messengers, as well as in a wide variety of other odd jobs.[25]

There is not enough evidence to establish how many of the children who were neither employed nor at school were engaged in "productive" (i.e., domestic chores or casual work) rather than leisure activity. A number of considerations suggest, however, that the proportion was significant. Many children would have been called on to do domestic chores because their mothers were working. If the mother in a working-class family was employed, frequently someone was hired to prepare meals and look after children.[26] Because the fees for these surrogates were not insubstantial, there was an incentive for families to have children do these tasks. Census data indicate that a modest but not negligible proportion of children would have had a working mother. Michael Anderson, using manuscript census material, found that in Preston in 1851, 26 percent of all married women had full-time jobs and 15 percent of all wives with children were working away from home.[27] The published census did not clearly classify married women as working or not, making it difficult to generalize Anderson's findings; according to the 1851 census, however, 25.5 percent of all married women in England and Wales reported some occupation besides wife.[28] No reliable guide to the extent of casual employment is available, although a number of contemporary sources, including the Newcastle Commission report cited above, agree that it was substantial.

A related point is that many children working on a part-time basis may have been recorded by the census as "at home" or even at school. Pamela Horn has argued that in Oxfordshire many children who worked part time in lace making were not recorded as employed by census takers.[29] Since much of this work would have been done in the home, it may have been difficult for census takers to classify them. Much lace work was done by children in so-called lace schools, whose primary purpose was not education but the production of lace with cheap labor. Even so, such children may well have frequently been recorded as scholars.

That the value of opportunities for children in casual and domestic work could exceed that of opportunities in the formal labor market was demonstrated by the passage of compulsory schooling laws in the 1870s, when restrictions on child labor in manufacturing firms were already in effect. Under compulsory schooling laws, it was illegal for children to be *at home* for any reason, and parents were fined for infractions. It was legal, however, as it had been under the child labor laws alone, for children to attend school part time and work part time. As a result, when the compulsory schooling laws were enacted, according to factory and school inspectors for a number of regions, parents who had previously kept their children out of the labor market to perform various domestic chores and odd jobs suddenly attempted to get their children positions as "half-timers" (that is, working part time and attending school part time). Apparently, then, without the threat of a fine, the value of children in casual tasks could exceed that in formal employment as half-timers.[30]

A final consideration in the impact of child labor on literacy is the importance of school attendance after the age of nine for acquiring literacy. Children who attended school for any length of time might have learned to read and write by the age of nine. But, if they attended school after the age of nine, they would have reinforced what they had learned earlier. And this would have been important, given that working-class school attendance appears to have been sporadic throughout childhood.[31] It is probable that the decision to acquire literacy, as suggested in previous chapters, was frequently not one of simply either/or, but rather a product of many choices made by parents or children as to whether to continue or resume schooling. This conclusion is supported by the cases mentioned in previous chapters of children who had learned to read and write and then lost the ability. And, school attendance rose markedly between 1851 and 1871, not just for children aged five through nine, but also for those aged ten through fifteen (see Table 7.2). Indeed, the rise at older ages was rather more important than the rise at younger ages for women.

The importance of children's attending school past the age of nine is suggested by cross-county regressions of signature rates at marriage in the 1860s on school enrollment rates in 1851 of both five- to nine-year-olds and ten- to fourteen-year-olds (see Table 7.3). For both males and females, school enrollment rates of the older age group explain far more of

Table 7.2

Percentage of Children at School, at Home, and at Work, 1851-71

	At School	*At Home*	*At Work*
Boys, 5 to 10			
1851	60.76	37.19	2.05
1861	69.02	28.99	1.99
1871	72.44	26.71	0.85
Girls, 5 to 10			
1851	56.07	42.50	1.43
1861	66.46	32.43	1.11
1871	63.42	35.84	0.74
Boys, 10 to 15			
1851	39.39	24.03	36.58
1861	45.32	17.82	36.86
1871	50.81	17.06	32.13
Girls, 10 to 15			
1851	41.41	38.68	19.91
1861	52.48	27.31	20.21
1871	55.27	24.22	20.51

Source: "Census of England and Wales, 1871, General Report, Vol. IV, Appendix A," PP 1873, vol. 71, pt. II, [C.-872-I], 112, Table 106.

Table 7.3

Regressions of Literacy on School Enrollment by Age

Independent Variables	Dependent Variables	
	Logodds Male Literacy 1869	Logodds Female Literacy 1869
Constant	-0.639	-1.130
	(-2.04)	(-2.80)
Mschol5-9	0.884	
	(1.42)	
	[.163]	
Mschol10-14	3.530	
	(6.01)	
	[.690]	
Fschol5-9		0.630
		(0.67)
		[.100]
Fschol5-14		4.460
		(4.33)
		[.641]
R²	.632	.509
F-statistic	36.10	21.76
Degrees of Freedom	(42,2)	(42,2)
N	45	45

(continued)

the variation in literacy rates across counties than do enrollments for the younger age group.[32] These results suggest, but do not prove, that school attendance at the older ages contributed to higher literacy; other factors correlated with school attendance could have caused these results.[33]

The importance of attending school toward the end of childhood for fully mastering literacy, the extensive employment opportunities for older children, the existence of some regions with extensive employment oppor-

Table 7.3 (continued)

Sources: "Census of Gt. Britain, 1851, Population Tables II, Vols. I and II," PP 1852-3, vols. 88, pt. I, and 88, pt. II, [1691-I], [1691-II], tables under individual counties for "Occupations of the People"; 32nd ARRG (Abstract for 1869), PP 1871, vol. 15, [C.453], lxvi.

Note: Definition of variables: The dependent variables are the logarithm of the odds ratio of the percentage of brides or grooms signing the marriage register in 1869. The odds ratio of a percentage x is $x/(1 - x)$. The dependent variables are expressed as log odds ratios so that they vary from minus to positive infinity. The regressions provide for an 18-year lag between school attendance at ages 5-9 and marriage at ages 25-29. The unit of observation is the registration county. Mschol5-9 = the proportion of the male population aged 5 to 9 reported as scholars in the 1851 census. Mschol10-14 = the proportion of the male population aged 10 to 14 reported as scholars in the 1851 census. Fschol5-9 and Fschol10-14 are analogous variables for females. Figures in parentheses are T-statistics. Figures in brackets are beta coefficients. Beta coefficients reported in the table are intended to indicate the amount of variance in the dependent variable each independent variable can explain. They are estimated by dividing the estimated coefficient for an independent variable by the ratio of the sample standard deviation of the dependent variable to the sample standard deviation of the independent variable.

tunities for even younger children, and the value of children in domestic and casual work all help explain why Victorian educators' concern with the opportunity costs of children's time was neither groundless nor exaggerated. The value of children's time outside the classroom does, in fact, seem to have constituted a pervasive barrier to the acquisition of literacy.

Did the Demand for Child Labor Decline during the Victorian Period?

A number of obvious trends in the Victorian economy suggest that opportunities for child labor were decreasing. Economic activity was shifting from agriculture, which employed a lot of children, to the service sector, which employed relatively few. Technological progress was increasing the possibilities for substituting mechanical power for unskilled labor. Although Parliament conducted numerous inquiries into child labor conditions between 1840 and 1870, after 1880 its attention shifted to other issues.[34] This shift in attention seems justified in light of the fall in the labor force participation rates of children after 1850 (see Table 7.4).

Yet the fall in the demand for child labor was not as inevitable as it might appear. Transportation, coal mining, and domestic service all employed a high proportion of children in their labor forces compared with

Table 7.4

Labor Force Participation of Children Aged Ten to Fourteen, 1851-1911
(Percentage Employed)

Year	Boys	Girls
1851	36.6	19.9
1861	36.9	20.2
1871	32.1	20.4
1881	22.9	15.1
1891	26.0	16.3
1901	21.9	12.0
1911	18.3	10.4

Source: "Census Returns of England and Wales, 1911, Vol. X, pt. I,
Occupations and Industries," PP 1913, vol. 78, [Cd.-7018], cxli.

other sectors of the economy, and all three sectors were expanding in the second half of the nineteenth century. Technical change did not always lead to substitution away from unskilled labor. One of the major technological developments in cotton manufacture in the nineteenth century was the switch from mule to ring spinning, which substituted unskilled for skilled labor.[35] Even the fall in the labor force participation rates of children reported in Table 7.4 could have been due to the impact on the supply of children to the labor market of rising living standards and an increased demand for education. Thus, trends in the demand for child labor in the second half of the nineteenth century should be examined more carefully.

The economic theory of the derived demand for productive inputs suggests three factors that would have affected trends in the demand for child labor: (1) shifts in the composition of the demand for final products; (2) substitution possibilities between child labor and alternative inputs; and (3) the supply of alternative inputs. They will be considered in turn.

The Composition of Product Demand

Increased international specialization, resulting from falling transportation costs and rising living standards, was shifting the composition of the English economy after 1850 away from sectors that used child labor intensively. After 1850 agriculture and textiles, the two largest employers of children, were decreasing in their share of the labor force. Although mining, transportation, and domestic service were expanding their labor force shares after 1850 and although all three sectors employed a larger proportion of children in their labor forces than agriculture or textiles, they did not expand by enough to offset the decline in agriculture and textiles. Furthermore, the proportion of children in the mining and transportation labor forces fell markedly after 1851, further weakening any offset.

The effects on the demand for child labor of the shifting composition of economic activity can be examined more precisely by calculating the change in the proportion of children in the total labor force accounted for by sectoral shifts in the composition of the total labor force. In principle, the shifts in sectoral composition could have been caused by changes in the supply of child labor, in which case they would not truly reflect demand forces. But the shares of children in the labor forces of the various sectors seem to have been small enough to preclude rising wages of children owing to a shift back in the supply of child labor from driving sectoral shifts. Calculations of changes in the sectoral composition of the labor force with respect to the use of children confirm the shift of the English economy after 1850 away from activities intensive in the use of child labor. Twenty percent of the decline in the proportion of children aged five to nine, and over 60 percent of the decline in the proportion of children aged ten to fourteen in the English labor force between 1851 and 1871 can be accounted for by shifts that occurred in the broad sectoral composition of the labor force between those two dates. Compositional shifts within sectors, in particular the growth of railroads in the transportation sector, were also important, and allowing for these more detailed intrasectoral shifts further increases the contribution of compositional shifts.[36]

But for girls aged ten to fourteen, broad sectoral shifts implied only a very small decline in their labor force shares, the decline of agriculture and textiles being offset by the rise of domestic service. Furthermore, in the domestic service and textile labor forces, the proportion of ten- to fourteen-year-old girls was actually increasing, and this effect far outweighed the effect of broad compositional shifts.[37] Also, broad sectoral shifts between 1871 and 1891 account for only 9 percent of the decline in the proportion of ten- to fourteen-year-olds in the labor force.[38] (The employment of children under ten had reached negligible proportions by 1881.)[39] Still, on net, the English economy after 1851 clearly shifted away from activities intensive in the use of child labor, and this shift accounts for a substantial part of the decline in the role of children in the labor force.

Substitution between Child Labor and Other Productive Inputs
As a result of technological advance and economic development in Victorian England, new machinery and general changes in the organization of production were changing the way productive inputs were combined. Indeed, it has been suggested that in the mid-nineteenth century, technical change shifted from a "paleotechnic" tendency, which emphasized the use of unskilled labor engaged in simple repetitive tasks especially suited to women and children, to a "neotechnic" tendency, which emphasized the use of machinery to replace unskilled labor.[40]

Clearly, there were important instances where technical and industry-specific changes in nineteenth-century England lowered the demand for children. Machine-made lace appeared by the 1850s, thereby threatening the use of children in the lace industry. Although the so-called domestic lace trade provided extensive employment for children in Bedfordshire and Buckinghamshire through the 1870s, it had collapsed by the end of the decade in the face of competition from the machine-made branch of the trade.[41] Straw plaiting provided extensive employment for children in Bedfordshire and to a lesser extent in Hertfordshire. Here, it was not technical change but cheap competition from Italy, China, and Japan that displaced English production in the 1880s and 1890s and hence the demand for child labor for this purpose in Bedfordshire and Hertfordshire.[42] By the end of the nineteenth century, English production of straw plait had almost disappeared. In coal mining, ponies and then steam traction replaced children for haulage, and improvements in ventilation obviated the need for children to open trap doors.[43] These changes would primarily have affected the South Midlands region, where lace making and straw plaiting were concentrated, and mining areas. The South Midlands, especially Bedfordshire, reported unusually high rates of labor force participation for children aged five through nine in the 1851 and 1871 censuses, and the region had relatively high rates of adult illiteracy.[44] Mining areas also tended to have both relatively high rates of child labor force participation and adult illiteracy.

Nevertheless, trends in some sectors of the Victorian economy suggest that there was not a general tendency for technical change to displace child labor. In agriculture and cotton textile manufacture, technical and organizational change between 1840 and 1900 may actually have increased the demand for child labor. In agriculture, parliamentary investigators in the 1860s observed that drainage improvements and the introduction of root crops in arable regions were increasing the demand for children to weed and cultivate.[45] Although, the spread of self-binders in the 1890s reduced the demand for children at harvest time, and the shift from arable to livestock farming reduced the demand for children in such tasks as scaring birds, picking stones, and weeding, still, as late as World War I, a widespread demand by farmers for child labor during periods of peak labor demand was reported.[46]

Indications are also conflicting on whether there was substitution away from child labor in cotton textiles. Clark Nardinelli has noted that the introduction of the self-acting mule in the 1830s caused fewer breaks in the yarn and hence lowered the demand for piecers, who were commonly children.[47] William Lazonick, however, has argued that piecing was not primarily a child's task and that the self-acting mule was actually developed to substitute women and children for skilled adult male labor, although he is skeptical of the extent to which such substitution actually occurred.[48] The proportion of children in the cotton textile labor force increased between 1850 and 1875, suggesting a growing demand for child labor. Although Nardinelli argues that this increase was due to administrative improvements in the Factory Acts, it could also be attributed to technical change.[49] Nineteenth-century writers appear to have shifted positions over time on whether technical change in cotton textiles increased the demand for child labor. Factory inspectors in the 1830s and 1840s observed that new machinery was increasing the employment of children.[50] Then, in the 1850s, factory inspectors noted a declining demand for children in textiles.[51] But in the 1860s and 1870s, factory inspectors asserted once again that the demand for child labor was increasing.[52] Thomas Ellison, in *The Cotton Trade of Great Britain*, written in 1886, also argued that mechanical improvements had led to the substitution of women and children for men.[53]

Another important opportunity for child labor was street selling. Studies of continental Europe indicate that street selling was disappearing toward the end of the nineteenth century because of organizational changes in distribution.[54] Still, street selling by school-age children in

London and other large English cities was still sufficiently extensive at the end of the nineteenth century to be the subject of a number of government investigations.

In sum, it does not appear that there was any universal tendency in the Victorian economy for technical or organizational change to displace the employment of children, which would seem consistent with H. J. Habbakkuk's emphasis on the neglect of labor-saving technical change in England compared with America.[55] It also seems consistent with the findings of Claudia Goldin and Kenneth Sokoloff that in the United States in the early nineteenth century, technical change in manufacturing actually increased the use of women and children.[56] Studies of the so-called sweated trades in late nineteenth-century Britain have argued that mechanization permitted the continued subdivision of tasks with an accompanying reduction in the skills involved in each task.[57] These tendencies are likely to have continued to develop new opportunities for child labor. Still, the mechanization of lace manufacture, the effect of foreign competition on the English straw plaiting trade, and changes in mining should also be viewed as technological developments (or, in the case of straw plaiting, a change in market competitiveness) that caused major reductions in opportunities for child labor in areas of high illiteracy in England.

The Supply of Alternative Inputs to Child Labor
The rising standard of living in the English economy after 1850 was lowering the hours men and women worked and reducing the proportion of married women who were in the labor market.[58] At the same time, capital accumulation, resulting in part from the same standard-of-living increases, was increasing the English economy's capital-labor ratio.[59] The effects of these shifts in input supply on the demand for child labor would have depended on the extent to which the inputs were substitutes or complements for children.

Women and children seem to have been close substitutes in the nineteenth-century labor market. Both tended to be used in occupations requiring little skill or strength. The connection between the two types of labor is suggested indirectly by the numerous parliamentary commissions on the employment of women and children. Testimony in the reports of these commissions confirms the substitutability between women and children.[60] In particular, investigators noted that one effect of the restrictions on the employment of children imposed by the Factory Acts was the increased employment of women. Given the substitutability between women and children, the reduced supply of women to the English labor market brought about by rising living standards would have increased the demand for child labor.[61]

Women and children were probably also substitutes in the household because they performed the same tasks. By spending less time in the labor force, women were spending more time in the household, thus lowering the demand for children to perform domestic tasks. The net result would have been no clear change in the opportunity cost of children's time from the declining labor force participation of their mothers. The effect of the declining labor force participation of mothers on raising the demand of employers for children would have been offset by a declining demand for children to do domestic tasks.

It is difficult to classify adult male labor as either a substitute for, or complement to, child labor. The extent to which it was either seems to have varied across sectors of the economy. In coal mining, adult and child labor were clearly complementary. In cotton spinning, they were probably complementary in the short run, although in the longer run, allowing for technical change, they could have been substitutes. A common complaint about "sweated" domestic production of clothing or clothing accessories was that such activity replaced skilled labor with unskilled. It is not obvious, then, if men's declining hours of work affected the demand for child labor.

Capital, as embodied in machinery, did not consistently displace children from the labor force, as was concluded above; however, industries such as lace making and mining, although they initially made extensive use of children, then introduced machinery which made their use unnecessary. Thus, the one trend in the supply of inputs that had a significant impact on reducing the demand for child labor may have been the accumulation of capital in the Victorian economy. And, even here, the impact may not have been consistent. In the textile industry, as noted previously, some of the new machinery associated with capital accumulation may have raised rather than lowered the demand for child labor.

General Indicators of Trends in the Demand for Child Labor
The various forces affecting the demand for child labor in Victorian England appear to have acted in offsetting directions. While the composition of economic activity was shifting away from sectors in which children

were a major part of the work force, technical change in important sectors of the economy may have been substituting child for adult labor. While women were spending more time in the household, lowering the demand for children to do domestic tasks, they spent less time in the labor force, thus raising the demand for children as substitutes.

One indicator of the conflicting forces affecting the demand for child labor was that children's wages did not fall. A comparison of children's wages in the 1840s and 1860s in industries investigated by the parliamentary commissions on children's employment in manufactures indicates, if anything, a slight upward trend (see Table 7.5). Investigators into wage trends in textiles following the Factory Acts also noted that children's wages did not fall, and other investigators reported a similar finding in agriculture.[62]

In general, the demand of the English economy for child labor seems to have declined in the second half of the nineteenth century. Even so, opportunities for child labor were still abundant in 1900. Some twenty-nine thousand children under fourteen in 1901 were still employed as half-timers in wool and cotton manufacture; in the textile towns of Blackburn, Burnley, and Halifax, approximately 30 percent of all children aged ten to fourteen were classified as employed in both the 1901 and 1911 censuses.[63] In 1909, advertisements for farm hands in Dorset indicated that adults applying for work should be prepared to offer the labor of their children as well.[64] In London and other major cities, street selling and similar employments for children noted above were common enough to be the subject of government inquiries. And, according to the 1901 census, 17 percent of all children aged ten to fourteen were employed (see Table 7.4). Moreover, child labor opportunities had been extensive enough as late as the 1870s to spur Parliament in that decade to restrict such employment and to directly force children into the schoolroom.

Could School Attendance Be Legislated?

Nineteenth-century reformers were not content to simply leave the opportunity costs of literacy to be lowered by secular trends in the labor market. Over the course of the century, Parliament restricted the ages at which children could work, required part-time school attendance for children that did work, and, ultimately, required all children of certain ages to attend school.

Table 7.5

Weekly Wages of Children in Manufacturing in 1843, 1863-65
(In Shillings and Pence)

Industry	1843	1863-65
Earthenware and pottery		
children, 8-13	2*s*.	1*s*. to 2*s*. 6*d*.[a]
		3-5*s*.[b]
Pillow lace		
girls	1-2*s*.	1*s*.[c]
Hosiery		
all children	1-4*s*.	3-5*s*.[d]
Glass manufacture		
all children	4-9*s*.	5-9*s*.[e]
Metal trades (Birmingham)		
boys, 9-13	2*s*.4*d*.	3*s*.4*d*.-4*s*.6*d*.[f]
girls, 9-13	2*s*.3*d*.	2*s*.6*d*.-3*s*.6*d*.[g]

Sources: "Appendix to Second Report on Children's Employment--Trades and Manufactures--Pt. I," PP 1843, vol. 14, [431], 93-97; "Appendix to First Report on Children's Employment," PP 1863, vol. 18, [3170], 4, 247, 268, 272, 274, 284, 288, 291; "Appendix to Third Report on Children's Employment," PP 1864, vol. 22, [3414-I], 58; "Appendix to Fourth Report of the Commissioners on the Employment of Children and Young Persons in Trades and Manufactures," PP 1865, vol. 20, [3548], 199.
[a]Wages reported are for boys, 9-11 in 1863.
[b]Wages reported are for boys, 12-14 in 1863.
[c]Wages reported are for girls, 11-12 in 1863.
[d]Wages reported are for all children in 1863.
[e]Wages reported are for all children in 1865.
[f]Wages reported are for boys, 10-13 in 1863.
[g]Wages reported are for girls, 10-13 in 1863.

In 1802 Parliament enacted the Health and Morals of Apprentices Act, which limited the number of hours that children could work in factories and required that they receive instruction. It did not, however, contain provisions for effective enforcement. In 1833 Parliament enacted further legislation restricting the employment of children in textile factories, and these restrictions were made stricter by legislation in 1844. More serious efforts were made to enforce the provisions of this legislation. The 1844 act prohibited the employment of any child under the age of eight in textile factories and required that children between the ages of eight and thirteen who were employed attend school a minimum number of hours per week, the so-called half-time provisions. Between 1860 and 1870, similar restrictions were extended to mining and to most manufacturing industries. Acts passed in 1867 restricted the employment of children both in establishments employing more than fifty people and in workshops and businesses employing under fifty. In 1873 child labor restrictions were extended to agriculture. Lord Sandon's act of 1876 prohibited all employment of children under the age of ten. These restrictions encouraged parents to send their children to school in order for them to legally qualify for employment, either under half-time provisions or under provisions exempting children who had passed a given standard at school from employment restrictions. Legislation was also introduced requiring that parents send their children to school to qualify to receive poor relief. These measures were frequently referred to as indirect compulsion.[65]

By 1870 there was considerable support among education reformers for direct compulsion as well.[66] The Education Act of 1870 gave school boards the power, if they wished to use it, to require children between the ages of five and thirteen to attend school and, at their discretion, to set standards for exempting children between the ages of ten and thirteen. In 1872, 35 percent of the population of England and Wales resided in areas where school boards had established bylaws requiring school attendance.[67] Lord Sandon's act of 1876 provided for the establishment of school attendance committees in areas where school boards had not been established. These committees were given the power to require school attendance as well as to enforce the child labor restrictions of Lord Sandon's act. By 1880, 72 percent of the population of England and Wales were governed by school attendance laws. In 1881 all school boards and school attendance committees in England and Wales were charged with enforcing compulsory school attendance for children, although each local authority determined at what age or level a child could leave school. At this point school attendance for a period long enough to allow mastery of basic reading and writing skills was no longer a matter of private choice or even of public priority; it had become a legal obligation.[68]

But passing laws restricting child labor or requiring school attendance did not ensure compliance with, or enforcement of, such laws. As long as these laws significantly altered what behavior would have been in the absence of the laws, that is, as long as child labor had not disappeared and school attendance during childhood had not become universal, then enforcement would have been required to ensure compliance. Reports of factory and school inspectors in the nineteenth century commonly contain a standard litany of complaints about the difficulty of enforcing both child labor restrictions and compulsory schooling laws.[69]

Enforcement required the presence of both factory inspectors to determine who was violating child labor restrictions and of school attendance officers to determine who was violating the compulsory schooling laws. The former were funded by the national government, whereas the latter were paid by local school boards and school attendance committees.[70] These local agencies determined how many officers would be hired and what their salaries would be. Two common complaints were that in a given district too few attendance officers had been hired relative to the population to be patrolled and that the salary had been set so low that the officers were either disgruntled or, more commonly, performed the job only on a part-time basis. As a result enforcement was at best half-hearted.[71]

It has been suggested that this lack of provision for school attendance officers reflected apathy or even hostility toward compulsory schooling laws, both by school board and attendance committee members and by the elite in local communities. For example, in agricultural districts, it was commonly noted that farmers, who were frequently members of these boards and committees, wanted to hire school-age children to do farm work and thus had a vested interest in not enforcing school attendance laws.[72] Indeed, on occasion it was reported that school boards and attendance committees were set up with the intention of seeing that the laws were ignored.[73]

Even when child labor and school inspectors tried to do their jobs, they found it difficult to catch violators. In textile factories, where enforcement appears to have been relatively more effective than in other sectors of the economy, there were still problems in determining a child's true age and, thus, whether he or she was in violation of the law.[74] In domestic workshops, lookouts could be posted and child workers would flee or go into hiding at the first sight of the inspector.[75] As for truants, school attendance officers in urban areas had to cope with bands of children in generally hostile neighborhoods. Well-dressed school attendence officers stood out in the working-class neighborhoods they entered and were not only viewed with suspicion but could be greeted with a variety of thrown objects, impeding all the more the search for nimble-footed children scurrying in and out of dark passageways they knew much better than the intruding school inspectors.[76]

When truants were caught, further expenditures had to be made on prosecuting them, and there were complaints that the fines levied on those convicted were far less than these costs. Local rate payers were then likely to grumble about the charge on the rates for prosecution.[77]

When the effort was made to prosecute the parents of truant children, there were frequent complaints that magistrates were reluctant to convict them no matter how strong the case for guilt.[78] Patrick Cumin, head of the Department of Education in the mid-1880s, reported to the Cross Commission that "a considerable number of complaints have come before us of magistrates not enforcing the law sufficiently strictly."[79] Their reluctance has been attributed to a number of motives.

First, some magistrates were sympathetic to the plight of poor parents and appreciated the importance of children's earnings to their families.[80] One London magistrate, Montagu Williams, was notorious for paying the fines set by other magistrates, and similar behavior was mentioned elsewhere.[81] And in the troublesome case for the London School Board of *School Board for London v. Duggan*, the court held in 1884 that the necessity of a girl's employment for supporting her family could be "reasonable excuse" for not attending school. The prominent justice Sir James Fitzjames Stephens, in upholding the verdict of a lower magistrate, stated that the girl in question "has been discharging the honourable duty of helping her parents. . . . there is nothing I should read with greater reluctance in any Act of Parliament than that a child was bound to postpone the direst necessity of her family to the advantage of getting a little more elementary instruction for herself."[82]

Second, some magistrates may have faced a conflict of interest. In textile districts, it has been suggested that the magistrates who ajudicated the Factory Acts may also have either directly employed children or at least had a financial stake in enterprises that employed children, although the extent to which this occurred has been disputed.[83] The school inspector for the Sunderland district reported in 1900, "At a certain country railway station boys regularly congregate for the purpose of attending on golfers who arrive by train . . . I complained to the village schoolmaster. 'Would it not I asked be possible to prosecute one of these gentlemen?' The answer I got was significant: 'He might be a J.P.'"[84]

Finally, magistrates may have been concerned about their own unpopularity if they convicted too vigorously. A report from the Boston district in 1882 stated that magistrates were reluctant to impose fines for fear of "endangering their seats at the municipal elections."[85] And a report on Surrey in 1878 stated of at least one country district that magistrates "are actually 'afraid' to convict even incorrigible offenders, or at least to enforce their convictions 'lest their haystacks should be set on fire in all directions.'"[86]

Even when an offender was convicted of violating compulsory schooling laws, the fine was often lower than what a child could earn in the labor market or the value of a child's time in doing domestic tasks. Under the Education Act of 1870, the maximum fine for violating compulsory schooling laws was five shillings, and it remained at this level until 1900, when it was raised to twenty shillings.[87] But, as the figures in Table 7.5 suggest, wages of five shillings a week were not uncommon for children of ten or older by the 1870s. Given that chances of evading conviction were high, even eight- or nine-year-olds who may have earned only one or two shillings per week would still have found that the yearly income of fifty to one hundred shillings they could command would more than justify the risk of getting caught, convicted, and fined once each year. Factory and school inspectors frequently complained that violation of compulsory schooling laws was widespread because the expected penalty was less than expected earnings.[88] A report to the Education Department from Kent in 1883 noted that parents would tell attendance officers that they gained more from their children's work at home than the maximum cost of a fine for truancy.[89] Children convicted of repeated truancy could be placed in a residential reformatory. But a school inspector in Middlesex reported that the response to this threat was that "parents, seeing a prospect of thus cheaply and easily getting rid of their responsibilities, besiege the board with entreaties that they may be summoned."[90]

In these circumstances, it is hardly surprising that parents were frequently willing to risk conviction and generally ignored compulsory schooling laws.[91] A school manager in Purbeck attempted to point out to a stonemason who did not send his sons to school regularly that if they did not pass the specified standards it would delay the age at which they could be legally employed. The manager attempted to clinch her argument by adding, "The Queen says so." The stonemason's reply was, "Never mind, Ma'am, we'll risk it; perhaps the Queen will change her mind before that."[92]

The consequence of all these difficulties of enforcement was recurrent reports from many regions that child labor restrictions and compulsory schooling laws were a dead letter and had no positive impact on school attendance. A school manager in Bournemouth, Dorsetshire, stated in the report to the Committee of Council on Education in 1878 that he was "unable to trace to the action of the attendance committee either the admission or the improved attendance of a single child at any one of our 11 schools."[93] A report on a union in the Bristol district in 1881 stated, "There is nearly unanimous opinion that the action of the school attendance committee has very little influence in improving the attendance."[94] Similar reports recurred not only through the 1880s but even up through the late 1890s.[95]

In many areas, however, there was a clear perception that compulsion had sizably increased school attendance. In Birmingham, school attendance rates in 1876 were reported to have doubled as a consequence of compulsory schooling laws, and a report for Nottingham in the same year indicated a two-thirds rise in enrollments associated with the introduction of compulsory schooling.[96] Even in Staffordshire, where resistance was initially high, compulsory schooling ultimately seems to have been successful.[97] There were numerous other cases where school inspectors and witnesses before the Cross Commission reported marked increases in the numbers attending school as compulsion was introduced.[98] These differences in perceptions concerning the effectiveness of compulsory schooling laws can be reconciled if one allows for both local differences in enforcement and increased effectiveness in enforcement over time.

School inspectors who surveyed local school boards and attendance committees to determine the effectiveness of compulsory schooling found considerable variation in the results.[99] For example, in his report to the Committee of Council on Education for 1882 on South Dorset and Hampshire, W. F. Tregarthen found that the number of poor law unions where compulsion had been effective was about the same as the number where it had not. When Tregarthen asked thirty-nine unions whether the school enrollments had increased since compulsion was introduced, twenty-two unions replied "yes" and seventeen replied "no." To the question whether average attendance had increased, twenty unions replied "yes" and nineteen replied "no." And on whether attendance had become continuous rather than sporadic, fifteen answered "yes" and twenty-four

answered "no."[100] Even in 1900, A. G. Legard reported of the Aberystwyth district in Wales:

> The attendance in some parts of this district has shown a marked improve-
> ment as a result of greater activity on the part of the responsible authorities.
> In a few places I regret to say that things have gone from bad to worse. The
> persistent neglect of some local authorities to perform their statutory duties
> is an evil which urgently calls for remedy. The worst offenders in this respect
> are the small country School Boards.[101]

Legard's conclusion about Aberystwyth in 1900 was commonly made
for districts throughout England and Wales: When concerted efforts were
made to enforce the laws, enrollment and attendance responded.[102] Thus,
with regard to school attendance committees, J. Rice Byrne stated in his report to the Committee of Council on Education for 1878 on Surrey, "Their
success is dependent for the most part on the energy and tact evinced by
the committee or board, as the case may be, on the qualifications possessed
by the attendance officer for his very peculiar office, and on the readiness or
reluctance of the magistrates to enforce the law."[103] There were exceptions.
For example, in one case in the Bristol district previously cited, it was
reported that, despite the school attendance committees' efforts to enforce
the law, they had little impact on attendance.[104]

It also appears that if enforcement was not sustained, parents and
children would catch on, and enrollment and attendance would fall back
to the level that prevailed before schooling was made compulsory. Thus,
George French stated in his report on a Yorkshire district in 1878:

> There was at starting [a school attendance committee] a sort of spasmodic
> action which just frightened the people for a little while, but they are keen
> enough hereabouts to learn very quickly whether a thing be real or not. The
> people soon found out that very little notice was taken after the first great
> effort, and ceased to pay any heed to the admonitions of managers and teach-
> ers as to what awaited those persons who failed to comply with the demands
> of the Act in regard to the education and employment of their children.[105]

And, in London during the six to eight weeks when school attendance
officers were occupied with taking censuses of the children residing in
their districts rather than with enforcement, the average attendance was
reported to have fallen off as much as 10 percent.[106]

There are a number of reasons why enforcement of compulsory
schooling laws probably improved over time. First, it took time to set in

place an efficient mechanism for enforcement. William Landes and Lewis Solmon, in their study of compulsory schooling in America, attribute the lag to the time "required to hire and train truant officers, devise ways of detecting violators, disseminate information on the law to school officials and parents, and test in courts the legality of schooling laws."[107] Second, the social classes affected by compulsory schooling may have changed over time. John Hurt has suggested that initially, compulsory schooling laws affected primarily the respectable working poor.[108] This group was attending school with enough frequency for their names to appear on school registers, and so they were easily picked up by school attendance officers. Since they valued education enough to put their children in school with some regularity, they were likely to have been influenced by the threat of a fine, even if enforcement was improbable. Once this group was in compliance, the less respectable poor remained to be dealt with.[109]

Getting this latter group—sometimes referred to as the "residuum"—into school seems to have been more difficult. First, a much lower proportion was initially enrolled in school, making them more difficult to identify. In their annual reports in the 1880s, school inspectors noted the existence of a sizable group of children who did not appear on any school register for most if not all of their childhood.[110] One report from Hampshire in 1878 noted, "there has been during the past year, under the action of the school attendance committees, a large number of backward and neglected children brought into the account for the first time."[111] Second, this group put less value on education and may have been actively opposed to it. Finally, because of this group's poverty, the earnings of their children may have been more important to family survival. The first consideration would have made it more difficult to convict this group of truancy; the second and third considerations would have raised this group's incentive to violate the law even if violators could be caught.

The compliance of the less respectable poor with the Education Acts began to improve for two reasons. First, the sustained efforts of school attendance officers became increasingly effective. Among the steps they took was to take a house-by-house census of school-age children to determine who was subject to compulsory schooling laws.[112] This census could take several years to complete initially; and then, several weeks a year were commonly set aside in major urban areas to update the census to allow for the migration so common in urban areas. One mark of the reliability of these censuses was that they were used in investigations of various social conditions in large urban areas, Charles Booth's famous survey of London being one notable example.[113] As such censuses were compiled, it became increasingly feasible to aim for comprehensive enforcement of school attendance laws.[114]

Second, improved compliance may have been due to the gradual diffusion of education and the increasing perception of its value, even among the lowest status segments of English society.[115] As it became increasingly uncommon for children to be outside of the classroom during the school-week, it became easier to catch truants. Some accounts suggest that the bands of youths that roamed the streets of cities in the mid-nineteenth century became more and more rare, and parents must have come to realize that a child kept out of school would stand out, raise suspicion, and be subject to prosecution for truancy.[116] Finally, the ethos among the lower classes may have come increasingly to favor education. A school inspector's report for 1901 stated of a southeastern village that "owing to some happy train of circumstances in past years it has become the correct thing to send the children [to school] with regularity, and the parents who fail to do so act contrary to the general notions of propriety existing in the place. Such a feeling is far more powerful than any attendance officer, summons or fine."[117] And the inspector's report on the Southwest division noted of one school in 1900, "illegal employment has almost ceased because of the sharp look out kept by the scholars. Boys who willfully absent themselves are very effectively made to feel that they have offended and injured their school mates and the punishment is not always verbal."[118]

A gradual change in attitudes toward education seems quite plausible. There is some evidence, however, that compulsory schooling had a more immediate impact. The means for enforcing compulsory schooling laws may not have taken long to set in place; by the mid-1880s, prosecutions for violation of the Education Acts were close to their peak (see Figure 7.1). But although prosecutions were level after this point, it cannot be inferred that there was no further development in enforcement activity. After the 1880s continued improvements in enforcement would have been offset by increased compliance, owing in part to the deterrent effect of enforcement. Nevertheless, the trends suggest that an active mechanism for enforcement was in place throughout much of England by the mid-1880s.

The commonly voiced complaint throughout the period about the unwillingness of magistrates to convict may also have been overstated. Judicial statistics reported in the British Parliamentary Papers indicate that, of violations of the Elementary Education Acts determined summarily

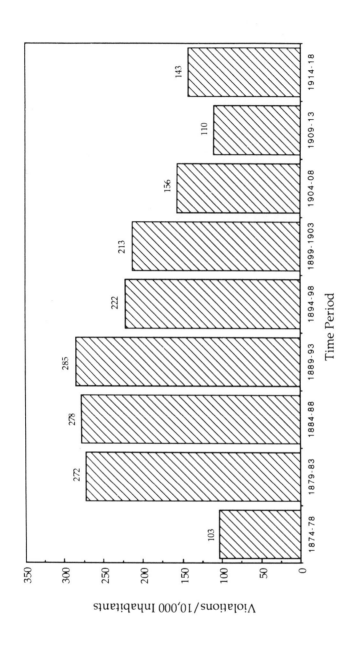

Figure 7.1. Prosecution rates for violation of the Education Acts in England and Wales, 1874–1918 (per 10,000 inhabitants).

Sources: "Judicial Statistics (England and Wales): Pt. I," PP 1895, vol. 108, [C.-7725], 75, 114; "Judicial Statistics (England and Wales): Pt. I, Criminal Statistics, 1898," PP 1900, vol. 103, [Cd.-123], 41; "Judicial Statistics (England and Wales), 1918, Pt. I–Criminal Statistics," PP 1920, vol. 50, [Cmd.-684], 8.

before justices, the conviction rate was 91 percent in 1874, 88 percent in 1883, and 89 percent in 1892.[119] Allowance must be made for reports that school attendance authorities dropped many cases before they reached the courts because they expected that magistrates would dismiss them and that even in some cases where convictions were obtained, trivial fines of only a few pennies were imposed. Still, the figures indicate that cases that made it to court had a high probability of resulting in conviction.

Compulsory schooling laws do not appear to have had their primary impact in areas where literacy rates were high initially, contrary to what would be expected if relatively more educated groups were significantly more likely to comply with the laws than relatively poorly educated groups. The correlation across counties between the percentage reduction in *illiteracy* and initial literacy rates between 1884 and 1900 was −.355 for grooms (statistically different from zero with a probability of 98 percent) and −.0611 for brides (statistically different from zero with a probability of 31 percent). The correlation between the percentage reduction in illiteracy and initial literacy between 1895 and 1905 was −.295 for grooms (with a probability of 95 percent of being different from zero) and −.311 for brides (with a probability of 96 percent of being different from zero). During the period 1864 to 1884, before compulsion would have exhibited an influence on literacy trends, the correlation between the percentage reduction in illiteracy and initial literacy was +.14 for grooms (with a probability of 64 percent of being different from zero) and +.57 for brides (with a probability of over 99 percent of being different from zero). These correlations suggest that compulsory schooling laws may have had a strong impact in areas where *illiteracy* was initially relatively high and that, furthermore, the introduction of compulsory schooling may have reversed a previous tendency for illiteracy to fall fastest in areas where literacy rates were initially relatively high. This interpretation can only be taken as suggestive since it does not control for the many other changes that were made in educational policy and, indeed, for exogenous influences on literacy. These changes and influences were also generally present during the period before compulsion, however.

School officials indicated, in numerous accounts, that the impact of compulsory schooling was sudden rather than gradual because the primary result of compulsion in their areas was not to improve the attendance of children who were already enrolled but to get previously unregistered children on the books.[120] These assertions are supported by aggregate trends in attendance rates, which show little upward tendency immediately after the introduction of compulsory schooling (see Figure 7.2). The trend in the percentage of registered scholars who were actually in attendance in inspected schools was approximately level between 1865 and 1878 at between 67 and 69 percent. The Newcastle Commission had found in 1858 and 1859 that the average attendance rate was 76.1 percent.[121] This static attendance trend was an apparent source of puzzlement and frustration to some witnesses who appeared before the Cross Commission.[122] Some school officials attributed it to the entry into their schools of children whose parents were more apathetic or even hostile toward education than those previously on the books.[123]

The provisional estimates of enrollment and the attendance trends reported in Table 7.6 indicate that enrollment rates rose by more between 1871 and 1896 and from initially lower levels than did attendance rates.[124] This in turn implies that the majority of the rise after 1870 in the percentage of school-age children attending school can be accounted for by a rise in enrollment rather than a rise in the attendance rate of those enrolled. Attendance rates did ultimately go up, however, and the estimated trends in Table 7.6 do imply that this rise made a significant contribution to the overall increase in the percentage of school-age children who attended.[125]

The difficulty in enforcing compulsory schooling may have been more in increasing the attendance rates of those enrolled than in increasing enrollment rates. Despairing remarks about enforcement of compulsory schooling laws seem, toward the end of the century, with greater frequency to refer more to the low attendance rate and, at the very end of the century, to keeping children in school long enough to educate them properly than to getting them into school at all.[126] All of this suggests that the most important impact of compulsion was its initial "shock" effect of getting children enrolled in school who otherwise would not have been.

Given the conflicting evidence from different regions and at different times that child labor restrictions and compulsory schooling laws were effectively enforced, consideration should be given to more aggregate evidence that the laws mattered and that the magnitude of their impact was sizable. This examination will begin with the impact of the restrictions on the employment of children in textiles in the 1830s. After enactment of the 1833 legislation restricting child labor in textiles, the number of children employed in textile factories fell by half in the course of three years. Over the next forty years, the percentage of children in the textile labor force increased. After 1878 employment again fell, but at a far more modest pace (see Table 7.7).

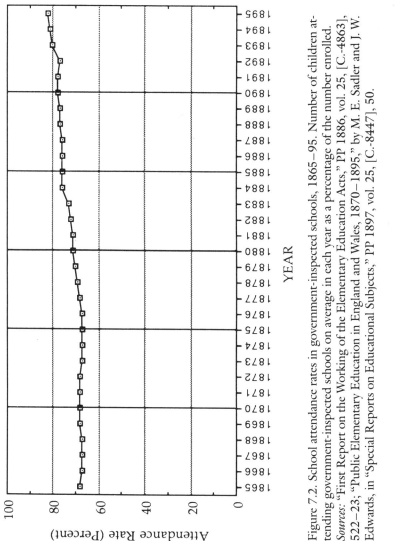

Figure 7.2. School attendance rates in government-inspected schools, 1865–95. Number of children attending government-inspected schools on average in each year as a percentage of the number enrolled. *Sources:* "First Report on the Working of the Elementary Education Acts," PP 1886, vol. 25, [C.-4863], 522–23; "Public Elementary Education in England and Wales, 1870–1895," by M. E. Sadler and J. W. Edwards, in "Special Reports on Educational Subjects," PP 1897, vol. 25, [C.-8447], 50.

Table 7.6

School Enrollment and Attendance Rates among Working-Class Children,
1871-96 (Percentage of Population in Age Group Enrolled and of Those
Enrolled in Attendance)

| | Enrollment Rate of Children | | |
| | | | Average |
Year	Aged 5-9	Aged 10-14	Attendance Rate
1871	57.3	37.3	68.0
1888-89	79.0	52.0	77.4
1896	82.6	56.4	81.5

Sources: The enrollment figures for 1871 are calculated based on the percentage of each
age group reported as scholars in "Appendix A to Report, Census of England and Wales,
1871, General Report, vol. IV," PP 1873, vol. 71, pt. II, [C.-872-I], 112 (Table 106).
These percentages are then adjusted to estimate working-class enrollments by assuming that
25 percent of the children aged 5-14 were from the upper and middle classes (the
percentage suggested by the 1851 Census of Education; see "Census of Gt. Britain, 1851,
Education," PP 1852-3, vol. 90, [1692], xxviii) and that all of these children were enrolled
in school. The 1888-89 and 1896 enrollment figures are the percentage of each age group
enrolled in state-inspected schools; they are taken from AR 1889-90, PP 1890, vol. 28,
[C.-6079-I], 274; and AR 1896-97, PP 1897, vol. 26, [C.-8544], xxiii. Attendance rates
are taken from "Public Elementary Education in England and Wales, 1870-1895," PP
1897, vol. 25, [C.-8447], 50 and AR 1896-97, PP 1897, vol. 26, [C.-8544], xxiii.

Between 1840 and 1870, literacy rates increased faster in a sample of
five textile districts covered by the Factory Acts than in a sample of nine
other districts with similar literacy and child labor force participation rates
in 1840. The comparison between the textile and nontextile areas was
based on five-year averages of bride and groom signature rates for the
1840s and 1870s from five textile districts (Bolton, Bradford, Bury, Halifax, and Preston) and nine nontextile districts (the Stafford districts: Bur-
ton, Cheadle, Stoke-Upon-Trent, Stone, W. Bromwich, and Wolstanton;
and the Hertford-Bedford districts: Hertford, Luton, and St. Albans). The
comparison includes those who migrated to these areas after leaving
school and does not capture those who emigrated from these areas after
attending school there. There is no reason to think that the literacy rate of

TABLE 7.7

Age and Sex Composition of the Textile Labor Force, 1835-90
(Percentage of the Textile Labor Force in Each Category)

Year	Children (8-12)	Young Men (13-17)	Women (13 and Over)	Men (18 and Over)
1835	15.9	12.2	47.3	25.5
1838	7.9	15.3	54.0	22.8
1847	7.9	11.8	54.9	25.4
1850	6.8	11.4	55.3	26.3
1856	7.7	10.3	56.2	25.8
1861	9.0	9.2	55.8	26.0
1867	10.0	8.7	56.1	25.1
1871	8.9	9.0	56.0	26.1
1874	12.5	8.4	54.4	24.7
1878	11.3	7.4	55.6	25.7
1885	8.9	7.9	56.2	27.1
1890	7.8	8.2	56.3	27.6

Source: Clark Nardinelli, "Child Labor and the Factory Acts," *Journal of Economic History* 40 (1980): 744, table 2. The table from Nardinelli's article is reprinted here with the permission of Cambridge University Press.

migrants relative to natives differed between the two types of districts, however.

Initial illiteracy rates were similar for males (42 percent in the textile areas; 40.2 percent in the Stafford districts; 46 percent in the Hertford-Bedford region) and somewhat higher for females in the textile districts than in the nontextile districts (74 percent in the textile districts in the 1840s versus 57 percent in the Stafford district and 53 percent in the Hertford-Bedford districts). The increase between the 1840s and the 1870s was 21 percentage points for males and 33 percentage points for females in the textile districts, compared with 10 percentage points for males and 18 percentage points for females in the nontextile districts. A t-test for differences in proportions revealed that the difference between textile and nontextile districts was statistically significant at the 99.5-percent level, although when nontextile districts were broken down into Stafford versus Hertford and Bedford, the difference between the two areas was significant only at the 90-percent level.[127] This last result can be explained by the demise of the lace making and straw plaiting industries in Hertford and Bedford, which reduced the demand for child labor.

At the national level, the impact of compulsory schooling laws was evident in trends in the distribution of scholars by age and standard. (The standard is the term used in the English educational system to refer to the level of instruction that is supposed to be covered during each year of enrollment as laid down by Education Department guidelines.) Secular forces behind educational expansion should generally have led to an even growth across all levels of the educational system. Compulsory schooling laws, however, applied primarily to children aged five to thirteen and in Standards I to III. After 1872 the proportion of scholars aged five to thirteen and in these standards increased markedly (see Figure 7.3). A greater secular decline in the demand for labor of children aged five to thirteen than of older children could also have led to this result. But examination of the impact of sectoral shifts on the demand for child labor indicates that compositional changes produced a larger decline in the demand for older rather than for younger children.[128]

Compulsory schooling legislation appears to have been the dominant force after 1850 that lowered children's participation in the labor force as a whole. Between 1851 and 1911 the proportion of boys aged ten to fourteen who were classified by the census as employed fell from 37 percent to 18 percent, and of girls, from 20 percent to 10 percent (see Table 7.4). For both sexes, about one-half of the decline occurred between 1871 and 1881, coinciding with the enactment of compulsory schooling laws. One should be cautious, however, in attributing all of this decline to compulsory schooling laws. The census changed classifications between 1871 and 1881; thus, some of this change may be a statistical artifact. Also, compulsory schooling laws were not universal throughout England until 1881; one might therefore expect a lag before these laws began to take their full effect. Nevertheless, the decline in the labor force participation of children between 1851 and 1911 suggests how strong the impact may have been (see Table 7.4).

The importance of compulsory schooling is also suggested by the decline in *illiteracy* after compulsion was introduced in counties where *illiteracy* was relatively high, compared with its decline in counties whose *illiteracy* levels were initially similar during the period just before compulsion would have begun to show an effect. Compulsion would have begun to be

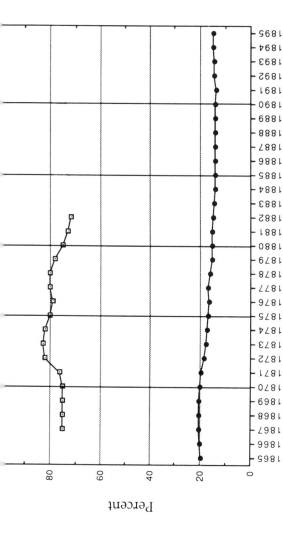

Figure 7.3. Percentage of all students enrolled in government-inspected schools who were in standards I to III and the percentage who were younger or older students, 1865–95: *open squares*, percentage of all students who were in standards I to III; *solid circles*, percentage of all students who were under age five or over age thirteen. *Standard* refers to the level of instruction set down by the Department of Education as appropriate for each year of enrollment.

Sources: "Return for Each of the Last 20 Years with Respect to Schools under Inspection in England and Wales," PP 1883, vol. 53, [C.-107]; AR 1867–68, PP 1867–68, vol. 25, [4051], 3, 7–9; AR 1868–69, vol. 20, [4139], 3, 7–9; AR 1869–70, PP 1870, vol. 22, [C.-165], 1, 8–11; AR 1870–71, PP 1871, vol. 22, [C.-406], 1, 4, 9–12; AR 1871–72, PP 1872, vol. 22, [C.-601], 1, 7–9; "Public Elementary Education in England and Wales, 1870–1895," PP 1897, vol. 25, [C.-8544], 51.

reflected in marriage register signature trends (allowing a ten- to fifteen-year lag between school attendance at ages seven to twelve in the early 1870s and marriage at ages twenty to twenty-five in the early to mid-1880s) in the mid-1880s. In 1884 the proportion of grooms making a mark on the marriage register was 12 percent, and that of brides was 14 percent. There were thirteen counties where over 15 percent of the grooms made marks, with a range from 16.1 percent to 24.6 percent and a mean across counties of 18.6 percent.[129] There were twelve counties in 1884 where more than 15 percent of brides made marks at marriage, with a range from 16.4 percent to 25.5 percent and a mean of 20.1 per-cent.[130] By 1895 the mean percentage of grooms making marks had fallen to 6.3 percent in the thirteen counties, and that of brides, to 6.5 percent in the twelve counties. Thus, on average the proportion making marks in these counties where illiteracy was relatively high fell by 12.3 percentage points for grooms and by 13.6 percentage points for brides. This implies, for both brides and grooms in these counties, a two-thirds reduction in the percentage making marks over the decade 1884–95.

In contrast, progress between 1874 and 1884 was much slower for counties with signature rates for brides and grooms in the same range as those just mentioned. In 1874 the proportion of grooms making marks at marriage was between 15 and 25 percent in twenty-seven counties, and that of brides was in the same range in nineteen counties. The average proportion making marks across the twenty-seven counties was 19.2 per-cent for grooms and 20.3 percent for brides. By 1884 the percentage had fallen only to 12.6 percent for grooms and to 12.15 percent for brides in these counties. This implies a reduction of only 34.5 percent for grooms and 40.06 percent for brides in these counties.

Signature ability at marriage during 1884–95 would cover schooling activity during the 1870s just as compulsion was being introduced. To consider the possibility that compulsion was not fully established through-out England and Wales until the 1880s, one can compare the progress of high illiteracy counties between 1895 and 1905 (again allowing for a fif-teen-year lag between schooling and marriage) with that of counties with similar levels of illiteracy before the influence of compulsion would have been felt. In 1895 the proportion of all grooms making a mark at marriage was 4.0 percent, and that of brides, 4.8 percent. In fifteen counties in 1895, the proportion of grooms making a mark was 5 percent or higher, with a mean across counties of 6.33 percent and a range across counties of 5.2 to 7.6 percent. For brides in 1895, there were thirteen counties in which 5 percent or more made marks, with a mean across counties of 6.4 percent and a range of 5.0 to 7.8 percent. By 1905 the percentage making marks at marriage had fallen to 2.2 percent in the fifteen counties just mentioned for grooms and to 2.4 percent in the thirteen counties just mentioned for brides. This implies a reduction in illiteracy over this decade from the 1895 level of 64.6 percent for grooms and 62.7 percent for brides.

In contrast, in 1874, before compulsion would have exercised any influence on marriage register signature ability, there were only two counties where the proportion of grooms making marks was below 10 percent, and 3 counties where fewer than 10 percent of brides made marks. In these counties, the mean proportion making marks of 8 percent for grooms and 9.4 percent for brides in 1874 had fallen by 1884 to 5.4 percent for grooms and 4.6 percent for brides. This implies a reduction in illiteracy from the 1874 level of 33 percent for grooms and 52.6 percent for brides during the decade just before compulsion would have exercised an influence. Thus, counties whose initial levels of illiteracy were similar experienced a much greater reduction in illiteracy in the decades just after compulsion would have exhibited an influence on marriage register trends than during the decade just before it would have shown an influence.[131]

If child labor and compulsory schooling laws had an impact on literacy trends, the issue still remains of how large it was. On the one hand, child labor restrictions alone probably had only a slight overall impact on literacy trends. Not only is there conflicting evidence on how effectively they were enforced, but the number of children employed in industries covered by these restrictions was quite small relative to the total school-age population.[132]

Compulsory schooling laws, on the other hand, applied to large segments of the English population; as already noted, by 1873, 40 percent of the English population resided in areas where compulsory schooling laws were in effect and by 1881 the coverage was universal. Still, it is difficult to draw any clear inference from schooling or literacy trends about the impact of compulsory schooling. There is the obvious problem of controlling for other influences on educational trends. Trying to spot a clear break in these trends that can be attributed to compulsory schooling is problematic because of the other marked changes that occurred in school provision and policy in the 1870s. Moreover, the data on schooling are not continuous or fully comparable, making it difficult to locate clear turning points in trends. One reason for the lack of comparability is that the main source of data on schooling is on inspected schools, which gain in share at the expense of noninspected schools over time. Continuous and comparable data are available annually for signature ability at marriage. Although the data reveal no clear change in trends in signature ability during the 1870s and 1880s, allowance should probably be made for the possibility that after 1870, the groups that had yet to acquire literacy were those who were most resistant to its acquisition.

Despite these uncertainties, one can set upward bounds on the impact of compulsory schooling by comparing literacy and schooling attendance rates immediately before compulsion was introduced in 1871 and at the end of the century when its longer-term results should have been completed. The percentage of children aged five to nine reported as scholars in the 1871 census was 68 percent. Using the procedure described in the notes to Table 7.6, one can estimate the *working-class* enrollment rate for this year at 57.3 percent. The Education Department report for the 1888–89 school year indicates that in that year 79 percent of children aged five to nine were enrolled in government-inspected schools.[133] By 1896 the enrollment rate in inspected schools had reached 82.6 percent for this group.[134]

For children aged ten through fourteen, the 1871 census reported that 53 percent were scholars. Using the procedure described in the notes to Table 7.6, one can estimate the *working-class* enrollment for this year at 37.3 percent. The Education Department report for the 1888–89 school year indicates that 52 percent of this group was enrolled in inspected schools; by 1896 this proportion had reached 56.4 percent.[135] The growth in enrollment rates between 1871 and 1896 increased by more, relative to the growth in enrollments between 1851 and 1871, for five- to nine-year-olds than for ten- to fourteen-year-olds. Thus, for the prime school-age group—children five to nine—these estimates suggest that enrollments may have grown somewhat faster after compulsory schooling went into effect. If one considers that segments of the population not enrolling regularly by 1871 were probably more apathetic, or even hostile, toward education than segments that had come to enroll earlier, then sustaining a faster growth in enrollment during the later period was no mean accomplishment.

Compulsory schooling laws were established at a relatively late stage in the rise of signature ability during the Victorian period so that their impact on literacy trends was attenuated. The laws were first established in the 1870s, became universal in the 1880s, and would have only begun to influence marriage register signature rates in the mid-1880s. In 1884, as previously noted, 88 percent of grooms and 86 percent of brides were able to sign their names. Still, areas where illiteracy was particularly high could have been significantly affected by compulsory schooling laws. By 1884, when compulsion would have only begun to show its effects, there were thirteen counties in England and Wales where the percentage of grooms making marks at marriage was over 15 percent; these counties included 17.6 percent of the total population of England and Wales in 1881. In twelve counties, the proportion of brides making marks was over 15 percent; these counties included 42.9 percent of the population of England and Wales in 1881. And, in some registration districts within counties, the proportion of brides or grooms making marks in 1884 exceeded 30 percent.[136] Thus, although in some areas of England compulsory schooling may have had a sizable effect on literacy trends, its overall impact was attenuated by its relatively late introduction.

The late introduction of compulsory schooling laws was probably not fortuitous. It could be argued that passage of these laws, along with their *effective* enforcement, was feasible only after literacy was widespread. Effective compulsory schooling laws appear to have required not just a national consensus for Parliament to enact them but also widespread local support for local authorities to enforce them. The delay in introducing compulsory schooling in England may well have reflected the reluctance of politicians to enact legislation that could not be enforced without widespread popular support for education.

This could lead one to conclude that rather than local authorities' improving the enforcement of the laws, parents and children may have become increasingly willing to comply with the laws because of a rising demand for schooling. But this point raises the question of how much of the increase in enrollment can be attributed to compulsion. The laws could, in fact, have been ultimately redundant, with compliance reflecting, rather than creating, an increase in demand. This point was emphasized by Landes and Solmon in their study of compulsory schooling in the United States.[137] If one concludes that compulsion was not completely redundant, because some recalcitrant parents were influenced by the laws to send their children to school, the issue remains of whether compulsion could influence even these parents before they had developed a sense of the value of education.

The Best Attendance Officer

The opportunity costs of acquiring literacy were declining during the Victorian period because both the number of jobs open to children was decreasing and the legal penalties that parents could incur if their children worked were increasing. Since the opportunity costs were initially quite large relative to school fees, their reduction surely did much to lower the total cost of acquiring literacy. The reduction of opportunity costs probably did not influence individuals who placed no value whatever on literacy, however. Even at the end of the Victorian period, a child's time continued to have some value despite the drying up of formal labor market opportunities. If education was not valued, the occasional threat of a fine of lower value than that of the child's time was unlikely to prod parents to send their children to school. Only as more of the working classes began to value education, influenced perhaps by compulsory schooling laws, could compulsion contribute, over the longer term, to raising school attendance or literacy.

The difficulties created by the combination of the low value placed on schooling by much of the working classes and the high value placed on children's time outside the classroom were evident in the minimal effect that laws restricting specific types of child labor frequently had on school attendance. These difficulties were often exacerbated by a high elasticity of substitution between machinery and older unskilled labor with child labor. As a result, children displaced from one group of occupations by legal restrictions readily found work at only slightly lower wages in other occupations or preferred to play in the streets rather than attend school.[138] There are a number of indications that, on the one hand, the abundance of substitutes for child labor led to a high elasticity of demand for child labor and the possibility of new job opportunities as children's wages fell and that, on the other hand, parents and children were so apathetic to education that even a marked decline in opportunity costs often had little impact on school attendance.

A high elasticity of demand for child labor was evident in the impact of child labor restrictions in the textile industry, which were first enacted in 1833.[139] They prohibited the employment of children under the age of nine, restricted the employment of children aged nine to twelve to forty-eight hours per week, and required them to attend school part time. Many mill owners found the educational provisions of the legislation burdensome and substituted older children and women for children under thirteen.[140] Consequently, the number of children under thirteen employed in cotton textile manufacture fell from twenty-nine thousand in 1835 to twelve thousand in 1838, while the number employed in wool manufacture fell from fourteen thousand in 1835 to ten thousand in 1838.[141]

There is no evidence that school enrollments increased as children left the textile mills. Factory inspectors' reports suggest instead that children so displaced found other jobs, did domestic chores, or, in some cases, simply idled in the streets. Although there is no direct evidence on school attendance trends immediately after the Factory Acts went into effect, it is noteworthy that investigations on the subject made no mention of children enrolling in school who had been displaced from textile mills.[142] The spillover of displaced children from textile employment into other full-time employment must have been limited because, even after the Factory Acts, over 60 percent of those children who were employed in many textile towns were working in textile manufacture.[143] The greater displacement of girls than boys by the Factory Acts is suggestive of movement into domestic and casual occupations.[144]

Some children under thirteen remained in textile factories and attended school part time to comply with the law, but the education they received was frequently only nominal. Factory inspectors noted numerous complaints of factory children crammed into makeshift schoolrooms with illiterate teachers.[145] This situation seems to have reflected the parents' apathy toward education as well as the mill owners' attempts to minimize costs.[146] Parental apathy continued to be evident in the 1860s and 1870s: factory inspectors noted that when the legal minimum age for employment in textile factories as a half-timer was raised during this period, the amount of schooling received by children in textile mills decreased since their parents sent them to school only to comply with the law.[147] Similarly, adult school attendance soared in Lancashire during the cotton famine as relief payments to adults were made contingent on school attendance. For children, however, school attendance increased by only 10 percent in areas hit by the famine, and this was despite the complete remission of school fees.[148]

As child labor restrictions were extended to other industries in the 1860s, factory inspectors noted that the result was similar to that in textiles: there was substantial substitution of machinery and older labor for children covered by the provisions of the legislation, with little improvement in school attendance owing to parental apathy.[149]

The modest impact of trends in opportunity costs on schooling during the mid-Victorian period is suggested by trends in school enrollments compared with the employment of children between 1851 and 1871. For children under the age of ten and for girls aged ten to fifteen, less than 10 percent of the increase in school attendance between 1851 and 1871 can be accounted for by a decline in the proportion reported by the census as employed (see Table 7.2). Even for boys aged ten to fifteen, the proportion was only 40 percent (see Table 7.2). Although the extent of the decline in opportunities for casual and domestic tasks not captured by the census is obscure, there is no reason to think that these opportunities changed much more than formal work opportunities. Moreover, of the total increase in school attendance rates between 1851 and 1871 for five- to fifteen-year-old children, about half is accounted for by children under the age of ten; and, between 1861 and 1891, the percentage of all scholars in government-inspected schools who were between the ages of ten and fifteen only rose from 30 to 34 percent.[150] One would expect that children over the age of ten had higher opportunity costs than those under the age of ten. Thus, if declining opportunity costs were an important factor in enrollment growth, enrollment should have grown faster for older children. But enrollment rates for older children do not appear to have grown at a markedly faster pace than for younger children.

On the other hand, simply getting children into schools did not guarantee that they would learn anything if they had no interest in what was being taught. After compulsory schooling was introduced, there were frequent complaints about the adverse influence on instruction of the irregular attendance of the residual elements newly brought into the schools; even the learning of children who attended regularly was said to have been disrupted.[151]

On the other hand, increasing children's interest in what was taught appears to have done much to gain compliance with child labor restrictions and compulsory schooling laws. In textile areas, factory inspectors noted that improved school provision in the 1840s and increased parental concern for their children's education in the 1860s and 1870s increased the impact of child labor restrictions on education.[152] And, after the introduction of compulsory schooling, school inspectors frequently noted that the most effective way to ensure compliance with school attendance laws was to get parents and children alike to value what was done in schools and that this was best accomplished through good teachers.[153] As school inspectors often phrased it, "a good teacher is the best attendance officer."[154]

This raises the question of whether the resources devoted to establishing and enforcing compulsory schooling and other restrictions on child labor would have been better devoted to improving the quality of the public schooling that was offered. Friendlier teachers and more attractive classrooms may have gotten children into schools more rapidly and effectively than truant officers and fines. This question will not be answered here. Compulsion may have been necessary to at least get portions of the "residuum" into schools. However, the decline in the opportunity costs of schooling was likely to have a long-term effect only if it led parents and children to appreciate the value of education. The value society placed on education could go only so far to compensate for the lack of value that individual parents and children placed on it. As Inspector J. G. Fitzmaurice stated in his report on the North-Central division in 1900, "The good teacher is the best attendance officer, . . . the man who says persuasively 'come in' is more potent than he who says compulsorily 'go in'."[155]

8. Becoming a Literate Society: Both a Private and a Public Decision

BETWEEN 1830 AND 1900 IN ENGLAND, both public educational policy and secular forces influencing the private demand for literacy were changing. Ensuring that all English children were within a short walk from a subsidized elementary school became not just the goal of increased state, church, and philanthropic funding but also a legal obligation for local school boards and attendance committees. Attending school became a legal obligation as well. On the demand side, the labor force was shifting away from agriculture and manufacturing and into the clerical, commercial transport, and service occupations that were probably making some use of literacy. Newspaper circulations and letters delivered per capita also increased many times over as newspaper prices and postal fees fell (reflecting, as Chapter 3 suggested, public policy perhaps even more than secular forces).

The previous chapters indicate that the impact of public policy on Victorian literacy trends was more visible and pervasive than that of secular changes in private demand. The thousands of new subsidized schools, the extensive bureaucracy that emerged to administer them, and the thousands of prosecutions for truancy touched, in one way or another, most of the English population. In Chapter 4, it was estimated that between 1840 and 1900, 40 to 70 percent of the English population gained access to subsidized schooling. Although child labor legislation affected a small proportion of the English population, compulsory schooling laws applied to 40 percent of the population by 1873; they were universal by 1881. In the last quarter of the nineteenth century, violation of the Elementary Education Acts was second only to offenses related to drunkeness as a cause of criminal prosecution.[1]

In contrast, it is far more difficult to establish what the private benefits of literacy were and how widespread they became. Chapter 2 estimated that, in the second half of the nineteenth century, the percentage of either men or women in the English labor force in occupations requiring, or likely to use, literacy rose by 7 to 10 percent. By 1891 just over 33 percent of male workers and 15 percent of female workers were in such occupations. Even for these jobs there is much uncertainty over the exact extent to which literacy was required; for virtually all jobs in the labor market, literacy was only one of many characteristics that might have influenced a worker's performance. The working classes probably used literacy skills—reading newspapers and writing letters—more during their leisure hours than they did at work. Although the working classes read newspapers and wrote letters far more in 1900 than in 1840, it is difficult to determine if these practices were universal at the end of the nineteenth century. Daily newspapers and work-related memos and forms aimed at working-class readers were less visible features of late Victorian society than board schools and truant officers.

Visibility, however, did not necessarily imply importance. For those segments of the English population for whom literacy clearly improved their earnings ability, this gain was almost certainly likely to outweigh the costs of acquiring literacy, and it contributed more to the rise in literacy than did changes in educational policy. Even the benefits associated with reading a daily paper could outweigh the costs of acquiring literacy because the benefits would have extended for decades, while the costs of acquiring literacy were incurred for several years at most. Even allowing for the discounting of benefits, they were still likely to outweigh the costs.

The point can be illustrated by using the information from previous chapters to estimate the costs and benefits of acquiring literacy. Appendix D explains how these estimates were obtained. The range of discounted direct and opportunity costs of schooling implied by the estimates in Chapters 5, 6, and 7 of school fees, children's wages, and time spent in school to acquire literacy is reported in Tables 8.1 and 8.2. The discounted direct costs reported in Table 8.1 ranged from well under a pound to just over seven pounds, and the opportunity costs reported in Table 8.2 ranged from four pounds to twenty-eight pounds. Intermediate estimates for costs based on three years of attendance for twenty-five weeks and school fees between two and six pence per week indicate ranges of half a pound to two pounds for direct costs and six to twelve pounds for opportunity costs. Intermediate estimates of the total combined costs of acquiring literacy, obtained by combining the intermediate results reported in Tables 8.1 and 8.2, range from six and a half to fourteen pounds.[2]

The present value of the wage premium associated with literacy implied by various weekly wage premiums, lengths of working life, and

Table 8.1

Present Value of the Direct Costs of Schooling by Discount Rate, Length of Schooling, and School Fees (In English Pounds)

	Length of Schooling			
Weekly School Fees	One 40-Week Year	Three 25-Week Years	Five 25-Week Years	Six 40-Week Years
	Discount Rate of .05			
Subsidized range				
1 pence	0.17	0.30	0.47	0.89
2 pence	0.33	0.60	0.95	1.78
4 pence	0.67	1.19	1.89	3.55
Unsubsidized range				
6 pence	1.00	1.79	2.84	5.32
8 pence	1.33	2.38	3.78	7.10
	Discount Rate of .20			
Subsidized range				
1 pence	—	0.26	0.37	0.67
2 pence	—	0.53	0.75	1.33
4 pence	—	1.05	1.50	2.66
Unsubsidized range				
6 pence	—	1.58	2.24	3.99
8 pence	—	2.10	2.99	5.32

discount rates is reported in Table 8.3. The wage premiums considered are based on likely values of the weekly amount by which literacy raised wages for workers whose wages were definitely raised by literacy.[3] The present values for the pecuniary benefits of literacy reported in Table 8.3 ranged from eleven pounds to well over one hundred pounds.

Chapter 3 suggested that the benefits from reading newspapers and books during leisure hours and using the mails for personal affairs had a

Table 8.2

Present Value of the Opportunity Cost of Acquiring Literacy by Discount Rate and Length of Schooling (In English Pounds)

Length of Schooling and Age When Attended	Discount Rate	
	.05	.20
40 weeks under age 10	4.00	—
Three 25-week years under age 10	7.13	6.32
Two 25-week years under age 10 and one 25-week year during age 10 or over	9.42	8.06
One 25-week year under age 10 and two 25-week years during age 10 or over	11.80	10.14
Four 40-week years under age 10 and two 40-week years during age 10 or over	27.74	19.50

Note: Calculations assume a wage rate of 2 shillings per week for children under age 10 and 4 shillings per week for children aged 10 and over.

present value ranging from under a pound to well over ten pounds, depending on how frequently these items were used.

For children who definitely could expect to receive higher wages because of literacy, the estimates reported in Tables 8.1 through 8.3 indicate that the benefits of literacy were almost sure to exceed the costs of acquisition. Even the lowest annual wage premium and working life and highest discount rate reported in Table 8.3 implies a present value of wage benefits of over ten pounds. Combined direct and opportunity costs of acquiring literacy in three years or less, however, ranged from a low of just over four pounds to only as high as just over fourteen pounds. Chapter 3 found that the value of nonpecuniary benefits associated with literacy was commonly only a pound or so, making it much less likely that these benefits by themselves would exceed the costs of acquiring literacy. But as the century wore on and the working classes read newspapers and wrote letters more

Table 8.3

Present Value of Wage Premium for Literacy by Discount Rate, Length of Working Life, and Wage Premium (In English Pounds)

Years of Working Life	*Wage Premium (Shillings per Week)*				
	1	*2*	*5*	*7.5*	*15*
	Discount Rate of .05				
10	19.7	39.4	98.5	147.8	295.5
15	26.4	52.8	132.0	198.0	396.0
20	31.6	63.2	158.0	237.0	474.0
25	35.7	71.4	178.5	267.8	535.5
30	38.8	77.6	194.0	291.0	582.0
35	41.3	82.6	206.5	309.8	619.5
40	43.2	86.4	216.0	324.0	648.0
45	44.7	89.4	223.5	335.3	670.5
50	45.9	91.8	229.5	344.3	688.5
	Discount rate of .20				
10	10.8	21.8	54.0	81.0	162.0
15	11.9	23.8	59.5	89.3	178.5
20	12.3	24.6	61.5	92.3	184.5
25	12.4	24.8	62.0	93.0	186.0
30	12.5	25.0	62.5	93.8	187.5
35	12.5	25.0	62.5	93.8	187.5
40	12.5	25.0	62.5	93.8	187.5
45	12.5	25.0	62.5	93.8	187.5
50	12.5	25.0	62.5	93.8	187.5

Note: Calculations assume a 50-week work year and are based on continuous discounting.

frequently, the value of the nonpecuniary benefits increased sizably, increasing the likelihood that these benefits would outweigh the costs of acquiring literacy. The influence of an excess of benefits over costs on the acquisition of literacy would have been muted by the likelihood that the costs were primarily incurred by parents while the benefits were received by their children. Nevertheless, both altruism of parents for the future prospects of their children and the prospect of enhanced support during old age would have tended to prevent a complete dampening of the consideration by parents of the benefits of literacy to their children.

Some people did not rely on help from their parents in obtaining an education but acquired literacy when adults. The person receiving the benefits of literacy in this situation would have been the same as the one who incurred the costs of acquisition, and the dampened incentive faced by parents providing literacy for their children would thus be avoided. The adult acquiring literacy would have faced a higher opportunity cost of acquiring literacy, however. Even though instruction was likely to have occurred during leisure hours, the demands of domestic life, fatigue after a hard day's work, and the difficulty of pursuing instruction part time would have made the opportunity cost of instruction higher during adulthood than childhood. For these reasons, evening schools do not seem to have been very successful during the Victorian period in teaching reading and writing.[4] Furthermore, acquiring literacy during adulthood would have reduced the number of years during which the benefits of literacy would be received. At any rate, Chapter 6 indicated that by the mid-Victorian period, literacy was primarily obtained during childhood.

In contrast to changes in the benefits of literacy, the impact of policy was likely to be far weaker. Access to subsidized schools was likely to provide savings of perhaps several shillings per year and perhaps a few pounds total (see Table 8.1). The fine for violating compulsory schooling laws was also a matter of several shillings.[5] If no value was placed by parents or children on education and opportunity costs were sizable, as they frequently were, then it is understandable that such laws were commonly violated, as Chapter 7 indicated, and that subsidized schools were sometimes half empty, as Chapter 6 indicated.

Estimates of costs and benefits do not fully explain why almost all of the English working classes decided by the end of the nineteenth century to learn how to read and write. Even then, there were sizable segments of the working classes for whom literacy would provide no obvious financial benefits and who were making at best occasional use in their daily lives of the ability to read and write (see Chapters 2 and 3). If large segments of the population were apathetic to education and placed no value on it, then why would educational policy measures alone have induced these groups to attend school or to acquire literacy?

Educational policy focused primarily on lowering the direct costs of literacy, but it would have had little impact on the balance of benefits over costs to people who perceived no potential benefits. Even fines for truancy could hardly have prodded these people to attend school because, as Chapter 7 indicated, these fines were commonly less than the opportunity costs of school attendance. If sizable groups continued to perceive that being literate had no benefits, how did lower school fees or the threat of minimal fines for truancy induce them to attend school?

One possiblity is that not only public authorities but also many working-class parents perceived that schools did more than teach reading and writing. These parents may have valued habits of orderliness and discipline that they believed schools instilled in their children as well as instruction in reading and writing. The combined value to parents of both the literacy skills and the behavioral habits that schools conveyed to their children may have exceeded the costs of schooling, while the value of literacy instruction alone did not. Parents may also have valued other cognitive instruction that schools conveyed, such as knowledge of history or science. Throughout most of the nineteenth century, however, few working-class children received instruction in cognitive subject matter other than basic literacy and arithmetic.[6] And as Chapter 6 noted, many working-class parents seem to have preferred private schools because of their greater emphasis on basic literacy skills compared with public schools.

Another possible explanation for rising school attendance among those receiving few actual benefits from literacy is that they may still have perceived that benefits were possible but uncertain. Many working-class parents may have thought that the probabilities were low that their children would aspire to jobs where literacy would be useful or would have much occasion to read and write during leisure hours. Only 3 percent of literate sons of laborers in the early Victorian period entered occupations clearly making use of literacy, and only a further 35 percent entered occupations where literacy was of possible use (see Table 2.4). Still, parents may have been willing to take the gamble that literacy might pay off for their offspring if the costs of acquiring literacy were low enough. Subsidized schools and fines for truancy may have convinced parents that the gamble was worthwhile.

That the benefits of literacy were uncertain takes on added significance when one considers that working-class parents did not simply decide, after weighing the benefits and costs a single time, whether or not to send their child to school for long enough to become literate. Instead, whether the child learned to read and write was the cumulative outcome of numerous parental decisions as to whether to send the child to school for any given day or week. Low school fees and the existence of penalties for truancy could have induced parents with at least a faint perception of the benefits of literacy to keep their children in school for enough additional months for them to learn to read and write. J. S. Winder's report to the Newcastle Commission in 1858 on the textile districts of Rochdale and Bradford contains passages consistent with this view:

> Indifference is a much more extensive cause of neglect [of schooling] than poverty; indifference not verbally avowed, for all but the most degraded admit that education is good, but proved unmistakeably by practical neglect . . . *education is ordinarily looked on as a matter of secondary importance, and made to give way to the convenience or interest of the moment without scruple or hesitation . . . the indifference which has the widest operation is not absolute, but comparative,* showing itself in a refusal, for the sake of schooling, to forego the wages which the child can earn, or the assistance which it can give in household affairs. . . . *There seems . . . to be no conventional standard, either of time to be spent or of accomplishments to be acquired there.* The child is sent to work when opportunity offers, and in districts such as mine he has not long to wait.[7] (Italics added)

Observers throughout the Victorian period asserted that virtually all children attended school at some point in their lives.[8] If this assertion was true, then the main schooling decision was not whether to attend school at all but for how long and how frequently. And if virtually all parents were sending their children to school for at least a limited period of time, then presumably virtually all of them placed at least some value on education. As the Newcastle Commission said in its 1861 report, "The great mass of the population recognizes its [education's] importance sufficiently to take advantage to some extent of the opportunities thus afforded [to obtain education] to their children."[9]

Some observers, however, did not agree that all children saw the inside of a schoolroom at some point in their lives.[10] And some groups in the mid-nineteenth century did not seem to value literacy, for example—according to the Newcastle Commission report—the prosperous Black Country metal workers.[11] Yet, over the next few decades literacy rates rose markedly in the Black Country, a puzzling trend in light of the Newcastle Commission observations. Thus, it seems that more evidence is required to confirm that by the early Victorian period virtually everyone perceived at least dimly that literacy had some benefits to offer.

This uncertainty as to the diffusion of benefits to the individual from literacy could have reflected the influence of sociological factors that would not show up in a narrow weighing of costs and benefits to the individual. These factors could include the influence of peers and social environment, changes in working-class culture, and class conflict.[12] While these factors cannot be completely dismissed and deserve further consideration, there are a number of reasons for not exploring them more fully in this study. The evidence considered in previous chapters suggested that their impact was at best modest. Chapter 3, for example, indicated that political and religious trends had a limited effect on working-class reading habits.

There are some indications, discussed in previous chapters, that rising literacy rates in English society could have generated further incentives for acquiring literacy. As literacy became more common, some occupations were redefined to make use of literacy skills. The growth of a mass readership increased the profitability of developing books and newspapers for the working classes. And, as a greater proportion of parents became literate, their children were more likely to acquire literacy.

However, the importance of the rise of literacy in generating further benefits from literacy should not be overstated. The extent to which occupations were redefined to incorporate literacy and the impact of rising literacy on the profitability of popular publications were probably modest; and their effects, moreover, were primarily felt quite late in the nineteenth century after the main rise in literacy had occurred. Furthermore, illiterates were not socially ostracized, according to the material considered in Chapter 3. Although the rising literacy of parents did significantly raise the probability that their children would be literate, some initial rise in literacy among recalcitrant parents had to take place before their children could be influenced. The self-generating forces behind literacy existed but were not strong; this is confirmed by the stagnant literacy trends in the century before 1840.[13]

Further evidence against any simple overarching sociological factor is the diversity of regional literacy trends. Regional patterns suggest considerable variation in the balance of forces raising literacy. In some areas, the lead of female over male literacy suggests the attraction of domestic service and migration opportunities.[14] In other areas, the marked jump in literacy trends corresponding to the establishment of compulsion suggests the importance of policy and its impact on attitudes. Such a fillip resulting from compulsion was apparent in Staffordshire between 1884 and 1895, where grooms' signature rates at marriage jumped from 79.4 percent to 94.5 percent and that of brides from 74.9 percent to 93.1 percent. It was also apparent in Monmouth, where during the same period signature rates for grooms jumped from 75.4 to 92.9 percent and for brides from 76.2 to 91.1 percent, and in South Wales, where signature ability jumped from 74.5 to 92.5 percent for brides.[15] Thus, in some regions rising literacy seems to have been generated by the pull of the private benefits to literacy, in other regions by the push of public educational policy. This diversity may also reflect diverse cultural and sociological influences, and despite the restricted attention given to these factors in this study, they do deserve further investigation.

The importance of both public policy and private incentive to the rise of literacy can nevertheless be shown by using the results of previous chapters to account for their contributions. A summary of such an accounting is presented in Table 8.4. Signature rates for grooms rose by about 40 percentage points and for brides by about 50 percentage points between 1840 and 1900. On the private benefit side, Chapter 2 estimated that 7 to 10 percent of both the male and female labor forces between 1840 and 1890 shifted from occupations unlikely to use literacy toward those likely to use it. On the policy side, Chapter 5 estimated that school enrollments rose by 10 to 50 percent as a result of improvements in the provision of subsidized schooling. On this basis one could attribute approximately 4 to 25 percentage points of the rise in signature rates to this factor. Finally, one could argue that compulsory schooling and child labor restrictions, the development of mass circulation newspapers, rising incomes, and the effects of rising parental literacy influenced signature rates primarily from the 1880s to the end of the century. The 10- to 15-percentage point rise in literacy that occurred during this period can then be allocated among these factors; at either extreme, one could reasonably attribute most of this rise either to increases in benefits or to policy measures, or as a middle ground estimate it can be attributed equally to changes in private incentives and in public policy.

The estimates presented in Table 8.4 vary widely in their upper and lower limits, due to uncertainty about their magnitudes, and they are admittedly quite provisional. Nevertheless, they do suggest that changes in both private benefits and public policy contributed significantly. For

Table 8.4

Estimates of the Contribution of Changes in Private Benefits and Public Policy to the Rise in English Literacy Rates, 1840-1900 (Percentage Points)

I. Total Change in Signature Rates, 1840-1900

Grooms	40
Brides	50

II. Contribution of Private Benefits and Public Policy to Increasing Literacy

Changes in literacy attributable to private benefits	
Shift to occupations more likely to use literacy	7 to 10
Rise of mass circulation newspapers and increased parental literacy	0 to 15
Total due to changes in private benefits	7 to 25
Changes in literacy attributable to public educational policy	
Improvements in the provision of subsidized schools	4 to 25
Compulsory schooling and child labor restrictions	0 to 15
Total due to changes in policy	4 to 40

example, changes in benefits could account for just over 60 percent of the increase in literacy that grooms experienced during the Victorian period, and changes in public policy could account for as much as 100 percent. But, the wide range in these estimates leaves open the possibility that one set of factors was far more important than the other; for example, the allocations reported in Table 8.4 indicate that changes in policy could have accounted for as much as 40 percentage points of the rise, and changes in benefits, as little 7 percentage points.

Nevertheless, consideration of the characteristics of each set of factors suggests that each made significant contributions. The pervasiveness of public policy has already been noted, and Part 2 of this study indicates that Victorian educational policy measures drew some response from the large segments of the population that they reached. Subsidized schools were not totally empty; compulsory schooling laws were not completely evaded. A smaller percentage of the Victorian population, especially of working-class families, may have perceived changes in the benefits of literacy, but they would have found these changes more decisive than changes in public policy. The prospect of raising one's wages by 10 percent or more per year for the rest of one's life provided far more incentive to acquire literacy than did the reduction of a few pennies a week in school fees or the imposition of a fine of a few shillings for truancy. The allocations reported in Table 8.4 suggest that at least 15 percent of the segment of Victorian society that had not yet acquired literacy (that is the 7 percentage point increase in job opportunities using literacy divided by the 50 percentage point rise in literacy for women) would have found improved job opportunities over the course of the Victorian period if they acquired literacy. A much larger percentage may have thought they had a chance of getting such opportunities. Surely, significant numbers in Victorian society became newly aware of the benefits that literacy could offer.

The benefits that literacy offered also provided important reinforcement for educational policy measures. Raising taxes for school boards and imposing fines on truants were considerably easier when the local population saw the value of education. Indeed, it may be that the million or so pounds a year the state sacrificed by repealing the stamp tax on newspapers ultimately accomplished more than the roughly similar amount it spent each year in the second half of the nineteenth century to provide schooling.[16] The availability of cheap newspapers offered direct positive incentives to learn to read and write. And, at least for those who read papers daily, the present value of the surplus they derived from the lower prices as estimated in Chapter 3 may well have exceeded the subsidy of a pound or so that each student in a state-funded school received.[17]

There is a final reason for emphasizing the contributions of both private demand and public policy to the rise of popular literacy. The division between public and private motives for raising literacy ultimately narrowed over the Victorian period. Social control or class hegemony may have motivated early Victorian educational policymakers.[18] But in the broadly based democracy that England was becoming in the Victorian period, the actual benefits the working classes received from education inevitably assumed increasing weight. As the working classes gained political power, educational policy was subject to increasing pressure to benefit the recipient as well as the provider.

There were alternative routes to the development of popular literacy than the balance between public policy and popular demand that emerged in Victorian England. In the United States the development of educational policy was subject to far more local control and thus possibly more popular influence than it was in Victorian England.[19] In seventeenth- and eighteenth-century Sweden and Prussia, the development of public policy was far more centralized and subject to less local influence than in Victorian England. Indeed, in these countries as well as in the Soviet Union, policy efforts were so intense as to have been labeled by some historians as literacy campaigns.[20] The case of Victorian England illustrates that near universal adult literacy could be achieved with a mix of public policy and popular demand intermediate between that of grass-roots popular support and an elite-sponsored literacy campaign.

Appendix A: Occupations Included in Each Category of Occupational Literacy Usage

Appendix A reports the specific occupational categories from W. A. Armstrong, "The Use of Information about Occupation," in *Nineteenth Century Society*, ed. E. A. Wrigley (Cambridge: Cambridge University Press, 1972), 255–81, that were included under each of the four categories of occupational literacy usage in Tables 2.1 and 2.2.

Literacy Required

All occupations classified under: Art and amusement (painting); education; industrial service sector—banking, insurance, accounts; literature; medicine; public service—administration (central and local); public service—police and prisons; religion; science.

Also these subclassifications: army officers; auctioneers, appraisers, valuers; brokers, agents, factors; commercial travellers; merchants; navy officers; salesmen and buyers.

Literacy Likely to be Useful

All occupations classified under: breeding; building sector—management; dealing sector—except buttermen, cheesemongers, coal heavers and laborers, cowkeepers, fruiterers, greengrocers, hawkers, hucksters and costers, milksellers, and potato dealers; manufacturing sector—copper, tin, lead; manufacturing sector—dyeing; manufacturing sector—furniture; manufacturing sector—gold, silver, jewelry; manufacturing sector—machinery; manufacturing sector—printing and bookbinding; manufacturing sector—shipbuilding; manufacturing sector—watches, instruments, and toys; transport sector—railways; transport sector—warehouses and docks, except harbor, dock, and lighthouse service.

Also these subclassifications: actors; blacksmiths; carpenters, joiners; coachmakers, railway carriage makers; farm bailiffs; farmers, graziers; mine service; musicians; ocean navigation—pilots.

Occupations with Possible (or Ambiguous) Use of Literacy

All occupations classified under: building sector—operative, except carpenters; domestic service—indoor service; land service; manufacturing sector—baking; manufacturing sector—chemical; manufacturing sector—coals and gas; manufacturing sector—earthenware; manufacturing sector—lace; manufacturing sector—sundries connected with dress; manufacturing sector—tools; manufacturing sector—unspecified; manufacturing sector—woodworkers; transport sector—roads.

Also these subclassifications: art, music, and theater service; billiards, cricket, and other games service; cheesemongers and buttermen; cooks; corn millers; curriers; farmers' sons, grandsons, nephews; fishmongers; gardeners; greengrocers, fruiters, potato dealers, milksellers and cowkeepers; nurserymen, seedsmen, and florists; performers, showmen, exhibition service; saddle, harness, and whip makers; wheelwrights.

Occupations Unlikely to Use Literacy

All occupations classified under: building sector—roadmaking; domestic service sector—extra service, except cooks; domestic service sector—outdoor service; manufacturing sector—cotton and silk; manufacturing sector—drink preparation; manufacturing sector—flax, hemp; manufacturing sector—floorcloth and waterproof; manufacturing sector—food preparation, except corn millers; manufacturing sector—furs and leather, except curriers; manufacturing sector—glue, tallow; manufacturing sector—hair; manufacturing sector—iron and steel, except blacksmiths; manufacturing sector—paper; manufacturing sector—smoking; mining sector, except mine service; public administration—army, except army officers; public administration—navy, except navy officers; transport sector—inland navigation; transport sector—ocean navigation, except pilots.

Also these subclassifications: agricultural laborers, farm servants; coal heavers and laborers; fishermen; general laborers; harbor, dock, wharf, and lighthouse service; hawkers, hucksters, costers; shepherds; town drainage and scavenging; woodmen.

Appendix B: The Sample of Marriage Registers and the Ranking of Occupations Reported in That Sample

Description of the Marriage Register Sample

One segment of the marriage register samples used in this study was designed to provide evidence on England as a whole. This segment of the sample consists of records of 4,208 marriages from the years 1839–43 and 3,959 marriages from the years 1869–73. Information from marriage certificates on the ability of brides and grooms to sign their names; occupations of brides, grooms, and their fathers; and ages of brides and grooms (where listed) was transcribed from microfilms in the Parish and Vital Records Collection for England, Genealogy Library, Salt Lake City, Utah. This sample was taken from twenty-nine of the forty-five counties of England and Wales distinguished by the Registrar General; the Genealogy Library did not have registers for the remaining sixteen counties. The twenty-nine counties in the sample are Bedford, Berkshire, Buckinghamshire, Cambridgeshire, Chestershire, Cornwall, Cumberland, Derbyshire, Durham, Gloucestershire, Hampshire, Hereford, Hertford, Lancashire, Leicestershire, Lincolnshire, London, Monmouth, Northumberland, Shropshire, Staffordshire, Suffolk, Surrey, Sussex, Warwickshire, Westmoreland, Wiltshire, Worcestershire, and the North Riding of Yorkshire. The sample was constructed so as to weight the proportion of samples taken from each county in England and Wales according to the proportion of the total population of England in that county. In addition to this national sample, additional samples of particular types of regions were taken and are referred to in the text.

The sample of twenty-nine counties is not a random sample of all marriage certificates from England and Wales for the two time periods in question. Not only was it necessary to omit sixteen counties, but samples of parishes from particular counties depended on availability in the

Genealogy Library. The counties defined by the Registrar General are arbitrary units for stratification, given the wide variation in social and economic conditions possible within a given county. The parishes used within each county both for the national sample and for the sample of particular types of regions are listed at the end of this section. In addition, the certificates contained in the Genealogy Library were largely from Church of England registers. Thus, no civil marriages were included in the sample. Civil marriages constituted 3 percent of all marriages in England and Wales in 1844 and 11 percent in 1874, but the incidence was considerably higher in some regions. For a further discussion of civil marriages, see Olive Anderson, "The Incidence of Civil Marriage in Victorian England and Wales," *Past and Present* 69 (1975): 50–87.

Nevertheless the twenty-nine-county sample does have features that suggest it is approximately representative of national conditions. First, the signature rates for the samples (used as measures of literacy rates) were in all cases within 4 percentage points of the signature rates for all brides and grooms married in England and Wales as reported by the Registrar General (see Table B.1). Another way of gauging the representativeness of the twenty-nine-county sample is to compare, for each of the two time periods, the proportions of grooms in broad sectors of the labor force in the twenty-nine-county sample with the proportions of males in those sectors in the nearest census for each of the two time periods (see Table B.2). The age distribution of grooms at marriage would have differed from that of the labor force as a whole, but one would not expect drastic differences in the distribution across basic sectors of the labor force for the two groups. Despite differences between the two sources, the relative importance of the various sectors of the labor force is similar.

LIST OF PARISHES IN THE TWENTY-NINE-COUNTY SAMPLE
OF MARRIAGE REGISTERS

Bedfordshire: Battlesden; Biggleswade; Caddington; Bedford, St. Cuthperts.

Berkshire: Abingdon; South Hinksey.

Buckinghamshire: Ashendon; Chearsley; Eton.

Cambridgeshire: Croxton; Eltisley.

Chestershire: Stockport; Disley, St. Mary, Stockport.

Cornwall: Bodmin; Blisland; Breage.

Cumberland: Alston; Bewcastle; Brampton; Carlisle, St. Cuthpert.

Derby: Ault Hucknall; Croxall; Edlaston; Heath; Long Eaton; North Wingfield; Pleaseley.

Table B.1

Signature Rates in the Marriage Register Sample and in the Registrar General's
Reports (Percentage Signing Their Names at Marriage)

	Marriage Register Sample	Registrar General's Report on All Marriages in England and Wales
Grooms		
1839-43	69.3	67.2
1869-73	82.5	80.6
Brides		
1839-43	53.6	51.0
1869-73	77.2	73.4

Notes and Sources: Signature rates for the sample were calculated from the proportion of
brides and grooms signing in the twenty-nine-county sample of marriage registers.
Signature rates reported by the Registrar General were taken from 7th ARRG (Abstract
for 1843), PP 1846, vol. 19, [727], 40-41; 32nd ARRG (Abstract for 1869), PP 1871,
vol. 15, [C.-453], ix; 33rd ARRG (Abstract for 1870), PP 1872, vol. 17, [C.667], xli;
34th ARRG (Abstract for 1871), PP 1873, vol. 20, [C.-806], lxvi; 35th ARRG (Abstract
for 1872), PP 1875, vol. 18, pt.I, [C.-1155], lxix; 36th ARRG (Abstract for 1873), PP
1875, vol.18, pt. I, [C.-1312], lxix.

Durham: Billingham; Esh; Haughton Le Skerne; Heworth; St. Andrew
Auckland.
Gloucestershire: Alderton; Arlingham; Berkeley; Brookthorpe; Bulley;
Leonard Stanley; Upleadon; Woodchester.
Hampshire: Bedhampton, St. Thomas; Farlington, St. Andrew; Havant;
Portchester; South Hayling; Wymering.
Herefordshire: Ashton Ingham; King's Pyon; Hertford; Hemel Hemp-
stead; Little Wymondley.
Kent: Deptford, St. Paul.
Lancashire: Blackley; Brindle; Bury; Chorley; Church Kirk; Cockerham;
Croston; Didsbury, St. James; Gorton; Great Harwood; Hindley;
Leyland; Liverpool, St. Nicholas; Manchester, Blackley Chapel;
Manchester, Cathedral; Preston; St. Michael on Wyre; West Derby.

Table B.2

Occupational Distribution of Grooms in the Marriage Register Sample and of the Male Labor Force in Census Reports

Occupational Sector	1839-43 Marriage Register Sample	1841 Census	1869-73 Marriage Register Sample	1871 Census
Agriculture and general labor	34.0	35.0	32.4	28.3
Mining	6.4	4.6	8.4	6.5
Manufacturing and construction	35.5	37.3	34.0	38.6
Transport	4.5	3.3	5.9	7.2
Dealing	9.4	6.6	8.7	9.2
Public Service, professional, aristocracy	6.0	8.0	6.9	8.4
Domestic service	4.2	5.2	4.0	1.8

Note: Occupational distributions for marriage registers were tabulated from occupations reported by grooms in the sample of marriage registers. Occupational distributions for census reports were calculated from the summaries in W. A. Armstrong, "Information about Occupation" in *Nineteenth Century Society*, Table A, 255-81.

Leicestershire: Coston; Dunton Bassett; Goadby near Market; Harborough; Humberstone; Keyham; Loughborough, All Saints; Ratby.

Lincolnshire: Claxby by Normanby; Coleby in Kesteven; Holbeach; Stainton Le Vale; Waddingworth.

London: All Hallows, London Wall; Christ Church, St. Leonard's Foster Lane; St. Benet's in Paul's Wharf; St. Dunstan in the East; St. Helen's Bishopsgate; St. Lawrence Jewry and St. Mary; Magdalene Milk Street; St. Mary Somerset; St. Mary the Virgin, Aldermanbury; St. Michael Bassishaw; St. Olave, Hart Street.

Middlesex: Enfield, St. Andrew; Feltham; Friern Barnet; Great Stanmore; Harmondsworth, St. Mary; Hoxton, Christ Church; Isleworth; Stepney, St. Thomas; Sunbury.

Monmouth: Llanfihangel-Tor-Y-Mynnydd.

Northumberland: Corsenside; Haltwhistle; Kirkharle; Kirknewton; Long Horsley.

Shropshire: Bitterley; Cheswardine; Church Preen; Cressage; Edgmond; Hughley; Kenley; Leaton by Shrewsbury; Long Stanton; Melverley; Sheinton; Shipton.

Staffordshire: Betley; Bushbury; Castle Church; Codsall; Elford; Grindon; Keele; Lichfield, Christ Church; Longdon by Lichfield; Maer; Newbourough; Pattingham.

Suffolk: Denham near Bury St. Edmunds; Felixstowe; Grundisburgh; Nacton; Nedging; Tostock.

Surrey: Abinger; Banstead; Bermondsey, St. Mary Magdalene; Bermondsey, St. Olave; Lambeth; Richmond, St. Mary.

Sussex: Cowfold.

Warwickshire: Ansty; Bearley; Brinklowe; Hampton in Arden; Knowle; Solihull; Weddington; Wolfhamcote; Wootton Wawen.

Westmoreland: Crosby Garrett; Crosby Ravensworth.

Wiltshire: Bremhill; Overton; Southbroom, St. James.

Worcestershire: Belbroughton; Broadway; Churchill in Oswaldslow; Doddenham; Eastham; Knightwick.

Yorkshire: Arkendale; Barningham; Bowes; Clapham; Coverham with Horsehouse; Eston; Grinton in Swaledale; Ingleton; Nidd; Sedbergh.

In addition to the twenty-nine-county sample of marriage registers just described, marriage registers were also sampled from certain types of regions within England in order to examine how specific regional circumstances influenced literacy.

LIST OF PARISHES IN THE SAMPLE OF SPECIAL TYPES OF REGIONS, BY COUNTY

Agricultural Regions

Buckinghamshire: Beaconsfield; Chetwode; Great Kimble; Great Missenden; Lane End; Latimer; Little Kimble.

Cumberland: Bridekirk; Castle Carrock; Croglin; Crosby upon Eden; Cumrew; Cumwhitten; Great Orton; Kirk near Penrith; Lanercost.

Hertfordshire: Chipping Barnet; King's Walden; Stanstead Abbots; Tring; Willian.

Wiltshire: Chippenham.

Industrial Districts

Worcestershire: Halesowen.

Lancashire: Bury.

Mining Districts

Durham: Gateshead.

Cornwall: Constantine; Gulval; Kenwyn.

Commercial and Maritime District
Hampshire: Catherington; Chalton; Clanfield; North Hayling; Yateley.

Mixed Industrial, Agricultural, Commercial Districts
Bedfordshire: Apsley Guise; Bedford, St. Cuthpert; Bedford, St. Paul; Bedford, St. Peter; Bedford, St. Peter Martin; Biggleswade; Eaton Socon; Goldington; Leighton Buzzard; Lidlington; Luton; Marston Moretaine; Maulden; Meppershall; Northill; Odell; Potsgrove; Roxton; Sundon; Tempsford; Upper Stondon; Woburn; Wootton.
Staffordshire: Edingale; Elford; Lichfield Cathedral; Newcastle under Lyme, St. Giles; Rocester; Sheen; Stafford, St. Chad; Stafford, St. Mary's; Stowe.
Warwickshire: Barford; Caldecote; Wroxhall.
Worcestershire: Norton Juxta Kempsey; Stoke Prior; Tardebigge, St. Bartholomew; Upton Snodsbury; Whitehaven, St. Michael; Worcester, St. Albans.

Ranking Occupations

To rank occupations reported in the marriage register sample, the five-category hierarchy of occupations proposed by the Registrar General's office is used in this study. This ranking scheme is described in W. A. Armstrong, "The Use of Information about Occupation, Part 1. A Basis for Social Stratification," in *Nineteenth Century Society. Essays in the Use of Quantitative Methods for the Study of Social Data*, ed. E. A. Wrigley (Cambridge: Cambridge University Press, 1972), 198–214. The five categories used in this study are similar to those described in Armstrong but with some modifications. They can briefly be described as follows:

   I: Those of aristocratic status, including gentlemen, esquires, and military officers
  II: Professional and administrative occupations, farmers, commercial occupations except those involving little capital
 III: Skilled manual occupations and petty commercial occupations
  IV: Semiskilled manual occupations
   V: Unskilled labor

A variety of sources, including the *Oxford English Dictionary*, occupational dictionaries issued by the census office, and parliamentary reports, were used to classify occupations. Such a classification is not totally objective and involves some use of judgment. Contemporary sources were used as much as possible in classification. Of a total of 4,208 marriage records in the 1839–43 sample, 195 were excluded either because no occupation was reported or because the occupation could not clearly be assigned to a category. Of 3,959 observations in the 1869–73 sample, 190 were excluded for these reasons.

Appendix C: Estimating the Consumer's Surplus from Books, Newspapers, and the Mails

If the typical consumer is assumed to have had a linear demand curve, then a simple formula can be used to estimate the consumer's surplus derived from the price fall.[1] Define P^H as the maximum price at which any of the product would be purchased or what could also be defined as the entry price for using. Define P^L as the price after the price fall and Q^L as the yearly quantity of the product the consumer would purchase at the price after the decline. Then the consumer's surplus from a given product whose price had fallen is given by:

$$(1/2) \times (P^H - P^L) \times Q^L.$$

This expression would indicate the net annual value to the consumer of access to the skills needed to use the product.

The lifetime present value of access to the product can be estimated by specifying how many years the flow of value was received and the rate at which future consumption was discounted relative to present consumption. Define n as the number of years that the product was used and r as the rate at which future consumption was discounted relative to the present. Assume that the annual flow of value was constant over time. Then the lifetime present value of the series of annual flows with continuous compounding was:

$$(1/2) \times (P^H - P^L) \times Q^L \times \left(\frac{1 - e^{-rn}}{r} \right).[2]$$

For an individual the total value of literacy induced by price falls from a variety of products would be the sum of present values from all the different products involved:

$$\sum_i (1/2) \times (P_i^H - P_i^L) \times Q_i^L \times \left(\frac{1 - e^{-rn}}{r} \right).$$

There are four reasons why this last expression might overstate the value of the consumer's surplus from the products under consideration. First, P^H and Q^L may have differed for those consumers who would have acquired literacy when the products were sold for P^H and those who would have been induced to acquire literacy by the fall in price of the products. Nothing definite can be said a priori about the direction of difference. But perhaps the most plausible possibility is that intended consumption at any given price and the price at which that consumption would begin was greater for the consumer who was already literate before the price fall. Such a consumer would have more familiarity with using literacy and perhaps greater knowledge of the full benefits of using literacy-related products.

Second, the annual flow of value from using the products may have risen over time for the consumer, both because of rising use with the life cycle and because of secular trends increasing the use of literacy-related products. If the expression above was an estimate for the average value over the consumer's life, then this average would have been pulled up by later consumption, which in fact the consumer would have discounted relative to consumption earlier in life.

Third, the summation procedure assumes either that the demand for each of the products was independent of the prices of the others, or that the prices fell in sequence. If the prices changed simultaneously and there were significant substitution effects, then this procedure will overstate gains from the price falls.[3] In fact it was likely that use of the mails was independent of the price of reading materials. Although books and newspapers may have been substitutes, the large fall in the price of books came before some of the critical fall in the price of newspapers.[4] This would reduce the extent of overestimate.

Finally, sharing or borrowing reading materials was probably common, in which case the cost of purchase would overstate the value received.

All of these biases reinforce the emphasis in the text on the modest value derived from using books, newspapers and the mails. In the absence of evidence that their magnitude was large, however, the existence of these biases does not preclude the conclusion in the text that in many situations the value derived from using books, newspapers, and the mails may have exceeded the costs of acquiring literacy.

Newspapers and Periodicals

The upper limits for annual reading Q^L for newspapers and periodicals were probably set by the 365 annual issues for a given daily newspaper and the 52 annual issues for a given weekly. These limits could have been exceeded through reading more than one publication per day or week. This was surely not a common practice for the working-class reader, however. Indeed, some accounts suggest that until the 1880s or 1890s, working-class readers primarily read weeklies rather than dailies.[5] It also appears that reading newspapers or at least daily newspapers did not become a nearly universal practice among working-class readers until after World War I. For an intermediate range, values for Q^L of one hundred and two hundred papers per year—roughly semi-weekly and every other day—will be used. For a lower limit, a value for Q^L of twenty papers per year—roughly every third week—will be used.

The plausible upper limit for P^H, the maximum price a working-class reader would pay for a newspaper, is given by the four-pence maximum price at which working-class newspapers sold in the 1830s and 1840s. This entry price was probably far less than four pence for many working-class readers, however. This is suggested by evidence of frequent multiple readership of a single copy. Estimates for the extent of such multiple readership per copy have ranged from as low as three or four readers per copy to ten or more.[6] Indeed, with multiple readership some readers of a newspaper could have been unwilling to pay anything at all for the newspaper. Such readers may have persisted after the fall in prices. Furthermore, even after the stamp tax on newspapers was reduced to a penny, Francis Place found widespread support in arguing that "the last penny was the worst penny" in deterring working-class purchase of newspapers.[7] The actual price after the price fall, P^L, was as low as a halfpenny, and halfpenny papers became increasingly common in the second half of the nineteenth century.[8] Thus, values of P^H of two pence and a penny will also be considered.

Books

It is not beyond the realm of possibility that some working-class readers devoured three or four novels a day or paid out thirty shillings for a new copy of *Ivanhoe* in the 1830s; Such occurrences were surely quite rare, however. Some guidance on usage after the 1830–50 price reductions—that is Q^L—is provided by Flora Thompson's description of the reading habits in the 1880s of women in her Oxfordshire hamlet.[9] Thompson suggests that each woman purchased a penny novelette each week, implying purchases of fifty-two per year. Thompson's description refers to swapping among readers, suggesting that an avid reader in a situation where reading matter could not be exchanged would have purchased even more. Other accounts of active working-class readers of novelettes suggest roughly a weekly purchase or at least a weekly reading. Florence Bell, in her survey of Middleborough in the early twentieth century, mentions one couple "all very fond of reading and [who] get books from the library every week."[10] John Leigh, in his description of what working-class people read in four Lancashire towns in the early twentieth century, refers to novelette purchases on roughly a weekly basis.[11] Richard Jeffries refers to city readers obtaining "their weekly London novelette."[12] Jeffries also suggests, however, that books and novelettes were still difficult to obtain for country readers in the last quarter of the nineteenth century.

Based on this description, fifty-two books will be used as an estimate for Q^L for an avid working-class reader in the nineteenth century. Many in the working classes were clearly less than avid in their reading habits. Bell's survey indicated that only one-fourth of working-class readers in the city she examined read books as well as newspapers, one-half read only newspapers, and one-fourth read nothing at all.[13] She suggests that women were even more infrequent readers than men.[14] But Leigh's survey suggests that novelettes were read with as much if not more frequency than newspapers.[15] This would suggest allowing for one segment of readers that read novelettes and other inexpensive books and pamphlets with the frequency of one per week, and for another segment that made little or no use of such material.

Especially avid working-class readers might have purchased the five-shilling reprints aimed at the middle classes, and so five shillings will be used here as an upper limit to P^H. Mayhew reports that used books aimed at working-class readers in London sold for one or two shillings, and he asserts that working-class readers would not have bought these books new.[16] So one to two shillings is definitely in the range of possibility as an entry price for London. Jefferies also suggested such a range for rural villages: "Books intended for the villages must be cheap. . . . Six-pence, a shilling, eighteenpence; nothing must be more than two shillings, and a shilling should be the general maximum. For a shilling how many clever little books are on sale on London bookstalls!"[17] The entry price for many was perhaps even lower.

One ambiguity concerns what type of publication should be considered. According to Victor Neuberg, penny and halfpenny chapbooks were being sold in the eighteenth century.[18] But such literature would be eight pages or so. Longer material of twenty pages or more does not seem to have made its way onto the streets before the early nineteenth century for under sixpence.[19] Referring to fiction selling for one shilling in the early nineteenth century, Neuberg states that this was "a price clearly beyond the reach of those who had to think twice before laying out a copper or two on a street ballad or a lurid piece of fiction."[20] And Charles Knight said of nonfiction aimed at a popular audience, "The millions were not ready to buy such books at a shilling, nor even at six-pence."[21] Thus, values for P^H of sixpence and threepence will be considered. The lower range for book prices after 1850—that is, P^L—would seem to be the one to six pence charged for pamphlets and novelettes with one-penny purchases perhaps more common than sixpenny ones.[22] In fact, some novelettes went for as little as a half penny.[23] Thus, values for P^L of six, three, and one half pence will be considered.

Letters

Postal statistics indicate that in 1881, 40 letters per capita were delivered. This could translate into as many as 144 letters per literate adult.[24] However, a disproportionate amount of the annual volume of letters was almost surely accounted for by the middle and upper classes as well as by commercial mail. Flora Thompson provides some guidance on working-class letter-writing patterns in the 1880s. In describing her village, she referred to young men writing weekly love letters and to daughters in domestic service sending home money once a month. She also referred to the postman telling one hamlet resident particularly eager for mail that she had received a letter "just last week." Jefferies, in his 1884 description of country reading habits, also suggests relatively infrequent receipt of letters in rural areas:

> A townsman picks up twenty letters, snatches the envelopes open, and casts them aside. The letters delivered in the countryside have marvellously multiplied but still the country people do not treat letters offhand. The arrival of a letter or two is still an event; it is read twice or three times, put in the pocket, and looked at again. Suburban residents receive circulars by every post of every kind and description, and cast them contemptuously aside. In the country the delivery of a circular is not so treated. It is certain to be read.[25]

An estimate of average delivery in the hamlet can be made from Thompson's statement that for the entire hamlet consisting of about thirty cottages, daily delivery was "at best 2 or 3 letters."[26] Assuming 250 delivery days per year, Thompson's statement would suggest a maximum delivery of 750 letters per year for the hamlet, or 25 per household. Thus, Thompson's statement would suggest that an upper limit for Q^L was probably no more than 100 letters (or two per week), with few working-class households receiving more than one letter per week. The rising use of the halfpenny postcard at the end of the century may have increased this frequency. David Vincent, as mentioned in the text, refers to one case where cards were exchanged a number of times per day. But it remains to be shown that such a practice was common.[27] Five letters per year will be used as a lower bound for Q^L. If the frequency was lower than this, the inconvenience or expense of getting others to read and write letters would have been insignificant.

Rowland Hill, as mentioned in the text, estimated the average charge for a letter in the 1830s at 6.25 pence per letter.[28] This was probably toward the upper limit for P^H since contemporary reports indicate that the working classes were not willing to pay prevailing postal rates at this time. Thus, more intermediate entry prices should also be considered. After the postal reform, a letter could cost as little as a penny to send anywhere in England. After 1870, postcards could be sent for a halfpenny. Thus, between a penny and a halfpenny is the range considered for P^L.[29] Another indication of the consumer's surplus from being able to write (and perhaps to read) letters over and above postage is the charge commonly made for writing letters for others. A street stationer interviewed by Mayhew indicated that he charged one or two pence for writing letters for others, although for a very poor person he charged nothing.[30]

Years the Flow of Value Was Received

The number of years the flow of value from using a literacy-related product would have been received can be taken to be the same as the years of life remaining once literacy had been acquired. During the period 1839–54, according to estimates by Warren Thompson, a ten-year-old boy in England and Wales could expect to live to age 47 and a ten-year-old girl to age 47.7.[31] For the period 1891–1900, according to Thompson's estimates, a ten-year-old boy could expect to live to age 49.6 and a ten-year-old girl to age 52. Thus, Thompson's estimates indicate that if literacy was acquired at age ten, a person in the nineteenth century acquiring literacy could expect to receive benefits from it for an average of thirty-five to forty years. To allow for variation in expectations, benefit streams will be considered here ranging from twenty-five to fifty years.

Internal Discount Rate

The rate at which working-class families would have discounted future consumption was subject to considerable variation. Middle-class observers in the late nineteenth century commonly criticized the working classes for their improvidence; one commented that "their mental horizon tends to be limited to a stretch of seven days."[32] Paul Johnson, however, has recently argued that such critics misunderstood working-class consumption strategies. For example, he points out that consumer durables were used as a source of liquidity at the pawn shop and that there was a lack of acceptable financial outlets for saving. His discussion suggests a wide range of possible discount rates for future relative to present consumption.[33] Postal savings banks in the late nineteenth century paid only 2.5 percent.[34] The rate on consol bonds in the nineteenth century ranged from 3 to 5 percent.[35] Legislation controlling pawnshops effectively set a nominal annual interest rate between 20 and 25 percent, depending on the size of the loan.[36] But the effective interest charge on a good pawned and redeemed week by week throughout the year would have come to 260 percent per year. And the annual interest rates charged by moneylenders could exceed 400 percent per year.[37] The willingness to accept such exorbitant credit charges would suggest an extremely high rate of time preference. But Johnson has suggested that loans or pawns at such rates were usually not continued throughout the year. Instead such loans were usually obtained during temporary periods when cash was especially short.[38]

To allow for a wide range of possible attitudes toward future consumption, four discount rates will be considered. The lowest discount rate will be for a thrifty consumer and will be set at 5 percent. For a consumer with a moderate rate of preference for present consumption, the discount rate will be set at 25 percent. A consumer with a high rate of preference for the present will be assigned a discount rate of 50 percent. Finally, a consumer will be considered who would have discounted consumption past the current year down to a value of zero. Once the discount rate exceeded 100 percent, as Johnson suggests it may have, the consumer would seem to be placing close to a negligible value on any future consumption relative to the present.

Calculations of the consumer's surplus gain at various life expectancies and discount rates demonstrate that life expectancy had a relatively small effect on the present value of the consumer's surplus gain, while the discount rate had a major impact.[39] Life expectancy only had a noticable influence at low discount rates. When the discount rate was 5 percent, increasing life expectancy from 25 to 50 years increased the present value by a third. But at higher discount rates, the values derived from additional years of life were discounted too heavily relative to the present to have any significant impact on present value. At a 25-percent discount rate, the effect of increasing life expectancy was negligible. Even at a 10-percent discount rate, doubling life expectancy in this manner only increased the present value by about 10 percent. On the other hand, raising the discount rate from 5 percent to 25 percent cut the present value by about three-quarters. Johnson suggests that many families may have faced short-term credit rates of 25 percent or higher, although the longer term trade-off may have been at a lower discount rate.[40]

Appendix D: The Costs and Benefits of Acquiring Literacy in Victorian England

To assess the impact of the various changes in English society in the second half of the nineteenth century that could have influenced the acquisition of literacy, one can begin by weighing the costs and benefits of acquiring literacy. Since benefits and costs were accrued over time, literacy should be viewed as a capital asset. The perspective taken here will be that of a person on the verge of acquiring literacy, and the discounting of costs and benefits will be taken back to that point. It should be kept in mind that a person's acquisition of literacy was not strictly the result of an either/or decision; it could frequently result from a sequence of decisions as to how regularly to attend school. It should also be noted that the costs of children becoming literate were likely to have been incurred primarily by their parents, while the benefits of literacy were received by the children themselves. The parents could have received indirect benefits in the form of enhanced support in old age, and they would also naturally take an altruistic interest in the future prospects of their children. Still the probability that different parties were incurring the costs than were receiving the benefits would have muted the impact of a given level of benefits relative to costs. No direct allowance is made for secular changes in costs or benefits, although, as note 2 to Chapter 8 indicates, the estimates reported in Tables 8.1 through 8.3 encompass the likely range that occurred during the Victorian period.

The Costs of Acquiring Literacy

Tuition Costs

The basic determinants of tuition costs would have been the length of time school was attended, whether the school was subsidized, and the level of school fees in subsidized and unsubsidized schools. The present value of tuition costs would also be influenced by the discount rate used.

Chapters 5 and 6 provided evidence on fees in subsidized and unsubsidized schools. In the 1850s, mean fees in subsidized schools were approximately two pence per week and in unsubsidized schools roughly sixpence per week. Although access to subsidized schooling was the most visible source of variation in school fees, it should be noted that fees in subsidized schools could commonly range from one to four pence per week and in unsubsidized schools from four to eight pence per week.

The length of time a child had to attend school to acquire literacy would have depended on the degree of mastery desired, the aptitude of the student, and the quality of the school. A number of sources provide guidance on the likely range of time required in school in order to master basic reading and writing skills, although this time is inherently subject to uncertainty and variability. In the 1831 Kerry Commission inquiry, the director of a teachers' training college stated that in twelve months of school attendance, a student could learn "to read well and write tolerably."[1] This testimony is consistent with recent statements by directors of adult literacy campaigns in developing countries.[2] Because both the nineteenth- and the twentieth-century directors just cited were promoters of literacy projects, however, they were perhaps prone to be optimistic; their statements should thus be regarded as presenting lower-bound estimates of school time required to acquire literacy.

At the other extreme, six years seems to have been the usual upper limit for working-class schooling in the nineteenth century. The curriculum guidelines as set down by the Department of Education allowed for six levels of instruction; each level, referred to as a "standard," was comparable to a year of attendance. Although after 1870 additional standards were introduced, they primarily involved training in specialized subjects. Even Standard VI often involved specialized subjects, although the basic level of competence involved literacy skills.[3] The 1862 Revised Code (the guidelines and regulations established by the Department of Education for curriculums and for distributing grants) provided that scholars examined in Standard VI should be able to both read and write from slow dictation short paragraphs from a newspaper and to do "a sum in practice or bills of parcels." Although some scholars could have taken longer than six years to reach Standard-VI proficiency, a minority of scholars do seem to have reached this level. Throughout the nineteenth century, of all scholars examined in any year, under 5 percent were examined at the Standard-VI level, compared with the 8 to 9 percent that should have been examined if over half of all students were passing through Standard VI.

Three years can tentatively be taken as the average amount of time a working-class child needed to master basic reading and writing skills. According to the Revised Code, a student examined in Standard III was supposed to be able to read a short paragraph from an elementary reading book, write a sentence dictated from the same, and do a "sum in any simple rule as far as short division."[4] It seems reasonable to consider the student who could accomplish these tasks to be literate. Standard III was considered by the public and by the authors of child labor and compulsory schooling legislation as the proper stopping point for the average scholar, with only the more apt proceeding further. Many students took longer than three years to attain Standard III competence, and in general, students could vary greatly in the amount of time they took to reach a given level of competence. Allowance must also be made for variation in attendance within a given school year. The Newcastle Commission report indicated that out of a forty-four-week school year, the mean number of weeks attended was twenty-five, though with considerable dispersion around this mean.[5]

Based on this evidence, a plausible lower-bound estimate of the length of time a student had to attend school full time in order to acquire literacy is forty weeks (the twenty-five-week average reported by the Newcastle Commission would almost surely not have been sufficient to acquire literacy in one year); a plausible upper-bound estimate is six years of attendance at forty weeks per year; and a plausible average estimate is three years of twenty-five weeks each.

Opportunity Costs

The opportunity costs of acquiring literacy were determined by the length of time required to acquire literacy as well as by the value per unit of time, which would have depended, among other things, on the age at which literacy was acquired and the prevailing wage rate in the region in question.

One indicator of the value of children's time was the prevailing wage rates for child labor. It was noted in a previous chapter that wage rates for child labor rose markedly with age. Thus, to measure properly the value of time sacrificed to attend school, the ages at which school was typically attended should also be considered. The evidence presented in Chapter 7 indicated that in the 1840s wages for children aged eight to ten ranged from one to three shillings per week, with an average of two shillings per week, while wages for children aged ten to thirteen ranged from one and a half to five shillings per week, with an average of four shillings per week. The census evidence considered in a previous chapter indicated that school attendance peaked at ages seven through nine, with attendance rates almost as high for those aged five, six, ten, and eleven.

The amount of time used to acquire literacy was discussed above in the section on tuition costs. When opportunity costs are considered, the ages when school was attended must also be discussed. First, the wages children could earn rose with their age. By attending school between ages five and eight, a child could conceivably acquire basic literacy without incurring any significant opportunity costs because few opportunities for employment existed at these ages. As noted in the text, an adult was likely to have had a far higher opportunity cost than a child, even if the adult obtained instruction during leisure hours. But by the mid-Victorian period, as Chapter 6 indicated and as noted in the text above, literacy instruction was primarily obtained during childhood.

It is also likely that younger children received far less literacy training than did older children, however. Many observers stated that infant and dame schools aimed at children under age eight were primarily providing child-minding services; these reports suggest that, at best, a child would emerge from such schools with a cursory knowledge of the alphabet. It is also reasonable to suppose that a child who attended school for any length of time past age eight, when a positive opportunity cost would have been present, would be more likely to retain and reinforce any literacy training he or she had obtained earlier. Regression results in Chapter 7 suggested the importance of school attendance after age ten relative to before age ten for the acquisition of literacy. Thus, it seems that allowance should be made for at least one year of time spent in school after age eight, when the child's time would have had a positive value in the labor market.

A school year could consist of fewer weeks than a work year for a child fully employed. The formal school year was commonly forty-four weeks, with average attendance at around twenty-five weeks. Employment in textile factories, however, seems to have involved over fifty weeks per year.[6] The question arises, then, of whether the opportunity costs of schooling consisted only of time directly in school or also of lost employment opportunities during the remaining part of the year. The answer to this question depends on whether work was available on a part-year basis, on the difference in wages between full-year and part-year work, and on the value placed on either leisure or work in the household. In agricultural regions and in London, most children's work was seasonal or casual, and earnings from the fraction of the year the children were not in school did not have to be sacrificed. In textile areas, employers appeared to favor the child who would be available for the full work year. But evidence considered in Chapter 7 suggested that even in textile areas, casual work outside the mills was available at only slightly lower wages and that the value of the child's work at home could exceed the going wage at the mill. Thus, the existence of casual and seasonal work and the value of household work and leisure suggest that only time spent in school was an opportunity cost.

Although the percentage variation in present values for opportunity costs was not as great as for direct costs, the absolute range was greater. Indeed, under any set of assumptions, opportunity costs dominated direct costs in importance. This is apparent from the commonsense observation made by a number of nineteenth-century observers that school fees were measured in pence while opportunity costs were measured in shillings.

The Pecuniary Benefits of Acquiring Literacy

The value of the conceivable pecuniary benefits from acquiring literacy varied widely. In Chapter 2, it was found that for a substantial proportion of literate workers the ex post premium for literacy was zero. Yet, at least some workers could have obtained a premium associated with acquiring literacy of fifteen shillings a week or more; for example, a male worker could have doubled his earnings by advancing from a fifteen-shilling-per-week job as an agricultural laborer to a thirty-shilling-per-week position as a clerk. Between these extremes, a premium in the range of two to five shillings per week was probably quite common. The ex post difference between literate and illiterate sons of laborers in 1839–43 was estimated in Chapter 2 at two shillings per week, an average that included those receiving no apparent wage premium whatever. And, a worker could realistically anticipate that by learning to read and write he could advance from being an unskilled laborer to being a semiskilled worker or petty artisan, and his earnings could then rise by between five and ten shillings per week.[7]

The range of weekly premiums commonly associated with literacy was probably similar for females. The ex post premium for literacy estimated for daughters of laborers was one shilling per week. A premium of five shillings per week was possible if, by learning to read and write, a woman advanced from work as a farm laborer or unskilled manufacturing worker to work as a dressmaker or housekeeper. Even a premium of ten shillings was conceivable if a woman could advance to a position as cook or housekeeper in a prominent household or as a certificated teacher.[8] Many women may have been in the labor force only from the time they left school until they married. This interval would have been ten to fifteen years, if they left school between the ages of ten and fifteen and married at about age twenty-five.

Notes

ABBREVIATIONS:

AR   "Annual Report of the Committee of Council on Education"
ARRG *Annual Report of the Registrar General of Births, Deaths, and Marriages in England and Wales*
PP   *House of Commons Sessional Papers*

Preface

1. For assessments of early modern literacy rates, see Harvey Graff, *Legacies of Literacy* (Bloomington: Indiana University Press, 1987), chap. 4; and R. A. Houston, *Literacy in Early Modern Europe* (London: Longman, 1988), 150–54.

2. See Graff, *Legacies of Literacy*, chap. 7.

3. On the economic consequences of literacy, see Mary Jean Bowman and C. Arnold Anderson, "Concerning the Role of Education in Development," in *Old Societies and New States: The Quest for Modernity in Africa and Asia*, ed. Clifford Geertz (Glencoe, Ill.: Free Press, 1963), 247–79; Richard Easterlin, "Why Isn't the Whole World Developed?" *Journal of Economic History* 41 (1981): 1–19; Lars Sandberg, "Ignorance, Poverty and Economic Backwardness in the Early Stages of European Industrialization: Variations on Alexander Gerschenkron's Grand Theme," *Journal of European Economic History* 11 (1982): 675–97; and Rondo Cameron, "A New View of European Industrialization," *Economic History Review* 2d ser., 38 (1985): 1–23. On the relation of mass schooling to the delineation of social classes, see Samuel Bowles and Herbert Gintis, *Schooling in Capitalist America* (New York: Basic Books, 1976); R. K. Webb, *The British Working Class Reader 1790–1848: Literacy and Social Tension* (London: Allen and Unwin, 1955); and Richard Johnson, "Notes on the Schooling of the English Working Class, 1780–1850," in *Schooling and Capitalism: A Sociological Reader*, ed. Roger Dale, Geoff Esland, and Madeleaine MacDonald (London: Routledge and Kegan Paul, 1976), 44–54.

4. For an example of the use of literacy rates to establish social status, see Eric Hobsbawm, "The Labour Aristocracy in Nineteenth-Century Britain," in *Labouring Men: Studies in the History of Labour*, ed. Eric Hobsbawm (London: Wiedenfeld and Nicolson, 1964), 311–15.

5. For surveys of traditional approaches to educational history see Harold Silver, "Aspects of Neglect: The Strange Case of Victorian Popular Education,"

Oxford Review of Education 3 (1977): 57–69; and John E. Talbott, "The History of Education," *Daedalus* 100 (1971): 133–50.

6. For a survey of trends in the public provision of mass education, see David Mitch, "The Rise of Popular Literacy in Europe," in *The Political Construction of Education: The State, School Expansion, and Economic Change*, ed. Bruce Fuller and Richard Rubinson (New York: Praeger, 1992).

7. For surveys illustrating this point, see Silver, "Aspects of Neglect"; and Ira Katznelson and Margaret Weir, *Schooling for All: Class, Race, and the Decline of the Democratic Ideal* (Berkeley: University of California Press, 1985), chap. 1.

8. The distinction between public and private used in this study is similar to the distinction between corporate and primary actors used by John Craig in "The Expansion of Education," in *Review of Research in Education*, vol. 9, ed. David C. Berliner (Washington, D.C.: American Educational Research Association, 1981), 157, 167–68. According to Craig, "corporate actors [are] organized groups united by a shared and self-conscious commitment to specific goals: to egalitarian reform, economic growth, national integration, social control, or whatever . . . primary actors [are] defined either as discrete individuals or . . . groups, notably the family, that are organized on the basis of primary rather than secondary relationships and hence have diffuse rather than specific functions." The distinctions are similar in their focus on primary versus secondary relationships. They differ, however, in that the public-private distinction focuses on the difference between the general public interest versus those of particular individuals whereas the corporate-primary distinction focuses on specific versus diffuse functions.

9. See, for example, "Census of Gt. Britain, 1851, Education," PP 1852–3, vol. 90, [1692], xliv. The Education Act of 1870 gave a more restricted definition of a public elementary school as a school that did not place certain requirements on students for religious worship or instruction but that did meet conditions for receiving parliamentary grants even if not actually receiving such grants. See AR 1870–71, PP 1871, vol. 22, [C.-406], xxii–xxiii.

10. On the contrast yet similarity between progressive and revisionist accounts, see Katznelson and Weir, *Schooling for All*, chap. 1; Silver, "Aspects of Neglect," 23–29 ; and Konrad Jarausch, "The Old 'New History of Education': A German Reconsideration," *History of Education Quarterly* 26 (1986): 225–41.

11. For studies emphasizing this theme, see Mary Jo Maynes, *Schooling in Western Europe* (Albany: State University of New York Press, 1985); Ben Eklof, *Russian Peasant Schools* (Berkeley: University of California Press, 1986); and E. G. West, "Resource Allocation and Growth in Early British Education," *Economic History Review*, 2d ser., 23 (1970): 69–95.

12. See Katznelson and Weir, *Schooling for All;* and William Reese, *Power and the Promise of School Reform: Grass-roots Movements during the Progressive Era* (Boston: Routledge and Kegan Paul, 1986).

13. See, for example, Eklof, *Russian Peasant Schools;* Maynes, *Schooling in Western Europe;* John S. Hurt, *Elementary Schooling and the Working Classes 1860–1918* (London: Routledge and Kegan Paul, 1979); and Grace Belfiore,

"Family Strategies in Essex Textile Towns 1860–1895: The Challenge of Compulsory Elementary Schooling" (D. Phil. thesis, Oxford University, 1987).

14. See E. G. West, "Educational Slowdown and Public Intervention in Nineteenth-Century England," *Explorations in Economic History* 12 (1975): 61–85; Phil Gardner, *The Lost Elementary Schools of Victorian England* (London: Croom Helm, 1984).

15. See, for example, David Vincent, *Literacy and Popular Culture: England 1750–1914* (Cambridge: Cambridge University Press, 1989); and Eklof, *Russian Peasant Schools*.

16. For surveys of official motives for public education, see Houston, *Literacy in Early Modern Europe*, 40–48; and Maynes, *Schooling in Western Europe*, chap. 3.

17. For essays emphasizing this theme, see Katznelson and Weir, *Schooling for All*; Reese, *Power and Promise*; David Hogan, review of *Ethnic Differences*, by Joel Perlman, *History of Education Quarterly* 30 (1990): 108–12; and David Hogan, "Making It in America: Work, Education, and Social Structure," in *Work, Youth, and Schooling*, ed. Harvey Kantor and David Tyack (Stanford: Stanford University Press), 142–79.

18. For summaries of the key features and issues involved in the Baker plan, see "Newsfocus: Education Reform Act," *Times Educational Supplement*, 29 July 1988, pp. 9–12.

19. For one influential statement of the case for choice and competition in school provision, and a survey of educational issues in the United States in the late 1980s and early 1990s, see John Chubb and Terry Moe, *Politics, Markets and America's Schools* (Washington, D.C.: The Brookings Institution, 1990).

20. See "Picking up the Bill for the Disruption," *Times Educational Supplement*, 22 April 1988, p. 4; "Assessment Mars Exam's Success Say Inspectors," *Times Educational Supplement*, 12 August 1988, p. 3; *Times Educational Supplement* 1 July 1988, p. 7; George Dearsley, "NUT finds Room for Subversion," *Times Educational Supplement*, 1 July 1988, p. 7; "Final Report on the Elementary Education Acts," PP 1888, vol. 35, [C.-5485], 177–78.

21. See "Soft at the Centre," *Times Educational Supplement*, 19 August 1988, p. 4; "Towards a New Education Act," advertisement in *Times Educational Supplement*, 26 January 1990, p. 7; and Chapter 5 below on filling in the gaps.

22. See R. S. Schofield, "Dimensions of Illiteracy, 1750–1850," *Explorations in Economic History* 10 (1973): 442–46.

23. See Chapters 3 and 4 below.

24. See Silver, "Aspects of Neglect," for a survey.

25. See "Report of the Commissioners on Popular Education," PP 1861, vol. 21, pt. I, [2794-I], 96; West, "Resource Allocation"; E. G. West, *Education and the Industrial Revolution* (London: Batsford, 1975); Gardner, *Lost Schools*.

26. See, for example, Johnson, "Notes on Schooling," 45–46, 48–51.

27. See Hurt, *Elementary Schooling*; Belfiore, "Family Strategies."

28. Estimating the actual proportion of the population who received some form of secondary education is complicated by the diverse types of secondary

education offered during the Victorian period, ranging from the elite public schools to higher-grade elementary schools. One indication of the limited extent of secondary schooling before 1900 is that even in 1901, only 9 percent of fourteen-year-olds were enrolled in some form of schooling. It should be noted that a marked expansion in secondary education did occur in the second half of the nineteenth century—in 1870 only 2 percent of fourteen-year-olds were in some form of school—and to a limited extent reached at least children of the skilled manual classes. Nevertheless, the overall numbers involved were small. For enrollments of fourteen-year-olds, see David Reeder, "The Reconstruction of Secondary Education in England, 1869–1920," in *The Rise of the Modern Educational System*, ed. Detlef Müller, Fritz Ringer, and Brian Simon (Cambridge: Cambridge University Press, 1987), 143. Reeder's essay also provides a general discussion of the expansion of secondary education.

29. See, for example, *The Oxford English Dictionary*, s.v. "literacy."

30. R. K. Webb, "Working Class Readers in Early Victorian England," *English Historical Review* 65 (1950): 350.

31. See Vincent, *Literacy and Popular Culture*, 10, 90.

32. The *Oxford English Dictionary* only includes reading and writing in its definition of literacy. For discussions of the notion of numeracy and its history, see Patricia Cline Cohen, *A Calculating People: The Spread of Numeracy in Early America* (Chicago: University of Chicago Press, 1982), 3–12; and Keith Thomas, "Numeracy in Early Modern England," *Transactions of the Royal Historical Society*, 5th ser., 37 (1987): 103–32.

33. In earlier times religion would have been accorded a more prominent role as well. For a survey of the history of the elementary school curriculum in Europe, see Maynes, *Schooling in Western Europe*, chap. 4.

34. W. B. Hodgson, "Exaggerated Estimates of Reading and Writing as Means of Education" (1867), reprinted in *History of Education Quarterly* 26 (1986): 383.

35. See Jack Goody, *The Logic of Writing and the Organization of Society* (Cambridge: Cambridge University Press, 1986), 65; and Roy Harris, *The Origin of Writing* (La Salle, Ill.: Open Court Press, 1986), chap. 5.

36. See Chapter 7 below.

37. See C. A. Birchenough, *History of Elementary Education in England and Wales from 1800 to the Present Day* (London: University Tutorial Press, 1914), 279.

38. See, for example, Hodgson, "Exaggerated Estimates," 381–93.

39. See Daniel P. Resnick, "Minimum Competency Testing Historically Considered," in *Review of Research in Education*, vol. 8, ed. David C. Berliner (Washington, D.C.: American Educational Research Association, 1981), 3–29; and Daniel Resnick and Lauren Resnick, "The Nature of Literacy: An Historical Exploration," *Harvard Educational Review* 47 (1977): 370–85.

40. See Donald L. Fisher, "Functional Literacy and the Schools," Educational Resources Information Center (ERIC) Report 151.760, Washington, D.C., National Institute of Education (1978), 10–11.

41. See Hodgson, "Exaggerated Estimates," 386.

42. See Egil Johansson, *The History of Literacy in Sweden in Comparison with*

Some Other Countries, Educational Reports Umea, no. 12 (Umea, Sweden: Umea University and Umea School of Education, 1977), 18–20; and John Morgan, *Godly Learning: Puritan Attitudes towards Reason, Learning and Education, 1560–1640* (Cambridge: Cambridge University Press, 1986), 159–69.

43. See Maynes, *Schooling in Western Europe*, chap. 3; and Vincent, *Literacy and Popular Culture*, chap. 3.

44. See, for example, Alex Inkeles and David Smith, *Becoming Modern: Individual Change in Six Developing Countries* (Cambridge: Harvard University Press, 1974), 283–84, 304; and Daniel Lerner, *The Passing of Traditional Society* (Glencoe, Ill.: Free Press, 1963), 57–64.

45. See, for example, Jack Goody, *The Domestication of the Savage Mind* (Cambridge: Cambridge University Press, 1977); and Ruth Finnegan, *Literacy and Orality* (Oxford: Basil Blackwell, 1988), chaps. 1, 2, 8, 9.

46. See Sylvia Scribner and Michael Cole, *The Psychology of Literacy* (Cambridge: Harvard University Press, 1981), chap. 14; and Shirley Brice Heath, *Ways with Words: Language, Life, and Work in Communities and Classrooms* (Cambridge: Cambridge University Press, 1983), 343–69.

47. R. S. Schofield, "The Measurement of Literacy in Pre-Industrial England," in *Literacy in Traditional Societies*, ed. Jack Goody (Cambridge: Cambridge University Press, 1968), 324.

48. See criticisms along similar lines in Hogan's review of *Ethnic Differences*, 108–12.

49. A similar argument is made in Craig, "Expansion of Education," 157–68.

Chapter 1: Interpreting the Rise of Literacy in Victorian England

1. See Graff, *Legacies of Literacy*, 95–106.

2. See Schofield, "Dimensions of Illiteracy," 445; and David Cressy, *Literacy and the Social Order: Reading and Writing in Tudor and Stuart England* (Cambridge: Cambridge University Press, 1980), chap. 7.

3. See Schofield, "Dimensions of Illiteracy," 445.

4. See 7th ARRG (Abstract for 1843), PP 1846, vol. 19, [540], 40–41.

5. See Graff, *Legacies of Literacy*, chap. 7; François Furet and Jacques Ozouf, *Reading and Writing: Literacy in France from Calvin to Jules Ferry* (Cambridge: Cambridge University Press, 1982), chap. 1; Lee Soltow and Edward Stevens, *The Rise of Literacy and the Common School in the United States* (Chicago: University of Chicago Press, 1981), chap. 2; Marjorie Lamberti, *State, Society, and the Elementary School in Imperial Germany* (New York: Oxford University Press, 1989), chap. 1; and Johansson, *History of Literacy in Sweden*, 64–73.

6. In 1900, only 2.8 percent of all grooms and 3.2 percent of all brides made a mark on the marriage register. See 63d ARRG (Abstract for 1900), PP 1901, vol. 15, [Cd.-761], lix.

7. See Gillian Sutherland, *Policy Making in Elementary Education, 1870–95* (London: Oxford University Press, 1973), 361.

8. For a study that focuses specifically on the growth of government involvement in education for the early Victorian period, see John Hurt, *Education in Evolution: Church, State, Society and Popular Education 1800–1870* (London: Rupert Hart-Davis, 1971). For the later Victorian period, see Sutherland, *Policy Making in Elementary Education*. For studies on the more general growth of the role of government in Victorian society that make specific reference to elementary education, see Gillian Sutherland, ed., *Studies in the Growth of Nineteenth Century Government* (London: Routledge and Kegan Paul, 1972), chaps. 5, 7; David Roberts, *Victorian Origins of the British Welfare State* (New Haven: Yale University Press, 1960), chaps. 2, 6; and S. G. Checkland, *British Public Policy 1776–1939: An Economic, Social and Political Perspective* (Cambridge: Cambridge University Press, 1983), 141–45, 155, 159.

9. "Census of Gt. Britain, 1851, Education," PP 1852–3, vol. 90, [1692], xl–xli; and "Report on Popular Education," PP 1861, vol. 21, pt. I, [2794], 179. For post-World War II histories, see, for example, Mary Sturt, *The Education of the People: A History of Primary Education in England and Wales in the Nineteenth Century* (London: Routledge and Kegan Paul, 1967), 210, 326–27; and Hurt, *Elementary Schooling*, chap. 2.

10. A. C. O. Ellis, "Influences on School Attendance in Victorian England," *British Journal of Educational Studies* 21 (1973): 313–26; W. P. McCann, "Elementary Education in England and Wales on the Eve of the 1870 Education Act," *Journal of Educational Administration and History* 2 (1969): 20–29; R. Pallister, "The Determinants of Elementary School Attendance about 1850," *Durham Research Review* 5 (1969): 384–98; and Nancy Ball, "Elementary School Attendance and Voluntary Effort before 1870," *History of Education* 2 (1973): 19–34.

11. Hurt, *Elementary Schooling*, chap. 2.

12. W. B. Stephens, *Education, Literacy and Society, 1830–70: The Geography of Diversity in Provincial England* (Manchester: Manchester University Press, 1987), 121–38, 174–84, 223–36.

13. E. G. West, "Resource Allocation."

14. Thomas Laqueur, *Religion and Respectability: Sunday Schools and Working Class Culture, 1780–1850* (New Haven: Yale University Press, 1976).

15. Gardner, *Lost Schools*, chaps. 6, 7.

16. West, "Educational Slowdown"; and West, *Education and the Industrial Revolution*, 198–203.

17. See West, *Education and the Industrial Revolution*, 200.

18. Michael Sanderson, "The Basic Education of Labour in Lancashire, 1780–1839" (Ph.D. diss., University of Cambridge, 1963); and Michael Sanderson, "Literacy and Social Mobility in the Industrial Revolution in England," *Past and Present* 56 (1972): 82–95.

19. See Richard Altick, *The English Common Reader. A Social History of the Mass Reading Public 1800–1900* (Chicago: University of Chicago Press, 1957); Webb, *British Working Class Reader*; and Raymond Williams, *The Long Revolution*, rev. ed. (New York: Harper Torchbooks, 1966), pt. 2, chaps. 2, 3.

20. Vincent, *Literacy and Popular Culture*.

21. See John S. Hurt, "Professor West on Early Nineteenth-Century

Education," *Economic History Review* 24 (1971): 624–32; and H. J. Kiesling, "Nineteenth-Century Education According to West: A Comment," *Economic History Review*, 2d ser., 36 (1983): 416–25. For defenses of the effectiveness of private school provision, see West, "Resource Allocation"; and Gardner, *Lost Schools*, chaps. 4, 5.

Part 1: Private Choice and the Benefits of Literacy

1. On the possibility of access to the written word through an intermediary in ancient and medieval times, see Graff, *Legacies of Literacy*, 23–24, 29, 68. For examples from American legal cases of situations where illiterates were expected to have others read documents to them and of the greater reliability of being able to read the document oneself, see Edward W. Stevens, Jr., *Literacy, Law, and Social Order* (DeKalb: Northern Illinois University Press, 1987), 137, 140, 150, 174–76. For general discussions of the various functions of literacy, see Daniel Resnick and Lauren Resnick, "Varieties of Literacy," in *Social History and Issues in Human Consciousness: Some Interdisciplinary Connections*, ed. A. E. Barnes and P. N. Stearns (New York: New York University Press, forthcoming); and Carl F. Kaestle, "The History of Literacy and the History of Readers," *Review of Research in Education*, vol. 12, ed. Edmund S. Gordon (Washington, D.C.: American Educational Research Association, 1985), 14–20, 36–45.

2. Jacob Larwood and John Camden Hotten, *The History of Signboards from Earliest Times to the Present Day*, 7th ed. (London: Chatto and Windus, 1870), v, 5, 11, 25–32; and Ambrose Heal, *Signboards of Old London Shops* (London: Batsford, 1947), 2.

3. Norman Wymer, *Country Folk* (London: Odhams Press, 1953), 131.

Chapter 2: The Benefits of Literacy in the Workplace

1. For England, see Schofield, "Dimensions of Illiteracy," 437–54; and Cressy, *Literacy and the Social Order*, chap. 7. For surveys of European studies, see Graff, *Legacies of Literacy*, 97, 166, 217, 230–50, 303–10, 320–50; Craig, "Expansion of Education," 173; and Rab Houston, "Literacy and Society in the West, 1500–1850," *Social History* 8 (1983): 269–93.

2. See Sanderson, "Literacy and Social Mobility," 75–104; and Michael Sanderson, "Social Change and Elementary Education in Industrial Lancashire, 1780–1840," *Northern History* 3 (1968): 131–40.

3. AR 1869–70, PP 1870, vol. 22 [C.-165], 98; AR 1864–65, PP 1865, vol. 42, [533], 38–39.

4. On the extent of literacy before 1500, see Graff, *Legacies of Literacy*, 36, 52, 63, 67.

5. On carpenters, see P. E. Razzell and R. W. Wainwright, eds., *The Victorian Working Class: Selections from Letters to the Morning Chronicle* (London: F. Cass, 1973), 125; and "Minutes of Evidence taken before the Royal Commission

on Labour, Group C," PP 1892, vol. 36, pt. II, [C.-6795-VI], 237 (item 16874). On glass workers, see "Fourth Report of the Commissioners on the Employment of Children in Trades and Manufactures," PP 1865, vol. 20, [3548], xxxi.

6. See Robert Colls, "'Oh Happy English Children': Coal, Class and Education in the North-East," *Past and Present* 73 (1976): 75–99; but also see A. J. Heesom, Brendan Duffy, and Robert Colls, "Debate: Coal, Class and Education in the North-East," *Past and Present* 90 (1981): 136–65. For similar arguments for North America, see Harvey Graff, *The Literacy Myth* (New York: Academic Press, 1979), 200–17, 228–33; and Alexander J. Field, "Educational Expansion in Mid-Nineteenth Century Massachusetts," *Harvard Educational Review* 46 (1976): 521–52.

7. For examples of employer interest in the moral effects of education, see "Children's Employment Commission, Second Report. Trades and Manufactures," PP 1843, vol. 13, [430], 182–191. For concern over practical aspects dominating the moral, see AR 1869–70, PP 1870, vol. 22, [C.-165], 98.

8. See V. H. Galbraith, "The Literacy of Medieval English Kings," *Proceedings, British Academy* 21 (1935): 205–6, 210–11; J. W. Thompson, *The Literacy of the Laity in the Middle Ages* (Berkeley: University of California Press, 1939), 5, 29, 82; and Kenneth Levine, *The Social Context of Literacy* (London: Routledge and Kegan Paul, 1986), 135–42.

9. See T. W. Schultz, "The Value of the Ability to Deal with Disequilibria," *Journal of Economic Literature* 13 (1975): 835.

10. The labor force distributions reported in Table 2.1 rely on the allocations of the labor force across occupations between 1841 and 1891 made by Armstrong. See W. A. Armstrong, "The Use of Information about Occupation," in *Nineteenth Century Society. Essays in the Use of Quantitative Methods for the Study of Social Data*, ed. E. A. Wrigley (Cambridge: Cambridge University Press, 1972), 253–83. Comparison of the 1841 figures with those for later dates in Table 2.1 may be biased because of differences in the way the 1841 census gathered information about occupation compared with later censuses. See ibid., 193, 208.

Edward Higgs has proposed revising Armstrong's allocations by occupational category for the female labor force in order to allow for possible overstatement by census enumerators of the number of female servants and for understatement of females employed in other occupations. See Edward Higgs, "Women, Occupations and Work in the Nineteenth Century," *History Workshop: A Journal of Socialist Historians* 23 (1987): 59–80. Higgs's revision markedly lowers the relative importance of domestic service as a source of female employment, although even with his revision it would account for over a fifth of female employment in the Victorian period. His revision also sizably raises the relative importance of female employment in agriculture and dealing. Since dealing would probably have made more use of literacy than service, increasing the share of dealing relative to service would raise the extent to which females would have been in occupations using literacy. Increasing the relative proportion of females in agriculture has more ambiguous effects on the use of literacy depending on the shift to farm proprietary work using literacy versus the shift to less farm service or labor using less literacy.

11. See Michael Glover, *Wellington's Army in the Peninsula, 1808–1814* (New York: Hippocrene Books, 1977), 36; and Michael Lewis, *The Navy in Transition 1814–1864: A Social History* (London: Hodder and Stoughton, 1965), 107–8. On educational requirements for non-commissioned officers, see W. H. Goodenough and J. C. Dalton, *The Army Book for the British Empire: A Record of the Development and Present Composition of the Military Forces and Their Duties in Peace and War* (London: HMSO, 1893), 419–20.

12. See Clive Elmsley, *Policing and Its Context 1750–1870* (New York: Schocken Books, 1984), 62, 66, 85; "Minutes of Evidence before the Select Committee on the Police of the Metropolis," PP 1834, vol. 16, [600], 78 (item 1231), 97 (item 1500), 302 (item 4183); "Minutes of Evidence for the First Report from the Select Committee on Police," PP 1852–3, vol. 36, [603], 24 (items 325–26); and "Minutes of Evidence for the Second Report from the Select Committee on Police," PP 1852–3, vol. 36, [715], 54 (item 3346), 88 (item 3662).

13. P. W. Kingsford, *Victorian Railwaymen* (London, Frank Cass and Co., 1970), 9; Frank McKenna, "Victorian Railway Workers," *History Workshop: A Journal of Socialist Historians* 1 (1976): 27, 30, 38–39; and Frank McKenna, *The Railway Workers, 1840–1970* (London: Faber and Faber, 1980), 31, 37–38.

14. See Henry Mayhew, *London Labour and the London Poor*, 4 vols. (1861–62; reprint, New York: Dover, 1968), 1: 4, 22; and John Benson, *The Penny Capitalists* (New Brunswick, N.J.: Rutgers University Press, 1983), 2.

15. See Thomas, "Numeracy," 119–20, 122.

16. Thomas, "Numeracy," 107, 109–12.

17. See "Reports of the Assistant Commissioners Appointed to Inquire into the State of Popular Education in England," PP 1861, vol. 21, pt. II, [2794–II], 252. On the importance of record keeping for the tradesman, also see David Alexander, *Retailing in England during the Industrial Revolution* (London: The Athelone Press, 1970), 165; and Daniel Defoe, *The Complete English Tradesman*, vol. 1 (1745; reprint, New York: Burt Franklin, 1970), vol.1, chap. 31. For American examples of problems encountered by illiterates in business transactions, see Stevens, *Literacy, Law, and Social Order*, 131–44, 178–81, 188–93.

18. See John Wilson, ed., *The Rural Cyclopedia* (Edinburgh: A. Fullarton and Co., 1852), 2: 224, 226; R. J. Colyer, "The Use of Estate Home Farm Accounts as Sources for Nineteenth Century Agricultural History," *The Local Historian* 11 (1975): 406. Also see James Obelkevich, *Religion and Rural Society* (Oxford: Clarendon Press, 1976), 49.

19. See "Appendix, Pt. II to First Report on the Employment of Children, Young Persons, and Women in Agriculture (1867), Evidence from the Assistant Commissioners," PP 1867–68, vol. 17, [4068–I], 41, 44.

20. Stuart MacDonald, "The Diffusion of Knowledge among Northumberland Farmers, 1780–1815," *Agricultural History Review* 27 (1979), part 1: 30–39; and H. S. A. Fox, "Local Farmer's Associations and the Circulation of Agricultural Information in Nineteenth Century England," in *Change in the Countryside: Essays on Rural England, 1500–1900*, Institute of British Geographers Special Publication, no. 10, ed. H. S. A. Fox and R. A. Butlin (London: Institute of British Geographers, 1979), 43–63.

21. See Sanderson, "Literacy and Social Mobility," 93; "Reports of Assistant Commissioners appointed on Popular Education," PP 1861, vol. 21, pt. II, [2794-II], 203–4.

22. See "Appendix to First Report of Children's Employment Commission. Mines. Reports and Evidence from Subcommissioners," PP 1842, vol. 17, [382], 465; and "Report on the State of the Population in the Mining Districts, 1850," PP 1850, vol. 22, [1248], 33–34.

23. See "Report and Minutes of Evidence on the State of the Woollen Manufacture in England," PP 1806, vol. 3, [268], 6, 69; "Appendix to Second Report on Children's Employment—Trades and Manufactures—Pt. I. Reports and Evidence from Subcommissioners," PP 1843, vol. 14, [431], b8; Esme Howard, "Dyeing and Cleaning," in *Life and Labour of the People in London*, 2d ser.: Industry, vol. 2, ed. Charles Booth (1903; reprint, New York: AMS Press, 1970), 328.

24. In the 1839–43 sample of marriages, 61 percent of dyers could sign their names compared with 69 percent of all grooms; in the 1869–73 sample, 75 percent of dyers could sign their names compared with 82 percent overall.

25. See Michael Guillou, "Technical Education, 1850–1914," in *Where Did We Go Wrong? Industrial Performance, Education and the Economy in Victorian Britain*, ed. Gordon Roderick and Michael Stephens (Barcombe, Lewes, Sussex: Falmer, 1981), 175, 179; and "New York Industrial Exhibition. Special Report of Mr. George Wallis," PP 1854, vol. 36, [1717], 65.

26. Ernest Aves, "The Hours of Labour," in *Life and Labour of the People in London*, 2d ser.: Industry, vol. 5, ed. Charles Booth (1903; reprint, New York: AMS Press, 1970), 201–14; and "General Report on the Wages of the Manual Labour Classes. Tables of the Average Rates of Wages and Hours," PP 1893–94, vol. 83, pt. II, [C.-6889], 93, 95, 101, 105, 111, 121.

27. Calculated from the census figures as reported in Armstrong, "Information about Occupation," 255–81.

28. R. A. Church, *The History of the British Coal Industry, Vol. 3. 1830–1913: Victorian Pre-eminence* (Oxford: Clarendon Press, 1986), 556; and B. R. Mitchell, *Economic Development of the British Coal Industry, 1800–1914* (Cambridge: Cambridge University Press, 1984), 168–70.

29. "Appendix to Fourth Report of the Commissioners on the Employment of Children and Young Persons in Trades and Manufactures," PP 1865, vol. 20, [3548], 53, 233; "Appendix to Third Report on the Employment of Children and Young People, Reports and Evidence of Assistant Commissioners," PP 1864, vol. 22, [3414-I], 190; and "Appendix to Second Report on Children's Employment—Trades and Manufactures—pt. I," PP 1843, vol. 14, [431], f169 (item 477). It should be noted that these examples come from children's employment commissions' hearings and that some employers may have overstated education requirements of child employees to minimize the apparent need for further regulation. Nevertheless, it is of interest to note that employers chose this reason for requiring literacy even if the extent of any requirement was exaggerated.

30. "Minutes of Evidence on Stoppage of Wages (Hosiery)," PP 1854–5, vol. 14, [421], 420 (items 7124, 7126); and "Appendix to Report on Framework

Knitters. Pt. II, Nottinghamshire and Derbyshire," PP 1845, vol. 15, [641], 68–69.

31. "Minutes of Evidence taken before the Commission on the Truck System," PP 1871, vol. 36, [C.-327], 865 (item 43653).

32. See Church, *History of Coal Industry, Vol. 3*, 702–4; Mitchell, *Economic Development of Coal Industry*, 234–35; and Dave Douglass, "The Durham Pitman," in *Miners, Quarrymen and Saltworkers*, ed. Raphael Samuel (London: Routledge and Kegan Paul, 1977), 244–46.

33. J. Geraint Jenkins, *The Craft Industries* (London: Longman, 1972), 112.

34. E. S. Turner, *What the Butler Saw* (New York: St. Martin's Press, 1963), 117; and Pamela Horn, *The Rise and Fall of the Victorian Servant* (New York: St. Martin's Press, 1975), 43–44.

35. Cited in Turner, *What the Butler Saw*, 108–9.

36. See "Evidence on Agricultural Gangs collected by Mr. J. E. White: Appendix to Sixth Report of the Children's Employment Commission," PP 1867, vol. 16, [3796], 109; and "Appendix, Pt. II to Second Report on the Employment of Children, Young Persons, and Women in Agriculture, Evidence from the Assistant Commissioners," PP 1868–9, vol. 13, [4202-I], 433.

37. Edward Higgs, *Domestic Servants and Households in Rochdale 1851–1871* (New York: Garland, 1986), 180, 204.

38. See Stephens, *Education, Literacy and Society*, 29, 79–80.

39. See Alan Everitt, "Country Carriers in the Nineteenth Century," *Journal of Transport History*, n.s., 3 (1976): 180–81.

40. "Reports of Assistant Commissioners on Popular Education," PP 1861, vol. 21, pt. II, [2794-II], 246.

41. See Stanley Chapman, "The Textile Industries," in *Where Did We Go Wrong?* ed. Roderick and Stephens, 125–38.

42. P. W. Musgrave, *Technical Change, the Labour Force, and Education* (Oxford: Pergamon Press, 1967), 27.

43. On seamen, see David Alexander, "Literacy Among Canadian and Foreign Seamen, 1863–1899," Maritime Studies Research Unit, Memorial University of Newfoundland, St. John's, Working Paper, 4. On watermen, see Wymer, *Country Folk*, 131. On the army, see Alan Skelley, *The Victorian Army at Home: The Recruitment and Terms and Conditions of the British Regular, 1859–1899* (London: Croom Helm, 1977), chap. 2; and Henry Marshall, *On the Enlisting, Discharging and Pensioning of Soldiers, with the Official Documents on these Branches of Military Duty*, 2d ed. (Edinburgh: A. and C. Black, 1839), 9–10. On the navy see "Statistical Return of the Education and Religious Denomination of Petty Officers, Seamen, and Marines serving in the Navy for 1865," PP 1867, vol. 44, [36].

44. See David Mitch, "The Spread of Literacy in Nineteenth Century England" (Ph.D diss., University of Chicago, 1982), 33–49.

45. "New York Industrial Exhibition. Special Report of Mr. Joseph Whitworth," PP 1854, vol. 36, [1718], 42.

46. "Appendix to First Report on Children's Employment. Mines," PP 1842, vol. 17, [382], 465; and "Appendix, Pt. II to First Report on the Employment

of Children, Young Persons, and Women in Agriculture," PP 1867–8, vol. 17, [4068-I], 41, 44.

47. See Schofield, "Measurement of Literacy," 320.

48. The wage estimates are taken from R. Dudley Baxter, *National Income: The United Kingdom* (London: Macmillan, 1868), app. part 2, 88–93. It should be noted that wage comparisons were not for all those whose fathers were of occupational status V (unskilled occupations) but only for those whose fathers reported the occupation of laborer on the marriage register. In the 1869–73 sample, 90 percent of grooms whose fathers were of occupational status V had fathers who reported the occupation of laborer.

49. These literacy rates are calculated from Table 2.3 by multiplying the number of all literate grooms whose fathers were of a given occupational status by the proportion of such grooms reporting occupational status III, then multiplying the number of all illiterate grooms whose fathers were of a given occupational status by the proportion of such grooms reporting occupational status III, and finally dividing the number of literate grooms of occupational status III and with fathers of a given status by the number of all grooms of occupational status III with fathers of a given status.

50. "Appendix, Pt. II to First Report on the Employment of Children, Young Persons, and Women in Agriculture," PP 1867–8, vol. 17, [4068-I], 41, 44.

51. "Report of Joseph Whitworth," PP 1854, vol. 36, [1718], 42.

52. Kingsford, *Victorian Railwaymen*, 9.

53. "Appendix, Pt. II to Third Report on the Employment of Children, Young Persons, and Women in Agriculture, Evidence Accompanying Reports of the Assistant Commissioners," PP 1870, vol. 13, [C.-70], 120.

54. "Minutes of the Committee of Council on Education, 1840–41," PP 1841, vol. 20, [317], 74; and "Reports of Assistant Commissioners on Popular Education," PP 1861, vol. 21, pt. II, [2794-II], 249–52.

55. "Reports of Assistant Commissioners on Popular Education," PP 1861, vol. 21, pt. II, [2794-II], 151, 203–4, 249; and "Further Reports of Assistant Commissioners on Popular Education in England," PP 1861, vol. 21, pt. III [2794-III], 94–95, 312–13, 399, 561.

56. Francis George Heath, *The English Peasantry* (London: F. Warne and Co., 1874), 129. Also see "Appendix, Pt. I to Second Report on the Employment of Children, Young Persons, and Women in Agriculture, Reports from Assistant Commissioners," PP 1868–9, vol. 13, [4202], 119.

57. The mining districts were excluded because of the small number of observations for sons of unskilled workers. These correlations were calculated from samples of marriage registers from each of the five remaining districts. These samples are described in Appendix B. Grooms included in the calculations were those whose fathers were in unskilled occupations.

58. See Schofield, "Measurement of Literacy," 320.

59. See Mitch, "The Spread of Literacy," 33–49. Also on seamen, see Alexander, "Literacy Among Canadian and Foreign Seamen," 28–29.

60. Ernest Aves, "Irregularity of Earnings," in *Life and Labour of the People*

in London, 2d ser.: Industry, vol. 5, ed. Charles Booth (1903; reprint, New York: AMS Press, 1970), 234; and "Appendix to First Report on Children's Employment (1862). Evidence of Assistant Commissioners," PP 1863, vol. 18, [3170], 146, 152.

61. "Appendix to First Report on Children's Employment," PP 1863, vol. 18, [3170], 267, 213, 214, 215; "Appendix to Third Report on Children's Employment," PP 1864, vol. 22, [3414-I], 107; and "Appendix to Fourth Report on the Employment of Children and Young Persons in Trades and Manufactures," PP 1865, vol. 20, [3548], 119.

62. Higgs, *Domestic Servants and Households,* 77–90; and Leone Levi, *Wages and Earnings of the Working Classes* (London: John Murray, 1867), 24–26, 69–93, indicate that clothing and service occupations paid more than textile occupations. The statistics presented in G. H. Wood, "The Course of Women's Wages during the Nineteenth Century," in *A History of Factory Legislation,* by B. L. Hutchins and A. Harrison (London: P. S. King and Son, 1903), app. A, 257–308, indicate more uncertainty.

63. Higgs, *Domestic Servants and Households,* 153, 137–45.

64. Wood, "Course of Women's Wages," 262; and Asher Tropp, *The School Teachers* (New York: Macmillan, 1956), 273–76.

65. See "Census of England and Wales, 1861, Population Tables, Vol. II, Ages, Civil Condition, Occupations, and Birth-Places of the People," PP 1863, vol. 53, pt. I, [3221], lvi–lxv; and N. L. Tranter, "The Labour Supply, 1780–1860," in *The Economic History of Britain since 1700,* vol. 1, ed. Roderick Floud and Donald McCloskey (Cambridge: Cambridge University Press, 1981), 207.

66. Sally Alexander, *Women's Work in Nineteenth Century London* (London: Journeyman Press, 1983), 52.

67. Sanderson, "Literacy and Social Mobility," 78–79, 89–91.

68. Although, as noted below, mine supervisors over the course of the nineteenth century did increasingly recognize the value of the ability to read safety instructions and diagrams, literacy never seems to have been commonly expected for the ordinary miner. See Neil Buxton, "The Coal Industry," in *Where Did We Go Wrong?* ed. Roderick and Stephens, 92–93, 97; Church, *History of Coal Industry, Vol. 3,* 201–15; and Mitchell, *Economic Development of Coal Industry,* 113, 121–30.

69. These estimates were obtained by using the detailed occupational classifications in Booth's unpublished tables for "Occupations of the United Kingdom 1801–1881," printed in Armstrong, "Information about Occupation," 255–81. The change of the proportion of the labor force in each occupational category between 1841 and 1871 was multiplied by an estimate of the literacy for that category from the 1839–43 marriage register sample. Of the additional amount of the increase in literacy explained over and above that due to broad sectoral shifts, virtually all of the within-sector shifts were due to agriculture, transport, and manufacturing. Of the contribution of compositional changes within these sectors, 54 percent was due to agriculture, 35 percent to transportation, and 11 percent to manufacturing.

70. Indexes of wages in occupations using and those not making use of

literacy were based on the occupational wage estimates in Jeffrey Williamson, "Structure of Pay in Britain, 1710–1911," *Research in Economic History*, vol. 7, ed. Paul Uselding (Greenwich, Conn.: JAI Press, 1982), 36–49. The following occupational groups from Williamson's study were classified as not making use of literacy: 1L, 2L, 6L, 5H. The following occupational groups were classified as making use of literacy: messengers and porters, government low wage, police, guards, compositors, teachers, 2H, 3H, 4H. In addition, farmers, clerks, and those in dealing occupations were classified as making use of literacy and were included in the wage estimates for occupations making use of literacy. Income estimates for farmers were taken from J. R. Bellerby, "National and Agricultural Income: 1851," *Economic Journal* 69 (1959): 103. Income estimates for clerks were taken from Gregory Anderson *Victorian Clerks* (Manchester: Manchester University Press, 1976), 68–70, 85–86, 109–11, 130. For income estimates for clerks, use was also made of extrapolations from Williamson, "Structure of Pay," 47. Estimates for dealing occupations were taken from Geoffrey Crossick, "The Petite Bourgoisie in Nineteenth-Century Britain: The Urban and Liberal Case," in *Shopkeepers and Master Artisans in Nineteenth-Century Europe*, ed. Geoffrey Crossick and Heinz-Gerhard Haupt (London: Methuen, 1984), 62–94. To calculate the wage indexes, the wage for each occupational group in each year was weighted by its share of the total labor force in that year, based on the estimates in Armstrong, "Information about Occupation," 255–81.

71. Higgs, *Domestic Servants and Households*, 77–90; W. T. Layton, "Changes in the Wages of Domestic Servants during Fifty Years," *Journal of the Royal Statistical Society* 72 (1908): 515–24; and Tropp, *The School Teachers*, 273–76.

72. "Appendix, Pt. I to First Report from the Commissioners on the Employment of Children, Young Persons, and Women in Agriculture, Reports from Assistant Commissioners," PP 1867–8, vol. 17, [4068], 102; and "Appendix, Pt. II to First Report on the Employment of Children, Young Persons, and Women in Agriculture, Evidence from the Assistant Commissioners," PP 1867–8, vol. 17, [4068-I], a16, 439.

73. Musgrave, *Technical Change*, 74. It has also been noted that in machinery and machine tool firms elementary education was required of workers after it had become virtually universal. See Charles More, *Skill and the English Working Class, 1870–1914* (New York: St. Martin's Press, 1980), 67–68.

74. Buxton, "The Coal Industry," 92–93, 97.

75. See W. H. Goodenough and J. C. Dalton, *The Army Book for the British Empire* (London: HMSO, 1893), 419–20; W. H. Goodenough and J. C. Dalton, *The Army Book for the British Empire* (London: HMSO, 1907), 62. In W. H. Goodenough and J. C. Dalton, *The Army Book for the British Empire* (London: HMSO, 1912), 54, it was stated that every recruit must be able to read and write. Also see Skelley, *Victorian Army at Home*, 85–92, 94. On the navy, see Sir Thomas Brassey, *The British Navy: Its Strengths, Resources, and Administration*, vol. 5, pt. 5 (London: Longmans, Green and Co., 1883), 32. An 1844 naval handbook made no mention of reading and writing requirements for enlisted personnel except for gunners; see Gt. Britain Admiralty, *The Queen's Regulations for the Government of*

Her Majesty's Naval Service (London: HMSO, 1844), app., 15. An 1862 naval handbook stated a preference for boys who could read and write, although literacy was not a strict requirement; see Gt. Britain Admiralty, *The Queen's Regulations and the Admiralty Instructions for the Government of Her Majesty's Naval Service* (London: HMSO, 1862), 78. An 1895 naval handbook stated that both able-bodied seamen and ordinary seamen were expected to take Morse code; see Gt. Britain Admiralty, *Queen's Regulations. Addenda (1895)* (London: HMSO, 1895), 91, 93. A 1923 naval handbook stated that able-bodied seamen were required to read, write, and do arithmetic, but no such requirement was stated for ordinary seamen. See Gt. Britain Admiralty, *The King's Regulations and Admiralty Instructions for the Government of His Majesty's Naval Service*, vol. 2 (London: HMSO, 1924), 537.

76. See Levine, *Social Context of Literacy*, 143–49, for examples of large British employers in the 1970s and 1980s who tested applicants' literacy skills. Also see R. M. Blackburn and Michael Mann, *The Working Class in the Labour Market* (London: Macmillan, 1979), 103–4. One can compare this with Booth's industry surveys in turn-of-the-century London where no mention is made of literacy requirements in manufacturing, or with statements to parliamentary commissions of large employers in the late 1860s who did not examine applicants' educational backgrounds. See "Minutes of Evidence to Report from the Select Committee on Scientific Instruction," PP 1867–68, vol. 15, [432], 234 (item 4611), 293 (item 5793).

77. See C. E. Parsons, *Clerks: Their Position and Advancement* (London: Provost, 1876), 7, 14; Henry Tuckley, *Masses and Classes: A Study of Industrial Conditions in England* (Cincinatti: Cranston and Curtis, 1893), 41 ; and John Stuart Mill, *Principles of Political Economy*, ed. W. J. Ashley (London: Longmans and Green, 1909), 392.

78. The figures reported in Table 2.3 indicate that the proportion of grooms with fathers of occupational status V who signed their names rose from $413/(413 + 624) = 40$ percent in 1839–43 to $643/(643 + 348) = 65$ percent in 1869–73.

79. The figures reported in Table 2.3 indicate that in the 1839–43 sample, the total number of grooms with fathers of occupational status V who signed their names was 413, and the proportion of literate grooms with fathers of occupational status V who had an occupational status higher than V was $1 - .506$. From these figures, one can calculate the number of upwardly mobile literate grooms with fathers of occupational status V in 1839–43 as $(1 - .506) \times 413 = 204$. The total number of grooms with fathers of occupational status V in 1839–43 reported in Table 2.3 is $413 + 624 = 1,037$. Thus, the proportion of all grooms with fathers of occupational status V in 1839–43 who were literate and upwardly mobile was $204/1037 = 19.7$ percent. In the 1869–73 sample, Table 2.3 indicates that the total number of grooms with fathers of occupational status V who signed their names was 643, and the proportion of these grooms who were upwardly mobile was $(1 - .521)$. Hence the number of upwardly mobile literate grooms with fathers of occupational status V in the 1869–73 sample was $(1 - .521) \times 643 = 308$. The total number of grooms with fathers of occupational status V in 1869–73 reported in Table 2.3 was $643 + 348 = 991$. Thus, the proportion of

all grooms with fathers of occupational status V in 1869–73 who were literate and upwardly mobile was 308/991 = 31.1 percent.

80. The figures in Table 2.3 indicate that in 1839–43 the number of illiterate grooms with fathers of occupational status V was 624 and that the proportion of these grooms with an occupational status higher than V was (1 − .80). These figures imply that the number of upwardly mobile illiterate sons of fathers of occupational status V in 1839–43 was (1 − .80) × 624 = 125. The total number of grooms with fathers of occupational status V in 1839–43 was 413 + 624 = 1,037. Hence, in 1839–43, the proportion of grooms with fathers of occupational status V who were upwardly mobile was 125/1037 = 12.05 percent. In 1869–73, the number of illiterate grooms with fathers of occupational status V was 348 and the proportion of these grooms with an occupational status higher than V was (1 − .782). These figures imply that the number of upwardly mobile illiterate sons of fathers of occupational status V in 1869–73 was (1 − .782) × 348 = 76. The total number of grooms with fathers of occupational status V in 1869–73 was 643 + 348 = 991. Hence, in 1869–73, the proportion of grooms of occupational status V who were upwardly mobile was 76/991 = 7.67 percent. And the decline between 1839–43 and 1869–73 in the proportion of upwardly mobile, illiterate grooms with fathers of occupational status V was 12.05 − 7.67 = 4.38 percent.

81. The figures in Table 2.3 indicate that in 1839–43, the number of literate sons of fathers of occupational status V was 413 and the proportion of these sons who were upwardly mobile was (1 − .506). Thus, the number of literate, upwardly mobile grooms with fathers of occupational status V in 1839–43 was (1 − .506) × 413 = 204. The number of illiterate sons of fathers of occupational status V in 1839–43 was 624 and the proportion of these sons who were upwardly mobile was (1 − .800). Thus the number of illiterate upwardly mobile grooms of fathers of occupational status V in 1839–43 was (1 − .80) × 624 = 125. The literacy rate among upwardly mobile sons of the unskilled in 1839–43 can thus be calculated as 204/(204 + 125) = 62 percent. In 1869–73, the number of literate sons of occupational status V was 643, and the proportion of these sons who were upwardly mobile was (1 − .521). Thus, the number of literate, upwardly mobile grooms with fathers of occupational status V in 1869–73 was (1 − .521) × 643 = 308. The number of illiterate sons of fathers of occupational status V in 1869–73 was 348, and the proportion of these sons who were upwardly mobile was (1 − .782). Thus, the number of illiterate, upwardly mobile grooms with fathers of occupational status V in 1869–73 was (1 − .782) × 348 = 76. The literacy rate among upwardly mobile sons of the unskilled in 1869–73 can thus be calculated as 308/(308 + 76) = 80.2 percent.

82. The figures in Table 2.3 indicate that the number of literate grooms of occupational status V whose fathers were also of occupational status V in 1839–43 was .506 × 413 = 209, and the number of illiterate grooms of occupational status V whose fathers were also of occupational status V in 1869–73 was .800 × 624 = 499. Hence, in 1839–43, the literacy rate among grooms of occupational status V whose fathers were also of occupational status V was 209/(209 + 499) = 29.5 percent. The number of literate grooms of occupational

status V whose fathers were also of occupational status V in 1869–73 was .521 × 643 = 335 and the number of illiterate grooms of occupational status V whose fathers were also of occupational status V in 1869–73 was .782 × 348 = 272. Hence, in 1869–73, the literacy rate among grooms of occupational status V whose fathers were also of occupational status V was 335/(335 + 272) = 55.2 percent.

83. In the 1839–43 sample, 24.2 percent of all grooms reported occupations of occupational status V. In the 1869–73 sample, 22.7 percent of all grooms reported occupations of occupational status V. Thus, the percentage reduction was 1 − (22.7/24.2) = 6.2 percent.

84. The change in the proportion of grooms with fathers of occupational status V retaining their father's status is calculated as follows. Table 2.3 indicates that in 1839–43, the number of literate grooms whose fathers were of occupational status V was 413. Of these, the proportion retaining their father's status was .506, implying that the number of illiterate grooms of fathers of occupational status V who retained their father's status in 1839–43 was .506 × 413 = 209. Using a similar procedure, the figures in Table 2.3 indicate that the number of illiterate grooms with fathers of occupational status V retaining their father's status was .800 × 624 = 499. The total number of grooms with fathers of occupational status V in 1839–43 was 413 + 624 = 1037. Thus, the proportion of grooms with fathers of occupational status V retaining their father's status was (209 + 499)/1037 = 68.27 percent. In 1869–73, the number of literate grooms with fathers of occupational status V who retained their father's status was .521 × 643 = 335, and the number of illiterate grooms of occupational status V retaining their father's status was .782 × 348 = 272. The total number of grooms with fathers of occupational status V in 1869–73 was 991. Thus the proportion of grooms with fathers of occupational status V retaining their father's status in 1869–73 was (335 + 272)/991 = 61.25 percent. Thus, the percentage fall in the proportion of grooms with fathers of occupational status V retaining their father's status was (68.27 − 61.25)/68.27 = 10.28 percent.

85. This proportion can be determined by first calculating the proportion of the percentage increase in upward mobility for sons of the unskilled not explained by the reduction in unskilled positions in the total sample—[1 − (6.20/10.28)] = .397. This proportion is then multiplied by the increase in the percentage of grooms with fathers of occupational status V who were upwardly mobile (7.05 percent), resulting in an estimate of .397 × 7.05 = 2.80 percent.

86. These signature rates are for grooms who reported the occupation of laborer in the twenty-nine-county marriage register sample described in Appendix B.

Chapter 3: Literacy as an Equipment for Living

The title of Chapter 3 owes apologies to the essay by Kenneth Burke, "Literature as an Equipment for Living," *Direction* 1 (1938): 10–13, reprinted in Kenneth Burke, *The Philosophy of Literary Form* (Berkeley: University of California

Press, 1973), 293–304. The title is intended to point to the broad range of situations in which literacy may be useful rather than to Burke's theme of how literature can be used to categorize situations that arise in life.

1. This sample is described in Appendix B.

2. "Minutes of Evidence taken before the Select Committee on Newspaper Stamps," PP 1851, vol. 17, [558], 353 (item 2366).

3. F. Liardet, "State of the Peasantry in the County of Kent," in *Third Publication of 1839*, Central Society of Education (1839; reprint, London: Woburn Books, 1969), 108, 119, 122. The survey was taken of families in Herehill Parish, the village of Dunkirk and the village of Boughton under the Blean. In the case of Dunkirk the report indicated that in "two cottages only did parents employ their evening in reading." In arriving at the figure of 15 parents in the text, these two cottages were assumed to contain 4 parents who were added to the 11 parents mentioned in the survey for the other two areas.

4. "Minutes of Evidence. Second Report from the Select Committee on Postage," PP 1837–8, vol. 20, pt. II, [658], 209 (item 9099).

5. Statistical Society of London, "Conditions of the Working Classes in St.George's Hanover Square," *Journal of the Statistical Society of London* 6 (1843): 21; Statistical Society of London, "Report of an Investigation into the State of the Poorer Classes of St. George's-in-the-East," *Journal of the Statistical Society of London* 11 (August 1848): 216.

6. Statistical Society of London, "Report on St. George's-in-the-East," 217.

7. Statistical Society of London, "Report of a Committee of the Statistical Society of London on the State of the Working Classes in the Parishes of St. Margaret and St. John, Westminister," *Journal of the Statistical Society of London* 3 (April 1840): 14–24.

8. See T. S. Ashton, *Economic and Social Investigations in Manchester, 1833–1933. A Centenary History of the Manchester Statistical Society* (London: P. S. King and Son, 1934), 18–19. Although volume of sales in the thousands is suggestive of an active demand, it requires comparison with the potential population of demanders for proper evaluation. In 1841 the population age twenty and over in Manchester borough was 136,513, according to the 1841 census. See "Population, Enumeration Abstract, 1841," PP 1843, vol. 22, [496], 149. The percentage of those getting married signing their names in 1841 in the Manchester registration district according to the Annual Report of the Registrar General for 1841 was 54 percent. See 4th ARRG (Abstracts for 1841), PP 1842, vol. 19, [423], 23. Assuming no change across cohorts in literacy and using signature ability as a measure of reading ability, the number of adults with reading ability in 1841 can then be estimated as .54 × 136,513, or 73,717. Thus, weekly sales of literature in the 1830s of three thousand was equal to about 4 percent of the literate adult population of Manchester in 1841. Although not a high proportion, it is not negligible either, especially allowing for exchanges among readers.

9. "Appendix to First Report of the Children's Employment Commission. Mines. Evidence from Subcommissioners," PP 1842, vol. 16, [381], 71 (item 21). A sixteen-year-old boy from Shropshire also reported reading books ranging from the Bible to *Robinson Crusoe*. See ibid., 83 (item 53).

10. Ibid., 72 (item 24).

11. Ibid., 86 (item 58); also see ibid., 85 (item 56), 86 (item 61).

12. See Liardet, "Peasantry in Kent," 108, 118, 122. For an insightful discussion of Liardet and the concerns he brought to these surveys, see David Vincent, "Reading in the Working Class Home," in *Leisure in Britain, 1780–1939*, ed. John K. Walton and James Walvin (Manchester: Manchester University Press, 1983), 207–26.

13. G. R. Porter, "Results of an Inquiry into the Condition of the Labouring Classes in 5 Parishes in the County of Norfolk," in *Third Publication of 1839*, Central Society of Education (1839; reprint, London: Woburn Books, 1969), 372. Also see G. R. Porter, "Statistical Inquiries into the Social Condition of the Working Classes and into the Means Provided for the Education of their Children," in *Second Publication of 1838*, Central Society of Education (1838; reprint, London: Woburn Books, 1969), 259–60. A survey of Monmouth in 1840 found that 80 percent of the houses surveyed owned Bibles. See G. S. Kenrick, "Statistics of the Population in the Parish of Trevethin (Pontypool) and at the Neighbouring Works of Blaenavon in Monmouthshire, chiefly employed in the Iron Trade, and inhabiting part of the District recently disturbed," *Journal of the London Statistical Society* 3 (January 1841): 373.

14. Liardet, "Peasantry in Kent," 108.

15. Florence Bell, *At the Works* (1907; reprint, New York: A. M. Kelley, 1969), 146, 148–49, 156 (#131), 157 (#139, #140, #149), 161 (#190).

16. Flora Thompson, *Lark Rise to Candleford: A Trilogy* (1945; reprint, Harmondsworth: Penguin Books, 1973), 471.

17. "Minutes from the Select Committee on Postage," PP 1837–8, vol. 20, pt. II, [658], 215 (item 9167).

18. See Heath, *Ways with Words*, 198–99, 218, 220, 258–59.

19. See Larwood and Hotten, *History of Signboards*, v, 5, 11, 25–32; and Heal, *Signboards of Old London Shops*, 2.

20. Cited in Michael Sanderson, "Basic Education of Labour," 436. The original source, a biography of Parnell, is J. Taylor, *Apostles of Fylde Methodism* (London, 1885), 117.

21. John Lowerson and John Myerson, *Time to Spare in Victorian England* (Hassocks, Sussex: Harvester Press, 1977), 14.

22. T. R. Nevett, *Advertising in Britain: A History* (London: Heiman, 1982), 55. A notable illustration of poster-covered walls in London is John Orlando Parry's "A London Street Scene." It has been reproduced in the end leaves in Max Gallo, *The Poster in History* (New York: American Heritage, 1974). For an insightful interpretation of Parry's painting see Richard L. Stein, "1837: The Writing on the Walls," *Victorian Poetry* 25, nos. 3–4 (Autumn-Winter 1987): 75–88. For other drawings of poster-covered streets in early Victorian London, see Nevett, *Advertising in Britain*, 54, and the plates between pp. 82–83; and Diana Hindly and Geoffrey Hindly, *Advertising in Victorian England, 1837–1901* (London: Wayland, 1972), plates 1.1 and 1.2. On the timing of the spread of the poster see Nevett, *Advertising in Britain*, 53–56.

23. "Minutes of Evidence before the Commission on the Truck System," PP 1871, vol. 36, [C.-327], 497–98 (items 25510 to 25520). For an example of a miner's wife who kept detailed independent records of the family's truck account, see ibid., 715 (item 36461). As noted in the text, in both cases the people involved would seem to have been able to do arithmetic as well as to read and write. Still, the ability to do arithmetic would have done little good in these cases without the ability to read and write. For an example of an illiterate apparently deceived because he could not read a truck agreement, see ibid., 717 (items 36543–36565).

24. The 1841 census indicates that the ninety-one billstickers reported for England and Wales were heavily concentrated in major urban areas. Two-thirds of the billstickers were reported from the counties of Middlesex, Surrey, Kent, Lancashire, and the West Riding of Yorkshire, even though these counties contained only 35 percent of the population of England and Wales. Rutland, Leicestershire, Lincoln, Oxford, Shropshire, Somerset, Westmoreland, and all of Wales reported no billstickers in the 1841 census. See "Population: Occupation Abstract, Census of Gt. Britain, 1841," PP 1844, vol. 27, [587], 1–269. Although billsticking could have been done in these other areas on a part-time basis and thus escaped the census enumerators, the pattern of distribution of billstickers suggests that the heavily posted walls depicted in pictures of early Victorian London did not prevail elsewhere in England. Nevett, *Advertising in Britain*, 56, supports this conclusion.

25. "Further Reports of Assistant Commissioners on Popular Education," PP 1861, vol. 21, pt. III, [2794-III], 116.

26. "Minutes before Select Committee on Newspaper Stamps," PP 1851, vol. 17, [558], 159 (item 980); and "Appendix to First Report of Children's Employment Commission. Mines," PP 1842, vol. 16, [381], 40 (item 323).

27. "Minutes from the Select Committee on Postage," PP 1837–8, vol. 20, pt. II, [658], 216 (item 9175).

28. "Minutes of Evidence. Report from the Select Committee on Public Libraries," PP 1849, vol. 17, [548], 128–29 (item 2012).

29. These ranges are based on the estimates in A. L. Bowley, *Wages in the United Kingdom in the Nineteenth Century* (Cambridge: Cambridge University Press, 1900), 32–33, 82–83, and, at the end of the book, the table on farm laborers and the figure on London building trades.

30. For a survey of the development of the newspaper tax, see Arthur A. Aspinall, *Politics and the Press, 1780–1850* (London: Home and Vanthal, 1949), 18–23.

31. For newspaper prices, see Altick, *English Common Reader*, chaps. 14, 15, and app. A. Also see Henry Richard Fox Bourne, *English Newspapers: Chapters in the History of English Journalism*, vol. 2 (London: Chatto and Windus, 1887), 112, 122–24, 235, 253–54.

32. Rowland Hill, *Post Office Reform: Its Importance and Practicability* (London: Charles Knight, 1837), 63.

33. See Victor Neuberg, *Popular Literature: A History and Guide* (Harmondsworth: Penguin Books, 1971), 114–16, for examples of late-eighteenth and early-nineteenth-century prices of street literature.

34. Altick, *The English Common Reader*, 288–89.

35. "Minutes from the Select Committee on Public Libraries," PP 1849, vol. 17, [548], 85 (item 1308).

36. "Minutes before Select Committee on Postage," PP 1837–8, vol. 20, pt. II, [658], 213 (item 9149).

37. Ibid., 49 (item 6696).

38. See Martin Daunton, *Royal Mail* (London: Athlone Press, 1985), 18.

39. For trends in newspaper prices, see Altick, *English Common Reader*, chaps. 14, 15, and app. A. Also see Bourne, *English Newspapers* 2:112, 122–24, 235, 253–54.

40. J. C. Hemmeon, *The History of the British Post Office* (Cambridge: Harvard University Press, 1912), chap. 8.

41. For a survey of postal rates, see George Frederick Kay, *Royal Mail: The Story of the Mail from the Time of Edward IV to the Present Day* (London: Rockliff, 1951), 78–79; and Hemmeon, *British Post Office*, 147.

42. For a discussion of book prices in the nineteenth century, see Altick, *English Common Reader*, chaps. 12, 13; and Charles Knight, *The Old Printer and the Modern Press*, (London: J. Murray, 1854), pt. 2, chaps. 4, 6. For a survey of changes in working-class penny literature in the nineteenth century, see Neuberg, *Popular Literature*, chap.4; and Louis James, *Fiction for the Working Man, 1830–1850* (Oxford University Press, 1974), chaps. 2–4. In surveying the fall in prices of reading materials and postage, allowance should be made for changes in the general level of prices. Between 1830 and 1870, the main period under consideration here, there was no clear trend in the general price level. See B. R. Mitchell and P. Deane, *Abstract of British Historical Statistics* (Cambridge: Cambridge University Press, 1962), 471–72.

43. For evidence on the movement of circulation with the stamp tax, see A. P. Wadsworth, "Newspaper Circulations, 1800–1954," *Transactions of the Manchester Statistical Society*, session 1954–55 (March 1955): 3–23; Bourne, *English Newspapers* 2:67; Altick, *English Common Reader*, chaps. 14, 15, and app. C. Also see "Minutes before Select Committee on Newspaper Stamps," PP 1851, vol. 17, [558], 160–62 (items 985–990), 182 (item 1121).

44. For Lloyd's price and circulation see Bourne, *English Newspapers* 2:122, 254; and Altick, *English Common Reader*, 394–95.

45. See Altick, *English Common Reader*, 342.

46. "Reports of Assistant Commissioners on Popular Education," PP 1861, vol. 21, pt. II, [2794-II], 109–10.

47. Ibid., 110, 163.

48. See Mayhew, *London Labour* 1:297.

49. Thompson, *Lark Rise to Candleford*, 109.

50. "Minutes from the Select Committee on Postage," PP 1837–8, vol. 20, pt. II, [658], 211 (item 9134).

51. See Daunton, *Royal Mail*, 19–25, 79; and Vincent, *Literacy and Popular Culture*, 35, 39.

52. "Appendix A to Twenty-Ninth Report of the Postmaster General of the Post Office," PP 1883, vol. 22, [C.-3703], 26.

53. See Vincent, *Literacy and Popular Culture*, 38–39.

54. "Reports from Assistant Commissioners on Popular Education," PP 1861, vol. 21, pt. II, [2794-II], 106.

55. "Further Reports of Assistant Commissioners on Popular Education," PP 1861, vol. 21, pt. III, [2794-III], 116.

56. See Vincent, *Literacy and Popular Culture*, 44–46. Vincent also refers to an instance where halfpenny postcards were used for short-distance communication, several times a day, between parties. See ibid., 51.

57. See Alan J. Lee, *The Origins of the Popular Press 1855–1914* (Totowa, N.J.: Rowman and Littlefield, 1976), 39 n.84. The original source is H. W. Massingame, *The London Daily Press* (London: The Religious Tract Society, 1892), 10.

58. Bell, *At the Works*, 144.

59. See John Leigh, "What Do the Masses Read?," *Economic Review* 14 (1904): 174–75.

60. See Lucy Brown, *Victorian News and Newspapers* (New York: Oxford University Press, 1985), 48.

61. J. R. Marshall and J. K. Walton, *The Lake Counties* (Manchester: Manchester University Press, 1981), 156. Also see Richard Jefferies, *The Life of the Fields* (Philadelphia: J. B. Lippincott, 1908), 186–87.

62. "The Agricultural Labourer, Reports by Mr. C. M. Chapman," PP 1893–94, vol. 35, [C.-6894-II], 83.

63. P. J. Lucas, "Furness Newspapers in Mid-Victorian England," in *Victorian Lancashire*, ed. S. P. Bell (Newton Abbot, Devon: David and Charles, 1974), 91.

64. Lee, *Origins of the Popular Press*, 40.

65. Bell, *At the Works*, 162.

66. Thompson, *Lark Rise to Candleford*, 109.

67. Leigh, "What Do the Masses Read?" 177.

68. Ibid., 174–76.

69. Bell, *At the Works*, 144.

70. Ibid., 166–67, 236.

71. Robert Roberts, *The Classic Slum: Salford Life in the First Quarter of the Century* (Harmondsworth: Penguin Books, 1973), 166. Further evidence of the limited extent of working-class reading is that although Parliament gave authority to local communities to levy funds for public libraries in 1850, by the end of the century libraries were used by only a small minority of the English population. Private rental libraries and reading rooms attached to other institutions were common in England by 1800. Not much use was made of the authority to levy funds for public libraries until after 1900. Only in the largest cities such as London and Manchester was there sizable political support for public libraries. By 1900 some forty-six areas with populations of over twenty thousand had defeated propositions to levy a library rate. Even where public libraries were established, they were not heavily patronized by the working classes. Returns from five towns in the 1890s indicate that active borrowers were only 3 to 8 percent of the population. And surveys of the occupations of borrowers in Manchester in the 1850s and Bristol in the 1890s show that the largest groups of adult borrowers were skilled artisans and clerks. See Altick, *English Common Reader*, 227, 236–39.

72. According to Richard Hoggart, "There is no diary, no book of engage-ments, and few letters are sent or received. If a member of the family is away a weekly letter is somewhat painfully put together on Sunday. Relatives or very close friends who have gone to live away are likely to be communicated with only by Christmas card, unless there is a special family event" (*The Uses of Literacy: Chang-ing Patterns in English Mass Culture* [Fairlawn, N.J.: Essential Books, 1957], 135).

73. Roberts, *Classic Slum*, 131, 165.

74. Hoggart, *Uses of Literacy*, 135.

75. On the possible connection between Methodism and education, see Charles Thomas, *Methodism and Self Improvement in Nineteenth Century Cornwall*, Cornish Methodist Historical Association, Occasional Publication, no. 9 (Red-ruth, Cornwall: Cornish Methodist Historical Association, 1965), 6–15.

76. On possible links between literacy and radical political activity, see Webb, *British Working Class Reader*, chap. 2; and E. P. Thompson, *The Making of the English Working Class* (New York: Vintage Books, 1963), 711–46.

77. For a comparison of rural and urban social ties, see Michael Anderson, *Family Structure in Nineteenth Century Lancashire* (Cambridge: Cambridge Uni-versity Press, 1971), chaps. 6, 7.

78. For a discussion of the relationship between cultural change and educa-tion, see Williams, *Long Revolution*, pt. 2, chap. 1.

79. For surveys of standard of living trends in the last half of the nineteenth century, see Jeffrey G. Williamson, *Did British Capitalism Breed Inequality* (Lon-don: Allen and Unwin, 1985), 28; and B. E. Supple, "Income and Demand 1860–1914," in *The Economic History of Britain Since 1700*, vol. 2, ed. Roderick Floud and Donald McCloskey (Cambridge: Cambridge University Press, 1981), 121–31.

80. In his report for the Newcastle Commission on mining districts in Dur-ham and Cumberland, A. F. Foster suggested that lead miners exhibited more interest in education and in literature than more highly paid coal miners. See "Re-ports of Assistant Commissioners on Popular Education," PP 1861, vol. 21, pt. II, [2794-II], 323. Also see George Coode's report on the Black Country of War-wick and Stafford in ibid., 249–51, 253, 264–65.

81. "Minutes from the Select Committee on Public Libraries," PP 1849, vol. 17, [548], 88 (item 1358). For other assessments of the apathy toward intellectual activities in the midland mining and manufacturing districts, see Stephens, *Edu-cation, Literacy and Society*, 131.

82. On the decline of Methodism relative to the Church of England after 1850, see Alan Gilbert, *Religion and Society in Industrial England. Church, Chapel and Social Change, 1790–1914* (New York: Longman, 1976), chap. 2.

83. On the indifference to religion of the rural laboring classes at the turn of the century, see Michael Winstanley, "Voices from the Past: Rural Kent at the Close of an Era," in *The Victorian Countryside*, vol. 2, ed. G. E. Mingay (London: Routledge and Kegan Paul, 1981), 633. On industrial areas at the turn of the century and in the early twentieth century, see Roberts, *Classic Slum* , 173, 175; and Hoggart, *Uses of Literacy*, 112. For skepticism on the extent to which Meth-odism or religion penetrated very deeply into working-class life, see Henry Pelling,

Popular Politics and Society in Late Victorian Britain: Essays (London: Macmillan, 1968), chap. 2; Kevin Stanley Inglis, *Churches and the Working Classes in Victorian England* (London: Routledge and Kegan Paul, 1963), 3–20; and C.D. Field, "The Social Structure of English Methodism: Eighteenth to Twentieth Centuries," *British Journal of Sociology* 28 (1977): 199–225.

84. Obelkevich, *Religion and Rural Society*, 79.

85. For contemporary statements deploring the vulgar character of working-class reading material, see Knight, *The Old Printer*, 289; Walter Montagu Gattie, "What English People Read," *The Fortnightly Review* 52 (n.s., 46) (1889): 307–21; Thomas Wright, "On a Possible Popular Culture," *Contemporary Review* 40 (1881): 25–44; Joseph Ackland, "Elementary Education and the Decay of Literature," *Nineteenth Century Society* 35 (1894): 412–23; George R. Humphrey, "The Reading of the Working Classes," *Nineteenth Century Society* 35 (1894): 412–23; George R. Humphrey, "The Reading of the Working Classes," *Nineteenth Century* 33 (1893): 690–701; and Alexander Strahan, "Our Very Cheap Literature," *The Contemporary Review* 14 (1870): 439–60. A bookseller in the East Riding of Yorkshire reported that "the class of books that he was most able to sell was not the best for the morality of the people." See "Appendix, Pt. II to First Report on the Employment of Children, Young Persons, and Women in Agriculture," PP 1867–68, vol. 17, [4068-I], 386. For surveys of London working class reading habits see Statistical Society of London, "Report on St. George's-in-the-East," 218, and Statistical Society of London, "Moral Statistics of the Parishes of St. James, St. George, and St. Anne Soho, in the City of Westminster," *Journal of the Statistical Society of London* 1 (1838): 485.

86. On the circulation of religious periodicals in Wales, see "Reports of the Commissioners of Inquiry into the State of Education in Wales," PP 1847, vol. 27, pt. I, [870], 235; vol.27, pt. II, [871], 66–67, 72, 264; and vol.27, pt. III, [872], 45, 60, 61, 322. On the thriving trade for sensational literature, see Altick, *English Common Reader*, 286–93.

87. For a detailed review of individual cities and types of cities and towns and the educational tendencies of their populations, see Stephens, *Education, Literacy and Society*, 28–42. Stephens reports the same ambiguity concerning the relation between urbanization and literacy as that noted here. Studies of early modern Europe and eighteenth- and nineteenth-century North America have found stronger correlations between measures of literacy and measures of urbanization or population density. See Houston, "Literacy and Society," 269–93; and Soltow and Stevens, *Rise of Literacy*, 22–23, 39–42, 167–71, 175–76. The stronger correlations reported in these studies reflect both larger variations in population density than were present in Victorian England and the difficulty of areas with very low population density in supporting schools. This latter point, emphasized in Soltow and Stevens (*Rise of Literacy*, 41–42), is a different issue than the cultural and environmental issues discussed in this chapter; it is considered, with regard to Victorian England, in Chapter 6 below. For a survey of this issue in Europe generally see Mitch, "The Rise of Popular Literacy in Europe."

88. "Reports from Assistant Commissioners on Popular Education," PP 1861, vol. 21, pt. II, [2794-II], 250–51.

89. See Vincent, *Literacy and Popular Culture*, chap. 2.

90. Calculated from the census of 1841, "Population, Enumeration Abstract, 1841," PP 1843, vol. 22, [496], 14; and "Census of England and Wales, 1881, vol. IV, General Report," PP 1883, vol.80, [C.-3797], 98.

91. See Dudley Baines, *Migration in A Mature Economy: Emigration and Internal Migration in England and Wales, 1861–1900* (Cambridge: Cambridge University Press, 1985), 10.

92. "Minutes from the Select Committee on Public Libraries," PP 1849, vol. 17, [548], 207 (item 3202).

93. Ibid., xi.

94. Joseph Arch, *The Story of His Life Told by Himself* (London: Hutchinson and Co., 1898), 9.

95. Thompson, *Lark Rise to Candleford*, 471.

96. Roberts, *Classic Slum*, 132. Hoggart, describing working-class habits in the mid-twentieth century, refers to payment books kept behind an ornament to record how much of a debt had been paid off. See Hoggart, *Uses of Literacy*, 133. Also see Hoggart, *Uses of Literacy*, 43–44, for a discussion of how useful accurate record keeping could be for keeping tight working-class budgets in balance.

97. Paul Johnson, *Saving and Spending: The Working-Class Economy in Britain, 1870–1939* (Oxford: Clarendon Press, 1985), 147–48. For an eighteenth-century example see Defoe, *The Complete English Tradesman* 1:311–13.

98. Hoggart, *Uses of Literacy*, 133. For an example of an illiterate tradesman cheated despite using an elaborate tally system, see "Reports of Assistant Commissioners on Popular Education," PP 1861, vol. 21, pt. II, [2794-II], 252.

99. Bell, *At the Works*, 54.

100. Roberts, *Classic Slum*, 202.

101. Kathleen Dayus, *Her People* (London: Virago, 1982), 167.

102. This theme is emphasized in Robert W. Malcolmson, *Popular Recreation in English Society, 1700–1850* (Cambridge: Cambridge University Press, 1973), chaps. 6–8. Also see Alun Howkins, *Whitsun in Nineteenth Century Oxfordshire*, History Workshop Pamphlet, no. 8 (Oxford: History Workshop, 1973), 1–27; Marshall and Walton, *Lake Counties*, chap. 7; Obelkevich, *Religion and Rural Society*, 92; and Douglas Reid, "The Decline of Saint Monday 1766–1876," *Past and Present* 71 (1976): 76–101.

103. See Marshall and Walton, *Lake Counties*, 157; and Howkins, *Whitsun*, 1–27.

104. For trends in hours of work see M.A. Bienefeld, *Working Hours in British Industry: An Economic History* (London: Weidenfeld and Nicolson, 1972), chap. 4. For a discussion of how the gain of the Saturday half-holiday by working men influenced the spread of football, see Tony Mason, *Association Football and English Society 1863–1915* (Hassocks, Sussex: The Harvester Press, 1980), 3.

105. See Armstrong, *Farmworkers*, 121.

106. See Marshall and Walton, *Lake Counties*, 166–68; and Mason, *Association Football*, chaps. 1, 5.

107. See Bell, *At the Works*, 254; Marshall and Walton, *Lake Counties*, 156–57, 169; Helen Elizabeth Meller, *Leisure and the Changing City, 1870–1914*

(London: Routledge and Paul, 1976), 226; Raymond Williams, "The Press and Popular Culture: An Historical Perspective," in *Newspaper History from the Seventeenth Century to the Present Day*, ed. George Boyce, James Curran, and Pauline Wingate (London: Constable, 1978), 50; James Walvin, *The People's Game: A Social History of British Football* (London: Allen Lane, 1975), 59; and Brown, *Victorian News*, 245.

108. For a survey of the extent of working-class betting on horses as well as other forms of gambling in the late Victorian and Edwardian periods, see Ross McKibbin, "Working-Class Gambling in Britain, 1880–1939," *Past and Present* 82 (1979): 147–78.

109. See for example, Bell, *At the Works*, 258, 262; and Lee, *Origins of the Popular Press*, 40, who cites James Haslam's survey of Manchester.

110. On the timing of the development of bookmaking, see Wray Vamplew, *The Turf: A Social and Economic History of Horse Racing* (London: Allen Lane, 1976), 208, 215–16.

111. Roberts, *The Classic Slum*, 164.

112. See Vincent, *Literacy and Popular Culture*, 29–32.

113. Some of this advantage may reflect factors associated with literacy rather than any direct influence or value of literacy as such as a quality in a marriage partner. There are indications that some of this advantage was an apparent one. For sons and daughters of those in the lowest social category (class V) the advantage to literacy in marrying a higher status-spouse was noticeably lower than the advantage it provided to sons in the labor market (compare Table 3.4 with Table 2.3). In tabulations of the marriage register sample not reported in this study, the advantage to literacy in marriage for sons narrowed considerably after controlling for the occupation of the sons. The advantage to literacy in marrying a higher-status spouse also fell markedly for daughters between the two time periods (see Table 3.4). One interpretation of these declines is that as literacy became more widespread, its value as an indicator of other desirable characteristics in a spouse diminished. But the advantage to literacy in marriage was about the same as in the labor market for sons and daughters of those in category III (skilled and relatively well paid manual labor) (see Tables 3.4, 2.3, and 2.7). And for daughters of those in category III, the advantage to literacy in marriage does not appear to have fallen by much as literacy rates rose between the two periods (see Table 3.4).

114. In some cases these differences between groups were as much as 5 to 20 percent.

115. Perkin has written a useful survey of historians arguing for the importance of the 1870 Education Act in the development of the popular press, although Perkin actually argues against this point of view. See Harold Perkin, "The Origins of the Popular Press," *History Today* 7 (1957): 425–26. Other useful critical surveys are provided by Williams, *Long Revolution*, 173–75; and Lee, *Origins of the Popular Press*, 29–30, 244 nn. 41, 42. Some accounts supporting the importance of the Education Act in the rise of the popular press include F. Williams, *Dangerous Estate* (London: Longmans, Green, 1957), 129; and Harold Herd, *The March of Journalism* (London: Allen & Unwin, 1952), 236–43.

116. See Perkin, "Origins of the Popular Press," 425–35; R. Williams, *Long*

Revolution, 173–79; Lee, *Origins of the Popular Press*, 26–41; Brown, *Victorian News*, 7, 29–30, 62; and Michael Schudson, *Discovering the News* (New York: Basic Books, 1978), 35–39.

117. See Perkin, "Origins of the Popular Press," 426–32; and Williams, *Long Revolution*, 167.

118. See Perkin, "Origins of the Popular Press," 431–32; and Williams, *Long Revolution*, 175–76.

119. See Williams, *Long Revolution*, 166; and Lee, *Origins of the Popular Press*, 55.

120. Wadsworth provides the most detailed and authoritative estimates of newspaper circulations for the nineteenth century. See Wadsworth, "Newspaper Circulations," 3–23. His estimates are primarily for individual publications. Although he attempts some more aggregate circulation estimates, he is aware of the lack of comprehensive evidence for total newspaper circulations.

121. Calculated by multiplying Raymond Williams's percentages by 1861 census estimates of the population of England over age nineteen. For Williams's estimates, see his *Long Revolution*, 67. For census estimates of the population over age nineteen in 1861 see "Census of England and Wales, 1861, Vol. III, General Report, Appendix," PP 1863, vol. 53, pt. I, [3221], 107 (Table 55).

122. Lee, *Origins of the Popular Press*, 34.

123. See James, *Fiction for the Working Man*, 21; and Lee, *Origins of the Popular Press*, 89, 179.

124. These circulation estimates are taken from Williams, *Long Revolution*, 191, 194.

125. Brown, *Victorian News*, 30.

126. See Williams, *Long Revolution*, 196, 204; Alan J. Lee, "The Structure, Ownership, and Control of the Press, 1855–1914," in *Newspaper History*, ed. Boyce, Curran, and Wingate, 123–24; and James Curran and Jean Seaton, *Power without Responsibility: The Press and Broadcasting in Britain* (London: Fontana, 1981), 54.

127. Brown, *Victorian News*, 30.

128. For further discussion of the importance of large circulations to compensate for low prices, see Brown, *Victorian News*, 62. On the importance of large circulations generally, see Lee, *Origins of the Popular Press*, 56; Williams, *Long Revolution*, 201–23; Brown, *Victorian News*, 8, 61–62, 65; and James Curran, "The Press as an Agency of Social Control: An Historical Perspective," in *Newspaper History*, ed. Boyce, Curran, and Wingate, 68.

129. By the 1890s a rotary printing press could cost upwards of £3,500 and a linotype machine for composing upward of £350. See A. E. Musson, "Newspaper Printing in the Industrial Revolution," *Economic History Review*, 2d ser., 10 (1958): 420, 423–24. For surveys of developments in printing technology, see ibid., 411–26; Ellic Howe, *Newspaper Printing in the Nineteenth Century* (London: Privately printed, 1943); G. A. Isaacs, *The Story of the Newspaper Printing Press* (London: Co-operative Printing Society, 1931); and W. J. Gordon, "The Newspaper Printing Press of Today," *Leisure Hour* 39 (1890): 263–68, 333–37. Also see Lee, "Structure," 118; and Alan J. Lee, "Franklin Thomasson and the

Tribune: A Case-Study in the History of the Liberal Press, 1906–1908," *The Historical Journal* 16 (1973): 348.

130. Musson, "Newspaper Printing," 412.

131. Lee, "Structure," 119, 124–25.

132. On rising capital costs and their relation to circulation increases, see Curran, "Press as an Agency of Social Control," 68; Wadsworth, "Newspaper Circulations," 27; Brown, *Victorian News*, 8, 61, 65; and Lee, *Origins of the Popular Press*, 56. As Lee mentions, advertising revenue as well as increasing circulations played an important role in meeting increasing capital costs. These points are also discussed in Williams, *Long Revolution*, 201–3; and in Lee, "Structure," 117–29.

133. On the increase in circulation required for successful newspaper publishing in the later nineteenth century, see Williams, *Long Revolution*, 201–3; and Curran, "Press as an Agency of Social Control," 68. Also see James, *Fiction for the Working Man*, 21; and Lee, *Origins of the Popular Press*, 89, 179.

134. See Lee, *Origins of the Popular Press*, 56.

135. See Perkin, "Origins of the Popular Press," 429.

136. See ibid. For similar arguments, see Williams, *Long Revolution*, 177; Lee, *Origins of the Popular Press*, 67.

137. See Brown, *Victorian News*, 48.

138. See Perkin, "Origins of the Popular Press," 434. On the importance of rising living standards, also see Massingame, *London Daily Press*, 178.

139. See Virginia Berridge, "Content Analysis and Historical Research on Newspapers," in *The Press in English Society from the Seventeenth to Nineteenth Centuries*, ed. Michael Harris and Alan Lee (Rutherford, N.J.: Fairleigh Dickinson University Press, 1986), 207–9. Also see Virginia Berridge, "Popular Sunday Papers and Mid-Victorian Society," in *Newspaper History*, ed. Boyce, Curran, and Wingate, 247–64. Berridge argues in the latter article that the popular Sunday papers, although different in character, had elements of continuity with the earlier radical, unstamped, pauper press.

Accounts conflict on just how pervasive newspapers were among the working classes in the late nineteenth century up through the eve of World War I. Williams estimates that readership of the daily press was only at 11 percent of the adult population in 1875, 18 percent in 1900, and 19 percent in 1910. He estimates readership of the Sunday press at 19 percent of the population in 1875, 33 percent in 1900, and 60 percent in 1910. See Williams, *Long Revolution*, 209–10. Williams provides no details as to the sources for his estimates, however, and indeed the lacunae in the most detailed study, that of Wadsworth, "Newspaper Circulations," suggests that Williams's estimates must be based on a considerable amount of conjecture.

Other assessments suggest that newspaper reading was far more widespread among the working classes than Williams's estimates suggest. As already noted, Berridge has argued in a very detailed examination of both the content of large-circulation Sunday papers that emerged in the 1850s that while some drew primarily on lower-middle-class support, others were primarily supported by the working classes. See Berridge, "Popular Sunday Papers," 249–50; and Berridge, "Content Analysis," 207–9. Brown refers to surveys done at the end of the nineteenth century showing that elements of the working classes at a status level lower than the labor aristocrats took an active interest in newspapers. See Brown, *Victorian News*, 49. As previously noted, Bell found in her survey of two hundred workmen in turn-of-the-century Middleborough that three-quarters read a newspaper regularly, and a Cambridge farmer reported in the 1890s that almost all farm laborers in his district received weekly newspapers. See Bell, *At the Works*, 144; and "The Agricultural Labourer, Reports by Mr. C.M. Chapman," PP 1893–94, vol. 35, [C.-6894-II], 83. Also see, as previously noted, Massingame, *London Daily Press*, 10; Leigh, "What do the Masses Read?" 174–75; Lucas, "Furness Newspapers," 91; and Marshall and Walton, *Lake Counties*, 156.

Weeklies aimed at the lower working classes, such as the *News of the World*, emerged during the later nineteenth century, and reading the weekly on Sundays became a staple of working-class life. See "Agricultural Labourer," PP 1893–4, vol.35, [C.-6894-II], 83.

140. Berridge, "Popular Sunday Papers," 253–55.

141. Thomas Frost, *Forty Years' Recollections* (London: Sampson Low, 1880), 90.

142. The estimates of working-class literacy in Table 3.5, based on marriage register signature ability, probably overstate overall adult signature ability among the working classes because signature ability among those getting married was probably greater than among the general adult working-class population. This was probably especially true of the estimate for 1870 reported in Table 3.5 because of the marked rise in signature ability that occurred among those getting married during the three decades prior to 1870. Because of this rise, the signature rate for 1870 among those in the ages when marriage most commonly occurred was probably significantly higher than among all adults. The signature estimate for 1900 of 85 percent in Table 3.5 attempts to allow for the upward trend in signature ability. That is why the estimate is below the 97-percent signature rate reported for those marrying in 1900. See 63d ARRG (Abstract for 1900), PP 1901, vol. 15, [Cd.-761], lix. It should also be noted that ability to sign one's name is an uncertain guide to the fluency in literacy required for reading a newspaper.

Williams's estimates of the ratio of newspaper purchases among the literate population, reported in Table 3.5, should be regarded as conjectural since Williams does not report his method of estimation. See Williams, *Long Revolution*, 167, 176, 191, 193, 199, 204. His figures for the twentieth century are fairly consistent with those reported in Wadsworth, "Newspaper Circulations," however. As benchmarks for gauging the increase in the proportion of the literate population purchasing newspapers, one can note that Wadsworth's and Williams's estimates imply that the proportion of the literate population purchasing newspapers was, for daily papers: .50 in 1921; .59 in 1931; and .84 in 1951; and, for weekly papers: .74 in 1921; .76 in 1931; and .86 in 1951.

143. This procedure assumes that one component did not influence the magnitude of the others, an assumption open to challenge. For example, literacy rates may have risen because of an increased desire to purchase newspapers. But the procedure does indicate in an accounting sense how changes in each factor would have contributed to total changes in newspaper circulation.

144. On profits earned by mid-nineteenth-century newspapers, see Lee, *Origins of the Popular Press*, 89. For circulation levels, see Berridge, "Popular Sunday Papers," 263; and Wadsworth, "Newspaper Circulations." Both Lee, *Origins of the Popular Press*, 89; and Berridge, "Popular Sunday Papers," 253, cite the fact that Edward Lloyd's estate at his death was valued at over a half million pounds as evidence of the profitability of his newspaper.

145. The last calculation was done under the arguable assumption that the newly literate segment of the population purchased newspapers in the same proportion as the initially literate segment.

146. In the late nineteenth century, however, newly literate groups were probably more important to the development of mass weekly papers than to that of mass dailies. As previously noted, it may not have been until the early twentieth century that reading daily papers became common among the working classes.

147. Admittedly Lee does so somewhat grudgingly in "Structure," 119–20. Also see Williams, *Long Revolution*, 168.

148. Lee, *Origins of the Popular Press*, 130.

149. See ibid., 216; and Wadsworth, "Newspaper Circulations," 27.

150. "Minutes from the Select Committee on Postage," PP 1837–8, vol. 20, pt. II, [658], 215–16 (items 9175–76).

151. See Daunton, *Royal Mail*, 16 on postal reform. For accounts of the movement to repeal taxes on knowledge, see Bourne, *English Newspapers*, vol. 2, chaps. 15, 20; Collet Dobson Collett, *History of the Taxes on Knowledge* (London: T. F. Unwin, 1899); and Patricia Hollis, *The Pauper Press: A Study in Working-Class Radicalism of the 1830s* (London: Oxford University Press, 1970), chap. 3.

152. *Times*, 17 May 1854, cited in Bourne, *English Newspapers* 2:219. Bourne points out that the *Times* hypocritically reversed its position when it appeared that repealing the tax would eliminate its postal advantages and its national monopoly position.

Chapter 4: The Influence of the Family on Literacy Trends

1. J. S. Mill, *On Liberty* (1859; reprint, New York: W. W. Norton, Norton Critical Editions, 1975), 97–100.

2. Admittedly, the largest range in Table 4.2 is down the column of grooms of occupational status V in 1839–43, with a difference of 70.5 percentage points between grooms with fathers of occupational status I and grooms with fathers of occupational status V. However, in every other comparison, for a given occupational status, of the range across rows versus the range down columns, the range is greater across rows.

3. See Schofield, "Dimensions of Illiteracy," 451–54; West, *Education and the Industrial Revolution*, 200; Eric J. Hobsbawm, "The Standard of Living Debate," in *The Standard of Living in England in the Industrial Revolution*, ed. Arthur Taylor (London: Methuen, 1975), 183.

4. See George H. Wood, "Real Wages and the Standard of Comfort since 1850," *Journal of the Royal Statistical Society* 73 (1909): 91–103. For recent surveys

of the literature on this topic, see P. K. O'Brien and S. L. Engerman, "Changes in income and its distribution during the industrial revolution," in *The Economic History of Britain Since 1700*, vol. 1, ed. Roderick Floud and Donald McCloskey (Cambridge: Cambridge University Press, 1981), 164–81; and Supple, "Income and Demand 1860–1914," 121–43.

5. For a more detailed description of these estimates see Mitch, "Spread of Literacy," 342–64.

6. The source for this data is "Reports from Assistant Hand-loom Weavers Commissioners, Part II," PP 1840, vol.23, [43-I], 415–19, 424–30, 432–33. For a presentation of the regression estimates see Mitch, "Spread of Literacy," 343–46.

7. The source for this data is "Reports from Assistant Hand-loom Weavers Commissioners, Part V, Report of the Commission on Hand-loom Weavers," PP 1840, vol.24, [220], 440–47. For a presentation of the regression estimates see Mitch, "Spread of Literacy," 344, 347–51.

8. The source for this data is Statistical Society of London, "Report on St. George's-in-the-East," 200–201, 217, 221. For a presentation of the regression estimates see Mitch, "Spread of Literacy," 347, 352–56.

9. The source for this data is "Half-yearly Factory Inspectors Reports, December 31, 1866," PP 1867, vol.16, [3794], 116,117. For a presentation of the regression estimates see Mitch, "Spread of Literacy," 357–58.

10. Baxter, *National Income*, app. pt.4, 88–93.

11. For a presentation of the regression estimates see Mitch, "Spread of Literacy," 357, 360–64.

12. W. B. Stephens has made a detailed survey by region of contemporary views of the impact of poverty on schooling and income for mid-nineteenth-century England. See Stephens, *Education, Literacy and Society*, 91–92, 215, 223, 224, 226.

13. J. R. Wood, "Report on the State of Education in Birmingham," *Journal of the Statistical Society of London* 3 (1840): 26.

14. Henry Tremenheere, "Agricultural and Educational Statistics of Several Parishes in the County of Middlesex," *Journal of the London Statistical Society* 6 (1843): 129.

15. "Minutes of Evidence before Select Committee on Hand-loom Weaver's Petitions," PP 1834, vol. 10, [556], 41 (items 670–71), 192 (item 2526); "Minutes of Evidence, Appendix Part I (Leicestershire), Report on the Condition of the Framework Knitters," PP 1845, vol. 15, [618], 128 (items 2051–53); "Appendix to Second Report on Children's Employment—Trades and Manufactures—Pt. I," PP 1843, vol. 14, [431], A12 (item 99); and "Appendix to First Report on Children's Employment," PP 1863, vol. 18, [3170], 28.

16. "Reports of Special Assistant Poor Law Commissioners on the Employment of Women and Children in Agriculture," PP 1843, vol. 12, [510], 71, 78, 105, 132, 217, 238, 257, 343, 353, 363.

17. Manchester Statistical Society, "Report on Education in Pendleton," 69; and Manchester Statistical Society, "Report on the State of Education in Kingston-Upon-Hull," *Journal of the Statistical Society of London* 4 (1841): 161.

18. "Census of Gt. Britain, 1851, Education," PP 1852–3, vol. 90, [1692],

xxxix-xl; and "Report of Commissioners on Popular Education," PP 1861, vol. 21, pt. I, [2794-I], 178–79. The testimony in the Assistant Commissioners's Reports for the Newcastle Commission is somewhat conflicting. Fraser's report on rural districts suggests on page 68 that poverty was not a cause of low attendance, although on page 57 he suggests that it was a barrier. See "Reports of Assistant Commissioners on Popular Education," PP 1861, vol. 21, pt. II, [2794-II], 57, 68. Winder reporting on textile districts perceived poverty as an important barrier to school attendance for those in displaced trades. See "Reports of Assistant Commissioners on Popular Education," PP 1861, vol. 21, pt. II, [2794-II], 200. But the reports of Hedley on Eastern rural areas, Foster on mining districts, and Hodgson on London all minimized the contribution of poverty. For Hedley's report, see "Reports of Assistant Commissioners on Popular Education," PP 1861, vol. 21, pt. II, [2794-II], 146; for the reports of Foster and Hodgson, see "Further Reports of Assistant Commissioners on Popular Education," PP 1861, vol. 21, pt. III, [2794-III], 233, 517.

19. "Appendix to First Report on Children's Employment," PP 1863, vol. 18, [3170], 223.

20. "Appendix to First Report of Children's Employment Commission. Mines," PP 1842, vol. 16, [381], 714; also see ibid., 608–9, 649, 800. But some observers of mine conditions did perceive poverty to be a problem. See ibid., 484, 485, 804.

21. "Reports from Assistant Hand-loom Weavers Commissioners, part II," PP 1840, vol. 23, [43-I], 447; also see ibid., 493, 494; and "Reports from Assistant Hand-loom Weavers Commissioners, part III," PP 1840, vol. 23, [43-II], 543, 641.

22. "Appendix, Pt. II to First Report on the Employment of Children, Young Persons, and Women in Agriculture," PP 1867–8, vol. 17, [4068-I], 470, 487, 257; and "Appendix, Part II to Second Report on the Employment of Women and Children in Agriculture. Evidence from the Assistant Commissioners," PP 1868–9, vol. 13, [4202-I], 334.

23. "Appendix, Pt. II to First Report on the Employment of Children, Young Persons, and Women in Agriculture," PP 1867–8, vol. 17, [4068-I], 321, 404; and "Appendix, Part II to Second Report on the Employment of Children, Young Persons, and Women in Agriculture," PP 1868–9, vol. 13, [4202-I], 78, 112.

24. "Third Report on the Employment of Children, Young Persons, and Women in Agriculture," PP 1870, vol. 13, [C.-70], 6.

25. Mitchell and Deane, *Abstract of British Historical Statistics*, 29, 36, 37.

26. See E. A. Wrigley and R. S. Schofield, *The Population History of England, 1541–1871* (Cambridge: Harvard University Press, 1981), 230, 236, 413–14. This pattern for England contrasts with the patterns reported by Mary Jo Maynes in comparing villages in France and Baden in the late eighteenth and early nineteenth centuries. Maynes found that in the Baden villages, infant and child mortality rates fell at a faster pace at the same time as literacy and school attendance rates were rising at a faster pace than in the French villages. Since Maynes had only two sets of villages to compare, however, she viewed this finding as "suggestive" and "compatible" with the impact of mortality on literacy investments rather than a clear demonstration of the connection. See Mary Jo Maynes, *Schooling for the*

People: Comparative Local Studies of Schooling History in France and Germany, 1750–1850 (New York: Holmes and Meier, 1985), 124–28.

27. For estimates of the age of marriage, see Wrigley and Schofield, *Population History of England*, 255, 437.

28. See Schofield, "Dimensions of Illiteracy," 445–46.

29. For age-specific mortality trends, see Mitchell and Deane, *Abstract of British Historical Statistics*, 40–41.

30. Relaxing the assumption of a constant annual rental to literacy and instantaneous acquisition of literacy would probably further reduce the impact of mortality declines. The rental to literacy probably rose with age, and the gains at older ages would be more heavily discounted. Relaxing the instantaneous acquisition assumption would also lead to heavier discounting, as the literacy acquisition decision was being made. The results here challenge E. L. Jones's argument that mortality changes had potentially substantial effects on educational decisions. See E. L. Jones, "Demographic and Educational Interaction in Nineteenth-Century Europe and the Modern Third World," School of Economics, La Trobe University, mimeograph, 6–7.

31. The percentage increase in the discounted benefits of literacy due to mortality declines can be estimated by the following expression:

$$\frac{\sum_{i=1}^{24} \frac{(1 - M_1)^i}{1 + r} A - \sum_{i=1}^{24} \frac{(1 - M_0)^i}{1 + r} A}{\sum_{i=1}^{24} \frac{(1 - M_0)^i}{1 + r} A}$$

Where M_0 is the mortality rate of those aged five to thirty-four before the mortality decline and M_1 is the mortality rate of this age group after the mortality decline, A is the annual flow of benefit attributable to literacy, assumed here to be constant over time, and r is the annual discount rate, also assumed to be constant over time. The calculation assumes that literacy was acquired instantaneously at age ten. The mortality rate for those aged five to thirty-four was 10 per thousand in 1840 and 5 per thousand in 1900, thus giving values for M_0 and M_1. For these mortality estimates, see Mitchell and Deane, *Abstract of British Historical Statistics*, 40–41. The value of this expression varies as follows with the following discount rates:

	Discount Rate			
	.05	.10	.15	.20
Increase in discounted benefits as a proportion of initial benefits from literacy	.047	.041	.031	.027

The low impact of mortality changes on education decisions has been noted by Samuel Preston, "Causes and Consequences of Mortality Declines in Less Developed Countries during the Twentieth Century," in *Population and Economic Change in Developing Countries*, ed. Richard Easterlin (Chicago: University of Chicago Press, 1980), 324–26.

32. Wrigley and Schofield, *Population History of England*, 229.

33. Michael Teitelbaum, *The Fertility Decline in Britain* (Princeton: Princeton University Press, 1984), 182, 213, 218.

34. See Louise Tilly and Miriam Cohen, "Does the Family Have a History? A Review of Theory and Practice in Family History," *Social Science History* 6 (1982): 139.

35. There has long been interest in the possible interrelation between education and fertility. See Grace Leybourne and Kenneth White, *Education and the Birth-Rate: A Social Dilemma* (London: J. Cape, 1940), 52–64, 176–89. It is usual to emphasize the influence of education on fertility rather than the other way around, however. In fact, the two can be viewed as simultaneously determined, with the strength of the trade-off captured in the correlation between the two variables.

36. See Gary S. Becker and H. G. Lewis, "Interaction between Quantity and Quality of Children," *Journal of Political Economy* 81 (1973): S279–88. For a critique of the Becker and Lewis approach, see Harvey Graff, "Literacy, Education, and Fertility, Past and Present: A Critical Review," *Population and Development Review* 5 (1979): 105–40.

37. For a presentation of these correlations see Mitch, "Spread of Literacy," 334, 337–38.

38. For the fertility and child labor correlation, see David V. Glass, "Changes in Fertility in England and Wales, 1851 to 1931," in *Political Arithmetic: A Symposium of Population Studies*, ed. Lancelot Hogben (London: George Allen and Unwin, 1938), 209–11. On the literacy-child labor correlation, see W. B. Stephens, *Regional Variations in Education during the Industrial Revolution, 1780–1870: The Task of the Local Historian* (Leeds: The University of Leeds, 1973), 6–13. On both correlations also see Mitch, "Spread of Literacy," 337–38.

39. George R. Boyer and Jeffrey G. Williamson, "A Quantitative Assessment of the Fertility Transition in England, 1851–1911," in *Research in Economic History* 12 (1989), ed. Roger Ransom (Greenwich, Conn.: JAI Press, 1989), 99–110.

40. See the survey in Jee Peng Tan and Michael Haines, *Schooling and the Demand for Children: Historical Perspectives*, Washington, D.C.: World Bank Staff Working Papers, no. 697, Population and Development Series, no. 22 (1984), 14.

41. Ibid., 7–14.

42. Ibid., 14–15. Also see Graff, "Literacy, Education, and Fertility," 125–32. Maynes, in her comparison of villages in France and Baden found, literacy and schooling rates were higher in Baden despite high fertility in Baden and declining fertility in the French villages. See Maynes, *Schooling for the People*, 124. Leet, in his study of nineteenth-century Ohio, found that although the simple cross-county correlation between illiteracy and fertility was high, illiteracy explained little of the

variation in fertility after other controls were entered. See Don R. Leet, *Population Pressure and Human Fertility Response. Ohio, 1810–1860* (New York: Arno Press, 1978), 228–36.

43. See Tan and Haines, *Schooling and the Demand for Children*, 22–25; John Knodel and Etienne Van de Walle, "Lessons from the Past: Policy Implications of Historical Fertility Studies," *Population and Development Review* 5 (1979): 224; and Francine Van de Walle, "Education and the Demographic Transition in Switzerland," *Population and Development Review* 6 (1980): 463–64.

44. David Levine, *Reproducing Families: The Political Economy of English Population History* (Cambridge: Cambridge University Press, 1987), 126–28, 162, 185–91, 210–12.

45. See J. W. Innes, *Class Fertility Trends in England and Wales 1876–1934* (Princeton: Princeton University Press, 1938), 41–52.

46. The sources for these data sets are Statistical Society of London, "Report on St. George's-in-the-East," 200–201, 217, 221; "Reports from Assistant Hand-loom Weavers Commissioners, Part II," PP 1840, vol.23, [43-I], 423–30, 432–33; "Reports from Assistant Hand-loom Weavers Commissioners, Part V," PP 1840, vol. 24, [220], 440–47.

47. For a presentation of these correlations and regressions see Mitch, "Spread of Literacy," 331–38.

48. See Tan and Haines, *Schooling and the Demand for Children*, 14–16.

49. See Wrigley and Schofield, *Population History of England*, 229; and M. W. Flinn, *British Population Growth 1700–1850* (London: Macmillan, 1970), 24–37.

50. See Teitelbaum, *Fertility Decline in Britain*, 182, 213, 218.

51. See Michael Anderson, *Approaches to the History of the Western Family, 1500–1914*, Economic History Society Studies in Economics and Social History (London: Macmillan, 1980), 15. Another survey reviewing the three approaches that Anderson distinguishes is Tilly and Cohen, "Does the Family Have a History?"

52. Tilly and Cohen, "Does the Family Have a History?" 157–60. Another survey emphasizing this approach is Bruce Bellingham, "The History of Childhood since the 'Invention of Childhood': Some Issues in the Eighties," *Journal of Family History* 13 (1988): 347–58.

53. Michael Anderson, "The Emergence of the Modern Life Cycle in Britain," *Social History* 10 (1985): 82–84.

54. Richard Wall, "The Age of Leaving Home," *Journal of Family History* 3 (1978): 191, 193.

55. Michael Anderson, "Households, families and individuals: Some preliminary results from the national sample from the 1851 Census of Great Britain," *Continuity and Change* 3 (1988): 434.

56. See J. H. Plumb, "The New World of Children in Eighteenth-Century England," *Past and Present* 67 (1975): 64–95.

57. For useful surveys of criticism, see Anderson, *Approaches to History of the Family*, chap.3; Tilly and Cohen, "Does the Family Have a History?" 133, 142–46; and Bellingham, "History of Childhood," 348–50.

58. See J. R. Gillis, "Affective Individualism and the English Poor," review

of *The Family, Sex and Marriage in England, 1500–1800*, by Lawrence Stone, *Journal of Interdisciplinary History* 10 (1979): 121–28; and E. P. Thompson, "Happy Families," review of *The Family, Sex and Marriage in England, 1500–1800*, by Lawrence Stone, *New Society*, 8 September 1977, 499–501.

59. For evidence on this, see Michael Anderson, *Family Structure in Lancashire*, 70 n.18. Anderson concludes that heavy drinking did cause some parents to neglect their children, although he also concludes that middle-class observers may have overstated the extent of this. Studies of trends in drinking habits over the nineteenth century suggest there is ambiguity in the extent to which industrialization increased drinking. W. R. Lambert has argued that although conditions in industrial areas tended to encourage drunkenness, new production methods also led employers to be increasingly active in promoting temperance among their workers. See W. R. Lambert, "Drink and Work-Discipline in Industrial South Wales, c. 1800–1870," *Welsh History Review* 7 (1975): 289–306. Brian Harrison has also argued that industrialization had conflicting effects on drinking habits. See Harrison, *Drink and the Victorians* (London: Faber and Faber, 1971), 40–41, 62, 346–47. Sheila Ferguson has argued that per capita consumption of beer declined in the first half of the nineteenth century while consumption of spirits rose. See Ferguson, *Drink* (London: Batsford, 1975), 57, 61. A. E. Dingle has argued that consumption per head of alcoholic beverages rose between 1850 and 1870 and then declined until 1914. See Dingle, "Drink and Working-Class Living Standards in Britain, 1870–1914," *Economic History Review*, 2d ser., 25 (1972): 608–22.

60. For a discussion of the concept of family strategies, see Louise A. Tilly, "Individual Lives and Family Strategies in the French Proletariat," *Journal of Family History* 4 (1979): 137–52.

61. For a comparison of education strategies among Italian and Jewish immigrants to New York City, see Miriam Cohen, "Changing Education Strategies Among Immigrant Generations: New York Italians in Comparative Perspective," *Journal of Social History* 15 (1982): 443–66.

62. See Stephens, *Education, Literacy and Society*, 176, 177. Also see Neil Smelser, *Social Change in the Industrial Revolution: An Application of Theory to the Lancashire Cotton Industry* (Chicago: University of Chicago Press, 1959), chaps. 9–11, for a discussion of the role of child labor in textile areas as part of family strategies more generally and the relation of changes in the role of child labor to increases in schooling.

63. See Higgs, *Domestic Servants and Households*, 67–77.

64. Tilly, "Individual Lives and Family Strategies," 137–38.

65. Anderson, *Approaches to History of the Family*, 84.

66. Anderson, *Family Structure in Lancashire*, chap. 10.

67. Stephen Ruggles, *Prolonged Connections: The Rise of the Extended Family in Nineteenth-Century England and America* (Madison: University of Wisconsin Press, 1987), chap. 3.

68. See "Appendix to First Report on Children's Employment. Mines," PP 1842, vol. 17, [382], 244 (item 12), 372 (item 50); "Appendix, Pt. II to First Report from the Commissioners on the Employment of Women, Young Persons,

and Children in Agriculture," PP 1867–8, vol. 17, [4068-I], 66; and "Appendix to Fourth Report on the Employment of Children and Young Persons in Trades and Manufactures," PP 1865, vol. 20, [3548], 242.

69. For the argument and evidence from the U.S. that migration does not weaken extended family ties, see Eugene Litwak, "Geographic Mobility and Extended Family Cohesion," in *Social Demography*, ed. Thomas Ford and Gordon de Jong (Englewood Cliffs, N.J.: Prentice-Hall, 1970), 180–92.

70. John C. Caldwell, *Theory of Fertility Decline* (New York: Academic Press, 1982), 139–43.

71. For a survey of this approach, see Bellingham, "History of Childhood," 347–58.

72. Smelser, *Social Change in the Industrial Revolution*, chaps. 9–11.

73. Gardner, *Lost Schools*, 95–96, 161.

74. Levine, *Reproducing Families*, 185–91, 210–12.

75. See, for example, Arleen Leibowitz, "Home Investments in Children," *Journal of Political Economy* 82 (1974): S111–31; and for developing countries, Nancy Birdsall and Susan Hill Cochrane, "Education and Parental Decision Making: A Two-Generation Approach," in *Education and Development*, ed. Lascelles Anderson and Douglas Windham (Lexington, Mass.: Lexington Books, 1982), 189–94. For late-eighteenth- and early-nineteenth-century England, see David Levine, "Education and Family Life in Early Industrial England," *Journal of Family History* 4 (1979): 375–76. Kaestle and Vinovskis report a weak effect of parental literacy on school attendance in data on nineteenth-century Massachusetts, but they attributed this to the low proportion of illiterates in their sample. See Carl Kaestle and Maris Vinovskis, "From Fireside to Factory: School Entry and School Leaving in Nineteenth-Century Massachusetts," in *Transitions: The Family and the Life Course in Historical Perspective*, ed. Tamara Hareven (New York: Academic Press, 1978), 160, 169.

76. Levine, "Education and Family Life," 375–76.

77. Two features of the sample underlying Tables 4.5 and 4.6 suggest the possibility of selectivity bias: First, the literacy rate of witnesses with the same name as fathers was unusually high for brides but not for grooms. Witnesses with the same name as fathers of grooms had a signature rate only slightly above that of grooms in the marriage register sample (72.6 percent for witnesses compared with 69 percent for grooms in the 1839–43 sample, and 84 percent for witnesses compared with 85 percent for grooms in the 1869–73 sample). But witnesses with the same name as brides' fathers had markedly higher literacy rates than grooms (85.7 percent for witnesses in the 1839–43 sample compared with 69 percent for grooms, and 90.6 percent for witnesses in the 1869–73 sample compared with 85 percent for grooms).

Second, a much higher proportion of brides' fathers than grooms' fathers had the same name as a witness (4.0 percent for grooms' fathers and 8.1 percent for brides' fathers in the 1839–43 sample, and 4.3 percent for grooms and 12.6 percent for brides in the 1869–73 sample).

The second feature suggests that in certain social groups it may have been customary for the bride's father to act as witness, while the first feature suggests that such groups may not have been representative of the general English population.

78. The marriage register sample itself provides some evidence on the proportion of cases in which this assumption was incorrect. In some cases where a father had the same name as a witness, the marriage register indicated that the father was deceased, clearly demonstrating that the father and the witness of the same name were in fact different people. Comparing the proportion of fathers in the total sample who were deceased with the proportion of deceased fathers in the subsample with the same name as the witness provides a measure of the extent to which witnesses and fathers of the same name were in fact the same. If in a substantial proportion of cases witnesses and fathers of the same name were the same, then the proportion of fathers with the same name as witnesses who were also deceased should be noticeably lower than the proportion of deceased fathers in the total sample.

In the 1839–43 sample, no deceased father of a bride shared his name with a witness, while of 167 grooms' fathers sharing the same name as a witness, only 1 was deceased (.60 percent of the sample of grooms' fathers sharing the same name as a witness) compared with 26 of 4,013 grooms' fathers who were deceased in the rest of the sample (.65 percent). Given the slight differences in the fraction of deceased then, few of the grooms' fathers with the same name as a witness may actually have been the same. In the 1869–73 sample, 13 of 485 brides' fathers with the same name as witness were deceased (2.68 percent of the sample), while 212 of 3,248 remaining brides' fathers were deceased (6.53 percent of the sample). For grooms' fathers in the 1869–73 sample, 6 of 163 with the same name as a witness were deceased (3.68 percent of the sample) compared with 222 of 3,567 of the remaining fathers being deceased (6.22 percent of the sample). The sizable difference in the proportion of deceased between the total sample of fathers and those with the same name as a witness suggests that a substantial proportion of fathers with the same name as witness in the 1869–73 sample were in fact witnesses.

Finally one can conjecture that even if the witnesses in some cases were not the father, it was likely that they were related to the bride or groom. Thus, if nothing else, Tables 4.5 and 4.6 probably indicate the relation between literacy of a relative and literacy of the bride or groom.

79. For a presentation of these regression results see Mitch, "Spread of Literacy," 360–63.

80. For a presentation of these regression results see ibid., 348–51.

81. See Leibowitz, "Home Investments," S116.

82. See Birdsall and Cochrane, "Education and Parental Decision Making," 190–92.

83. For a presentation of these regression results see Mitch, "Spread of Literacy," 353–56.

84. "Third Report on Children's Employment," PP 1864, vol. 22, [3170], 37 (item 188). Also see "Appendix to Second Report on Children's Employment—Trades and Manufactures—Pt. I," PP 1843, vol.14, [431], B19 (items 135–37), E30, E31.

85. To demonstrate this, consider the following model of literacy transmission between generations. Define: P = probability a child of illiterate parents will be literate; δ = difference between probability a child of literate parents will be literate and probability a child of illiterate parents will be literate. If in one generation the proportion of the population literate is q_0; in the next generation, the proportion literate (q_1) will be:

$$q_1 = q_0(P + \delta) + (1 - q_0)P.$$

The steady state level of literacy will be given by:

$$q_1 = q_0 = q_0(P + \delta) + (1 - q_0)P.$$
$$q_1 = q_0 = P/(1 - \delta).$$

The effect on the steady state level of literacy of a change in P (ΔP) due to some exogenous force such as increased provision of subsidized schooling or an increased demand for literate workers will then be given by:

$$\Delta q = \Delta P/(1 - \delta).$$

The results considered in the text suggest that a reasonable estimate for δ would be .2, implying that the effect of parental education would amplify the impact of an exogenous force on the steady state level of literacy by $[1 - 1/(1 - .2)]$ or 25 percent.

86. This is evident if the beta coefficients are calculated for these regressions. See Mitch, "Spread of Literacy," 384–85. The beta coefficients indicate the percentage of the variance in the dependent variable accounted for by each independent variable.

Part 2: Public Policy and the Costs of Acquiring Literacy

1. For one account of the extent of activity of the Society for the Preservation of Christian Knowledge, see Mary Gwladys Jones, *The Charity School Movement: A Study of Eighteenth-Century Puritanism in Action* (Cambridge: Cambridge University Press, 1938). For a critical view of Jones that emphasizes the importance of local activity in the eighteenth century, see Joan Simon, "Was there a Charity School Movement?" in *Education in Leicestershire 1540–1940*, ed. Brian Simon (Leicester: Leicester University Press, 1968), 55–100. For an account of the funding of schools in the late eighteenth and early nineteenth centuries in one English city, see James Murphy, "The Rise of Public Elementary Education in Liverpool: Part One, 1784–1818," *Transactions of the Historic Society of Lancashire and Chesire for the Year 1964* 116 (1965): 165–95; and "The Rise of Public Elementary Education in Liverpool: Part Two, 1819–1835," *Transactions . . . for the Year 1966* 118 (1967): 105–38.

2. For an account of the establishment of the National Society, see H. J. Burgess, *Enterprise in Education* (London: National Society and SPCK, 1958). For accounts of parliamentary and government involvement in education during the nineteenth century, see Sturt, *Education of the People*; Birchenough, *History of Elementary Education*; Hurt, *Education in Evolution*; and Gillian Sutherland, *Elementary Education in the Nineteenth Century* (London: The Historical Association, 1971).

3. The 1818 enrollment in subsidized schools is obtained from "A Digest of Parochial Returns on the Education of the Poor, Vol.III," PP 1819, vol. 9, pt. III, [224], 1171, 1275. All endowed schools and "new" or monitorial schools were classified as subsidized. There is no way of determining whether any of the ordinary unendowed schools were subsidized. Enrollment in subsidized schools in 1880 is based on AR 1881–82, PP 1882, vol. 23, [C.-3312], iii. Witnesses before Parliament in the 1830s suggested that the annual cost per pupil in a National or British school was ten to twelve shillings. See "Minutes of Evidence before the Select Committee on Education of the Poorer Classes," PP 1837–8, vol. 7, [589], 71 (item 669). School fees were typically two pence a week. Assuming a forty-week year, this would imply a fee income of four shillings per year, making the subsidy per student six to eight shillings. In 1880, total income per scholar minus fee income, according to Education Department reports, was twenty-four shillings per year in voluntary schools and thirty-three shillings per year in Board schools. See AR 1881–2, PP 1882, vol. 23, [C.-3312], v.

4. For a survey of the evolution of the educational aims of the elementary school curriculum in nineteenth-century England, see Vincent, *Literacy and Popular Culture*, chap. 3.

5. See Sutherland, *Policy Making in Elementary Education*, 81–91.

6. See Birchenough, *History of Elementary Education*, 56.

7. W. L. Sargent, "On the Progress of Elementary Education," *Journal of the Royal Statistical Society* 30 (1867): 112–20.

8. For critical surveys of these histories, see Mark Blaug, "The Economics of Education in English Classical Political Economy: A Re-examination," in *Essays on Adam Smith*, ed. Andrew Skinner and Thomas Wilson (Oxford: Clarendon Press, 1975), 594–99; Thomas Laqueur, "Working Class Demand and the Growth of English Elementary Education, 1750–1850," in *Schooling and Society*, ed. Lawrence Stone (Baltimore: Johns Hopkins University Press, 1976), 193–95; and Silver, "Aspects of Neglect."

9. For estimates of government expenditure on education during this period, see Norman Morris, "Public Expenditure on Education in the 1860's," *Oxford Review of Education* 3 (1977): 3. For comments on gaps in school provision, see "Report of Commissioners on Popular Education," PP 1861, vol. 21, pt. I, [2794-I], 278–79, 285–87.

10. For an example, see David Wardle, *Education and Society in Nineteenth Century Nottingham* (Cambridge: Cambridge University Press, 1971), 51–53.

11. Manchester Statistical Society, "Report on Education in Pendleton," 73, 80.

12. "Reports of Assistant Commissioners on Popular Education," PP 1861, vol. 21, pt. II, [2794-II], 254, 268, 304, 312.

13. See AR 1876–77, PP 1877, vol. 29, [C.-1780-I], 640, 647; AR 1881–82, PP 1882, vol. 23, [C.-3312], 380; AR 1883–84, PP 1884, vol. 24, [C.-4091-I], 431; AR 1880–81, PP 1881, vol. 32, [C.-2948-I], 442, 443; and Sutherland, *Policy Making in Elementary Education*, 159–61.

Chapter 5: The Geographical Distribution of Public Schooling

1. "Third Report of the Royal Commission Appointed to Inquire into the Working of the Elementary Education Acts," PP 1887, vol. 30, [C.-5158], 446 (item 53998).

2. See Michael Sanderson, "The National and British School Societies in Lancashire 1803–1839: The Roots of the Anglican Supremacy in English Education," in *Local Studies and the History of Education: Papers from the 1971 Conference of the History of Education Society*, ed. T. G. Cook. (London: Methuen, 1972), 1–36.

3. The National Society, for example, during this period would in general only provide funds to defray building costs. See Burgess, *Enterprise in Education*, 27.

4. See National Society, *Twenty-Third Annual Report* (London, 1834), 19.

5. For description of the 1846 provisions, see Sturt, *Education of the People*, chaps. 9, 10.

6. National Society, *Thirty-First Annual Report* (London, 1842), 2.

7. Cited in Stephens, *Education, Literacy and Society*, 235.

8. National Society, *Forty-Sixth Annual Report* (London, 1857), xxiv-xxv. For further mention of this problem, see Stephens, *Education, Literacy and Society*, 90 n.235; "Final Report on the Elementary Education Acts," PP 1888, vol. 35, [C.-5485], 12; W. E. Marsden, *Unequal Educational Provision in England and Wales: The Nineteenth Century Roots* (London: Woburn, 1987), 33; and Birchenough, *History of Elementary Education*, 70, 86–87.

9. National Society, *Thirty-Third Annual Report* (London, 1844), 1–12. Pages 1 and 2 of the report indicate that the fund was set up in response to concerns about disturbances in mining and manufacturing districts in the autumn of 1842.

10. See National Society, *Thirty-Sixth Annual Report* (London, 1847), 5–10.

11. These enrollment rates are based on "Census of Gt. Britain, 1851, Education," PP 1852–53, vol. 90, [1692], 4–7.

12. National Society, "Summaries of Returns to the Inquiry into the State and Progress of Schools during the Years 1856–7, throughout England and Wales" (London, 1858), 54–59.

13. Calculated from "List of School Boards and Attendance Committees in England and Wales, 1st April, 1895," PP 1895, vol. 76, [C.-7687], 8–111. Also see Marsden, *Unequal Educational Provision*, 40.

14. See Sturt, *Education of the People*, 208–9.

15. See Burgess, *Enterprise in Education*, 106.

16. On problems of areas with low population densities see "Report of Commissioners on Popular Education," PP 1861, vol. 21, pt. I, [2794-I], 278, 285–87; Sutherland, *Elementary Education*, 32; "Minutes of Evidence before Royal Commission on Elementary Education, Third Report," PP 1887, vol. 30, [C.-5158], 590 (items 57436–57443); and "Final Report on the Elementary Education Acts," PP 1888, vol. 35, [C.-5485], 49.

17. "Report of Commissioners on Popular Education," PP 1861, vol. 21, pt. I, [2794-I], 386, 392.

18. As cited in Birchenough, *History of Elementary Education*, 115. For the history of payment by results and its critics, see Sutherland, *Policy Making in Elementary Education*, chaps. 7, 8.

19. Calculated from "Report of Commissioners on Popular Education," PP 1861, vol. 21, pt. I, [2794-I], 585.

20. Calculated from National Society, "Summaries of Returns to the Inquiry into the State and Progress of Schools during the Years 1856–7," 54–59.

21. If just the forty counties of England are considered, the Spearman coefficients reported in Table 5.1 are:

	1833 School Enrollment	1851 School Enrollment	1841 Illiteracy	1857 Illiteracy
Nonfee income, 1857	.319 (.045)	.567 (.0001)	-.196 (.225)	-.388 (.013)
Subscription income, 1857	.167 (.302)	.438 (.005)	-.098 (.549)	-.253 (.116)
Endowment income, 1857	.214 (.186)	.346 (.029)	-.140 (.390)	-.309 (.053)
Government income, 1857	.169 (.296)	.316 (.047)	.035 (.830)	-.016 (.924)
Cumulative parliamentary grants, 1833-59	-.061 (.708)	.142 (.381)	-.126 (.438)	-.070 (.666)
Percent assisted by government, 1866	-.381 (.015)	-.287 (.072)	-.064 (.697)	.014 (.934)

Note: Numbers in parentheses report the probability that the correlation coefficient is equal to zero.

22. See "Report of Commissioners on Popular Education," PP 1861, vol. 21, pt. I, [2794-I], 76, 278–79; and "Reports of Assistant Commissioners on Popular Education," PP 1861, vol. 21, pt. II, [2794-II], 217, 420. On the role of landowners and the clergy, see John S. Hurt, "Landowners, Farmers and Clergy and the Financing of Rural Education before 1870," *Journal of Educational Administration and History* 1 (1968): 6–13. The role of the clergy has also been examined in detail by Clark. See George Kitson Clark, *Churchmen and the Condition of England, 1832–1885: A Study in the Development of Social Ideas and Practice from the Old Regime to the Modern State* (London: Methuen, 1973), chap. 4.

23. National Society, *Twenty-Third Annual Report* (London, 1834), 19.

24. Sturt, *Education of the People*, 208–9.

25. See "Report of Commissioners on Popular Education," PP 1861, vol.21, pt. I, [2794-I], 69–71.

26. If all forty of the traditional English counties are considered, the rank order correlation between government income and subscription income is +.477 while between government income and endowment income it is +.08. If the forty English counties and the 12 Welsh counties are considered together, the two respective correlations are +.454 and +.132.

27. Roger R. Sellman, *Devon Village Schools in the Nineteenth Century* (Newton Abbot, Devon: David and Charles, 1967), 27.

28. Thus the National Society reported that in 1856, of operating income in Church of England schools financed by subsidies, only 4 percent came from government grants; in 1866, 37.3 percent came from government grants. See National Society, "Summaries of Returns to the Inquiry into the State and Progress of Schools during the Years 1856–7," 56–59; and National Society, "Statistics of Church of England Schools for the Poor in England and Wales for the Years 1866 and 1867," 2d ed. (London, 1868), 26.

29. See 7th ARRG (Abstract for 1843), PP 1846, vol. 19, [727], 40–41.

30. Calculated from "A Digest of Parochial Returns on the Education of the Poor," PP 1819, vol. 9, [224], pt. I, 229–44, 289–326, 327–50, 423–46, 475–532, 533–64; pt. II, 693–716, 853–76.

31. Calculated from "Abstract of Returns on the State of Education in England and Wales," PP 1835, vol. 41, [62], 240–73, 300–335, 336–53, 422–75; and PP 1835, vol. 42, [62], 504–53, 554–94, 712–37, 868–95.

32. Calculated from "Abstract of Returns on the State of Education," PP 1835, vol. 43, [62], 1218–15, 1228–35, 1238–47, 1278–89, 1292–95, 1320–23.

33. See Rev. Charles Richson, "On the Fallacies Involved in Certain Returns of the Number of Day Schools and Day Scholars in England and Wales in 1818, 1833 and 1851, etc.," *Transactions of the Manchester Statistical Society* (1853–54): 1–16. Also see West, "Resource Allocation," 78–79, 83–84.

34. See Jones, *Charity School Movement*, 28, 160–61; Simon, "Was There a Charity School Movement?" 95–99; Murphy, "Rise of Public Elementary Education in Liverpool: Part Two," 109–22.

35. Calculated from National Society, "Summaries of Returns to the Inquiry into the State and Progress of Schools during the Years 1856–7"; and National Society, "Statistics of Church of England Schools for the Poor in England and Wales for the Years 1866 and 1867."

36. Calculated from "Abstract of Returns on the State of Education," PP 1835, vol. 43, [62], 1326; and "Census of Gt. Britain, 1851. Education," PP 1852–3, vol. 90, [1692], 4–7.

37. "Report of the Commissioners on Popular Education," PP 1861, vol. 21, pt. I, [2794-I], 297–99.

38. "Further Reports of Assistant Commissioners on Popular Education," PP 1861, vol. 21, pt. III, [2794-III], 233, 351. Also see "Reports of Assistant

Commissioners on Popular Education," PP 1861, vol. 21, pt. II, [2794-II], 54, 199–210, 466.

39. "Reports of Assistant Commissioners on Popular Education," PP 1861, vol. 21, pt. II, [2794-II], 199–210.

40. Ibid., 54.

41. Ibid., 466.

42. Ibid., 304, 407, 415, 600, 603, 605.

43. On the passage of the Education Act of 1870, see Sturt, *Education of the People*, chap. 14.

44. Calculated from "Return of Civil Parishes not within Municipal Buroughs showing Returns under the Education Act," PP 1871, vol. 55, [C.-201], 46–53, 286–306.

45. "Report from the Select Committee on the Education of the Poorer Classes," PP 1837–38, vol. 7, [589], viii. On the one-in-six rule, see E. G. West, *Education and the Industrial Revolution*, chap. 3; and Sutherland, *Elementary Education*, 11.

46. See "First Report on the Elementary Education Acts," PP 1886, vol. 25, [C.-4863], 68 (item 1556) on Forster's speech. On the wording of the Education Act, see AR 1870–71, PP 1871, vol. 21, [C.-406], xxiii (sect. 8).

47. See "Final Report on the Elementary Education Acts," PP 1888, vol. 35, [C.-5485], 55–59; and "First Report on the Elementary Education Acts," PP 1886, vol. 25, [C.-4863], 419 (items 11160–63), 425 (items 11350–51), 421 (item 11242), 423 (item 11279), 424 (item 11304), 425 (items 11352–55, 11357–59). Also see Gardner, *Lost Schools*, chap. 6.

48. See Sutherland, *Policy Making in Elementary Education*, 88 (especially n. 56), 92–93.

49. Calculated from "List of School Boards and Attendance Committees in England and Wales," PP 1895, vol. 76, [C.-7687], 8–111.

50. See Sutherland, *Policy Making in Elementary Education*, 105, 353.

51. Sellman, *Devon Village Schools*, 61.

52. Ibid., 71.

53. Ibid., 35–37, 51–52.

54. Sutherland, *Policy Making in Elementary Education*, chaps. 7, 8.

55. Calculated from "A Digest of Parochial Returns on the Education of the Poor, Vol. III," PP 1819, vol. 9, pt. III, [224], 1171, 1275; "Education Department Return, Summary Tables of Educational Statistics," PP 1900, vol. 65, pt. I, [Cd.-109], 109 (Table 48).

56. Calculated by subtracting from private and public enrollments, estimates of middle-class enrollments in each type of school. Estimates of middle-class enrollments are contained in the "Census of Gt. Britain, 1851, Education," PP 1852–3, vol. 90, [1692], xxviii. These estimates are subject to considerable uncertainty. See the discussion in David Mitch, "The Impact of Subsidies to Elementary Schooling on Enrolment Rates in Nineteenth-Century England," *Economic History Review*, 2d ser., 39 (1986): 386 n.48.

57. This point has been made in Gardner, *Lost Schools*, chap. 3.

58. Ibid., chap. 2.

59. This estimate based on "First Report on the Elementary Education Acts," PP 1886, vol. 25, [C.-4863], 539.

60. AR 1881–82, PP 1882, vol. 23, [C.-3312-I], xlii.

Chapter 6: The Impact of Increased Public School Provision on Literacy Trends

1. Margaret Spufford, "First Steps in Literacy: The Reading and Writing Experiences of the Humblest Seventeenth-Century Spiritual Autobiographers," *Social History* 4 (1979): 416.

2. Abstracts of the biographies are contained in Sanderson, "Basic Education of Labour," appendix.

3. John Burnett, David Vincent, and David Mayall, *The Autobiography of the Working Class: An Annotated Critical Bibliography, Vol. I: 1790–1800* (New York: New York University Press, 1984). Although authors of autobiographies should not be viewed as fully representative of the working class as a whole, there is no reason to think that the heavy reliance on informal instruction was completely unrepresentative of working-class experience during this period. The introduction to the Burnett, Vincent, and Mayall volume provides a discussion of the characteristics of this genre.

4. Day and Sunday school enrollment trends are calculated from "Census of Gt. Britain, 1851, Education," PP 1852–3, vol. 90, [1692], cxviii-cxix. The growth of Sunday schools is discussed in Laqueur, *Religion and Respectability*, 42–61.

5. Reported in Laqueur, *Religion and Respectability*, 103. Chapters 4 and 5 of Laqueur's book discuss in detail the literacy instruction provided in Sunday schools. The question of how frequently Sunday schools offered literacy instruction and what statistical society surveys indicated about this issue had been debated prior to the publication of Laqueur's book in the exchange between Hurt and West. See Hurt, "Professor West on Early Nineteenth-Century Education," 629, in which he argues that Sunday schools in the 1830s primarily offered religious instruction; and E. G. West, "The Interpretation of Early Nineteenth-Century Education Statistics," *Economic History Review*, 2d ser., 24 (1971): 637, in which he argues that Sunday schools commonly offered literacy instruction in this period. Laqueur, who offers the most detailed review of the evidence, concludes that Sunday schools did commonly offer literacy instruction in the first half of the nineteenth century.

6. National Society, *Twenty-Fourth Annual Report* (1835), 59. Also see National Society, *Thirty-Second Annual Report* (1843), 45 (item 21). That working-class demand for literacy instruction put pressure on Sunday schools to offer it has also been argued by West, "Interpretation of Education Statistics," 637; and Laqueur, *Religion and Respectability*, 148–60.

7. See "Report of Commissioners on Popular Education," PP 1861, vol. 21, pt. I, [2794-I], 51; National Society, "Summaries of Returns to the Inquiry into the State and Progress of Schools during the Years 1856–7," v; and National

Society, "Statistics of Church of England Schools for the Poor in England and Wales for the Years 1866—67," 20.

8. "Evidence collected by W. R. Wood in the Collieries and Ironworks adjacent to Bradford and Leeds, Appendix to First Report on Children's Employment. Mines, Pt. II," PP 1842, vol. 17, [382], h11, h18, h24, h29, h31.

9. The text reports the correlation between *total* day school enrollment and Sunday school enrollment for 1833 and 1851 but the correlation for *public* day school enrollment and Sunday school enrollment for 1858 because the Newcastle Commission survey only reported public day enrollments. The correlation between *public* day enrollment and Sunday school enrollment was also negative for 1833 and 1851, however, compared with the positive correlation in 1858.

These correlations were calculated from the estimates reported in "A Digest of Parochial Returns on the Education of the Poor, Vol. III," PP 1819, vol. 9, pt. III, [224], 1171, 1275; "Abstract of Returns on the State of Education," PP 1835, vol. 43, [62], 1326; "Census of Great Britain, 1851, Education," PP 1852—3, vol. 90, [1692], 4—7; "Report of Commissioners on Popular Education," PP 1861, vol. 22, pt. I, [2794-I], 594—616.

10. Gardner, *Lost Schools*, 95—97, gives evidence of the continued importance of informal methods of instruction into the late nineteenth century.

11. Manchester Statistical Society, "Report on Education in Kingston-upon-Hull," 170.

12. "Report on Education in Pendleton," 81.

13. "Appendix, Pt. II to First Report on the Employment of Children, Young Persons and Women in Agriculture," PP 1867—8, vol. 17, [4068-I], 209—10.

14. "Appendix to First Report on Children's Employment. Mines, Pt. I, Reports and Evidence from Subcommissioners," PP 1842, vol. 16, [381], 758.

15. See, for example, D. W. Galenson, "Literacy and Age in Preindustrial England: Quantitative Evidence and Implications," *Economic Development and Cultural Change* 29 (1981): 813—39.

16. "Appendix to First Report on Children's Employment, Mines," PP 1842, vol. 17, [382], 77—86.

17. This point has been emphasized in Farley Grubb, "Colonial Immigrant Literacy: An Economic Analysis of Pennsylvania-German Evidence, 1727—1775," *Explorations in Economic History* 24 (1987): 67—72.

18. These profiles come from unpublished tables provided to the author by Professor Roderick Floud of City of London Polytechnic.

19. This issue is too complex to attempt to explore in any detail here. But for indications of this change, compare the following statement by Reverend Allen to the Committee of Council on Education in 1843 with that in the Newcastle Commission report in 1861.

Rev. Allen: "Next after the pains that are bestowed on the religious and moral training of children, the teaching them the chief matters of faith and duty, the impressing them with an abiding sense of their Maker's presence, and their own accountableness to him, the cultivation of habits of obedience, diligence, cleanliness, and order, no instruction seems to be more important that that which is occupied in leading children not only to understand but also to consider and profit by what they read." AR 1842–3, PP 1843, vol. 40, [520], 7.

The Newcastle Commission report, stating objectives for teaching in elementary schools: "First, that all the children who attend the elementary day schools of the country should be induced to attend with sufficient regularity to enable them, within a reasonable period, to obtain a mastery over the indispensable elements of knowledge, reading, writing, and the primary rules of arithmetic." "Report on Popular Education," PP 1861, vol. 21, pt. I, [2794-I], 295–96.

For an example of the controversy that has emerged over elite objectives in providing schools for the working classes and how these objectives may have changed in the mid-nineteenth century, see the debate between A. J. Heesom, Brendan Duffy, and Robert Colls in "Debate: Coal, Class and Education," 136–165. A statement of early government objectives in educational policy is contained in Richard Johnson, "Educational Policy and Social Control in Early Victorian Britain," *Past and Present* 49 (1970): 96–119. There is also a vast literature on the conflict between religious and secular objectives in the development of educational policy. One survey of this conflict is given in James Murphy, *Church, State and Schools in Britain, 1800–1970* (London: Routledge and Kegan Paul, 1971).

West has argued that the shift in emphasis from religious to literacy instruction in day schools occurred as early as the 1830s in response to parental pressure. See West, "Resource Allocation," 90–91.

20. "Abstract of Returns on the State of Education, Vol. III," PP 1835, vol. 43, [62], 1326.

21. Manchester Statistical Society, *Report of a Committee of the Manchester Statistical Society on the State of Education in the Borough of Bury in July, 1835* (London: James Ridgway and Son, 1835), 6–8, 17, General Summary Table; Manchester Statistical Society, *Report of a Committee of the Manchester Statistical Society on the State of Education in the City of York in 1836–1837* (London: James Ridgeway and Son, 1837), 9–11, xiv; Statistical Society of London, "Second Report of the Statistical Society of London, appointed to Inquire into the State of Education in Westminister," *Journal of the Statistical Society of London* 1 (1838): 196–200, 204, 205; Statistical Society of London, "Report of the Education Committee of the Statistical Society of London on the Borough of Finsbury," *Journal of the Statistical Society of London* 6 (1843): 29–34, 35, 43; Bristol Statistical Society, "Report on the Statistics of Education in Bristol," *Journal of the Statistical Society of London* 4 (1841): 251–53, 256–57; J.R. Wood, "Report on the State of Education in Birmingham," 26–35, 39; Manchester Statistical Society, "Report of a Committee of the Manchester Statistical Society on the State of Education in the County of Rutland in the Year 1838," *Journal of the Statistical Society of London* 2 (1839): 305–8. Also see West, *Education and the Industrial Revolution*, chap. 7; and West, "Resource Allocation," 78, 82, 84.

22. See Thomas Laqueur, "Working Class Demand," 197.

23. See Hurt, "Professor West on Early Nineteenth-Century Education," 625–26.

24. See ibid., 626–29; and Gardner, *Lost Schools*, 118–19.

25. *Hansard Parliamentary Debates*, 3d ser., vol. 91 (1847), cols. 1016–17.

26. For a critical discussion of the view that private teachers entered teaching as a last resort, see Gardner, *Lost Schools*, 108–26.

27. For a critical review of depictions of dame schools, see ibid., chaps. 4, 5.

28. Surveys of the development of denominational and state-supported schooling include Sturt, *Education of the People*; Birchenough, *History of Elementary Education*; and Hurt, *Education in Evolution*.

29. Calculated from evidence in "Report of Commissioners on Popular Education," PP 1861, vol. 21, pt. I, [2794-I], 591, 638–40. A more detailed discussion of this calculation is contained in Mitch, "Impact of Subsidies," 377 n.22.

30. For a further discussion, see Gardner, *Lost Schools*, 148–59.

31. Cited in ibid., 155–56.

32. Ibid., 171–72, 160, 164–65.

33. Ibid., 120.

34. Ibid., 133.

35. This division is suggested by the Newcastle Commission survey of what subject matter children studied in public and private schools. Over 90 percent of students in both private and public schools studied reading. A substantially lower proportion of students in private schools studied writing or arithmetic than in public schools, however. Students in private schools were on average younger than those in public schools. Thus, rather than simply acting as creches, private schools may have specialized in offering the first elements of instruction to younger students. See "Report of Commissioners on Popular Education," PP 1861, vol. 21, pt. I, [2794-I], 656, 660, 665.

36. Gardner, *Lost Schools*, 172; also see pp. 173, 163, 169.

37. Ibid., 165, 169; also see pp. 163, 172–73.

38. Cited in ibid., 94.

39. Cited in ibid., 95.

40. Cited in ibid., 95.

41. Cited in ibid., 176.

42. "Report of Commissioners on Popular Education," PP 1861, vol. 21, pt. I, [2794-I], 638–40, 591.

43. Gardner, *Lost Schools*, 167–70.

44. The value-added model could only be estimated at the county level, because of the absence of data at the registration district level on schooling for years before 1851. For an explanation of the value-added approach, see Eric Hanushek, "Conceptual and Empirical Issues in the Estimation of Educational Production Functions," *Journal of Human Resources* 14 (1979): 364–69.

45. A number of studies based on twentieth-century evidence of the determinants of instructional effectiveness have found that factors associated with nineteenth-century English educational reform in public schools such as teacher training, teacher experience, and pupil-teacher ratios make no difference to educational outcomes. See Eric Hanushek, "The Economics of Schooling," *Journal of Economic Literature* 24 (1986): 1141–77.

46. "Report of Commissioners on Popular Education," PP 1861, vol. 21, pt. I, [2794-I], 587, 590.

47. See Mitch, "Impact of Subsidies," 374.

48. See ibid., 374–77.

49. "Report of Commissioners on Popular Education," PP 1861, vol. 21, pt. I, [2794-I], 278; also see ibid., 285–87. On the difficulty of supporting schools in urban areas where the population was apathetic to education, see ibid., 339. Histories of literacy for both North America and continental Europe have also noted the difficulty of financing schools in areas with low population densities. For North America, see Kenneth Lockridge, *Literacy in Colonial New England* (New York: Norton, 1974), 65–67; and Soltow and Stevens, *Rise of Literacy*, 23, 37–42. For Europe, see Mary Jo Maynes, "The Virtues of Archaism: The Political Economy of Schooling in Europe, 1750–1850," *Comparative Studies in Society and History* 21 (1979): 611–25; Michel Vovelle, "Y-a-t'il eu une revolution culturelle au XVIIIe Siecle? A Propos de l'education populaire en Provence," *Revue d'histoire moderne et contemporaine* 22 (1975): 89–141; Furet and Ouzef, *Reading and Writing*, 147, 154–57; Mitch, "Rise of Popular Literacy in Europe."

50. Threshold population levels of the same size for maintaining a school have been reported for France and Russia. See Vovelle, "Y-a-t'il eu une revolution culturelle," 120–25; and Eklof, *Russian Peasant Schools*, 298.

51. Based on "First Report on the Elementary Education Acts," PP 1886, vol. 25, [C.-4863], 539.

52. Calculated from "Census of Gt. Britain, 1851, Population Tables I, Vol. I," PP 1852–3, vol. 85, [1631], division 3: 14–20, 50–52; division 5, 28–40; division 6: 30–38; and from "Census of Gt. Britain, 1851, Population Tables I, Vol. II," PP 1852–3, vol. 86, [1632], Division 7: 12–38, 68–79; division 10: 54–59. These calculations do not allow for the possibility of children in one settlement attending schools in neighboring settlements and thus may overstate the problem. They give some indication of its possible magnitude, however.

53. For mention of itinerant teachers in France, see Furet and Ozouf, *Reading and Writing*, 70.

54. See T. W. Bamford, *The Evolution of Rural Education*, Research Monographs, no. 1, Institute of Education, University of Hull, 1965, chap. 1. Bamford argues that in rural areas public schools supported by local philanthropy were more important than private schools; see ibid., 7–8. On the Black Country, see "Reports of Assistant Commissioners on Popular Education," PP 1861, vol. 21, pt. II, [2794-II], 254–60, 268, 292–307. On Lincolnshire, see Rex C. Russell, *A History of Schools and Education in Lindsey, Lincolnshire: 1800–1902* (Lindsey, Lincs.: County Council Education Committee, 1965–66), pt. I; pt. II, 3–9; pt. III, 9–11, 49–52.

55. "First Report on the Elementary Education Acts," PP 1886, vol. 25, [C.-4863], 534–35, app. C, XII, XIII. Also see Sutherland, *Policy Making in Elementary Education*, 110–11.

56. "Census of Gt. Britain, 1851, Education," PP 1852–53, vol. 90, [1692], xxiii.

57. There are instances where these measures do seem to have had a short-term impact. However, Ball has argued that in the long term, efforts at offering positive inducements to attend school were not effective. See Ball, "Elementary School Attendance," 19–37.

58. In a survey of twenty thousand adults in Hull in 1841, 69 percent said

that they had attended a day school at some point in their lives. In a survey of five thousand adults in Pendleton in 1839, 88 percent said that they had attended a day school. See Manchester Statistical Society, "Report on Education in Kingston-upon-Hull," 170; and Manchester Statistical Society, "Report on Education in Pendleton," 81. Also see the "Report of the Commissioners on Popular Education," PP 1861, vol. 21, pt. I, [2794-I], 86.

59. In addition to "Report on Education in Pendleton," 73 referred to in note 58 above; also see "Minutes before Select Committee on Newspaper Stamps," PP 1851, vol. 17, [558], 159 (item 980); "Appendix to First Report on Children's Employment. Mines," PP 1842, vol. 16, [381], 40 (item 323); "Minutes from the Select Committee on Postage," PP 1837–8, vol. 20, pt. II, [658], 134; "Appendix to First Report on Children's Employment, Mines. Pt. II," PP 1842, vol. 17, [382], 208, 617, 594, 804; and Gardner, *Lost Schools*, 177, 186 nn. 139, 140.

60. AR 1864–65, PP 1865, vol. 42, [3533], 141.

61. National Society, *Forty-Sixth Annual Report* (London, 1857), xxiv.

62. National Society, *Twenty-Eighth Annual Report* (London, 1839), 77.

63. "Reports on the State of Education in Wales," PP 1847, vol. 27, pt. I, [870], 54–60; PP 1847, vol. 27, pt. II, [871], 75–77; PP 1847, vol. 27, pt. III, [872], 1–6.

64. National Society, "Summaries of Returns to the Inquiry into the State and Progress of Schools during the Years 1856–57," 54–59; "Report of Commissioners on Popular Education," PP 1861, vol. 21, pt. I, [2794-I], 596–616.

65. "Statistical Report of the Commission on the Elementary Education Acts," PP 1888, vol. 36, [C.-5485-II], 175–487.

66. See Mitch, "The Impact of Subsidies," 375.

67. See ibid., 383–84.

68. The 1861 enrollment estimates are based on census evidence. Gardner has argued that the 1861 census underestimated enrollments by undercounting private schools. See Gardner, *Lost Schools*, chap. 2. If Gardner is correct, this would lower enrollment growth between 1861 and 1891 (based on the assumption that by 1891 private schools had been largely displaced by public schools; as Gardner notes in chapter 6, even by the end of the century the displacement had not been complete) then the relative growth between 1891 and 1900 would have been even greater.

69. For a discussion of enrollment trends see Mitch, "Impact of Subsidies," 389.

70. For examples of schools at full capacity, see J. W. Docking, *Victorian Schooling and Scholars: Church of England Schools in Nineteenth-Century Coventry*, Coventry and North Warwickshire History Pamphlets, no. 3 (Coventry: Coventry Branch of the Historical Association, 1967), 6–7; National Society, "Extracts from Reports Made to the General Committee of the National Society in the Year 1826 by the Diocesan and District Societies and Schools in the Unions, Report for Lichfield and Coventry," Appendix to *Fifteenth Annual Report* (London, 1826); National Society, *Twenty-Ninth Annual Report* (London, 1840), 154; National Society, *Twenty-Fifth Annual Report* (London, 1836), 75 (on Oldham); and National Society, *Twenty-Fourth Annual Report* (London, 1835), 57 (on Jersey).

For examples of half-empty schools, see Murphy, "Rise of Public Elementary Education: Part Two," 120; National Society, *Twenty-Seventh Annual Report* (London, 1838), 174; Stephens, *Education, Literacy and Society*, 127, 151, 254; and "Census of Gt. Britain, 1851, Education," PP 1852–3, vol. 90, [1692], xxxix.

71. "Report of Commissioners on Popular Education," PP 1861, vol. 21, pt. I, [2794-I], 83. For specific examples, see "Reports of Assistant Commissioners on Popular Education," PP 1861, vol. 21, pt. II, [2794-II], 54, 199–210.

72. National Society, *Thirty-First Annual Report* (London, 1842), 2.

73. "Report on Popular Education," PP 1861, vol. 21, pt. I, [2794], 83.

74. AR 1890–91, PP 1890–91, vol. 27, [C.-6438-I], 327.

75. Ibid., 327.

Chapter 7: The Changing Opportunity Costs of Acquiring Literacy

1. "Census of Gt. Britain, 1851, Education," PP 1852–53, vol. 90, [1692], xxiii.

2. Cited in Stephens, *Education, Literacy and Society*, 128. The original statement was made in AR 1851–52, PP 1852, vol. 40, [1480], 380.

3. "Census of England and Wales, 1871, General Report, Vol. IV, Appendix to Report, Appendix A," PP 1873, vol. 71, pt. II, [C.-872-I], 112.

4. See "Census of Gt. Britain, 1851, Population Tables II, Ages, Civil Condition, Occupations, and Birth-place of the People, Vol. I, Summary Tables," PP 1852–3, vol. 88, pt. I, [1691-I], clvii.

5. See P. M. Tillett, "Sources of Inaccuracy in the 1851 and 1861 Censuses," in *Nineteenth Century Society: Essays in the Use of Quantitative Methods for the Study of Social Data*, ed. E. A. Wrigley (Cambridge: Cambridge University Press, 1972), 121–24.

6. See Beryl Madoc-Jones, "Patterns of attendance and their social significance: Mitcham National School 1830–39," in *Popular Education and Socialization in the Nineteenth Century*, ed. Phillip McCann (London: Methuen, 1977), 41–66. Another source is provided by the school certificate book of the Belper Mills School, which cites reasons for pupils leaving school. Of thirty-seven boys who left school between 1841 and 1851, ten left to be kept at home compared with fourteen who went to work. Of forty-one girls who left the school during the same time, nine left to be kept at home while twenty went to work. See School Certificate Book, Records of Strutt Mills at Derby/9–47, Archives Department, Manchester Reference Library, Manchester, England. Madoc-Jones, in "Patterns of School Attendance," 47, found a low percentage of boys kept at home (3 percent) compared with those who went to work (57 percent); but a relatively high percentage of girls kept at home (10 percent) compared with those who went to work (10 percent).

7. On the use of sedatives for young children, see J. L. Hammond and Barbara Hammond, *The Skilled Laborer, 1760–1832* (New York: Harper and Row, Harper Torchbook Editions, 1970), 254; and Margaret Hewitt, *Wives and Mothers in Victorian Industry* (London: Rockliff, 1958), chap. 10. For evidence on the use

of schools as child-minding institutions, see Hurt, "Professor West on Early Nine-teenth-Century Education," 625–26.

8. Carolyn Tuttle, "Children at Work in the British Industrial Revolution" (Ph.D diss., Northwestern University, 1986), 211–14.

9. Stephens has emphasized this point. See Stephens, *Education, Literacy and Society*, 21–22.

10. Ibid., 23.

11. For evidence on the ages at which children started to work, see "Children's Employment Commission, Second Report," PP 1843, vol. 13, [430], 7–14; "First Report on the Employment of Children, Mines," PP 1842, vol. 15, [380], 38, 205, 208, 252; "Reports on the Employment of Women and Children in Agriculture," PP 1843, vol. 12, [510], 28, 150, 170, 237; "Appendix to First Report on Children's Employment," PP 1863, vol. 18, [3170], xi, xxxvi-xxxvii, 275, 280, 287, 290; and "Appendix to Third Report on Children's Employment," PP 1864, vol. 22, [3414-I], 3, 5.

12. For evidence on the low productivity of young children, see "Reports on the Employment of Women and Children in Agriculture," PP 1843, vol. 12, [510], 28.

13. For evidence on wages in agriculture, see "Reports on the Employment of Women and Children in Agriculture," PP 1843, vol. 12, [510], 31; for adult wages, see ibid., 13.

14. See "Appendix to First Report on Children's Employment. Mines, Pt. I," PP 1842, vol. 16, [381], 18, 153–64.

15. See "Children's Employment Commission, Second Report," PP 1843, vol. 13, [430], 93–99; and "Reports from each of the Four Factory Inspectors, on the Effects of the Educational Provisions of the Factories Act; together with Joint Report," PP 1839, vol. 42, [42], 63.

16. See C. H. Lee, *A Cotton Enterprise, 1795–1840: A History of M'Connel and Kennedy, Fine Cotton Spinners* (Manchester: Manchester University Press, 1972), 174.

17. See Anderson, *Family Structure in Lancashire*, 74–76.

18. See "Appendix, Pt. I to First Report of the Commissioners on the Employment of Children, Young Persons, and Women in Agriculture," PP 1867–8, vol. 17, [4068], 17 (items A.50-A.52); and "Appendix, Pt. II to First Report on the Employment of Children, Young Persons, and Women in Agriculture," PP 1867–8, vol. 17, [4068-I], 135–40.

19. See "Reports on the Effects of the Educational Provisions of the Factories Act," PP 1839, vol. 42, [42], 37; M. W. Thomas, *The Early Factory Legislation* (Westport, Conn.: Greenwood Press, 1970), 178; and "Reports of Assistant Commissioners on Popular Education," PP 1861, vol. 21, pt. II, [2794-II], 312 (items 5, 10), 408 (item 5), 203.

20. See "Reports of Assistant Commissioners on Popular Education," PP 1861, Vol.21, pt. II, [2794-II], 321–23.

21. See "Appendix, Pt. I to First Report of the Commissioners on the Employment of Children, Young Persons, and Women in Agriculture," PP 1867–8, vol. 17, [4068], 60 (item B.89), 13 (items A.43–44), 24 (item A.78).

22. See "Appendix to the Second Report on Children's Employ-ment—Trades and Manufactures—Pt. I," PP 1843, vol. 14, [431], e7 (item 11).

23. "Minutes from the Select Committee on Manchester and Salford Edu-cation," PP 1852, vol. 11, [499], 213 (items 1444–45).

24. Reported by Belfiore, "Family Strategies," 306.

25. "Further Reports of Assistant Commissioners on Popular Education," PP 1861, vol. 21, pt. III, [2794-III], 354, 518.

26. Hewitt, *Wives and Mothers*, 63–67.

27. Anderson, *Family Structure in Lancashire*, 71–74.

28. "Census of Gt. Britain, 1851, Population Tables II, Ages, Civil Con-dition, Occupations, and Birth-place of the People, Vol. I, Summary Tables," PP 1852–53, vol. 88, pt. I, [1691-I], ccv, ccxxv-ccxxvii; and "Census Returns of England and Wales, 1911, vol. 10, pt. II, Occupations and Industries: Pt. II," PP 1913, vol. 79, [Cd.-7019], 2 (Table 13).

29. Pamela Horn, "The Employment of Children in Victorian Oxfordshire," *Midland History* 4 (1977): 69.

30. On the impact of compulsory schooling laws in increasing the number of half-timers see "Report of the Commissioners Appointed to Inquire into the Working of the Factory and Workshops Acts with a View to their Consolidation and Amendment, Vol. I, Appendix C," PP 1876, vol. 29, [C.-1443], 28, 51, 61, 78, 85; "Reports of the Inspectors of Factories for the Half-Year ending 31st October, 1873," PP 1874, vol. 13, [C.-937], 86–91, 129; and "Reports of the Inspectors of Factories for the Half-Year ending 31st October, 1875," PP 1876, vol. 16, [C.-1434], 89, 90–91, 97.

31. See Ball, "Elementary School Attendance," 21–22.

32. Similar results obtain when the year 1864 is used for the dependent vari-ables, and also when 1861 and 1871 were used for the independent variables and a similar eighteen-year lag between school enrollment and marriage was specified.

33. It should also be noted that the collinearity between the independent variables in the regressions is high. For males, the correlation between the pro-portion who were scholars in the five-to-nine age range and ten-to-fourteen age range is $+.571$; for females, the correlation is $+.676$. When the regressions were run by using change in school enrollments between 1851 and 1871 for each age group as the independent variables along with signature ability at marriage in the 1860s and using signature ability at marriage in the 1880s as the dependent vari-able, then the change in school enrollment for the younger age group actually had a stronger impact than that for the older age group for females, while for males getting a statistically significant coefficient for change for the older group de-pended on the exact choice of time period. Thus the conclusion to be drawn from the results in the text is not that enrollment at the older ages is a more important determinant of literacy than enrollment at the younger ages under all circum-stances. It is rather that enrollment at older ages in certain situations is of possible importance for acquiring literacy.

34. The declining interest in child labor conditions was evident in factory inspectors' reports, which after 1885 focus almost exclusively on issues of factory safety rather than child labor conditions. Compare "Report of the Chief Inspector

of Factories and Workshops for the Year ending 31st October, 1887," PP 1888, vol. 26, [C.-5328], 3–112, with "Reports of the Inspectors of Factories for the Half-year ending 30th April, 1875," PP 1875, vol.16, [C.-1345], 7–32, 59–88.

35. See Lars Sandberg, *Lancashire in Decline: A Study of Entrepreneurship, Technology, and International Trade* (Columbus: Ohio State University Press, 1974), 215, 219; and John Jewkes and P. M. Gray, *Wages and Labour in the Lancashire Cotton Spinning Industry* (Manchester: Manchester University Press, 1935), 12.

36. The change in the employment of children accounted for by sectoral shifts was calculated by adding changes in sectoral proportions of the labor force weighted by the 1851 proportion of children of a given age range relative to the total labor force in each sector. The following sectoral categories were used in these calculations: agriculture, mining, building, metals, textiles, other manufacturing, transport, dealing, commerce, general labor, public service, and domestic service.

Census figures indicate that the total change in the proportion of the English labor force who were children aged five to nine between 1851 and 1871 was − .00241. The change in the employment of children aged five to nine that can be attributed to sectoral shifts using the calculation just described was − .00049, which is 20.2 percent of the total change in employment of children aged five to nine between 1851 and 1871. The total change in the proportion of the English labor force who were children aged ten to fourteen between 1851 and 1871, according to census figures, was − .00489. The change in the employment of children aged ten to fourteen that can be accounted for by sectoral shifts was − .0031, which is 63.4 percent of the total change in the employment of children aged ten to fourteen between 1851 and 1871.

Calculating the role of compositional shifts within the transportation sector with shifts away from the use of messengers and porters toward railroads, and within the textile labor force with the decline of the silk industry suggests the importance of compositional shifts within broad sectors of the economy.

The figures used in these calculations were taken from "Census of Gt. Britain, Population Tables II, Ages, Civil Condition, Occupations, and Birth-place of the People, Vol. I, Summary Tables," PP 1852–3, vol. 88, pt. I, [1691-I], ccxxii-ccxxvii; "Census of England and Wales, 1871, Population Abstracts: Age, Civil Condition, Occupations, and Birth-Places of the People, vol. III," PP 1873, vol.71, pt. I, [C.-872], xxxvii-xlviii; and Armstrong, "Information about Occupation," 280.

37. See "Census of Gt. Britain, Population Tables II, Ages, Civil Condition, Occupations, and Birth-place of the People, Vol. I, Summary Tables," PP 1852–3, vol. 88, pt. I, [1691-I], ccxxii-ccxxvii; "Census of England and Wales, 1871, Population Abstracts: Age, Civil Condition, Occupations, and Birth-Places of the People, Vol. III," PP 1873, vol. 71, pt. I, [C.-872], xxxvii-xlviii; and Armstrong, "Information about Occupation," 280.

38. The change in the proportion of the English labor force who were children aged ten to fourteen between 1871 and 1891 was − .0081. The change in the proportion of the English labor force aged ten to fourteen that can be accounted for by sectoral shifts, using the procedure described in note 36, was − .00074, which is 9.1 percent of the total change in the proportion of the English

labor force aged ten to fourteen between 1871 and 1891. The figures for these calculations were taken from "Census of England and Wales, 1871, Population Abstracts: Age, Civil Condition, Occupations, and Birth-Places of the People, vol. III," PP 1873, vol. 71, pt. I, [C.-872], xxxvii-xlviii; "Census of England and Wales, 1891, vol. III, Ages, Condition as to Marriage, Occupations, Birth-Places, and Infirmities," PP 1893–4, vol. 106, [C.-7058], x-xxv, Table 5; and Armstrong, "Information about Occupation," 280.

39. The disappearance of child labor for children under ten is suggested by census reports indicating that in 1871 only .8 percent of all children were classified as employed. See "Census of England and Wales, 1871, General Report, vol. IV, Appendix A," PP 1873, vol. 71, pt. II, [C.-872-I], 92–110. The report for the 1891 census declared that so few children under the age of ten were working that it was unnecessary to record these children. One should, however, allow for at least an element of wishful thinking, since the report attributed the low number of employed children under ten to the impact of compulsory schooling. See "Census of England and Wales, 1891, General Report," PP 1893–94, vol. 106, [C.-7222], 37, 59.

40. See Tuttle, "Children at Work," 68. In making the distinction between paleotechnic and neotechnic stages, Tuttle refers to Lewis Mumford, *Technics and Civilization* (New York: Harcourt, Brace and Co., 1934), 109, chaps. 4, 5.

41. See Pamela Horn, "Child Workers in the Pillow Lace and Straw Plait Trades of Victorian Buckinghamshire and Bedfordshire," *The Historical Journal* 17 (1974): 782, 788. Also see "Appendix of Evidence to Report on Lace Manufacture," PP 1861, vol. 22, [2797], 31, 54–69.

42. See Horn, "Child Workers in Pillow Lace and Straw Plait Trades," 782. This change reflected a shift in the market position of English producers rather than technological developments. It is considered in this section because it is an industry-specific change, not a change reflecting broad shifts in the composition of the English economy.

43. A. J. Taylor, "Labour Productivity and Technological Innovation in the British Coal Industry, 1850–1914," *Economic History Review*, 2d ser., 14 (1961): 57. Also see Church, *History of the British Coal Industry, Vol. 3*, 199.

44. Stephens has emphasized the role of domestic industry as a cause of illiteracy in these areas. See Stephens, *Education, Literacy and Society*, 179.

45. See "First Report of the Commissioners on the Employment of Children, Young Persons, and Women in Agriculture," PP 1867–8, vol. 17, [4068], xviii-xix (items 73–74); and "Report of Assistant Commissioners on Popular Education," PP 1861, vol. 21, pt. II, [2794-II], 147.

46. See Pamela Horn, *The Changing Countryside in Victorian and Edwardian England and Wales* (Rutherford, N.J.: Fairleigh Dickinson University Press, 1984), 165–66.

47. Clark Nardinelli, "Child Labor and the Factory Acts," *Journal of Economic History* 40 (1980): 745.

48. William Lazonick, "Industrial Relations and Technical Change: The Case of the Self-Acting Mule," *Cambridge Journal of Economics* 3 (1979): 236–46.

49. See Nardinelli, "Child Labor and the Factory Acts," 748–50.

50. "Reports of the Inspectors of Factories for the Half-year ending 31st December, 1836," PP 1837, vol. 31, [73], 12; "Reports of the Inspectors of Factories for the Half-year ending 31st December, 1841, Appendix no. 4 to the Report by L. Horner," PP 1842, vol. 22, [31], 83; and "Reports of the Inspectors of Factories for the Half-year ending 31st December, 1842," PP 1843, vol. 27, [429], 8. For similar testimony by school inspectors see AR 1846, PP 1847, vol. 45, [787], 225; and AR 1847–8, PP 1847–8, vol. 50, [998], 152.

51. "Reports of the Inspectors for the Half-year ending 31st October, 1856," PP 1857, vol. 3, [2153], 19.

52. "Reports of the Inspectors of Factories for the Half-year ending 30th April, 1875," PP 1875, vol. 16, [C.-1345], 11–13.

53. Thomas Ellison, *The Cotton Trade of Great Britain* (1886; reprint, London: Frank Cass and Co., 1968), 74.

54. See Louise Tilly and Joan Scott, *Women, Work, and Family* (New York: Holt, Rinehart and Winston, 1978), 197–98; and George Alter, "Women and Children in the Family Economy: Belgium, 1853 and 1891," Paper presented at the Economic History Workshop, Department of Economics, The University of Chicago, January 23, 1981, p. 18.

55. H. J. Habbakkuk, *American and British Technology in the Nineteenth Century* (Cambridge: Cambridge University Press, 1967), chap. 5.

56. Claudia Goldin and Kenneth Sokoloff, "Women, Children and Industrialization in the Early Republic: Evidence from the Manufacturing Censuses," *Journal of Economic History* 42 (1982): 741–74.

57. See Duncan Bythell, *The Sweated Trades* (New York: St. Martin's Press, 1978), 143–44; and James Schmiechen, *Sweated Industries and Sweated Labor* (Urbana: University of Illinois Press, 1984), 24–29, 185. Sweating was a term used to refer to certain manufacturing activities employing low-skill labor and providing low remuneration for long hours of work, with the general implication that employers were in a position to exploit their workers. The work referred to was done both in workshops and domestically, commonly with piecework compensation.

58. For trends in hours of work, see Bienefield, *Working Hours in British Industry*, 82–84; and E. H. Hunt, *British Labour History 1815–1914* (London: Weidenfeld and Nicolson, 1981), 77–81. For trends in female labor force participation, see Hewitt, *Wives and Mothers*, chaps. 2, 3; Viola Klein, *Britain's Married Women Workers* (New York: Humanities Press, 1965), 12; C. E. V. Leser, "The Supply of Women for Gainful Work in Britain," *Population Studies* 9 (1955): 142–47; and Hunt, *British Labour History*, 18–19.

59. For trends in the capital-labor ratio, see C. H. Feinstein, *Statistical Tables of National Income, Expenditure, and Output of the U.K., 1855–1955* (Cambridge: Cambridge University Press, 1976), T-51 (Table 20).

60. For evidence on the substitutability between women and children see "Reports of the Inspectors of Factories for the Half-year ending 31st December, 1841, Appendix no. 4 to the Report by L. Horner," PP 1842 vol. 22, [31], 19; "Minutes of Evidence, Third Report on the Regulation of Mills and Factories," PP 1840, vol. 10, [314], 40 (item 4621). The substitutability is evident in the sharp increase in employment both of children aged thirteen to eighteen and of

women in cotton textiles along with the sharp decline in employment of children under thirteen between 1835 and 1838. See Mitchell and Deane, *Abstract of British Historical Statistics*, 188.

61. It is possible, however, that a declining supply of adult female labor led to the development of machinery and other substitutes for unskilled labor that ultimately displaced children. But the impact of such indirect effects would be reflected in the impact of technological change considered in the previous section.

62. For wage trends in textile areas following the Factory Acts, see G. H. Wood, "Factory Legislation, Considered with Reference to the Wages etc. of the Operatives Protected Thereby," *Journal of the Royal Statistical Society* 65 (1902): 284–324. For children's wage trends in agriculture, compare "Reports on the Employment of Women and Children in Agriculture," PP 1843, vol. 12, [510], 31–33, 165–92, 235–36, 245–46, 251–59, 288–89; with "Returns of Wages Published between 1830 and 1886, Pt. II," PP 1887, vol. 89, [C.-5172], 411–19. Although these comparisons do not control for changes in the price level, over the period in question (1830 to 1870) there appears to have been no clear trend in the price level. See Mitchell and Deane, *Abstract of British Historical Statistics*, 471–72.

63. For evidence on the number of half-timers, see Mitchell and Deane, *Abstract of British Historical Statistics*, 188, 199. For child employment rates in large textile towns, see "Census Returns of England and Wales, 1911, vol. 10, pt. I, Occupations and Industries," PP 1913, vol. 78, [Cd.-7018], cxli, cxlii.

64. See Horn, *Changing Countryside*, 163. On the continued demand of farmers for child labor in the later nineteenth century, also see Alan Armstrong, *Farmworkers*, 124.

65. For more detailed descriptions of legislation restricting child labor, see Sutherland, *Policy Making in Elementary Education*, 115–45; A. H. Robson, *The Education of Children Engaged in Industry in England, 1833–1876* (London: Kegan Paul, Trench, Trench, Trubner and Co., 1931), chaps. 2–4; and Frederic Keeling, *Child Labour in the United Kingdom: A Study of the Development and Administration of the Law Relating to the Employment of Children* (London: P. S. King and Son, 1914), xxv-xxxii.

66. For a discussion of the political trends leading to the establishment of compulsory schooling laws, see Sutherland, *Policy Making in Elementary Education*, chap. 5; and David Rubinstein, *School Attendance in London, 1870–1904: A Social History*, Occasional Papers in Economic and Social History no. 1, University of Hull, 1969, chap. 5.

67. M. E. Sadler and J. W. Edwards, "Public Elementary Education in England and Wales, 1870–1895, Education Department, Special Reports on Educational Subjects," PP 1897, vol. 25, [C.-8447], 15.

68. For more detailed descriptions of the legislation establishing compulsory schooling, see Sutherland, *Policy Making in Education*, chap. 5; and "Final Report on the Elementary Education Acts," PP 1888, vol. 35, [C.-5485], 30–36.

69. For one presentation of the problems encountered in enforcing this legislation, see "Final Report on the Elementary Education Acts," PP 1888, vol. 35, [C.-5485], 105–6. For surveys by twentieth-century historians of the problems

involved in enforcement, see, for example, Sturt, *Education of the People*, 323–30; Hurt, *Elementary Schooling*, chap.8; Sutherland, *Policy Making in Elementary Education*, 126, 145–51, 159–61; Rubinstein, *School Attendance in London*, chaps. 3, 5; Horn, *Changing Countryside*, 147–48, 164–65; Horn, "Child Workers in Pillow Lace and Straw Plait Trades," 788, 794–95; Horn, "Children in Victorian Oxfordshire," 63–64, 70; Pamela Horn, "Child Workers in the Victorian Countryside: The Case of Northamptonshire," *Northamptonshire Past and Present* 7 (1985–6): 175–78.

70. School boards were created to provide schools; between 1871 and 1880, they had the choice of passing bylaws compelling school attendance for children under their jurisdiction. School attendance committees were created in 1876 as part of Lord Sandon's act to allow areas that had not established school boards to have means of compelling school attendance. For a further account of the authority of each type of body to require school attendance, see Sutherland, *Policy Making in Elementary Education*, chap. 5.

71. For examples of the complaints that there were too few attendance officers for the size of the districts and more generally that their attempts at enforcement were half-hearted, see AR 1878–79, PP 1878–79, vol. 23, [C.-2342-I], 472, 566–67, 741; AR 1881–82, PP 1882, vol.23, [C.-3312-I], 235, 259, 293, 395; AR 1883–84, PP 1884, vol. 24, [C.-4091-I], 455.

72. For examples of these complaints in school inspector reports, see AR 1878–79, PP 1878–79, vol.23, [C.-2342-I], 638–39, 704; and AR 1881–82, PP 1882, vol. 23, [C.-3312-I], 218, 327, 432. Also see Stephens, *Education, Literacy and Society*, 138; and "First Report on the Elementary Education Acts," PP 1886, vol. 25, [C.-4863], 69–70 (items 1593–94), 272 (items 7486–87).

73. See AR 1875–76, PP 1876, vol. 23, [C.-1513-I], 305; and AR 1881–82, PP 1882, vol. 23, [C.-3312-I], 305.

74. See Hurt, *Elementary Schooling*, 190.

75. For examples of the problems of trying to catch truants, see Horn, "Child Workers in Pillow Lace and Straw Plait Trades," 793; Horn, *Changing Countryside*, 148; Horn, "Child Workers in Northamptonshire," 175–77; Alan Armstrong, *Farmworkers*, 124; and Hurt, *Elementary Schooling*, 193–96.

76. For examples of these problems in London, especially in the 1870s after compulsion was first introduced, see Rubinstein, *School Attendance in London*, 50–51. For an example in Liverpool, see AR 1881–82, PP 1882, vol. 23, [C.-3312-I], 313. In his report for 1900, W. P. Turnbull comments on the unwillingness of prosecuters to prosecute cases in areas where they lived. See Board of Education, W. P. Turnbull, "North-eastern Division General Report for the Year 1900," PP 1901, vol. 21, [Cd.-570], 7. J. J. Blandford, in his report on the Derby district, also comments on the hostility attendance officers encountered from parents. See AR 1882–83, PP 1883, vol. 25, [C.-3706-I], 249.

77. For examples, see AR 1878–79, PP 1878–79, vol. 23, [C.-2342-I], 472; AR 1881–82, PP 1882, vol. 23, [C.-3312-I], 327; AR 1882–83, PP 1883, vol. 25, [C.-3706-I], 381; AR 1884–85, PP 1884–5, vol. 23, [C.-4483-I], 351.

78. This problem was mentioned throughout the Cross Commission inquiry in the mid-1880s. See "Index to Evidence on the Working of the Elementary

Education Acts," PP 1888, vol. 37, [C.-5329-I], 86; "Minutes to Second Report on the Elementary Education Acts," PP 1887, vol. 29, [C.-5056], 160 (item 18839), 163 (items 18979–80), 373 (item 25919), 436 (item 27806). Also see AR 1875–76, PP 1876, vol. 23, [C.-1513-I], 312; AR 1878–79, PP 1878–79, vol. 23, [C.-2342-I], 640; AR 1881–82, PP 1882, vol.23, [C.-3312-I], 246, 344; AR 1882–83, vol. 25, [C.-3706-I], 381, 413. Sutherland has also discussed the problem. See Sutherland, *Policy Making in Elementary Education*, 159.

79. "First Report on the Elementary Education Acts," PP 1886, vol. 25, [C.-4863], 81 (item 1862a).

80. See, for example, Rubinstein, *School Attendance in London*, 98–99; and Alan E. Peacock, "The Successful Prosecution of the Factory Acts, 1833–55," *Economic History Review*, 2d ser., 37 (1984): 200.

81. See Rubinstein, *School Attendance in London*, 99. For another example of similar behavior, see AR 1883–84, PP 1884, vol. 24, [C.-4091-I], 456.

82. Cited in Rubinstein, *School Attendance in London*, 102.

83. See Peacock, "Successful Prosecution of the Factory Acts," 197–210; and Peter Bartrip, "Success or Failure? The Prosecution of the Early Factory Acts," *Economic History Review*, 2d ser., 38 (1985): 423–27; Clark Nardinelli, "The Successful Prosecution of the Early Factory Acts: A Suggested Explanation," *Economic History Review*, 2d ser., 38 (1985): 428–30; Alan E. Peacock, "Factory Act Prosecutions: A Hidden Consensus," *Economic History Review*, 2d ser., 38 (1985): 431–36.

84. From Board of Education, W. P. Turnbull, "North-Eastern Division General Report for the Year 1900," PP 1901, vol. 21, [Cd.-570], 6.

85. AR 1882–83, PP 1883, vol. 25, [C.-3706-I], 332–33.

86. AR 1878–79, PP 1878–79, vol. 23, [C.-2342-I], 521.

87. "Return of Notices during 1873 Requiring the Attendance of Children," PP 1873, vol. 52, [368], 2–9.

88. See AR 1878–79, PP 1878–9, vol. 23, [C.-2342-I], 471–72, 703–4; AR 1881–82, PP 1882, vol. 23, [C.-3312-I], 271; and "Reports of Inspectors of Factories for the Half-year ending 31st October, 1875," PP 1876, vol. 16, [C.-1434], 122.

89. Cited in Belfiore, "Family Strategies," 302.

90. AR 1878–79, PP 1878–79, vol. 23, [C.-2342-I], 754.

91. See, for example, AR 1878–79, PP 1878–79, vol. 23, [C.-2342-I], 566–67; AR 1881–82, PP 1882, vol. 23, [C.-3312-I], 194–95, 351, 354; and AR 1882–83, PP 1883, vol. 25, [C.-3706-I], 354, 457.

92. Cited in AR 1882–83, PP 1883, vol. 25, [C.-3706-I], 457.

93. AR 1878–79, PP 1878–79, vol. 23, [C.-2342-I], 702–3.

94. AR 1881–82, PP 1882, vol. 23, [C.-3312-I], 352.

95. See, for example, AR 1897–98, PP 1898, vol. 22, [C.-8987], 158; Board of Education, W. E. Currey, "Eastern Division General Report for 1900," PP 1901, vol. 21, [Cd.-566], 6, 9, 10, 11, 13; Board of Education, J. G. Fitzmaurice, "North-Central Division General Report for 1900," PP 1901, vol. 21, [Cd.-572], 3, 6; Board of Education, W. P. Turnbull, "North-Eastern Division General Report for 1900," PP 1901, vol. 21, [Cd.-570], 6–8; Board of Education,

J. Armine Willis, "South-Western Division General Report for the Year 1900," PP
1901, vol. 21, [Cd.-571], 4–6; and Board of Education, A. G. Legard, "Welsh
Division General Report for the Year 1900," PP 1901, vol. 21, [Cd.-622], 14, 19.
For other examples, see AR 1878–79, PP 1878–79, vol. 23, [C.-2342-I], 639,
703; AR 1881–82, PP 1882, vol. 23, [C.-3312-I], 419, 431; AR 1882–83,
PP 1883, vol. 25, [C.-3706-I], 277, 325; AR 1884–85, PP 1884–5, vol. 23,
[C.-4483-I], 326; AR 1889–90, PP 1890, vol. 28, [C.-6079-I], 385–86; AR
1892–93, PP 1893–4, vol. 26, [C.-7089-I], 5–7, 45–48, 54–55, 71–74,
96–97; "First Report on the Elementary Education Acts," PP 1886, vol. 25,
[C.-4863], 112 (item 2696); and "Second Report on the Elementary Education
Acts," PP 1887, vol. 29, [C.-5056], 148 (items 18280, 18285), 155 (18612). For
evidence on the difficulty of enforcing the Agricultural Children's Act and other
child labor restrictions see "Report of the Commissioners on the Factory and
Workshops Act, Vol. I, Appendix C," PP 1876, vol. 29, [C.-1443], 194–209.
Also see Hurt, *Elementary Schooling*, chap. 8.

96. See "Minutes of Evidence taken before the Commission to Inquire into
the Workings of the Factories and Workshops Act," PP 1876, vol. 30, [C.-1443-
I], 265 (item 5280), 396 (item 8003), 399 (item 8051), 574 (item 11887).

97. See AR 1875–76, PP 1876, vol. 23, [C.-1513-I], 324.

98. See, for example AR 1875–76, PP 1876, vol. 23, [C.-1513-I], 357; AR
1878–79, PP 1878–79, vol. 23, [C.-2342-I], 471, 503, 640–41, 670, 692, 712,
725–26, 733; AR 1881–82, PP 1882, vol. 23, [C.-3312-I], 216–17, 390; AR
1882–83, PP 1883, vol. 25, [C.-3706-I], 418, 444; AR 1883–84, PP 1884, vol.
24, [C.-4091-I], 343; AR 1884–85, PP 1884–5, vol. 23, [C.-4483-I], 324–25,
337–42; AR 1889–90, PP 1890, vol. 28, [C.-6079-I], 301–2; AR 1892–93,
PP 1893–4, vol. 26, [C.-7089-I], 4; and Board of Education, W. E. Currey,
"Eastern Division General Report for 1900," PP 1901, vol. 21, [Cd.-566], 7–9.
Also see "Second Report on the Elementary Education Acts," PP 1887, vol. 29,
[C.-5056], 84 (item 16198), 922 (item 41035); "First Report on the Elementary
Education Acts," PP 1886, vol. 25, [C.-4863], 103–4 (items 2345–52), 108–9
(2554–58), 112 (2695–2701), 121 (items 3036–43), 122–23 (items 3082–88);
and Rubinstein, *School Attendance in London*, 93. Rubinstein cites an example
where a skeptic on the impact of compulsion was pressed by the committee about
how compulsion could have had no impact if national attendance had risen by 15
percent in fifteen years.

99. For further examples of variation in the impact of compulsion than those
cited in this paragraph, see AR 1875–76, PP 1876, vol. 23, [C.-1513-I], 312;
AR 1878–79, PP 1878–9, vol. 23, [C.-2342-I], 670, 753; AR 1881–82, PP
1882, vol. 23, [C.-3312-I], 217, 301, 367; AR 1883–84, PP 1884, vol. 24, [C.-
4091-I], 200, 342; AR 1889–90, PP 1890, vol. 28, [C.-6079-I], 280–81; AR
1897–98, PP 1898, vol. 22, [C.-8987], 158, 186, 207, 216, 230, 244, 262–63,
227; AR 1901, PP 1902, vol. 25, [Cd.-1159], 16, 22, 40, 48, 63, 64, 66, 68,
123–25, 152–53.

100. AR 1882–83, PP 1883, vol. 25, [C.-3706-I], 456–57.

101. Board of Education, A. G. Legard, "Welsh Division General Report for
the Year 1900," PP 1901, vol. 21, [Cd.-622], 20.

102. For example, see AR 1881–82, PP 1882, vol. 23, [C.-3312-I], 301; AR 1882–83, PP 1883, vol. 25, [C.-3706-I], 294–97, 332–33; AR 1884–85, PP 1884–5, vol. 23, [C.-4483-I], 263–64, 299; AR 1889–90, PP 1890, vol. 28, [C.-6079-I], 386; Board of Education, J. G. Fitzmaurice, "North-Central Division General Report for 1900," PP 1901, vol. 21, [Cd.-572], 3; AR 1901, PP 1902, vol. 25, [Cd.-1159], 124.

103. AR 1878–79, PP 1878–9, vol. 23, [C.-2342-I], 520. Byrne goes on to provide specific examples of this principle from various districts in his area.

104. AR 1881–82, PP 1882, vol. 23, [C.-3312-I], 352.

105. AR 1878–79, PP 1878–9, vol. 23, [C.-2342-I], 567. Also see ibid., 471–72, 520–21, 566, 639, 704, 754; and "Second Report on the Elementary Education Acts," PP 1887, vol. 29, [C.-5056], 123 (item 17391). This theme is also touched on in Belfiore, "Family Strategies," 190–202, 281, 368, 390, 398–99.

106. Rubinstein, *School Attendance in London*, 46.

107. William Landes and Lewis Solmon, "Compulsory Schooling Legislation: An Economic Analysis of Law and Social Change in the Nineteenth Century," *Journal of Economic History* 32 (1972): 84. The flexibility and evolution of the system of compulsion in England is a central theme in Belfiore, "Family Strategies" (pp. 190–201, 205–6, 343–44, 361–63, 390, 399).

108. Hurt, *Elementary Schooling*, 155–57.

109. Extensive evidence for the differential impact of compulsory schooling laws on different social classes is also presented in Belfiore, "Family Strategies," 163, 190–202, 205–6, 251, 361–63, 385, 395, 399.

110. See, for example, AR 1882–83, PP 1883, vol. 25, [C.-3706-I], 477; and AR 1889–90, PP 1890, vol. 28, [C.-6079-I], 301.

111. AR 1878–79, PP 1878–79, vol. 23, [C.-2342-I], 716.

112. On the compilation of such censuses in London, see Rubinstein, *School Attendance in London*, 46–48. On their use in Liverpool, see AR 1889–90, PP 1890, vol. 28, [C.-6079-I], 297.

113. See Rubinstein, *School Attendance in London*, 52.

114. See Hurt, *Elementary Schooling*, 204.

115. For an insightful account of the evolution of both working-class response and policies of school officials and magistrates to compulsory schooling laws in a group of Essex villages, see Belfiore, "Family Strategies," chaps. 9, 10.

116. See Hurt, *Elementary Education*, 204–5.

117. AR 1901, PP 1902, vol. 25, [Cd.-1159], 124–25.

118. Board of Education, J. Armine Willis, "South-Western Division General Report for the Year 1900," PP 1901, vol. 21, [Cd.-571], 5–6.

119. See "Judicial Statistics. 1874, England and Wales, Pt. I, Police, Criminal Proceedings, Prisons," PP 1875, vol. 81, [C.-1315], 32 (Table 8); "Judicial Statistics, 1883 (England and Wales), Pt. I, Police, Criminal Proceedings, Prisons," PP 1884, vol. 86, [C.-4170], 32 (Table 8); "Judicial Statistics, 1892 (England and Wales), Pt. I, Police, Criminal Proceedings, Prisons," PP 1893–94, vol. 103, [C.-7168], 32 (Table 8).

120. See AR 1878–79, PP 1878–79, vol. 23, [C.-2342-I], 618; AR

1881–82, PP 1882, vol. 23, [C.-3312-I], 194, 394; and AR 1882–83, PP 1883, vol. 25, [C.-3706-I], 277, 324. Also see "Second Report on the Elementary Education Acts," PP 1887, vol. 29, [C.-5056], 155 (items 18766–68), 520 (items 30091–92), 970 (item 41906). Evidence on this issue is also presented in Belfiore, "Family Strategies," 190–202, 326, 377–78, 385, 389, 395, 398–99. In their study of the United States, Landes and Solmon also suggest that compulsory schooling may have had a stronger effect on enrollment than attendance rates. See Landes and Solmon, "Compulsory Schooling Legislation," 71.

121. See "Second Report on the Elementary Education Acts," PP 1887, vol. 29, [C.-5056], 504 (item 29644).

122. See, for example, Patrick Cumin's testimony as head of the Department of Education and J. R. Diggle's testimony as an official with the London School Board. These are recorded in "First Report on the Elementary Education Acts," PP 1886, vol. 25, [C.-4863], 70 (item 1605); and "Second Report on the Elementary Education Acts," PP 1887, vol. 29, [C.-5056], 504 (item 29646). Rubinstein also notes the perplexity of London school officials at the rather stagnant attendance trends between 1877 and 1900. See Rubinstein, *School Attendance in London*, 115.

123. See, for example, AR 1878–79, PP 1878–9, vol. 23, [C.-2342-I], 526–27, 618.

124. It should be noted that the enrollment figures for 1871 in Table 7.6 differ from those in later years because the 1871 figures are based on the census and include all those who were classified as scholars by the census no matter what type of school they attended. The enrollment figures for later years are based on Department of Education reports and include only scholars enrolled in state-inspected schools; they thus omit enrollment in private schools. If one accepts Gardner's conclusion that few working-class private schools remained in existence by the 1880s, this omission will be small. See Gardner, *Lost Schools*, 206. It should also be noted that to properly interpret the enrollment figures in Table 7.6 as working-class enrollments, it must be assumed that virtually all children enrolled in state-inspected schools were from working-class families.

125. The figures in Table 7.6 can be used as follows to estimate the relative contributions of increases in enrollment rates and attendance rates to the rise in the proportion of children attending school between 1871 and 1896. The percentage increase attributable to enrollment increases can be estimated by multiplying the change in the estimated working-class enrollment rate between 1871 and 1896 from Table 7.6 by the attendance rate in 1871 from Table 7.6 and dividing by the change between the two dates in the scholars in attendance per population. Using this procedure, the percentage of the total rise in attendance atributable to enrollment increases was 60.7 percent for children aged five to nine and 63.0 percent for children aged ten to fourteen.

The percentage increase attributable to increases in the attendance rate can be calculated by multiplying the change in attendance rate reported in Table 7.6 between 1871 and 1896 by the initial working-class enrollment rate and dividing by the change in attendance per population. Using this procedure, the percentage of the total rise in attendance attributable to the rise in the attendance rate was

27.3 percent for children aged five to nine and 24.4 percent for children aged ten to fourteen.

The contribution of the interaction between attendance and enrollment increases can be estimated by multiplying the change in enrollment rates by the change in attendance rates and dividing by the change in attendance per population. Using this procedure, the percentage of the total rise in attendance attributable to the interaction between rising enrollment and attendance rates was 12.0 percent for children aged five to nine and 12.6 percent for children aged ten to fourteen. These estimates assume that attendance rates were the same for children aged five to nine as for children aged ten to fourteen.

These estimates of the relative contribution of enrollment and attendance rate increases to rising attendance per population indicate that over half of the rise can be attributed to rising enrollment rates but that about one-fourth can attributed to rising attendance rates.

126. See, for example, "Board of Education, W. P. Turnbull, North-Eastern Division General Report for 1900," PP 1901, vol. 21, [Cd.-570], 30–31. Also see AR 1884–85, PP 1884–5, vol. 23, [C.-4483-I], 265; AR 1889–90, PP 1890, vol. 28, [C.-6079-I], 356–57; AR 1901, PP 1902, vol. 25, [Cd.-1159], 48; "Second Report on the Elementary Education Acts," PP 1887, vol. 29, [C.-5056], 158 (items 18766–68), 212 (20843). Useful evidence is also presented in Belfiore, "Family Strategies," 169 n.80, 190–202, 295, 399.

127. Literacy rates are calculated from proportions of brides and grooms able to sign their names as reported in 5th ARRG (Abstract for 1841), PP 1843, vol. 21, [516], 79–95; 6th ARRG (Abstract for 1842), PP 1844, vol. 19, [540], 6–19; 7th ARRG (Abstract for 1844), PP 1846, vol. 19, [727], 114–27, 162–75; 8th ARRG (Abstract for 1845), PP 1847–8, vol. 25, [967], 106–23; 35th ARRG (Abstract for 1872), PP 1875, vol. 18, pt. I, [C.-1155], 6–25; 36th ARRG (Abstract for 1873), PP 1875, vol. 18, pt. I, [C.-1312], 6–25; 37th ARRG (Abstract for 1874), PP 1876, vol. 18, [C.-1581], 6–25; 38th ARRG (Abstract for 1875), PP 1877, vol. 25, [C.-1786], 6–25; 39th ARRG (Abstract for 1876), PP 1878, vol. 22, [C.-2075], 6–25.

128. See the section "The Composition of Product Demand" earlier in this chapter.

129. These counties were Hertford, Buckingham, Huntingdon, Bedford, Cambridge, Suffolk, Norfolk, Cornwall, Hereford, Stafford, Monmouth, South Wales, and North Wales.

130. These counties were Bedfordshire, Cornwall, Staffordshire, Worcestershire, Warwickshire, Nottingham, Lancashire, West Riding, Durham, Monmouth, South Wales, and North Wales.

131. Signature rates at marriage are taken from 37th ARRG (Abstract for 1874), PP 1876, vol. 18, [C.-1581], xlii; 47th ARRG (Abstract for 1884), PP 1886, vol. 17, sess. I, [C.-4722], xli; 58th ARRG (Abstract for 1895), PP 1897, vol. 21, [C.-8403], xlv; 68th ARRG (Abstract for 1905), PP 1906, vol. 20, [Cd.-3279], 11.

132. See Hurt, *Elementary Education*, chap. 8. For a study arguing that at least the Factory Acts were effectively prosecuted, see Peacock, "Successful

Prosecution of the Factory Acts," 197–210. For a critique of Peacock, see Bartrip, "Success or Failure?" 423–27; and Nardinelli, "Successful Prosecution," 428–30. For estimates of the number of children employed in activities covered by the Factory Acts and other restrictions on child labor, see Hurt, *Elementary Education*, 44; Birchenough, *History of Elementary Education*, 145 n.1; and Sutherland, *Policy Making in Education*, 117.

133. AR 1889–90, PP 1890, vol. 28, [C.-6079-I], 274.

134. AR 1896–97, PP 1897, vol. 26, [C.-8544], 23.

135. AR 1889–90, PP 1890, vol. 28, [C.-6079-I], 274; and AR 1896–97, PP 1897, vol. 26, [C.-8544], 23.

136. See 47th ARRG (Abstract for 1884), PP 1886, vol. 17, sess. I, [C.-4722], xli, 6–25. For example the percentage making marks reported in the 1884 Registrar General's report for the following registration districts was as follows:

	Grooms	*Brides*
Staffordshire		
Dudley	33.8	44.5
South Wales		
Glamorgen		
Ponty Pridd	28.8	32.5
Methyr Tydfil	26.1	34.7
Cardigan		
Lampeter	20.0	44.0
Brecon		
Crickhowel	42.4	39.0
Monmouthshire		
Bedwelty	35.5	28.3

137. Landes and Solmon, "Compulsory Schooling Legislation," 86–89.

138. Hurt mentions this possibility in *Elementary Schooling*, 198–99.

139. For a discussion of the restrictions on child labor imposed by the Factory Acts, see Robson, *Education of Children*, chaps. 2–4; and Keeling, *Child Labour*, xxv-xxxii.

140. For evidence on mill owners' reluctance to hire children in accord with the educational provisions of the Factory Acts see "Minutes from the Select Committee on Manchester and Salford Education," PP 1852, vol. 11, [499], 14–16 (item 60); "Half-Yearly Reports of Inspectors of Factories dated August, 1835," PP 1836, vol. 45, [78], 7; "Reports of Inspectors of Factories," PP 1834, vol. 43, [596], 39; and "Third Report on the Regulation of Mills and Factories," PP 1840, vol. 10, [314], 28 (item 4402).

141. See Mitchell and Deane, *Abstract of British Historical Statistics*, 188, 199.

142. See, for example, "Minutes before Select Committee on the Education

of the Poorer Classes," PP 1837–8, vol. 7, [589], 12 (items 89, 92–93), 64–65 (items 558–77); and "Reports on the Effects of the Educational Provisions of the Factories Act," PP 1839, vol.42, [42], 3–6, 17–31, 65–70. For evidence on what children displaced from the textile mills did subsequently, see "Reports of Inspectors of Factories," PP 1834, vol. 43, [596], 39.

143. The 1851 census shows that of employed children under twenty, the proportion employed in textiles in Blackburn was 70 percent for boys and 84 percent for girls; in Bolton, it was 49 percent for boys and 72.2 percent for girls; in Oldham, 56 percent for boys and 80.5 percent for girls; in Preston, 55.4 percent for boys and 73.4 percent for girls; and in Bradford, 60 percent for boys and 84.3 percent for girls. See "Census of Gt. Britain, 1851, Population Tables II, Ages, Civil Condition, Occupations and Birth-place of the People, vol. II," PP 1852–3, vol. 88, pt. II, [1691-II], 648–53.

144. Factory inspectors' returns indicate that between 1835 and 1847, the number of boys under thirteen employed in cotton textile factories fell from fifteen thousand to eleven thousand, while the number of girls under thirteen employed in cotton textile factories fell from fourteen thousand to seven thousand. See Mitchell and Deane, *Abstract of British Historical Statistics*, 188.

145. See Robson, *Education of Children*, 25–35, 69–73, 83–107.

146. See Robson, *Education of Children*, 97, 99–100; "Reports of the Inspectors of Factories for the Year ending 31st December, 1837," PP 1837–8, vol. 28, [119], 15–16; "Minutes before Select Committee on Education of the Poorer Classes," PP 1837–8, vol. 7, [589], 65–66 (items 581–86); and "Reports on the Effects of the Educational Provisions of the Factories Act," PP 1839, vol. 42, [42], 37.

147. See "Minutes of Evidence taken before the Commissioners appointed to inquire into the Factory and Workshops Acts," PP 1876, vol. 30, [C.-1443-I], 100 (item 2048), 574 (item 11887), 831 (items 17467–68); "Reports of the Inspectors of Factories for the Half-year ending 30th April, 1875," PP 1875, vol. 16, [C.-1345], 67; and "Reports of Inspectors of Factories for the Half-year ending 30th April, 1876," PP 1876, vol. 16, [C.-1572], 66.

148. See "Appendix to Third Report on Children's Employment," PP 1864, vol. 22, [3414-I], 64–69; "Reports of the Inspectors of Factories for the Half-year ending 31st October, 1865," PP 1866, vol. 24, [3622], 110; and "Reports of the Inspectors of Factories for the Half-year ending 31st October, 1862," PP 1863, vol. 18, [3076], 33–34.

149. See "Appendix to Fourth Report on the Employment of Children and Young Persons in Trades and Manufactures," PP 1865, vol. 20, [3548], 9, 16, 52, 68; and "Reports of Inspectors of Factories for the Half-year ending 31st October, 1865," PP 1866, vol. 24, [3622], 30.

150. From the numbers of scholars by age group reported in "Appendix A to Report, Census of England and Wales, 1871, General Report, vol. IV," PP 1873, vol. 71, pt. II, [C.-872-I], 112 (Table 106), one can calculate that of the rise between 1851 and 1871 in the proportion of children aged five to fifteen reported as scholars, 47.7 percent can be attributed to a rise among children aged five to nine and 51.4 percent can be attributed to a rise among ten- to

fourteen-year-old children. The enrollment by age proportions between 1861 and 1891 were obtained from AR 1870–71, PP 1871, vol. 22, [C.-406], 5; and "Public Elementary Education in England and Wales, 1870–1895," PP 1897, vol. 25, [C.-8447], 51.

151. See AR 1875–76, PP 1876, vol. 23, [C.-1513-I], 305, 331; AR 1878–79, PP 1878–79, vol. 23, [C.-2342-I], 526–27, 752; AR 1897–98, PP 1898, vol. 22, [C.-8987], 201; and Board of Education, W. P. Turnbull, "North-Eastern Division General Report for the Year 1900," PP 1901, vol. 21, [Cd.-570], 7.

152. For evidence on improvements in school provision in the 1840s in textile regions, see Robson, *Education of Children*, 82–107. On the increased concern of parents for education and its effect on compliance with the Factory Acts, see "Reports of Inspectors of Factories for the Half-year ending 30th April, 1876," PP 1876, vol. 16, [C.-1572], 23–24, 97.

153. See AR 1875–76, PP 1876, vol. 23, [C.-1513-I], 271; AR 1878–79, PP 1878–9, vol. 23, [C.-2342-I], 320; AR 1881–82, PP 1882, vol. 23, [C.-3312-I], 313–14; AR 1882–83, PP 1883, vol. 25, [C.-3706-I], 278; AR 1883–84, PP 1884, vol. 24, [C.-4091-I], 268; AR 1884–85, PP 1884–5, vol. 23, [C.-4483-I], 264, 327; AR 1889–90, PP 1890, vol. 28, [C.-6079-I], 280, 331; AR 1892–93, PP 1893–4, vol. 26, [C.-7089-I], 6–7, 45–46, 70; and AR 1897–98, PP 1898, vol. 22, [C.-8987], 185, 187, 242, 244.

154. See AR 1889–90, PP 1890, vol. 28, [C.-6079-I], 299; AR 1897–98, PP 1898, vol. 22, [C.-8987], 185; Board of Education, J. G. Fitzmaurice, "North-Central Division General Report for 1900," PP 1901, vol. 21, [Cd.-572], 4; AR 1901, PP 1902, vol.25, [Cd.-1159], 62.

155. Board of Education, J. G. Fitzmaurice, "North-Central Division General Report for 1900," PP 1901, vol. 21, [Cd.-572], 4.

Chapter 8: Becoming a Literate Society

1. See "Judicial Statistics, 1874 (England and Wales), Pt. I, Police, Criminal Proceedings, Prisons," PP 1875, vol. 81, [C.-1315], 32; "Judicial Statistics, 1883 (England and Wales), Pt. I, Police, Criminal Proceedings, Prisons," PP 1884, vol. 86, [C.-4170], 32 (Table 8); "Judicial Statistics, 1892 (England and Wales), Pt. I, Police, Criminal Proceedings, Prisons," PP 1893–4, vol. 103, [C.-7168], 32.

2. The estimates reported in Tables 8.1 to 8.3 are for conditions that probably prevailed throughout the Victorian period. These tables and the text make no allowance for changes in costs and benefits that may have occurred throughout the Victorian period. In fact tuition costs clearly changed. The real tuition costs of schooling in subsidized schools appear to have at least doubled over the Victorian period before the establishment of free schools in 1891. See Mitch "Impact of Subsidies," 375. Whether other costs and the benefits changed is less obvious. Chapter 7 found no clear trend in children's wages during the mid-Victorian period. Chapter 2 found that the *percentage* wage premium associated with literacy fell over the Victorian period, but the effect of this on the *absolute* wage premium

would have been offset by generally rising wages during this period. The absolute wage premium would have been most relevant to the decision to acquire literacy. Chapter 3 found that the nonpecuniary benefits of literacy were markedly influenced by the falling prices of newspapers and postage. Although the text and tables make no direct mention of changes in costs and benefits, the values considered in the tables encompass the likely range that commonly occurred over the Victorian period.

3. These estimates assume a constant annual premium to literacy throughout one's working life. In fact, the premium probably rose with age. Insofar as these annual estimates are accurate as mean lifetime values, using them to estimate the present value overstates the present value of literacy. But the range of estimated present values corresponding to the range of constant annual premia does indicate the range of likely values of premia, even taking into account variation over the life cycle.

4. See "Report of Commissioners on Popular Education," PP 1861, vol. 21, pt. I, [2794-I], 39–51. For evidence on the low rate of evening school enrollment compared with enrollment in day schools, see Statistical Society of London, "State of Education in Westminister," 193–215; Statistical Society of London, "Report on Finsbury," 28–43; Bristol Statistical Society, "Report on Education in Bristol," 250–63; J. R. Wood, "Report on Education in Birmingham," 25–49; Manchester Statistical Society, "Education in Rutland," 303–15; Manchester Statistical Society, "Report on Education in Bury," 11; "Census of Gt. Britain, 1851, Education," PP 1852–3, vol. 90, [1692], cxxii. Also see John F. C. Harrison, *Learning and Living 1790–1860: A Study in the History of the English Adult Education Movement* (London: Routledge and Paul, 1961), 56–58, 65–74, 129–30.

5. See Chapter 7.

6. See Vincent, *Literacy and Popular Culture*, chap. 3.

7. "Reports of Assistant Commissioners on Popular Education," PP 1861, vol. 21, pt. II, [2794-II], 202–3.

8. As early as 1851, Horace Mann stated in the Census of Education that "very few children are *completely* uninstructed; nearly all, at some time or another of their childhood, see the inside of a schoolroom, though some do little more." "Census of Gt. Britain, 1851, Education," PP 1852–3, vol. 90, [1692], xxx. Ten years later the Newcastle Commission report asserted, "With these exceptions [children of outdoor paupers and parents viciously inclined] almost all children in the country capable of going to school receive some instruction." See "Report of Commissioners on Popular Education," PP 1861, vol. 21, pt. I, [2794-I], 84–86. The report proceeded to draw on assessments of the specimen districts examined for the commission to verify this claim. In the 1880s the Cross Commission reported the view of Patrick Cumin, head of the Education Department, as being that "at present almost every child goes to an efficient school for a certain time in its life." See "Final Report on the Elementary Education Acts," PP 1888, vol. 35, [C.-5485], 103; Cumin's original testimony is in "First Report on the Elementary Education Acts," PP 1886, vol. 25, [C.-4863], 87 (items 1954–65).

9. "Report of Commissioners on Popular Education," PP 1861, vol. 21, pt. I, [2794-I], 86.

10. Several surveys of the Victorian working classes indicate that school attendance was by no means close to universal. In a survey of twenty thousand adults in Hull, referred to in Chapter 6, 69 percent stated that they had attended a day school at some point in their lives. See Manchester Statistical Society, "Report on Education in Kingston-Upon-Hull," 170. In a survey of five thousand adults in Pendleton in 1838, referred to in Chapter 6, 88 percent indicated that they had attended a day school. See Manchester Statistical Society, "Report on the State of Education in Pendleton," 81. A survey of sixty teenage mining boys in the 1840s indicated that only twenty-two had ever attended a day school. See "Evidence Collected by W. R. Wood in the Collieries and Ironworks adjacent to Bradford and Leeds, Appendix to First Report on the Employment of Children. Mines, Pt. II," PP 1842, vol. 17, [382], h11, h18, h24, h29, h31. Of a group of Gloucester agricultural laborers surveyed in 1867, eighteen of twenty-four men had attended day school, as had nine of thirteen boys and six of eight women. See "Appendix, Pt. II to the First Report on the Employment of Women, Young Persons, and Women in Agriculture," PP 1867–68, vol. 17, [4068-I], 209–10.

Some school inspectors in the 1870s and 1880s acknowledged the existence of children who had never attended school. See AR 1883–84, PP 1884, vol. 24, [C.-4091-I], 415–16; AR 1878–79, PP 1878–9, vol. 23, [C.-2342-I], 716; AR 1889–90, PP 1890, vol. 28, [C.-6079-I], 301. John Hurt also states, "Although it had been possible as late as 1890 to find families here who had never sent a child to school, such parents became increasingly rarer." See Hurt, *Elementary Schooling*, 204. One inspector of the Middlesex district in 1882 estimated this group at about 10 percent of all children. See AR 1882–83, PP 1883, vol. 25, [C.-3706-I], 477.

11. "Reports of Assistant Commissioners on Popular Education," PP 1861, vol. 21, pt. II, [2794-II], 249–53.

12. For one study that considers such factors but ultimately minimizes their influence on working-class literacy trends, see Levine, *Reproducing Families*, 126–29, 192–93, 194–200, 208, 210–12.

13. See Schofield, "Dimensions of Illiteracy," 445–46.

14. See Stephens, *Education, Literacy and Society*, 21, 71, 79–80.

15. For trends in signature rates, see 47th ARRG (Abstract for 1884), PP 1886, vol. 17, sess. I, [C.-4722], xli; 58th ARRG (Abstract for 1895), PP 1897, vol. 21, [C.-8403], xlv.

16. Disraeli in the early 1850's estimated that the newspaper stamp tax brought in £1.5 million a year. See Collet, *History of the Taxes on Knowledge*, 92. Expenditure on education, science, and art by the government grew from £370,000 in 1850 to £4 million by 1880, and £12 million by 1900. See Mitchell and Deane, *British Historical Statistics*, 397–98. Education Department expenditure was reported at £760,000 in 1870, £2.5 million in 1880, and £6.66 million in 1895. See Sutherland, *Policy Making in Elementary Education*, 361.

17. For estimates of the subsidy per year received in state-funded schools, see Mitch, "Impact of Subsidies," 375.

18. See Richard Johnson, "Educational Policy and Social Control," 96–119; Richard Johnson, "Educating the Educators: Experts and the State, 1833–9," in

Social Control in Nineteenth Century Britain, ed. A.P. Donajgrodzki (London: Croom Helm, 1977), 77–107.

19. See Katznelson and Weir, *Schooling for All*; Reese, *Power and Promise*. For a respected account putting emphasis on tendencies toward centralization and systematization, however, see David Tyack, *The One Best System. A History of American Urban Education* (Cambridge: Harvard University Press, 1974).

20. See Richard Gawthorp, "Literacy Drives in Preindustrial Germany"; Rab Houston, "The Literacy Campaign in Scotland, 1560–1803"; and Ben Eklof, "Russian Literacy Campaigns, 1861–1939," all in *National Literacy Campaigns: Historical and Comparative Perspectives*, ed. Robert Arnove and Harvey Graff (New York: Plenum Press, 1987), 29–48, 49–64, 123–146.

Appendix C

1. The assumption that consumers had linear demand curves for the items being considered here does not impart any obvious bias to the estimation of consumer's surplus.

2. Continuous discounting would seem appropriate since the benefits of literacy would seem likely to have been distributed more or less evenly throughout the year, not at the end of the year. For a derivation of the formula for the present value of a flow with continuous discounting, see Alpha Chiang, *Fundamental Methods of Mathematical Economics*, 2d ed. (New York: McGraw-Hill, 1974), 457.

3. See Robin Boadway and David Wildasin, *Public Sector Economics*, 2d ed. (Boston: Little, Brown and Co., 1984), 34–38.

4. See Altick, *English Common Reader*, chaps. 12–15.

5. See ibid., 355; and Williams, *Long Revolution*, 193.

6. Lee, *Origins of the Popular Press*, 245 n.64, reports estimates of multiple readership ranging from three or four people per copy to as many as thirty people per copy. Hollis, *Pauper Press*, 119, estimates that "Readership exceeded sales perhaps by 20 times."

7. See Hollis, *Pauper Press*, 298; and Bourne, *English Newspapers* 2: 209–10.

8. See Altick, *English Common Reader*, chaps. 14, 15; Bourne, *English Newspapers* 2:253–54; and Wadsworth, "Newspaper Circulations," 18–28.

9. Thompson, *Lark Rise to Candleford*, 109.

10. Bell, *At the Works*, 155 (item 112).

11. Leigh, "What Do the Masses Read?" 170.

12. Jefferies, *Life of the Fields*, 193.

13. Bell, *At the Works*, 144.

14. Ibid., 166.

15. Leigh, "What Do the Masses Read?" 174–75.

16. Mayhew, *London Labour* 1:295–96.

17. Jefferies, *Life of the Fields*, 198.

18. Neuberg, *Popular Literature*, 114, 116.

19. Altick, *English Common Reader*, 288–89.

20. Neuberg, *Popular Literature*, 144.

21. Knight, *Old Printer*, 243.

22. See Altick, *English Common Reader*, chap. 13; Neuberg, *Popular Literature*, chap. 4; and James, *Fiction for the Working Man*, chap. 3.

23. Mayhew, *London Labour* 3:390, cites one example of halfpenny books.

24. Letter delivery statistics are taken from "Appendix A to Twenty-Ninth Report of the Postmaster General of the Post Office," PP 1883, vol. 22, [C.-3703], 26. The number of adult literates were calculated by multiplying the population over twenty by the 1840 literacy rate as reported in 7th ARRG (Abstracts for 1843), PP 1846, vol. 19, [727], 40–41; and Mitchell and Deane, *Abstract of British Historical Statistics*, 12. This is a clear understatement of adult literates and hence an overstatement of letters per literate incorporated to deal with a rising literacy rate across generations, or in other words, higher literacy rates for those marrying in 1881 than the adult population generally.

25. Jefferies, *Life of the Fields*, 201.

26. See Thompson, *Lark Rise to Candleford*, 101, 167, 165.

27. Vincent, *Literacy and Popular Culture*, 51.

28. See Hill, *Post Office Reform*, 63. George Frederick Kay estimated that the average charge was as high as 8.75 pence per letter. See Kay, *Royal Mail*, 78. J. C. Hemmeon indicates that fees for letters within England could exceed 10 pence; see Hemmeon, *British Post Office*, chap. 8.

29. See Kay, *Royal Mail*, 78–79; and Hemmeon, *British Post Office*, 147.

30. Mayhew, *London Labour* 1:268.

31. See Warren S. Thompson, *Population Problems*, 2d ed. (New York: McGraw-Hill, 1935), 221.

32. Helen Bosanquet, "Wages and Housekeeping," in *Methods of Social Advance*, ed. C. S. Loch (London: Macmillan, 1904), 136.

33. Johnson, *Saving and Spending*, chaps. 4, 6.

34. Ibid., 89.

35. Mitchell and Deane, *Abstract of British Historical Statistics*, 455.

36. Johnson, *Saving and Spending*, 165–66; also see page 153 for an instance of a 25-percent rate set by a credit club.

37. Ibid., 166, 190–91.

38. Ibid., 181–83.

39. See Mitch, "Spread of Literacy," 187.

40. Johnson, *Saving and Spending*, 153, 166, 181, 222–23.

Appendix D

1. See "Minutes of Evidence taken before the Select Committee on Education," PP 1834, vol. 9, [572], 120 (items 260–67).

2. See Mark Blaug, *An Introduction to the Economics of Education* (London: Penguin Books, 1970), 249, 258–65.

3. For a discussion of the curriculum of the nineteenth-century school, see Birchenough, *History of Elementary Education*, 275–84.

4. See ibid., 279–80.

5. "Report of Commissioners on Popular Education," PP 1861, vol. 21, pt. I, [2794-I], 651–52.

6. See Bienefield, *Working Hours in British Industry*, 43–48.

7. Based on the occupational wage estimates provided in Baxter, *National Income*, 88–93.

8. For women's wages, see ibid., 88–93; Tropp, *School Teachers*, 273; and Levi, *Wages and Earnings*, 24–26, 69–93.

Bibliography

MANUSCRIPT SOURCES

"School Certificate Book." Records of Strutt Mills at Derby/9–47. Archives Department. Manchester Reference Library, Manchester, England.

PRIVATELY PRINTED REPORTS

National Society for Promoting the Education of the Poor in the Principles of the Established Church. "Result of the Returns to the General Inquiry Made by the National Society, into the State and Progress of Schools for the Education of the Poor in the Principles of the Established Church during the Years 1846–7, Throughout England and Wales." London: Printed at the School-press, for the Society, 1849.
———. "Summaries of the Returns to the General Inquiry Made by the National Society into the State and Progress of Schools During the Years 1856–7, Throughout England and Wales." London, 1858.
———. "Statistics of Church of England Schools for the Poor in England and Wales for the Years 1866 and 1867." 2d ed. London, 1868.
———. *Annual Reports*. London: Printed for the Society.

BRITISH GOVERNMENT DOCUMENTS

PARLIAMENTARY PAPERS

"Report and Minutes of Evidence on the State of the Woollen Manufacture in England." PP 1806. Vol. 3. [268].
"Digest of Parochial Returns on the Education of the Poor." PP 1819. Vol. 9, pt. III. [224].
"Minutes of Evidence taken before the Select Committee on Education." PP 1834. Vol. 9. [572].
"Minutes of Evidence before Select Committee on Hand-loom Weaver's Petitions." PP 1834. Vol. 10. [556].
"Minutes of Evidence before the Select Committee on the Police of the Metropolis." PP 1834. Vol. 16. [600].

"Abstract of Returns on the State of Education in England and Wales." PP 1835. Vols. 41, 42, 43. [62].

"Minutes of Evidence before Select Committee on Education of the Poorer Classes." PP 1837–8. Vol. 7. [589].

"Minutes of Evidence. Second Report from the Select Committee on Postage." PP 1837–8. Vol. 20, pt. II. [658].

"Reports from Each of the Four Factory Inspectors, on the Effects of the Educational Provisions of the Factories Act; together with Joint Report." PP 1839. Vol. 42. [42].

"Minutes of Evidence, Third Report on the Regulation of Mills and Factories." PP 1840. Vol. 10. [314].

"Reports from Assistant Hand-loom Weaver Commissioners, Part II." PP 1840. Vol. 23. [43-I].

"Reports from Assistant Hand-loom Weavers Commissioners, Part III." PP 1840. Vol. 23. [43-II].

"Reports from Assistant Hand-loom Weaver Commissioners, Part V." PP 1840. Vol. 24. [220].

"Minutes of the Committee of Council on Education, 1840–41." PP 1841. Vol. 20. [317].

"First Report on the Employment of Children. Mines." PP 1842. Vol. 15. [380].

"Appendix to First Report on Children's Employment. Mines. Pt. I. Reports and Evidence from Subcommissioners." PP 1842. Vol. 16. [381].

"Appendix to First Report of Children's Employment Commission. Mines. Reports and Evidence from Subcommissioners." PP 1842. Vol. 17. [382].

"Reports of Special Assistant Poor Law Commissioners on the Employment of Women and Children in Agriculture." PP 1843. Vol. 12. [510].

"Children's Employment Commission, Second Report. Trades and Manufacturers." PP 1843. Vol. 13. [430].

"Appendix to Second Report on Children's Employment—Trades and Manufacturers—Pt. I. Reports and Evidence from Subcommissioners." PP 1843. Vol. 14. [431].

"Minutes of Evidence, Appendix Part I (Leicestershire). Report on the Condition of the Framework Knitters." PP 1845. Vol. 15. [618].

"Appendix to Report on Framework Knitters. Pt. II, Nottinghamshire and Derbyshire." PP 1845. Vol. 15. [641].

"Reports of the Commissioners of Inquiry into the State of Education in Wales." PP 1847. Vol. 27, pts. I, II, III. [870, 871, 872].

"Minutes of Evidence. Report from the Select Committee on Public Libraries." PP 1849. Vol. 17. [548].

"Report on the State of Population in the Mining Districts, 1850." PP 1850. Vol. 22. [1248].

"Minutes of Evidence taken before the Select Committee on Newspaper Stamps." PP 1851. Vol. 17. [558].

"Report from the Select Committee on Manchester and Salford Education; with the Proceedings of the Committee, Minutes of Evidence, Appendix." PP 1852. Vol. 11. [499].

"Minutes of Evidence for the First Report from the Select Committee on Police." PP 1852–3. Vol. 36. [603].

"Minutes of Evidence for the Second Report from the Select Committee on Police." PP 1852–3. Vol. 36. [715].

"Census of Gt. Britain, 1851, Education." PP 1852–3. Vol. 90. [1692].

"New York Industrial Exhibition. Special Report of Mr. George Wallis." PP 1854. Vol. 36. [1717].

"New York Industrial Exhibition. Special Report of Mr. Joseph Whitworth." PP 1854. Vol. 36. [1718].

"Minutes of Evidence on Stoppage of Wages (Hosiery)." PP 1854–5. Vol. 14. [421].

"Report of the Commissioners Appointed to Inquire into the State of Popular Education in England." PP 1861. Vol. 21, pt. I. [2794-I].

"Reports of the Assistant Commissioners Appointed to Inquire into the State of Popular Education in England." PP 1861. Vol. 21, pt. II. [2794-II].

"Further Reports of Assistant Commissioners on Popular Education in England." PP 1861. Vol. 21, pt. III. [2794-III].

"Appendix to First Report on Children's Employment (1862). Evidence of Assistant Commissioners." PP 1863. Vol. 18. [3170].

"Third Report on Children's Employment." PP 1864. Vol. 22. [3170].

"Appendix to Third Report on Children's Employment, Reports and Evidence of Assistant Commissioners." PP 1864. Vol. 22. [3414-I].

"Fourth Report on the Employment of Children and Young Persons in Trades and Manufactures." PP 1865. Vol. 20. [3548].

"Evidence on Agricultural Gangs collected by Mr. J. E. White: Appendix to Sixth Report of the Children's Employment and Commission." PP 1867. Vol. 16. [3796].

"Statistical Return of the Education and Religious Denomination of Petty Officers, Seamen, and Marines serving in the Navy for 1865." PP 1867. Vol. 44. [36].

"Minutes of Evidence to Report from the Select Committee on Scientific Instruction." PP 1867–8. Vol. 15. [432].

"First Report from the Commissioners on the Employment of Children, Young Persons, and Women in Agriculture with Appendix. Part I and Part II." PP 1867–8. Vol. 17. [4068, 4068-I].

"Second Report of the Commissioners on the Employment of Children, Young Persons, and Women in Agriculture with Appendix, Part I and Part II." PP 1868–9. Vol. 13. [4202, 4202-I].

"Third Report of the Commissioners on the Employment of Children, Young Persons, and Women in Agriculture with Appendix, Parts I and II." PP 1870. Vol. 13. [C.-70].

"Minutes of Evidence taken before the Commission on the Truck System." PP 1871. Vol. 36. [C.-327].

"Return of Civil Parishes not within Municipal Buroughs Showing Returns under the Education Act." PP 1871. Vol. 55. [C.-201].

"Return of Notices during 1873 Requiring the Attendance of Children." PP 1873. Vol. 52. [368].

"Report of Commissioners Appointed to Inquire into the Working of the Factory and Workshops Acts with a View to their Consolidation and Amendment. Vol. I, Report, Appendix, and Index." PP 1876. Vol. 29. [C.-1443].

"Vol. II. Minutes of Evidence taken before the Commission to Inquire into the Factory and Workshops Acts." PP 1876. Vol. 30. [C.-1443-I].

"Appendix A to Twenty-Ninth Report of the Postmaster General of the Post Office." PP 1883. Vol. 22. [C.-3703].

"Returns for each of the Last 20 years with Respect to Schools under Inspection in England and Wales." PP 1883. Vol. 63. [C.-107].

"First Report of the Royal Commission Appointed to Inquire into the Working of the Elementary Education Acts (England and Wales)." PP 1886. Vol. 25. [C.-4863].

"Second Report of the Royal Commission Appointed to Inquire into the Working of the Elementary Education Acts (England and Wales)." PP 1887. Vol. 29. [C.-5056].

"Third Report of the Royal Commission Appointed to Inquire into the Working of the Elementary Education Acts (England and Wales)." PP 1887. Vol. 30. [C.-5158].

"Returns of Wages Published between 1830–1886, Pt. II." PP 1887. Vol. 89. [C.-5172].

"Final Report of the Royal Commission Appointed to Inquire into the Working of the Elementary Education Acts." PP 1888. Vol. 35. [C.-5485].

"Statistical Report of the Royal Commission Appointed to Inquire into the Working of the Elementary Education Acts." PP 1888. Vol. 36. [C.-5485-II].

"Index to Evidence on the Working of the Elementary Education Acts." PP 1888. Vol. 37. [C.-5329-I].

"Minutes of Evidence taken before the Royal Commission on Labour, Group C." PP 1892. Vol. 36, pt. II. [C.-6795-VI].

"The Agricultural Labourer. Reports by Mr. C. M. Chapman." PP 1893–4. Vol. 35. [C.-6894-II].

"General Report on the Wages of the Manual Labour Classes. Tables of the Average Rates of Wages and Hours." PP 1893–4. Vol. 83, pt. II. [C.-6889].

"List of School Boards and Attendance Committees in England and Wales, 1ˢᵗ April, 1895." PP 1895. Vol. 76. [C.-7687].

"Public Elementary Education in England and Wales, 1870–1895." By M. E. Sadler and J. W. Edwards. In "Special Reports on Educational Subjects." PP 1897. Vol. 25. [C.-8447].

"Education Department Return. Summary Tables of Educational Statistics." PP 1900. Vol. 65-pt. I. [Cd.-109].

OTHER GOVERNMENT REPORTS

Gt. Britain Admiralty. *The Queen's Regulations for the Government of Her Majesty's Naval Service*. London: HMSO, 1844.

————. *The Queen's Regulations and the Admiralty Instructions for the Government of Her Majesty's Naval Service*. London: HMSO, 1862.

————. *The Queen's Regulations. Addenda (1895)*. London: HMSO, 1895.

————. *The King's Regulations and Admiralty Instructions for the Government of His Majesty's Naval Service*. Vol. 2. London: HMSO, 1924.

PUBLICATIONS, 1700–1914

Ackland, Joseph. "Elementary Education and the Decay of Literature." *Nineteenth Century Society* 35 (March 1894): 412–23.

Arch, Joseph. *The Story of his Life Told by Himself*. London: Hutchinson and Co., 1898.

Aves, Ernest. "The Hours of Labour." In *Life and Labour of the People in London*, 2d ser.: Industry, vol. 5, edited by Charles Booth, 182–214. 1903. Reprint. New York: AMS Press, 1970.

————. "Irregularity of Earnings." In *Life and Labour of the People in London*, 2d ser.: Industry, vol. 5, edited by Charles Booth, 228–62. 1903. Reprint. New York: AMS Press, 1970.

Baxter, R. Dudley. *National Income: The United Kingdom*. London: Macmillan, 1868.

Bell, Florence. *At the Works*. 1907. Reprint. New York: A. M. Kelley, 1969.

Bosanquet, Helen. "Wages and Housekeeping." In *Methods of Social Advance*, edited by C. S. Loch, 131–46. London: Macmillan, 1904.

Bourne, Henry Richard Fox. *English Newspapers: Chapters in the History of English Journalism*. 2 vols. London: Chatto and Windus, 1887.

Bowley, A. L. *Wages in the United Kingdom in the Nineteenth Century*. Cambridge: Cambridge University Press, 1900.

Brassey, Sir Thomas. *The British Navy: Its Strengths, Resources, and Administration*. 5 vols. London: Longmans, Green and Co., 1883.

Bristol Statistical Society. "Report on the Statistics of Education in Bristol." *Journal of the Statistical Society of London* 4 (1841): 250–63.

Collet, Collet Dobson. *History of the Taxes on Knowledge*. 2 vols. London: T.F. Unwin, 1899.

Defoe, Daniel. *The Complete English Tradesman*. 2 vols. 1745. Reprint. New York: Burt Franklin, 1970.

Ellison, Thomas. *The Cotton Trade of Great Britain*. 1886. Reprint. London: Frank Cass and Co., 1968.

Frost, Thomas. *Forty Years' Recollections*. London: Sampson Low, 1880.

Gattie, Walter Montagu. "What English People Read." *The Fortnightly Review*. 52 (n.s. 46) (1889): 307–21.

Goodenough, W. H., and J. C. Dalton. *The Army Book for the British Empire: A Record of the Development and Present Composition of the Military Forces and Their Duties in Peace and War*. London: HMSO, 1893.

————. *The Army Book for the British Empire*. London: HMSO, 1907.

————. *The Army Book for the British Empire*. London: HMSO, 1912.

Gordon, W. J. "The Newspaper Printing Press of Today." *Leisure Hour* 39 (1890): 263–68, 333–37.

Heath, Francis George. *The English Peasantry*. London: F. Warne and Co., 1874.

Hemmeon, J. C. *The History of the British Post Office*. Cambridge: Harvard University Press, 1912.

Hill, Rowland. *Post Office Reform: Its Importance and Practicability*. London: Charles Knight, 1837.

Hodgson, W. B. "Exaggerated Estimates of Reading and Writing as Means of Education." 1867. Reprinted in *History of Education Quarterly* 26 (1986): 377–93.

Howard, Esme. "Dyeing and Cleaning." In *Life and Labour of the People in London*, edited by Charles Booth, 2d ser.: Industry, vol. 2, 326–34. 1903. Reprint. New York: AMS Press, 1970.

Humphrey, George R. "The Reading of the Working Classes." *Nineteenth Century* 33 (1893): 690–701.

———. "The Reading of the Working Classes." *Nineteenth Century* 35 (1894): 412–23.

Jefferies, Richard. "Country Literature." In *The Life of the Fields*, 185–204. Philadelphia: J. B. Lippincott, 1908.

Kenrick, G. S. "Statistics of the Population in the Parish of Trevethin (Pontypool) and at the Neighbouring Works of Blaenavon in Monmouthshire, chiefly employed in the Iron Trade, and inhabiting part of the District recently disturbed." *Journal of the London Statistical Society* 3 (January 1841): 366–75.

Knight, Charles. *The Old Printer and the Modern Press*. London: J. Murray, 1854.

Larwood, Jacob, and John Camden Hotten. *The History of Signboards from Earliest Times to the Present Day*. 7th ed. London: Chatto and Windus, 1870.

Layton, W. T. "Changes in the Wages of Domestic Servants during Fifty Years." *Journal of the Royal Statistical Society* 72 (1908): 515–24.

Leigh, John. "What Do the Masses Read?" *Economic Review* 14 (1904): 166–77.

Levi, Leone. *Wages and Earnings of the Working Classes*. London: John Murray, 1867.

Liardet, F. "State of the Peasantry in the County of Kent." In *Third Publication of 1839*. Central Society of Education, 87–139. Reprint. London: Woburn Books, 1969.

Manchester Statistical Society. *Report of a Committee of the Manchester Statistical Society on the State of Education in the Borough of Bury in July, 1835*. London: James Ridgeway and Son, 1835.

———. *Report of a Committee of the Manchester Statistical Society on the State of Education in the City of York in 1836–1837*. London: James Ridgeway and Son, 1837.

———. "Report on the State of Education in the Township of Pendleton, 1838." *Journal of the Statistical Society of London* 2 (1839): 65–83.

———. "Report of a Committee of the Manchester Statistical Society on the State of Education in the County of Rutland in the Year 1838." *Journal of the Statistical Society of London* 2 (1839): 303–15.

———. "Report on the State of Education in Kingston-upon-Hull." *Journal of the Statistical Society of London* 4 (1841): 156–75.

Marshall, Henry. *On the Enlisting, Discharging and Pensioning of Soldiers, with the Official Documents on these Branches of Military Duty*, 2d ed. Edinburgh: A. and C. Black, 1839.

Massingame, H. W. *The London Daily Press*. London: The Religious Tract Society, 1892.

Mayhew, Henry. *London Labour and the London Poor*. 4 vols. 1861–62. Reprint. New York: Dover, 1968.

Mill, John Stuart. *On Liberty*. 1859. Reprint. New York: W. W. Norton, Norton Critical Editions, 1975.

———. *Principles of Political Economy*. Edited by W. J. Ashley. London: Longmans and Green, 1909.

Parsons, C. E. *Clerks: Their Position and Advancement*. London: Provost, 1876.

Porter, G. R. "Results of an Inquiry into the Condition of the Labouring Classes in 5 Parishes in the County of Norfolk." In *Third Publication of 1839*, Central Society of Education, 368–74. 1839. Reprint. London: Woburn Books, 1969.

———. "Statistical Inquiries into the Social Condition of the Working Classes and into the Means Provided for the Education of their Children." In *Second Publication of 1838*, Central Society of Education, 250–72. London: Taylor and Walton. 1838. Reprint. London: Woburn Books, 1969.

Richson, Rev. Charles. "On the Fallacies Involved in Certain Returns of the Number of Day Schools and Day Scholars in England and Wales in 1818, 1833 and 1851, etc." *Transactions of the Manchester Statistical Society*, 1853–54: 1–16.

Sargent, W. L. "On the Progress of Elementary Education." *Journal of the Royal Statistical Society* 30 (1867): 80–125.

Statistical Society of London. "Second Report of the Statistical Society of London, appointed to Inquire into the State of Education in Westminister," *Journal of the Statistical Society of London* 1 (1838): 193–215.

———. "Moral Statistics of the Parishes of St. James, St. George, and St. Anne Soho, in the City of Westminister." *Journal of the Statistical Society of London* 1 (1838): 478–92.

———. "Report of a Committee of the Statistical Society of London on the State of the Working Classes in the Parishes of St. Margaret and St. John, Westminister." *Journal of the London Statistical Society* 3 (April, 1840): 14–24.

———. "Report of the Education Committee of the Statistical Society of London on the Borough of Finsbury." *Journal of the Statistical Society of London* 6 (1843): 28–43.

———. "Conditions of the Working Classes in St.George's Hanover Square." *Journal of the Statistical Society of London* 6 (1843): 17–27.

———. "Report of an Investigation into the State of the Poorer Classes of St. George's-in-the-East." *Journal of the Statistical Society of London* 11 (August, 1848): 192–249.

Strahan, Alexander. "Our Very Cheap Literature." *The Contemporary Review* 14 (1870): 439–60.

Taylor, J. *Apostles of Fylde Methodism*. London, 1885.

Tremenheere, Henry. "Agricultural and Educational Statistics of Several Parishes in the County of Middlesex." *Journal of the London Statistical Society* 6 (1843): 120–30.

Tuckley, Henry. *Masses and Classes: A Study of Industrial Conditions in England*. Cincinnati: Cranston and Curtis, 1893.

Wilson, John, ed. *The Rural Cyclopedia*. Edinburgh: A. Fullarton and Co., 1852.

Wood, G. H. "Factory Legislation, Considered with Reference to the Wages etc. of the Operatives Protected Thereby." *Journal of the Royal Statistical Society* 65 (1902): 284–324.

———. "The Course of Women's Wages during the Nineteenth Century." In *A History of Factory Legislation*, by B. L. Hutchins and A. Harrison, Appendix A, 257–316. London: P. S. King and Son, 1903.

———. "Real Wages and the Standard of Comfort since 1850." *Journal of the Royal Statistical Society* 73 (1909): 91–103.

Wood, J. R. "Report on the State of Education in Birmingham." *Journal of the Statistical Society of London* 3 (1840): 25–49.

Wright, Thomas. "On a Possible Popular Culture." *Contemporary Review* 40 (1881): 25–44.

PUBLICATIONS SINCE 1914

BOOKS AND ARTICLES

Alexander, David. "Literacy Among Canadian and Foreign Seamen, 1863–1899." Maritime Studies Research Unit, Memorial University of Newfoundland, St. John's. Working Paper.

———. *Retailing in England during the Industrial Revolution*. London: The Athelone Press, 1970.

Alexander, Sally. *Women's Work in Nineteenth Century London*. London: Journeyman Press, 1983.

Alter, George. "Women and Children in the Family Economy: Belgium, 1853 and 1891." Paper presented at the Economic History Workshop, Department of Economics, The University of Chicago, January 23, 1981.

Altick, Richard. *The English Common Reader. A Social History of the Mass Reading Public 1800–1900*. Chicago: University of Chicago Press, 1957.

Anderson, Gregory. *Victorian Clerks*. Manchester: Manchester University Press, 1976.

Anderson, Michael. *Family Structure in Nineteenth Century Lancashire*. Cambridge: Cambridge University Press, 1971.

———. *Approaches to the History of the Western Family, 1500–1914*. Economic

History Society Studies in Economic and Social History. London: Macmillan, 1980.

——. "The Emergence of the Modern Life Cycle in Britain." *Social History* 10 (1985): 69–87.

——. "Households, Families, and Individuals: Some Preliminary Results from the National Sample from the 1851 Census of Great Britain." *Continuity and Change* 3 (1988): 421–38.

Armstrong, Alan. *Farmworkers in England and Wales: A Social and Economic History, 1770–1980.* Ames: Iowa State University Press, 1988.

Armstrong, W. A. "The Use of Information About Occupation." In *Nineteenth-century society. Essays in the use of quantitative methods for the study of social data.* Edited by E. A. Wrigley, 191–310. Cambridge: Cambridge University Press, 1972.

Arnove, Robert, and Harvey Graff, eds. *National Literacy Campaigns: Historical and Comparative Perspectives.* New York: Plenum Press, 1987.

Ashton, T. S. *Economic and Social Investigations in Manchester, 1833–1933. A Centenary History of the Manchester Statistical Society.* London: P. S. King and Son, 1934.

Aspinall, Arthur A. *Politics and the Press, 1780–1850.* London: Home and Vanthal, 1949.

Baines, Dudley. *Migration in A Mature Economy: Emigration and Internal Migration in England and Wales, 1861–1900.* Cambridge: Cambridge University Press, 1985.

Ball, Nancy. "Elementary School Attendance and Voluntary Effort before 1870." *History of Education* 2 (1973): 19–34.

Bamford, T. W. *The Evolution of Rural Education.* Research Monographs, no. 1, Institute of Education, University of Hull, 1965.

Bartrip, Peter. "Success or Failure? The Prosecution of the Early Factory Acts." *Economic History Review* 2d ser., 38 (1985): 423–27.

Becker, Gary S., and H. G. Lewis. "Interaction between Quantity and Quality of Children." *Journal of Political Economy* 81 (1973): S279–88.

Bellerby, J. R. "National and Agricultural Income: 1851." *Economic Journal* 69 (1959): 95–104.

Bellingham, Bruce. "The History of Childhood since the 'Invention of Childhood': Some issues in the Eighties." *Journal of Family History* 13 (1988): 347–58.

Benson, John. *The Penny Capitalists.* New Brunswick, N.J.: Rutgers University Press, 1983.

Berridge, Virginia. "Content Analysis and Historical Research on Newspapers." In *The Press in English Society from the Seventeenth to Nineteenth Centuries,* edited by Michael Harris and Alan Lee, 201–18. Rutherford, N.J.: Fairleigh Dickinson University Press, 1986.

——. "Popular Sunday Papers and Mid-Victorian Society." In *Newspaper History from the Seventeenth Century to the Present Day,* edited by George Boyce, James Curran, and Pauline Wingate, 247–64. London: Constable, 1978.

Bienefield, M. A. *Working Hours in British Industry: An Economic History*. London: Wiedenfeld and Nicolson, 1972.

Birchenough, C. A. *History of Elementary Education in England and Wales from 1800 to the Present Day*. London: University Tutorial Press, 1914.

Birdsall, Nancy, and Susan Cochrane. "Education and Parental Decision Making: A Two-Generation Approach." In *Education and Development*, Edited by Lascelles Anderson and Douglas Windham, 175–210. Lexington, Mass.: Lexington Books, 1982.

Blackburn, R. M., and Michael Mann. *The Working Class in the Labour Market*. London: Macmillan, 1979.

Blaug, Mark. "The Economics of Education in English Classical Political Economy: A Re-examination." In *Essays on Adam Smith*, edited by Andrew Skinner and Thomas Wilson, 568–99. Oxford: Clarendon Press, 1975.

———. *An Introduction to the Economics of Education*. London: Penguin Books, 1970.

Boadway, Robin, and David Wildasin. *Public Sector Economics*. 2d ed. Boston: Little, Brown and Co., 1984.

Bowles, Samuel, and Herbert Gintis. *Schooling in Capitalist America*. New York: Basic Books, 1976.

Bowman, Mary Jean, and C. Arnold Anderson. "Concerning the Role of Education in Development." In *Old Societies and New States: The Quest for Modernity in Africa and Asia*, edited by Clifford Geertz, 247–79. Glencoe, Ill.: Free Press, 1963.

Boyce, George, James Curran, and Pauline Wingate, eds. *Newspaper History from the Seventeenth Century to the Present Day*. London: Constable, 1978.

Boyer, George R., and Jeffrey G. Williamson. "A Quantitative Assessment of the Fertility Transition in England, 1851–1911." In *Research in Economic History* 12 (1989), edited by Roger Ransom, 93–117. Greenwich, Conn.: JAI Press, 1989.

Brown, Lucy. *Victorian News and Newspapers*. New York: Oxford University Press, 1985.

Burgess, H. J. *Enterprise in Education*. London: National Society and SPCK, 1958.

Burke, Kenneth. "Literature as an Equipment for Living." *Direction* 1 (1938): 10–13. Reprinted in Kenneth Burke, *Philosophy of Literary Form*. Berkeley: University of California Press, 1973.

Burnett, John, David Vincent, and David Mayall. *The Autobiography of the Working Class. An Annotated Critical Bibliography*. 2 vols. New York: New York University Press, 1984.

Buxton, Neil. "The Coal Industry." In *Where Did We Go Wrong? Industrial Performance, Education and the Economy in Victorian Britain*, edited by Gordon Roderick and Michael Stephens, 85–106. Barcombe, Lewes, Sussex: Falmer, 1981.

Bythell, Duncan. *The Sweated Trades*. New York: St. Martin's Press, 1978.

Caldwell, John C. *Theory of Fertility Decline*. New York: Academic Press, 1982.

Cameron, Rondo. "A New View of European Industrialization." *Economic History Review*, 2d ser., 38 (1985): 1–23.

Chapman, Stanley. "The Textile Industries." In *Where Did We Go Wrong? Industrial Performance, Education and the Economy in Victorian Britain*, edited by Gordon Roderick and Michael Stephens, 125–38. Barcombe, Lewes, Sussex: Falmer, 1981.

Checkland, S. G. *British Public Policy 1776–1939: An Economic, Social and Political Perspective*. Cambridge: Cambridge University Press, 1983.

Chiang, Alpha. *Fundamental Methods of Mathematical Economics*. 2d. ed. New York: McGraw-Hill, 1974.

Chubb, John, and Terry Moe. *Politics, Markets and America's Schools*. Washington, D.C.: The Brookings Institution, 1990.

Church, R. A. *History of the British Coal Industry, Vol. 3. 1830–1913: Victorian Pre-eminence*. Oxford: Clarendon Press, 1986.

Clark, George Kitson. *Churchmen and the Condition of England, 1832–1885: A Study in the Development of Social Ideas and Practice from the Old Regime to the Modern State*. London: Methuen, 1973.

Cohen, Miriam. "Changing Education Strategies Among Immigrant Generations: New York Italians in Comparative Perspective." *Journal of Social History* 15 (1982): 443–66.

Cohen, Patricia Cline. *A Calculating People: The Spread of Numeracy in Early America*. Chicago: University of Chicago Press, 1982.

Colls, Robert. "'Oh Happy English Children': Coal, Class and Education in the North-East." *Past and Present* 73 (1976): 75–99.

Colyer, R. J. "The Use of Estate Home Farm Accounts as Sources for Nineteenth Century Agricultural History." *The Local Historian* 11 (1975).

Craig, John. "The Expansion of Education." In *Review of Research in Education*, vol. 9, edited by David C. Berliner, 151–213. Washington, D.C.: American Educational Research Association, 1981.

Cressy, David. *Literacy and the Social Order: Reading and Writing in Tudor and Stuart England*. Cambridge: Cambridge University Press, 1980.

Crossick, Geoffrey. "The Petite Bourgeoisie in Nineteenth-Century Britain: The Urban and Liberal Case." In *Shopkeepers and Master Artisans in Nineteenth-Century Europe*, edited by Geoffrey Crossick and Heinz-Gerhard Haupt, 62–94. London: Methuen, 1984.

Curran, James. "The Press as an Agency of Social Control: An Historical Perspective." In *Newspaper History: Studies in the Evolution of the British Press*, edited by George Boyce, James Curran, and Pauline Wingate, 51–75. London: Constable, 1978.

Curran, James, and Jean Seaton. *Power without Responsibility: The Press and Broadcasting in Britain*. London: Fontana, 1981.

Daunton, Martin. *Royal Mail*. London: Athlone Press, 1985.

Dayus, Kathleen. *Her People*. London: Virago, 1982.

Dingle, A. E. "Drink and Working-Class Living Standards in Britain, 1870–1914." *Economic History Review*, 2d ser., 25 (1972): 608–22.

Docking, J. W. *Victorian Schooling and Scholars: Church of England Schools in Nineteenth-Century Coventry*. Coventry and North Warwickshire History Pamphlets, no. 3. Coventry: Coventry Branch of the Historical Association, 1967.

Douglass, Dave. "The Durham Pitman." In *Miners, Quarrymen and Saltworkers*, edited by Raphael Samuel, 205–95. London: Routledge and Kegan Paul, 1977.

Easterlin, Richard. "Why Isn't the Whole World Developed?" *Journal of Economic History* 41 (1981): 1–19.

Eklof, Ben. *Russian Peasant Schools*. Berkeley: University of California Press, 1986.

———. "Russian Literacy Campaigns, 1861–1939." In *National Literacy Campaigns: Historical and Comparative Perspectives*, edited by Robert Arnove and Harvey Graff, 123–45. New York: Plenum Press, 1987.

Ellis, A. C. O. "Influences on School Attendance in Victorian England." *British Journal of Educational Studies* 21 (1973): 313–26.

Elmsely, Clive. *Policing and Its Context 1750–1870*. New York: Schocken Books, 1984.

Everitt, Alan. "Country Carriers in the Nineteenth Century." *Journal of Transport History*, n.s., 3 (1976): 179–202.

Feinstein, C.H. *Statistical Tables of National Income, Expenditure, and Output of the U.K., 1855–1955*. Cambridge: Cambridge University Press, 1976.

Ferguson, Sheila. *Drink*. London: Batsford, 1975.

Field, Alexander J. "Educational Expansion in Mid-Nineteenth Century Massachusetts." *Harvard Educational Review* 46 (1976): 521–52.

Field, C. D. "The Social Structure of English Methodism: Eighteenth to Twentieth Centuries." *British Journal of Sociology* 28 (1977): 199–225.

Finnegan, Ruth. *Literacy and Orality*. Oxford: Basil Blackwell, 1988.

Fisher, Donald L. "Functional Literacy and the Schools." Educational Resource Information Center (ERIC) Report 151.760, Washington, D.C., National Institute of Education (1978).

Flinn, M. W. *British Population Growth 1700–1850*. London: Macmillan, 1970.

Fox, H. S. A. "Local Farmer's Associations and the Circulation of Agricultural Information in Nineteenth Century England." In *Change in the Countryside: Essays on Rural England, 1500–1900*, edited by H. S. A. Fox and R. A. Butlin, 43–63. Institute of British Geographers Special Publication no. 10. London: Institute of British Geographers, 1979.

Furet, François, and Jacques Ozouf. *Reading and Writing: Literacy in France from Calvin to Jules Ferry*. Cambridge: Cambridge University Press, 1982.

Galbraith, V. H. "The Literacy of Medieval English Kings." *Proceedings, British Academy* 21 (1935): 201–38.

Galenson, D. W. "Literacy and Age in Preindustrial England: Quantitative Evidence and Implications." *Economic Development and Cultural Change* 29 (1981): 813–39.

Gallo, Max. *The Poster in History*. New York: American Heritage, 1974.

Gardner, Phil. *The Lost Elementary Schools of Victorian England*. London: Croom Helm, 1984.

Gawthrop, Richard. "Literacy Drives in Preindustrial Germany." In *National Literacy Campaigns: Historical and Comparative Perspectives*, edited by Robert Arnove and Harvey Graff, 19–48. New York: Plenum Press, 1987.

Gilbert, Alan. *Religion and Society in Industrial England. Church, Chapel and Social Change, 1790–1914*. New York: Longman, 1976.

Gillis, J. R. "Affective Individualism and the English Poor." Review of *The Family, Sex and Marriage in England, 1500–1800*, by Lawrence Stone. *Journal of Interdisciplinary History* 10 (1979): 121–28.

Glass, David V. "Changes in Fertility in England and Wales, 1851 to 1931." In *Political Arithmetic: A Symposium of Population Studies*, edited by Lancelot Hogben, 161–212. London: George Allen and Unwin, 1938.

Glover, Michael. *Wellington's Army in the Peninsula, 1808–1814*. New York: Hippocrene Books, 1977.

Goldin, Claudia, and Kenneth Sokoloff. "Women, Children and Industrialization in the Early Republic: Evidence from the Manufacturing Censuses." *Journal of Economic History* 42 (1982): 741–74.

Goody, Jack. *The Domestication of the Savage Mind*. Cambridge: Cambridge University Press, 1977.

——. *The Logic of Writing and the Organization of Society*. Cambridge: Cambridge University Press, 1986.

Graff, Harvey. "Literacy, Education, and Fertility, Past and Present: A Critical Review." *Population and Development Review* 5 (1979): 105–40.

——. *The Literacy Myth*. New York: Academic Press, 1979.

——. *Legacies of Literacy*. Bloomington: Indiana University Press, 1987.

Grubb, Farley. "Colonial Immigrant Literacy: An Economic Analysis of Pennsylvania-German Evidence, 1727–1775." *Explorations in Economic History* 24 (1987): 63–76.

Guillou, Michael. "Technical Education, 1850–1914." In *Where Did We Go Wrong? Industrial Performance, Education and the Economy in Victorian Britain*, edited by Gordon Roderick and Michael Stephens, 173–84. Barcombe, Lewes, Sussex: Falmer, 1981.

Habbakkuk, H. J. *American and British Technology in the Nineteenth Century*. Cambridge: Cambridge University Press, 1967.

Hammond, J. L., and Barbara Hammond. *The Skilled Laborer, 1760–1832*. New York: Harper and Row, Harper Torchbook Editions, 1970.

Hanushek, Eric. "Conceptual and Empirical Issues in the Estimation of Educational Production Functions." *Journal of Human Resources* 14 (1979): 351–88.

——. "The Economics of Schooling." *Journal of Economic Literature* 24 (Sept. 1986): 1141–77.

Harris, Roy. *The Origin of Writing*. LaSalle, Ill.: Open Court Press, 1986.

Harrison, Brian. *Drink and the Victorians*. London: Faber and Faber, 1971.

Harrison, John F. C. *Learning and Living 1790–1860: A Study in the History of the English Adult Education Movement*. London: Routledge and Paul, 1961.

Heal, Ambrose. *Signboards of Old London Shops*. London: Batsford, 1947.

Heath, Shirley Brice. *Ways with Words: Language, Life, and Work in Communities and Classrooms*. Cambridge: Cambridge University Press, 1983.

Heesom, A. J., Brendan Duffy, and Robert Colls. "Debate: Coal, Class and Education in the North-East." *Past and Present* 90 (1981): 136–65.

Herd, Harold. *The March of Journalism*. London: Allen and Unwin, 1952.

Hewitt, Margaret. *Wives and Mothers in Victorian Industry*. London: Rockliff, 1958.

Higgs, Edward. *Domestic Servants and Households in Rochdale 1851–1871*. New York: Garland, 1986.

———. "Women, Occupations and Work in the Nineteenth Century." *History Workshop: A Journal of Socialist Historians* 23 (1987): 59–80.

Hindly, Diana, and Geoffrey Hindly. *Advertising in Victorian England, 1837–1901*. London: Wayland, 1972.

Hobsbawm, Eric. "The Labour Aristocracy in Nineteenth-Century Britain." In *Labouring Men: Studies in the History of Labour*, edited by Eric Hobsbawm, 272–315. London: Wiedenfeld and Nicolson, 1964.

———. "The Standard of Living Debate." In *The Standard of Living in England in the Industrial Revolution*, edited by Arthur Taylor, 179–88. London: Methuen, 1975.

Hogan, David. "Making It in America: Work, Education and Social Structure." In *Work, Youth, and Schooling*, edited by Harvey Kantor and David Tyack, 142–79. Stanford: Stanford University Press, 1982.

———. Review of *Ethnic Differences*, by Joel Perlman. *History of Education Quarterly* 30 (1990): 108–12.

Hoggart, Richard. *The Uses of Literacy: Changing Patterns in English Mass Culture*. Fairlawn, N.J.: Essential Books, 1957.

Hollis, Patricia. *The Pauper Press: A Study in Working-Class Radicalism of the 1830s*. London: Oxford University Press, 1970.

Horn, Pamela. "Child Workers in the Pillow Lace and Straw Plait Trades of Victorian Buckinghamshire and Bedfordshire." *The Historical Journal* 17 (1974): 779–96.

———. *The Rise and Fall of the Victorian Servant*. New York: St. Martin's Press, 1975.

———. "The Employment of Children in Victorian Oxfordshire." *Midland History* 4 (1977): 61–74.

———. *The Changing Countryside in Victorian and Edwardian England and Wales*. Rutherford, N.J.: Fairleigh Dickinson University Press, 1984.

———. "Child Workers in the Victorian Countryside: The Case of Northamptonshire." *Northamptonshire Past and Present* 7 (1985–86): 173–85.

Houston, Rab. "Literacy and Society in the West, 1500–1850." *Social History* 8 (1983): 269–93.

———. "The Literacy Campaign in Scotland, 1560–1803." In *National Literacy Campaigns: Historical and Comparative Perspectives*, edited by Robert Arnove and Harvey Graff, 49–64. New York: Plenum Press, 1987.

———. *Literacy in Early Modern Europe*. London: Longman, 1988.

Howe, Ellic. *Newspaper Printing in the Nineteenth Century*. London: Privately printed, 1943.

Howkins, Alun. *Whitsun in Nineteenth Century Oxfordshire*. History Workshop Pamphlet, no. 8. Oxford: History Workshop, 1973.

Hunt, E. H. *British Labour History 1815–1914*. London: Weidenfeld and Nicolson, 1981.

Hurt, John S. "Landowners, Farmers and Clergy and the Financing of Rural Education before 1870." *Journal of Educational Administration and History* 1 (1968): 6–13.

———. *Education in Evolution: Church, State, Society and Popular Education 1800–1870*. London: Rupert Hart-Davis, 1971.

———. "Professor West on Early Nineteenth-Century Education." *The Economic History Review* 24 (1971): 624–32.

———. *Elementary Schooling and the Working Classes 1860–1918*. London: Routledge and Kegan Paul, 1979.

Inglis, Kevin Stanley. *Churches and the Working Classes in Victorian England*. London: Routledge and Kegan Paul, 1963.

Inkeles, Alex, and David Smith. *Becoming Modern: Individual Change in Six Developing Countries*. Cambridge: Harvard University Press, 1974.

Innes, J. W. *Class Fertility Trends in England and Wales 1876–1934*. Princeton: Princeton University Press, 1938.

Isaacs, G. A. *The Story of the Newspaper Printing Press*. London: Co-operative Printing Society, 1931.

James, Louis. *Fiction for the Working Man, 1830–1850*. Oxford University Press, 1974.

Jarausch, Konrad. "The Old 'New History of Education': A German Reconsideration." *History of Education Quarterly* 26 (1986): 225–41.

Jenkins, J. Geraint. *The Craft Industries*. London: Longman, 1972.

Jewkes, John, and P. M. Gray. *Wages and Labour in the Lancashire Cotton Spinning Industry*. Manchester: Manchester University Press, 1935.

Johansson, Egil. *The History of Literacy in Sweden in Comparison with Some Other Countries*. Educational Reports Umea, no. 12. Umea, Sweden: Umea University and Umea School of Education, 1977.

Johnson, Paul. *Saving and Spending: The Working-Class Economy in Britain, 1870–1939*. Oxford: Clarendon Press, 1985.

Johnson, Richard. "Educational Policy and Social Control in Early Victorian Britain." *Past and Present* 49 (1970): 96–119.

———. "Notes on the Schooling of the English Working Class, 1780–1850." In *Schooling and Capitalism: A Sociological Reader*, edited by Roger Dale, Geoff Esland, and Madeleaine MacDonald, 44–54. London: Routledge and Kegan Paul, 1976.

———. "Educating the Educators: Experts and the State, 1833–9." In *Social Control in Nineteenth Century Britain*, edited by A. P. Donajgrodzki, 77–107. London: Croom Helm, 1977.

Jones, E. L. "Demographic and Educational Interaction in Nineteenth-Century and the Modern Third World." School of Economics, La Trobe University. Mimeograph.

Jones, Mary Gwladys. *The Charity School Movement: A Study of Eighteenth-Century Puritanism in Action*. Cambridge: Cambridge University Press, 1938.

Kaestle, Carl. "The History of Literacy and the History of Readers." *Review of Research in Education*, vol. 12, edited by Edmund S. Gordon, 11–53. Washington, D.C.: American Educational Research Association, 1985.

Kaestle, Carl, and Maris Vinovskis. "From Fireside to Factory: School Entry and School Leaving in Nineteenth-Century Massachusetts." In *Transitions: The Family and the Life Course in Historical Perspective*, edited by Tamara Hareven, 135–85. New York: Academic Press, 1978.

Katznelson, Ira, and Margaret Weir. *Schooling for All: Class, Race and the Decline of the Democratic Ideal*. Berkeley: University of California Press, 1985.

Kay, George Frederick. *Royal Mail: The Story of the Mail from the Time of Edward IV to the Present Day*. London: Rockliff, 1951.

Keeling, Frederic. *Child Labour in the United Kingdom: A Study of the Development and Administration of the Law Relating to the Employment of Children*. London: P. S. King and Son, 1914.

Kiesling, H. J. "Nineteenth-Century Education According to West: A Comment." *Economic History Review*, 2d ser., 36 (1983): 416–25.

Kingsford, P. W. *Victorian Railwaymen*. London: Frank Cass and Co., 1970.

Klein, Viola. *Britain's Married Women Workers*. New York: Humanities Press, 1965.

Knodel, John and Etienne Van de Walle. "Lessons from the Past: Policy Implications of Historical Fertility Studies." *Population and Development Review* 5 (1979): 217–45.

Lambert, W. R. "Drink and Work-Discipline in Industrial South Wales, c. 1800–1870." *Welsh History Review* 7 (1975): 289–306.

Lamberti, Marjorie. *State, Society, and the Elementary School in Imperial Germany*. New York: Oxford University Press, 1989.

Landes, William, and Lewis Solmon. "Compulsory Schooling Legislation: An Economic Analysis of Law and Social Change in the Nineteenth Century." *Journal of Economic History* 32 (1972): 54–91.

Laqueur, Thomas. *Religion and Respectability: Sunday Schools and Working Class Culture, 1780–1850*. New Haven: Yale University Press, 1976.

———. "Working Class Demand and the Growth of English Elementary Education, 1750–1850." In *Schooling and Society*, edited by Lawrence Stone, 192–205. Baltimore: John Hopkins University Press, 1976.

Lazonick, William. "Industrial Relations and Technical Change: The Case of the Self-Acting Mule." *Cambridge Journal of Economics* 3 (1979): 231–62.

Lee, Alan J. "Franklin Thomasson and the Tribune: A Case-Study in the History of the Liberal Press, 1906–1908." *Historical Journal* 16 (1973): 341–60.

———. *The Origins of the Popular Press 1855–1914*. Totowa, N.J.: Rowan and Littlefield, 1976.

———. "The Structure, Ownership, and Control of the Press, 1855–1914." In *Newspaper History from the Seventeenth Century to the Present Day*, edited by George Boyce, James Curran, and Pauline Wingate, 117–29. London: Constable, 1978.

Lee, C. H. *A Cotton Enterprise, 1795–1840: A History of M'Connel and Kennedy, Fine Cotton Spinners*. Manchester: Manchester University Press, 1972.

Leet, Don R. *Population Pressure and Human Fertility Response: Ohio 1810–1860.* New York: Arno Press, 1978.

Leibowitz, Arleen. "Home Investments in Children." *Journal of Political Economy* 82 (1974): S111–31.

Lerner, Daniel. *The Passing of Traditional Society.* Glencoe, Ill.: Free Press, 1963.

Leser, C. E. V. "The Supply of Women for Gainful Work in Britain." *Population Studies* 9 (1955): 142–47.

Levine, David. "Education and Family Life in Early Industrial England." *Journal of Family History* 4 (1979): 368–80.

———. *Reproducing Families: The Political Economy of English Population History.* Cambridge: Cambridge University Press, 1987.

Levine, Kenneth. *The Social Context of Literacy.* London: Routledge and Kegan Paul, 1986.

Lewis, Michael. *The Navy in Transition 1814–1864: A Social History.* London: Hodder and Stoughton, 1965.

Leybourne, Grace, and Kenneth White. *Education and the Birth-Rate: A Social Dilemma.* London: J. Cape, 1940.

Litwak, Eugene. "Geographic Mobility and Extended Family Cohesion." In *Social Demography*, edited by Thomas Ford and Gordon de Jong, 180–92. Englewood Cliffs, N.J.: Prentice-Hall, 1970.

Lockridge, Kenneth. *Literacy in Colonial New England.* New York: Norton, 1974.

Lowerson, John, and John Meyerson. *Time to Spare in Victorian England.* Hassocks, Sussex: Harvester Press, 1977.

Lucas, P. J. "Furness Newspapers in Mid-Victorian England." In *Victorian Lancashire*, edited by S. P. Bell, 83–102. Newton Abbot, Devon: David and Charles, 1974.

McCann, W. P. "Elementary Education in England and Wales on the Eve of the 1870 Education Act." *Journal of Educational Administration and History* 2 (1969): 20–29.

MacDonald, Stuart. "The Diffusion of Knowledge among Northumberland Farmers, 1780–1815." *Agricultural History Review* 27 (1979), part 1: 30–39.

McKenna, Frank. "Victorian Railway Workers." *History Workshop: A Journal of Socialist Historians* 1 (1976): 26–73.

———. *The Railway Workers, 1840–1970.* London: Faber and Faber, 1980.

McKibbin, Ross. "Working-Class Gambling in Britain, 1880–1939." *Past and Present* 82 (1979): 147–78.

Madoc-Jones, Beryl. "Patterns of attendance and their social significance: Mitcham National School 1830–39." In *Popular Education and Socialization in the Nineteenth Century*, edited by Phillip McCann, 41–66. London: Methuen, 1977.

Malcolmson, Robert W. *Popular Recreation in English Society, 1700–1850.* Cambridge: Cambridge University Press, 1973.

Marsden, W. E. *Unequal Educational Provision in England and Wales: The Nineteenth Century Roots.* London: Woburn, 1987.

Marshall, J. R., and J. K. Walton. *The Lake Counties.* Manchester: Manchester University Press, 1981.

Mason, Tony. *Association Football and English Society, 1863–1915*. Hassocks, Sussex: Harvester Press, 1980.

Maynes, Mary Jo. "The Virtues of Archaism: The Political Economy of Schooling in Europe, 1750–1850." *Comparative Studies in Society and History* 21 (1979): 611–25.

———. *Schooling for the People: Comparative Local Studies of Schooling History in France and Germany, 1750–1850*. New York: Holmes and Meier, 1985.

———. *Schooling in Western Europe*. Albany: State University of New York Press, 1985.

Meller, Helen Elizabeth. *Leisure and the Changing City, 1870–1914*. London: Routledge & Kegan Paul, 1976.

Mitch, David. "The Impact of Subsidies to Elementary Schooling on Enrolment Rates in Nineteenth Century England." *Economic History Review*. 2d ser., 39. (1986): 371–91.

———. "The Rise of Popular Literacy in Europe." In *The Political Construction of Education: The State, School Expansion, and Economic Change*, edited by Bruce Fuller and Richard Rubinson. New York: Praeger, 1992.

Mitchell, B. R. *Economic Development of the British Coal Industry, 1800–1914*. Cambridge: Cambridge University Press, 1984.

Mitchell, B. R., and P. Deane. *Abstract of British Historical Statistics*. Cambridge: Cambridge University Press, 1962.

More, Charles. *Skill and the English Working Class, 1870–1914*. New York: St. Martin's Press, 1980.

Morgan, John. *Godly Learning: Puritan Attitudes towards Reason, Learning and Education, 1560–1640*. Cambridge: Cambridge University Press, 1986.

Morris, Norman. "Public Expenditure on Education in the 1860's." *Oxford Review of Education* 3 (1977): 3–19.

Mumford, Lewis. *Technics and Civilization*. New York: Harcourt, Brace and Co., 1934.

Murphy, James. "The Rise of Public Elementary Education in Liverpool: Part One, 1784–1818 and Part Two, 1819–1835." *Transactions of the Historical Society of Lancashire and Chesire for the Year 1964 and for the Year 1966* 116 (1965): 165–95; 118 (1967): 105–38.

———. *Church, State and Schools in Britain, 1800–1970*. London: Routledge and Kegan Paul, 1971.

Musgrave, P. W. *Technical Change, the Labour Force and Education*. Oxford: Pergamon Press, 1967.

Musson, A. E. "Newspaper Printing in the Industrial Revolution." *Economic History Review*, 2d ser., 10 (1958): 411–26.

Nardinelli, Clark. "Child Labor and the Factory Acts." *Journal of Economic History* 40 (1980): 739–56.

———. "The Successful Prosecution of the Early Factory Acts: A Suggested Explanation." *Economic History Review*, 2d ser., 38 (1985): 428–30.

Neuberg, Victor. *Popular Literature: A History and Guide*. Harmondsworth: Penguin Books, 1971.

Nevett, T. R. *Advertising in Britain: A History*. London: Heiman, 1982.

Obelkevich, James. *Religion and Rural Society*. Oxford: Clarendon Press, 1976.

O'Brien, P. K., and S. L. Engerman. "Changes in income and its distribution during the industrial revolution." *The Economic History of Britain Since 1700*. Vol. 1, edited by Roderick Floud and Donald McCloskey, 164–81. Cambridge: Cambridge University Press, 1981.

Pallister, R. "The Determinants of Elementary School Attendance about 1850." *Durham Research Review* 5 (1969): 384–98.

Peacock, Alan E. "The Successful Prosecution of the Factory Acts, 1833–55." *Economic History Review*, 2d ser. 37 (1984): 197–210.

———. "Factory Act Prosecutions: A Hidden Consensus." *Economic History Review*, 2d ser., 38 (1985): 431–36.

Pelling, Henry. "Popular Attitudes to Religion." In *Popular Politics and Society in Late Victorian Britain: Essays*, edited by Henry Pelling, 19–36. London: Macmillan, 1968.

Perkin, Harold. "The Origins of the Popular Press." *History Today* 7 (1957): 425–35.

Plumb, J. H. "The New World of Children in Eighteenth-Century England." *Past and Present* 67 (1975): 64–95.

Preston, Samuel. "Causes and Consequences of Mortality Declines in Less Developed Countries during the Twentieth Century." In *Population and Economic Change in Developing Countries*, edited by Richard Easterlin, 324–26. Chicago: University of Chicago Press, 1980.

Razzell, P. E. and R. W. Wainwright, eds. *The Victorian Working Class: Selections from Letters to the Morning Chronicle*. (London: F. Cass, 1973).

Reeder, David. "The Reconstruction of Secondary Education in England, 1869–1920." In *The Rise of the Modern Education System*, edited by Detlef Müller, Fritz Ringer, and Brian Simon, 135–50. Cambridge: Cambridge University Press, 1987.

Reese, William. *Power and the Promise of School Reform: Grass Roots Movements during the Progressive Era*. Boston: Routledge and Kegan Paul, 1986.

Reid, Douglas. "The Decline of Saint Monday 1766–1876." *Past and Present* 71 (1976): 76–101.

Resnick, Daniel P. "Minimum Competency Testing Historically Considered." In *Review of Research in Education*, vol. 9, edited by David C. Berliner, 3–29. Washington, D.C.: American Educational Research Association, 1981.

Resnick, Daniel, and Lauren Resnick. "The Nature of Literacy: An Historical Exploration." *Harvard Educational Review* 47 (1977): 370–85.

———. "Varieties of Literacy." In *Social History and Issues in Human Consciousness: Some Interdisciplinary Connections*, edited by A. E. Barnes and P. N. Stearns. New York: New York University Press, forthcoming.

Roberts, David. *Victorian Origins of the British Welfare State*. New Haven: Yale University Press, 1960.

Roberts, Robert. *The Classic Slum: Salford Life in the First Quarter of the Century*. Harmondsworth: Penguin Books, 1973.

Robson, A. H. *The Education of Children Engaged in Industry in England, 1833–1876*. London: Kegan, Paul, Trench, Trench, Trubner and Co., 1931.

Roderick, Gordon, and Michael Stephens, eds. *Where Did We Go Wrong? Industrial Performance, Education, and the Economy in Victorian Britain*. Barcombe, Lewes, Sussex: Falmer, 1981.

Rubinstein, David. *School Attendance in London, 1870–1904: A Social History*. Occasional Papers in Economic and Social History, no. 1. University of Hull, 1969.

Ruggles, Stephen. *Prolonged Connections: The Rise of the Extended Family in Nineteenth-Century England and America*. Madison: University of Wisconsin Press, 1987.

Russell, Rex C. *A History of Schools and Education in Lindsey, Lincolnshire: 1800–1902*. 3 vols. Lindsey, Lincs.: County Council Education Committee, 1965–66.

Sandberg, Lars. *Lancashire in Decline: A Study of Entrepreneurship, Technology, and International Trade*. Columbus: Ohio State University Press, 1974.

———. "Ignorance, Poverty and Economic Backwardness in the Early Stages of European Industrialization: Variations on Alexander Gerschenkron's Grand Theme." *Journal of European Economic History* 11 (1982): 675–97.

Sanderson, Michael. "Social Change and Elementary Education in Industrial Lancashire, 1780–1840." *Northern History* 3 (1968): 131–40.

———. "Literacy and Social Mobility in the Industrial Revolution in England." *Past and Present* 56 (1972): 75–104.

———. "The National and British School Societies in Lancashire 1803–1839: The Roots of the Anglican Supremacy in English Education." In *Local Studies and the History of Education: Papers from the 1971 Conference of the History of Education Society*, edited by T. G. Cook, 1–36. London: Methuen, 1972.

Schmiechen, James. *Sweated Industries and Sweated Labor*. Urbana: University of Illinois Press, 1984.

Schofield, R. S. "The Measurement of Literacy in Pre-Industrial England." In *Literacy in Traditional Societies*, edited by Jack Goody, 311–25. Cambridge: Cambridge University Press, 1968.

———. "Dimensions of Illiteracy, 1750–1850." *Explorations in Economic History* 10 (1973): 437–54.

Schudson, Michael. *Discovering the News*. New York: Basic Books, 1978.

Schultz, T. W. "The Value of the Ability to Deal with Disequilibria." *Journal of Economic Literature* 13 (1975): 827–46.

Scribner, Sylvia, and Michael Cole. *The Psychology of Literacy*. Cambridge: Harvard University Press, 1981.

Sellman, Roger R. *Devon Village Schools in the Nineteenth Century*. Newton Abbot, Devon: David and Charles, 1967.

Silver, Harold. "Aspects of Neglect: The Strange Case of Victorian Popular Education." *Oxford Review of Education* 3 (1977): 57–69.

Simon, Joan. "Was there a Charity School Movement?" In *Education in Leicestershire 1540–1940*, edited by Brian Simon, 55–100. Leicester: Leicester University Press, 1968.

Skelley, Alan. *The Victorian Army at Home: The Recruitment and Terms and Conditions of the British Regular, 1859–1899*. London: Croom Helm, 1977.

Smelser, Neil. *Social Change in the Industrial Revolution: An Application of Theory to the Lancashire Cotton Industry*. Chicago: University of Chicago Press, 1959.

Soltow, Lee, and Edward Stevens. *The Rise of Literacy and the Common School in the United States*. Chicago: University of Chicago Press, 1981.

Spufford, Margaret. "First Steps in Literacy: The Reading and Writing Experiences of the Humblest Seventeenth-Century Spiritual Autobiographers." *Social History* 4 (1979): 407–35.

Stein, Richard. "1837: The Writing on the Walls." *Victorian Poetry* 25, nos. 3–4 (Autumn-Winter 1987): 75–88.

Stephens, W. B. *Regional Variations in Education during the Industrial Revolution, 1780–1870: The Task of the Local Historian*. Leeds: The University of Leeds, 1973.

———. *Education, Literacy and Society, 1830–70: The Geography of Diversity in Provincial England*. Manchester: Manchester University Press, 1987.

Stevens, Edward W., Jr. *Literacy, Law, and Social Order*. DeKalb: Northern Illinois University Press, 1987.

Sturt, Mary. *The Education of the People: A History of Primary Education in England and Wales in the Nineteenth Century*. London: Routledge and Kegan Paul, 1967.

Supple, B. E. "Income and Demand 1860–1914." In *The Economic History of Britain Since 1700*, Vol. 2, edited by Roderick Floud and Donald McCloskey, 121–43. Cambridge: Cambridge University Press, 1981.

Sutherland, Gillian. *Elementary Education in the Nineteenth Century*. London: The Historical Association, 1971.

———. *Policy Making in Elementary Education, 1870–95*. London: Oxford University Press, 1973.

———, ed. *Studies in the Growth of Nineteenth Century Government*. London: Routledge and Kegan Paul, 1972.

Talbott, John E. "The History of Education." *Daedalus* 100 (1971): 133–50.

Tan, Jee Peng, and Michael Haines. *Schooling and the Demand for Children: Historical Perspectives*. World Bank Staff Working Papers, no. 697. Population and Development Series, no. 22, Washington, D.C., 1984.

Taylor, A. J. "Labour Productivity and Technological Innovation in the British Coal Industry, 1850–1914." *Economic History Review*, n.s., 14 (1961): 48–70.

Teitelbaum, Michael. *The Fertility Decline in Britain*. Princeton: Princeton University Press, 1984.

Thomas, Charles. *Methodism and Self Improvement in Nineteenth Century Cornwall*.

Cornish Methodist Historical Association, Occasional Publication, no. 9. Redruth, Cornwall: Cornish Methodist Historical Association, 1965.

Thomas, Keith. "Numeracy in Early Modern England." *Transactions of the Royal Historical Society*, 5th ser., 37 (1987): 103–32.

Thomas, M. W. *The Early Factory Legislation*. Westport, Conn.: Greenwood Press, 1970.

Thompson, E. P. *The Making of the English Working Class*. New York: Vintage Books, 1963.

———. "Happy Families." Review of *The Family, Sex and Marriage in England, 1500–1800*, by Lawrence Stone. *New Society* (8 September, 1977): 499–501.

Thompson, F. M. L. *English Landed Society in the Nineteenth Century*. London: Routledge and Kegan Paul, 1963.

Thompson, Flora. *Lark Rise to Candleford: A Trilogy*. 1945. Reprint. Harmondsworth: Penguin Books, 1973.

Thompson, J. W. *The Literacy of the Laity in the Middle Ages*. Berkeley: University of California Press, 1939.

Thompson, Warren S. *Population Problems*. 2d ed. New York: McGraw-Hill, 1935.

Tillett, P. M. "Sources of Inaccuracy in the 1851 and 1861 Censuses." In *Nineteenth Century Society: Essays in the Use of Quantitative Methods for the Study of Social Data*, edited by E. A. Wrigley, 82–133. Cambridge: Cambridge University Press, 1972.

Tilly, Louise A. "Individual Lives and Family Strategies in the French Proletariat," *Journal of Family History* 4 (1979): 137–52.

Tilly, Louise, and Miriam Cohen. "Does the Family Have a History? A Review of Theory and Practice in Family History." *Social Science History* 6 (1982): 131–79.

Tilly, Louise, and Joan Scott. *Women, Work, and Family*. New York: Holt, Rinehart and Winston, 1978.

Tranter, N. L. "The Labour Supply, 1780–1860." In *The Economic History of Britain Since 1700*, vol. 1, edited by Roderick Floud and Donald McCloskey, 204–26. Cambridge: Cambridge University Press, 1981.

Tropp, Asher. *The School Teachers*. New York: Macmillan, 1956.

Turner, E. S. *What the Butler Saw*. New York: St. Martin's Press, 1963.

Tyack, David. *The One Best System: A History of American Urban Education*. Cambridge: Harvard University Press, 1974.

Vamplew, Wray. *The Turf: A Social and Economic History of Horse Racing*. London: Allen Lane, 1976.

Van de Walle, Francine. "Education and the Demographic Transition in Switzerland." *Population and Development Review* 6 (1980): 463–72.

Vincent, David. "Reading in the Working Class Home." In *Leisure in Britain, 1780–1939*, edited by John K. Walton and James Walvin, 207–26. Manchester: Manchester University Press, 1983.

———. *Literacy and Popular Culture: England 1750–1914*. Cambridge: Cambridge University Press, 1989.

Vovelle, Michel. "Y-a-t'il eu une revolution culturelle au XVIIIe Siecle? A propos de l'education populaire en Provence." *Revue d'histoire moderne et contemporaine*, 22 (1975): 89–141.

Wadsworth, A. P. "Newspaper Circulations, 1800–1954." *Transactions of the Manchester Statistical Society*, session 1954–55 (March, 1955): 1–40.

Wall, Richard. "The Age of Leaving Home." *Journal of Family History* 3 (1978): 181–202.

Walvin, James. *The People's Game: A Social History of British Football*. London: Allen Lane, 1975.

Wardle, David. *Education and Society in Nineteenth Century Nottingham*. Cambridge: Cambridge University Press, 1971.

Webb, R. K. "Working Class Readers in Early Victorian England." *English Historical Review* 65 (1950): 333–51.

———. *The British Working Class Reader 1790–1848: Literacy and Social Tension*. London: Allen and Unwin, 1955.

West, E.G. "Resource Allocation and Growth in Early British Education." *Economic History Review*, 2d ser., 23 (1970): 69–95.

———. "The Interpretation of Early Nineteenth-Century Education Statistics." *Economic History Review*, 2d ser., 24 (1971): 633–52.

———. *Education and the Industrial Revolution*. London: Batsford, 1975.

———. "Educational Slowdown and Public Intervention in Nineteenth-Century England." *Explorations in Economic History* 12 (1975): 61–85.

Williams, F. *Dangerous Estate*. London: Longmans, Green, 1957.

Williams, Raymond. *The Long Revolution*. New York: Columbia University Press, 1961. Rev. ed. New York: Harper Torchbooks, 1966.

———. "The Press and Popular Culture: An Historical Perspective." In *Newspaper History from the Seventeenth Century to the Present Day*, edited by George Boyce, James Carron, and Pauline Wingate, 44–50. London: Constable, 1978.

Williamson, Jeffrey. "Structure of Pay in Britain, 1710–1911." *Research in Economic History*, vol. 7, edited by Paul Uselding, 1–54. Greenwich, Conn.: JAI Press, 1982.

———. *Did British Capitalism Breed Inequality?* London: Allen and Unwin, 1985.

Winstanley, Michael. "Voices from the Past: Rural Kent at the Close of an Era." In *The Victorian Countryside*, vol. 2, edited by G. E. Mingay, 626–38. London: Routledge and Kegan Paul, 1981.

Wrigley, E. A., and R. S. Schofield. *The Population History of England, 1541–1871*. Cambridge: Harvard University Press, 1981.

Wymer, Norman. *Country Folk*. London: Odhams Press, 1953.

PH.D. DISSERTATIONS

Belfiore, Grace. "Family Strategies in Essex Textile Towns 1860–1895: The Challenge of Compulsory Elementary Schooling." D. Phil. thesis, Oxford University, 1987.

Mitch, David. "The Spread of Literacy in Nineteenth Century England." Ph.D. diss., University of Chicago, 1982.

Sanderson, Michael. "The Basic Education of Labour in Lancashire, 1780–1839." Ph.D. diss., University of Cambridge, 1963.

Tuttle, Carolyn. "Children at Work in the British Industrial Revolution." Ph.D. diss., Northwestern University, 1986.

Index

This book has been set in Linotron Galliard. Galliard was designed for Mergenthaler in 1978 by Matthew Carter. Galliard retains many of the features of a sixteenth-century typeface cut by Robert Granjon but has some modifications that give it a more contemporary look.

Printed on acid-free paper.